the city
after
property

Main Portion,

DETROIT

SCALE

0   ¼   ½   ¾ m.

Rand McNally & Co.'s 11 x 15 Map of the Main Portion of Detroit.
Copyright by Rand McNally & Co.

E T R O I T   R I V E R

FERRY

Post Office   City Hall

Union Depot

Michigan Central Depot

Grand Trunk
Lake Shore &
Depot

W I N D

Michigan Av.

Grand River Ave. Sta.

Lafayette St.

Sara Safransky
Abandonment and Repair
in Postindustrial Detroit

the city after property

Duke University Press Durham and London 2023

Project editor: Bird Williams | Designed by Aimee C. Harrison
Typeset in Untitled Serif and Helvetica Neue LT Std
by Westchester Publishing Services

Library of Congress Cataloging-in-Publication Data
Names: Safransky, Sara, author.
Title: The city after property : abandonment and repair in postindustrial
Detroit / Sara Safransky.
Description: Durham : Duke University Press, 2023. | Includes bibliographical references
and index.
Identifiers: LCCN 2022045620 (print)
LCCN 2022045621 (ebook)
ISBN 9781478020783 (paperback)
ISBN 9781478020028 (hardcover)
ISBN 9781478024613 (ebook)
Subjects: LCSH: Sociology, Urban—Michigan—Detroit. | Urban policy—Michigan—
Detroit. | Housing—Abandonment—Michigan—Detroit. | African Americans—
Michigan—Detroit—Social conditions—21st century. | Right of property—United States.
| Property—Social aspects—United States. | Detroit (Mich.)—Economic conditions—
21st century. | BISAC: SOCIAL SCIENCE / Sociology / Urban | SOCIAL SCIENCE / Ethnic
Studies / American / African American & Black Studies
Classification: LCC HN80. D6 S24 2023 (print)
LCC HN80.D6 (ebook)
DDC 307.7609774/34—dc23/eng/20230216
LC record available at https://lccn.loc.gov/2022045620
LC ebook record available at https://lccn.loc.gov/2022045621

Cover art: (*Front, top to bottom, left to right*) (1) 1971 Ford Torino convertible and
coupes. Photograph by Boulevard Photographic (Firm). © National Automotive
History Collection, Detroit Public Library. (2) Queen Anne style house located at
2170 Monroe. © Burton Historical Collection, Detroit Public Library. (3) Carol M.
Highsmith, *An abandoned and decaying home in Detroit*. Library of Congress.

(4) Members of the NAACP's Housing Committee, 1962. Detroit NAACP Photographs.
© Walter P. Reuther Library, Archives of Labor and Urban Affairs, Wayne State
University. (5) Edward Stanton, Children play in an opened fire hydrant, Detroit,
MI, c. 1930s–1940s. © Walter P. Reuther Library, Archives of Labor and Urban
Affairs, Wayne State University. (6) Growing Joy Community Garden. Photograph
by Summer in the City. Accessed via Flickr. (7) Ford automobiles on assembly line.
© National Automotive History Collection, Detroit Public Library. MAP: Plan
of Detroit, 1825. In collection at the William L. Clements Library. Accessed via
University of Michigan Museum of Art. (*Back*) MAP: Koerner, *Detroit and vicinity
before 1900* (1893 ed). Accessed via davidrumsey.com.

For Ashley, Eli, and June,
for Linda,
for beloved community

contents

abbreviations

AIM	American Indian Movement
ACLU	American Civil Liberties Union
BPP	Black Panther Party
CDFI	Community Development Financial Institution
CLR	Community Legal Resources
CRA	Community Reinvestment Act
DBRTF	Detroit Blight Removal Task Force
DFC	Detroit Future City
DPD	Detroit Police Department
D-REM	Detroiters Resisting Emergency Management
DRUM	Dodge Revolutionary Union Movement
DWP	Detroit Works Project
DWSD	Detroit Water and Sewerage Department
FHA	Federal Housing Administration
GM	General Motors
HOLC	Home Owners' Loan Corporation
HOPE	Home Ownership Opportunities for People Everywhere
HUD	Department of Housing and Urban Development
LRBW	League of Revolutionary Black Workers
MDTRC	Metropolitan Detroit Truth and Reconciliation Commission
MVA	Market Value Analysis
NAACP	National Association for the Advancement of Colored People
NAREB	National Association of Real Estate Boards
NDEDC	National Black Economic Development Conference
PA 123	Public Act 123
RECI	Riverfront East Congregation Initiative
RF	Reinvestment Fund
RNA	Republic of New Afrika
SNCC	Student Nonviolent Coordinating Committee
SOSAD	Save Our Sons and Daughters

TRC	Truth and Reconciliation Commission
UAW	United Auto Workers
UCHC	United Community Housing Coalition
URD	Urban Revitalization Demonstration
VA	Veterans Administration

acknowledgments

This book has taken a long time to write. Without the help and support I received from many people and places along the way, it would have taken far longer. Foremost, I am indebted to the insights and generosity of Detroiters. Many of the best ideas in this book come from them and rest on a long radical tradition of movement building. This book would be a very different one if not for the Uniting Detroiters project and for the mentorship and insight of Linda Campbell. I thank her for inviting me to collaborate and learn together. I'm grateful to Andrew Newman for the years we have spent thinking and writing together and to Tim Stallmann for joining us full spiritedly. Thanks to all those who contributed to the Uniting Detroiters project. A special thanks to those who assited with research and management and offered guidance, including Gregg Newsom, Jimmy Johnson, Ayana Rubio, Isra El-beshir, Jeremy Whiting, Emma Slager, Danielle Atkinson, Denis Sloan, Shea Howell, Shane Bernardo, Lottie Spady, Charity Hicks, and Heidi Bisson. Thanks to Baba Wayne Curtis and Mama Myrtle Thompson-Curtis of Feedom Freedom Growers, who generously opened their garden and home to strangers like me. Shea Howell and Monica White kindly took time to engage in conversation when this project was just the seed of an idea and provided encouragement. Jessi Quizar enriched my fieldwork through weekly dinners, lively discussion, and the Geographies of Justice reading group. In addition to Jessi, I am grateful for conversations with other scholars of Detroit, including Rebecca Kinney, Kimberley Kinder, Alesia Montgomery, Rae Baker, and Joshua Akers, and their collective expertise.

Writing is truly a collaborative process. This book would be a lesser one if not for two anonymous reviewers at Duke University Press who engaged with this work in the best spirit of critique. That they accepted the manuscript to review right before the COVID pandemic hit and still stayed on schedule leaves me especially indebted. Their generous comments helped me think more deeply about the substance and order of my arguments. Feedback from colleagues have sustained this project. Thanks to Erin Collins, Greta Marchesi, Tasha Rijke-Epstein, Aimi Hamraie, Kate Derickson, Nathan McKlintock, Rachel Brahinsky, Sophie Bjork-James, and Zoé Hamstead for constructive and incisive criticism and encouragement. Thanks to Elsa Noterman for supportive conversations during the finishing stages of this work. I also benefited immensely from a Robert Penn Warren Center Fellowship, where I received helpful feedback from Anand Vivek Taneja, Emily Greble, Candice Amich, Ruth Hill, Brandon Byrd, and We Jung Yi. Thanks to Malini Ranganathan, Anne Bonds, and Nik Heynen, who organized conference sessions and special issues that helped me advance the project.

Mentors and friends at the University of North Carolina at Chapel Hill provided support and read early drafts of chapters, including Brenda Baletti, Elizabeth Hennessy, Georgina Drew, Holly Worthen, Wendy Wolford, Lawrence Grossberg, Dorothy Holland, John Pickles, and Alvaro Reyes. A special thanks to Dottie, who joined the ancestors before she could see this book between covers but whose encouragement provided much sustenance. Early versions of several chapters benefited from constructive feedback from participants of the Summer Institute on Contested Landscapes at Cornell University and the Social Science Research Council Dissertation Proposal Development Program, including Jennifer Baka, Gabrielle Clark, Thomas Fleischman, Aaron Jakes, Pablo Lapegna, Greta Marchesi, and Tom Okie.

I am indebted to my colleagues in the Department of Human and Organizational Development at Vanderbilt University for their encouragement and good cheer. I am also grateful to my students for enriching conversation and enthusiasm. A special thanks to Amie Thurber, Jyoti Gupta, Sara Eccleston, Tessa Eidelman, Danielle Wilfong, Ashley Bachelder, Emily Barrett, and Gavin Crowell-Williamson. Tessa Eidelman, Gavin Crowell-Williamson, B. Balmer, and Madeleine Lewis provided instrumental research assistance at various stages.

This work has benefited from generous financial support from the American Council of Learned Societies Dissertation Completion Fellowship; Antipode Foundation Scholar-Activist Award; Landscape Architecture Foundation Dissertation Fieldwork Grant; National Science Foundation Graduate Research Fellowship; National Science Foundation Dissertation Development Research Initiative Award; Social Science Research Council Dissertation Proposal Development Program Grant; Wenner-Gren Dissertation Fieldwork Grant; and intramural grants from the University of North Carolina at Chapel Hill Graduate School.

At Duke University Press, I thank Gisela Fosado for believing in this project and for her patience and editorial guidance. Thanks to Alejandra Mejía for dealing with my numerous logistical questions with grace. The book has benefited from editorial advice from Anitra Grisales and Melanie Mallon. Thanks to Bird Williams for seeing it through production. Finally, thanks to Aimee Harrison for cover and interior design work.

Chapters 3, 5, 6, 7, and 8 significantly expand some of the ideas and empirical material that appear in articles published in the *International Journal of Urban and Regional Research*, *Antipode: A Radical Journal of Cartography*, *Geoforum*, and the *Annals of the Association of Geographers*.

It was not easy to continue with this project when the pandemic turned everything upside down. Conviviality and shared care duties with our pod family—Jyoti Gupta, Eric Gauen, Kai, Bhodi, and Ms. Teri—made it possible.

My family has offered their unwavering support over the years. Thank you to my four sisters, Mara, Leah, Rachel, and Gaela; my mother, Priscilla; my father, Sy; my stepmother, Norma; and my in-laws, Lib and Jim.

My children, Eli and June, have lived with this book since they were born. They have made writing and life immeasurably more joyful as they attune me to what matters in the present.

I have finished this book because of Ashley Carse. Not only did he create time and space for me to write, but he also read (and listened to) every word, more than once. Our conversations and his editing acumen have made it far more readable than it ever would have been. While many have contributed to this book, and it is better for it, all errors and shortcomings are mine alone.

A final note, all future royalties made on this book will be donated to the Transforming Power Fund of Detroit.

prologue

The crowd spilled out of the Cobo Center convention hall in downtown Detroit where the US Social Forum was being held. It was a sunny day in June 2010. I maneuvered along the normally subdued street through a line of buses and people. The World Social Forum had been hosting annual meetings since 2001, but this was only the second domestic event. The event slogan, "Another World Is Possible / Another US Is Necessary / Another Detroit Is Happening," underscored the relevance of Detroit to the forum's aim of developing alternatives to neoliberal globalization. In the wake of the subprime mortgage crisis, with growing anxieties about the precarity of late capitalism, Detroit stood as ground zero for economic collapse. With its rich social movement history, it was seen as a good place to think about what it means to build another world and a new global Left.

I wasn't in Detroit that summer specifically to attend the Social Forum. I was a graduate student from North Carolina who had come to do exploratory research on land politics in the city. After decades of deindustrialization and white flight, officials classified more than 150,000 parcels of land as "abandoned" or "vacant." I was interested in what happens when a private property system fails and how people endeavor to put it back together or reorder it.

I had chosen Detroit as a research site for many of the same reasons the Social Forum picked it for its assembly. I thought Detroit might offer models for progressive land policy and more socially and ecologically just forms of urbanism. At the time, I mostly thought about this in terms of redistribution. It wasn't until later that I began to appreciate the deeply moral and ethical questions surrounding urban land and property. These were questions about race and personhood. They were about abandonment and belonging. They were about reckoning and healing. This book is about these questions.

No single narrative explains how these concerns took hold in me and drew me to Detroit. I wasn't from the city. Nor was my family. I grew up in the Appalachian Mountains in the rural western corner of North Carolina, bordering Tennessee and Virginia. South-Central Appalachia and Detroit are very different places, though I would come to learn they shared some similarities and connections, not least of which was the migration of significant numbers of poor people from Appalachia to Detroit seeking work during the mid-twentieth century.

When I was young, property relations in my Appalachian *holler* materialized most memorably as "no trespassing" signs along roadways, hillsides, and, most surprisingly, tucked deep in the forest. I didn't understand the histories of race and power that these boundary objects signified. But I did sense a misapprehension in their possessive claims. To claim the woodlands as one's own seemed an act of folly—a madness born from the delusions of dominion that I am still seeking to understand. My rural all-white public primary school taught regional geography and history. We learned about Sir Walter Raleigh and the lost colony of Roanoke. We learned about the state bird (the red cardinal) and the state flower (the dogwood). But the history we learned barely acknowledged the most salient aspects that might have helped us understand our place in it.

This is to say, it left aside how race and property regimes established over centuries through colonialism, slavery, and capitalism facilitated the ownership of land and people. Despite the lore that there had been no slavery in the region—owing to its high elevation, steep slopes, narrow valleys, and distance from markets—slaveholders in my small county held almost four hundred people in bondage. The history we were taught left aside the fact that slave owners made up less than 7 percent of farmers but owned half the county's wealth; that by the mid-nineteenth century, a third of households had no real property; that the plantation aristocracy gave rise to divisions, sometimes between families, who ended up fighting on opposite sides of the Civil War; and that when men died at war, state law prohibited women from inheriting family property. We learned about the Trail of Tears and the civil rights movement but not how this history manifested locally in geographies of resistance, such as in Affrilachian freedmen settlements like the Hill or in Native resistors like the Eastern Band of Cherokee Indians who defied removal and refused to give up land.[1]

Such history of American race and property relations may have helped me better understand my own discomfort living in a place where white belonging was conferred by generations of settlement. When my mother, who was from the Northeast, relocated us to western North Carolina, we were considered outsiders from "off the mountain," as were my siblings who were born locally.

While I felt unease, I was ill equipped to understand how my ancestral lineage (Italian and Irish on my mother's side and Jewish Ukrainian and Russian on my father's) had enabled my family to assimilate into a regime of whiteness after immigrating to the United States at the turn of the twentieth century, if less seamlessly into a rural version of it decades later. I sensed class differences among my classmates but didn't understand why regional poverty was so grueling.

The history I learned said nothing of the political-economic forces that drew an estimated seven million Appalachians northward from the 1940s to the 1960s along the mythic Hillbilly Highway, many recruited by Northern industrialists at a time when the mechanization of mining, timber, and agriculture had reduced already sparse job opportunities. My history books left aside working-class insurgencies like the Appalachian Mine Wars of the 1920s, the interracial solidarity efforts like the Young Patriots in the 1960s, and how 1970s' theories of domestic colonialism rooted in the Black Power movement had profound importance for explaining underdevelopment and extractivism in Appalachia. When in the 1980s, my middle-school playmates began professing allegiance to American-owned cars, I didn't understand how the uncertainty in Detroit's auto industry, Cold War anxieties, union conservatism, and a broader movement demobilization fostered by the rise of middle-class suburban life defined the terms of such loyalty.[2]

Decades later, when I arrived in Detroit, these connections were not yet on my mind, at least not consciously. Detroit first caught my attention because the city had been making headlines as an urban agriculture mecca. In the aughts, the growth of the local food movement gave rise to fervor over urban farming as a site to enact sustainable political change, though often in ways that skirted long-standing issues of racial and economic equity. Activists in Detroit were challenging the movement to confront and deal with these paradoxes and limitations. In graduate school, I'd been steeped in literature on agrarian land reform movements in Latin America and postsocialist property transformations in Europe. I found myself wondering how land and property questions were being adjudicated in a radically different context. It was an inquiry that took on a new sense of urgency as the subprime mortgage crisis tore across the country and globe.

My first summer in Detroit impressed on me the generous ways people were engaging in collective study and seeking to build capacious theories of liberation. I was introduced to a world of radical thought that led me to reappraise my own disciplinary training as a lapsed planner and then a geographer. I sensed that Detroit was not only a good place to think about the land questions that preoccupied me but also a place to learn a version of American history I'd not learned in school.

Detroit, unlike Appalachia, occupies a central place in American history and mythology. I learned a version of Detroit's history that was intended to make sense of the American experience more generally—this was the history of the American dream, the melting pot, the might of industry—and later, in graduate school, the history of Fordism and post-Fordism. Yet as in my grammar school lessons, the margins of this history were elided. This book evolved from an attempt to think about land politics and battles over the future of urban America from these margins.

After the summer of the Social Forum, I returned to Detroit in the fall of 2011 for a year and a half of fieldwork. By then the city was inundated with journalists, documentarians, and researchers—myself among them. As re-development dollars poured into the city, there was also a sense of urgency around who was being left behind. Not only did many residents, activists, and city officials have to negotiate incessant requests for interviews, they were also facing the repercussions of how stories about the city's supposed renaissance were being told and who got to control the narrative. The saturation of outsiders studying and writing about Detroit forced me to grapple with important questions about why, for whom, and how to go about doing research, and particularly what it meant for me as a white woman from outside Detroit to try to do so in ways that were ethical, accountable, and, at best, potentially useful for the communities with whom I collaborated.

I set about meeting with activists to see if my research might connect with local organizing efforts. In conversations, community activists told me about their frustrations with "extractivist" journalism and research. They spoke of needing to defend against research and how the timelines of researchers were often at odds with community needs. Many expressed concerns about what was lost in translation, having stories told wrong, and never seeing what was written. One of the main concerns was about how the city's crisis was being analyzed, from whose perspective, and how the front lines of struggle were being covered.

As a result of how Detroit's story was being studied and narrated, some activists talked about developing models of research that empowered residents to share their own analyses and that benefited community work. They suggested that often the most necessary and urgent theory emerges from efforts to make sense of contemporary predicaments and better everyday life. This is a kind of theorizing that stems from lived experiences. It happens in meetings and study groups, in conversations on porches, while laboring in gardens and on factory lines, and over shared meals. It happens as a matter of survival. It is the kind of theorizing that anchors radical traditions by both analyzing power and fortifying the imagination.[3]

Amid grappling with my position in this charged political landscape, I attended a conference, "Reimagining Work," sponsored by the James and Grace Lee Boggs Center to Nurture Community Leadership. There I had a chance encounter with Linda Campbell that shaped my research trajectory in fundamental ways. Linda had been a community organizer in Detroit since the 1970s. At the time we met, she was the local director for a branch of a national organization called Building Movement.

When Linda and I struck up a conversation, she told me that she and her community partners were in the beginning stages of conceptualizing a project that would, on the one hand, elucidate significant political-economic changes in the city and, on the other hand, document and illuminate the work of progressive social justice and neighborhood-level groups pursuing alternative approaches to development. Linda had a no-nonsense approach and a healthy dose of skepticism about working with academics. During the HIV/AIDS crisis in Detroit, she had witnessed how academics came into communities of color and extracted information that enriched their knowledge and social standing but left the subjects of their research with nothing. At the same time, she was keenly aware that university resources could be leveraged for movement work.

In a series of meetings over several months, we discussed how my research might be strategically useful for and benefit from working on the landscape analysis. She invited Andrew Newman, an anthropology professor at Wayne State University, and me to be "learning partners" on the project. I always appreciated her naming us "learning partners" versus, for example, academic partners, because it suggested that we were learning together rather than academics providing expertise.

In the months and years that followed, Linda, Andy, and I talked about what it meant to coproduce knowledge across cultural and institutional borders and what types of analyses are useful for deepening on-the-ground struggles. We worked with other community activists to develop a participatory research project that came to be known as Uniting Detroiters. Its goals were to study and discuss the emerging development agenda in Detroit and how it fit into broader national and global trends, as well as to identify local challenges to and opportunities for transformative social change. The project aimed to use research activities to strengthen the infrastructure of the city's long-vibrant grassroots sector.

To this end, our research group, made up of activists, community leaders, scholars, students, and residents conducted interviews with individuals involved in social justice organizations and neighborhood groups. Our aim was to document and understand how Detroiters were analyzing and responding to urban restructuring. We approached the interviews as *one-on-ones*, a term used in community organizing that emphasizes identifying shared values, cultivating relationships, and fostering coalitions. As part of the project, we also hosted a series of workshops with the aim of creating a shared space in which to engage in collective analysis of the new conjuncture. The project yielded a documentary called *A People's Story of Detroit* and a book called *A People's Atlas of Detroit*, which together offer counternarratives of the city's redevelopment in the 2010s from the perspectives of residents on the front lines of struggle.[4]

This book extends the collective research that we conducted as part of the Uniting Detroiters project by analyzing in more depth the land and property questions that pervaded Detroit's urban planning and development landscape in the early 2010s. I draw on a diverse archive of sources. These include interviews that I conducted about land governance and use with city officials, urban planners, nongovernmental professionals, urban farmers, city maintenance workers, and residents involved in neighborhood groups that cared for their communities. These oral accounts were enriched by observations at over sixty meetings, including planning charettes, city council meetings, municipal financial review board meetings, community land meetings, and activist gatherings. I supplemented these contemporary data sources with historical research on transformations in the city's property regimes drawn from secondary literature, newspapers, oral histories, and activist and community archives. Finally, I collected and analyzed media representations of Detroit from local, national, and international news outlets, documentaries and films, websites, and books to understand the language, stories, and images used to describe the city's landscape, stake a particular vision for its development, and justify possession of it. To gain a deeper understanding of the tensions that surrounded planning for the city's future, I juxtaposed the experiential attachments to land and political aspirations voiced by Detroiters with the spatial imaginaries and practices that showed up in policy and planning documents, audit reports, maps and plans, media accounts of events, regulatory acts, and development agreements.

As this book's title suggests, *The City after Property* delves into the past, but it is mostly a work of recent history. Writing recent history comes with possibilities and challenges. One has much material at one's fingertips but less distance for reflection. The primary research and early writing for this book took place in the United States in the 2010s, a decade defined by the election of President Barack Obama and rapid technological advances. If heady optimism accompanied such "progress," it was betrayed by ballooning corporate profits, mounting ecological crisis, the rapid financialization of housing, brutal austerity measures, and ideological polarization that manifested in a rising tide of right-wing nationalism.

As I pen this prologue, ten years on, at the disorienting outset of the COVID-19 pandemic, it seems we've reached a new moment of societal reckoning. The pandemic has brought into stark relief the limits and inequities of our political, economic, and health care systems. At the same time, it has given rise to a groundswell of social movements calling for alternatives—land and housing justice among them. In the summer of 2020, the massive uprisings for Black lives following the murders of George Floyd, Ahmaud Arbery, and Breonna Taylor led to a new explosion of demands across the country to defund the police, take down white supremacist monuments, and decolonize curriculums. While protestors drew strong connections between anti-Black police violence and the violence of capitalist property relations, the mainstream media and feigned corporate attempts to unsettle America's racial hierarchy ignored them. Since then, a growing white racial backlash over perceived loss of power combined with a widening racial wealth gap suggest that the pandemic will come and go, but enduring questions about how to come together to build a more dignified and just world—and the crucial role of decommodifying land and social relationships therein—will remain. This book is a humble offering to these conversations.

Map 1 | This map of Michigan and its environs situates Detroit in regional context. It shows that Detroit, named Waawiiyaatanong by the Anishinaabe, occupies stolen land and is governed by the 1807 Treaty of Detroit between the United States and the Odawa, Ojibwe, Wyandot, and Potawatomi Nations. Other major treaties with the United States are represented by year and signing tribes. *Source:* Tim Stallmann.

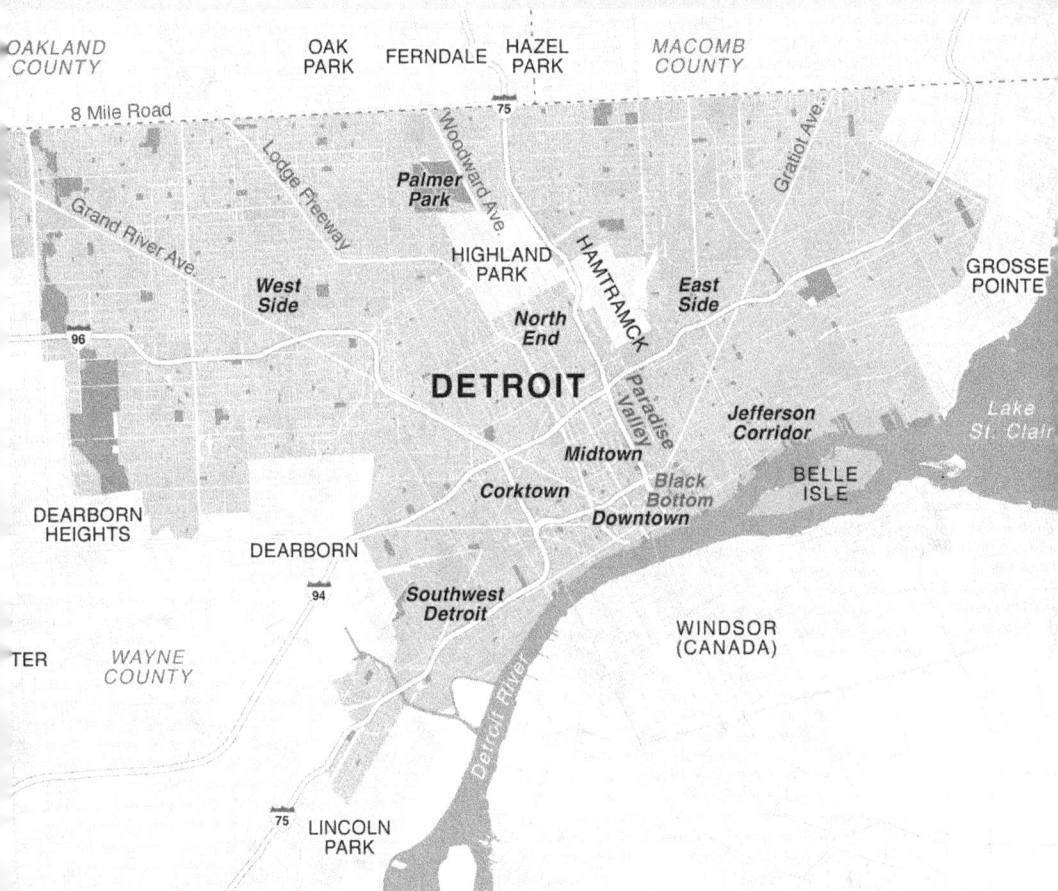

Map 2 | Detroit Metropolitan Area. *Source:* Tim Stallmann.

Figure 1.1 (opposite) | This 2016 aerial image depicts a portion of Detroit. Downtown is shown at the center, and the Ambassador Bridge is center left. A barge cruises down the Detroit River, which separates the city from Windsor, Canada, the land mass to the south. *Source:* Planet Labs, August 22, 2016.

Figure 1.2 | "They tried to buy us. They didn't know we were seeds," reads a mural by Brandan "BMike" Odums and Rick Williams at Eastern Market in Detroit. *Source:* Photo by wiredforlego, September 17, 2018, Flicker.com.

unbuilding a city

It was a quiet street. A meadow undulated in the breeze. Before the grass pushed through the concrete and erased visible markers of the property grid, streets like this were lined with the modest homes of Detroit autoworkers. This was more than a half century ago, before factory automation started to eliminate jobs, and the Big Three—Ford, Chrysler, and General Motors— started to relocate their factories down South and overseas. It was before the suburbs began to sprout up on the surrounding Michigan farmland, before the city went up in flames. It was before the exodus of white Detroiters, before one of the nation's largest cities became majority Black and too big for itself, before planners began to ask: How do you unbuild a city?

In the autumn of 2011, I moved to Detroit seeking answers to this question. It was a pivotal moment. The city that put the world on wheels had become a laboratory for postindustrial futures and a dramatic reterritorialization was underway. Reeling from the Great Recession, Detroit was on the precipice of emergency financial management and municipal bankruptcy. The Motor City, which once boasted almost 2 million residents, had grappled with de-population since the 1950s, when the postwar exodus to the suburbs began. As white people filled the suburbs around an increasingly Black city, Detroit became a site of persistent racialized poverty and a skeleton of its midcentury self. Officials classified a staggering 150,000 lots—more than a third of the city—as "vacant" or "abandoned."

Vociferous debates ensued over the city's budgetary challenges, austerity measures, and how to respond to the problem of too much land. It was, in short, a time of chaos at all levels of city government and of extreme uncertainty for residents. City officials had been working aggressively to attract inhabitants and transnational capital to the city. New public-private partnerships and philanthropic initiatives aimed to address the city's land problem through policies that focused on the acquisition, disposition, demolition, and regularization of the city's vacant properties.

The most sweeping initiative, launched by then-mayor David Bing, was a planning process called the Detroit Works Project that sought to fix the city's spatial mismatch by radically reconfiguring—or "rightsizing"—its urban footprint to match its smaller population. Controversially, it proposed stabilizing real estate markets by decommissioning some depopulated neighborhoods. In practice, this meant retracting public services (garbage pickup, transportation, water) and installing landscape features like wetlands, retention ponds, farms, forests, and greenways. Within this blue and green infrastructure paradigm, entrepreneurs began to envision Detroit's abandoned lots as sites for large-scale commercial food, fuel, and fiber production.

The unprecedented scale of the land crisis grabbed media headlines as an overwhelmed city government sought to offload property and housing at rock bottom prices. Meanwhile, a motley group of actors came out of the woodwork, proposing new ways to solve or exploit the city's surplus land problem. They often sought different political and economic ends. Schemes included a twenty-first-century homesteading program, an immigrant resettlement plan, developing a zombie theme park, and turning an iconic island park into an independent commonwealth and tax haven, among others. One investor even launched a billboard campaign in New York City that encouraged Brooklynites to move "west of Bushwick" to Detroit.[1]

In this context, a paradox emerged: government officials, planners, and the media characterized Detroit's land problem in terms of overabundance (too much vacant land and too little demand). At the same time, many residents faced foreclosures and evictions, which further increased the supply. They also faced barriers to gaining ownership over vacant de facto public land. The situation on the ground was complicated. Many property parcels were not actually "abandoned" or "vacant" but existed in liminal or contested states of ownership, characterized by foreclosure and eviction defenses, cloudy titles, squatting, and efforts to "take back" the land. For decades, residents had been mowing and maintaining city blocks, cleaning streets, fixing up and living in old buildings, and transforming unused lots into urban gardens on a scale unmatched in any other American city. This caretaking led to a widespread sense of collective ownership over de facto public lands poised for repurposing and privatization under planned shrinkage.

This paradox is at the heart of the empirical and ethical questions explored in this book: Why did the city have so much land when so many residents had so little? To whom did Detroit's "vacant" and "abandoned" lands belong? Whose land claims were validated by existing legal and juridical frameworks? Whose were not? Why? Could those frameworks be reformed? Was reform even the answer? How did competing notions of repair undergird land claims and portend different urban futures? And the more rudimentary if far from straightforward question: How had Detroit found itself in this situation?

Detroit's abandonment is often presented as a story of industrial decline, suburbanization, and white flight. And Detroit as *the* abandoned place is characterized by lack, absence, and inactivity.[2] As I talked to residents, activists, planners, and government officials, however, I realized this framing of abandonment reified the notion of surplus land and concealed the systematic abuses of power and arbitrary rules that produced scarcity. The enormous land questions facing postindustrial cities like Detroit are often approached as problems of depopulation and failed property markets that require technical fixes. Yet a reframing of the problem suggests different avenues for what is to be done in response. To better understand the visions, tensions, passionate responses, and complex questions of justice that arose as plans unfolded to unbuild and redevelop Detroit, I realized the very idea of "abandoned" land needed rethinking.

The City after Property takes the reader on a journey into the everyday land and property struggles that emerged over the city's so-called abandoned lands as planners, policy makers, and residents, among other actors, sought to reimagine Detroit. Debates were about use, distribution, and much more. Detroit's lands, even "abandoned" lands, were imbued with powerful memories, fears, aspirations, and visions for alternative futures. Efforts to unbuild Detroit, thus, upturned not only material detritus but also complex relationships of land, property, and race that often remained hidden from view.

Throughout the book, I argue that access to land is mediated by property formations that are cultural, racialized, historical, and contested. As this suggests, if we want to understand abandonment, we must get beyond seeing property as simply a thing (i.e., the land itself) that one owns and interrogate it as a political construct, an ideology, and a moral force that shapes selves and worlds. In other words, we must ask what comes *after property*?

A Laboratory for Postindustrial Futures

Narratives of abandonment can shape how urban problems are conceptualized and how solutions are imagined. When I started this project, there were three well-rehearsed explanations of Detroit's decline. The first and most widely circulating of these emphasized how the invisible hand of global capital and shifts in the political economy of the auto industry had emptied out the city. A second overtly racist narrative pinned Detroit's demise on Black cultural pathologies, the ineptitude and corruption of the Black municipal government, and a pervasive lawlessness that gripped the city.

In the early 2000s, new narratives began to emerge. Propagated by filmmakers, photographers, journalists, and tourists, they cast Detroit as empty, wasted, and underutilized. The iconic images of the abandoned factory as representative of the Motor City's working-class, industrial aesthetics came to compete with a potent new imaginary of "urban wilderness": houses ensnarled in vines (so-called feral houses), trees sprouting from the tops of deserted skyscrapers, dense groves of invasive Chinese "ghetto palms," and wildlife sightings. It was a landscape altered by but notably absent of humans. Rarely did the documentarians of these haunting and, at times, beautiful landscapes inquire into the historical conditions of their production.[3]

Detroit had long been called "America's wasteland" and its "most dramatically depopulated city," but it was not alone in its plight. Buffalo, Cleveland, Pittsburgh, and St. Louis, to name only a few cities, had all been in population decline since their industrial heydays, confounding planning models impelled by growth prerogatives. Policy makers commonly wrote off Detroit and other postindustrial cities as beyond salvation.

But something shifted at the turn of the century as millennial cultural fixation on end-time narratives and fantasies of renewal reached new heights. Now, in spite of (or, perhaps, because of) their myriad problems, many planners, policy makers, and publics began seeing Detroit and other cities with copious amounts of vacant land as exciting testing grounds for experimental urban futures within the context of collapse.

Detroit was no stranger to crisis, but the Great Recession of 2007–2009 served up its own unique hell. As foreclosures combined with welfare cuts, job losses, and relentless cutbacks in public education, the city hemorrhaged residents. Detroit had faced steady depopulation for a half century, but between 2000 and 2010 alone, the city lost an additional 25 percent of its residents. The loss reduced its population to 713,000, over 80 percent of whom identified as African American. Of the working-age residents who remained in the city, half were unemployed.[4]

Throughout history, cities have experienced booms and busts, even total population collapses. Their ruins—from Machu Picchu to the Acropolis—have long served as sites of contemplation on the ephemerality of civilizations. Postindustrial cities were just the latest sites of ruination. When the public fixed their gaze on Detroit, it was not just to imagine new futures but also to process or deflect generalized anxiety about the precarity of and experiences of dislocation that accompanied late capitalism.

Where better to grapple with the uncertainty that followed the fallout of the subprime foreclosure crisis than Detroit, the birthplace of Fordism and Fordist decline? Fordism was always more than an economic model of standardized production for Model Ts. It standardized an entire way of life and promised increased prosperity for all. Communities suffered stunning job losses with Fordist decline. Less noted, though, perhaps, even more devastating was the loss of social and political infrastructures propped up by union power.[5] Fordist prosperity did not simply come from mass production but was indelibly tied to unions, which exerted pressure on company management and the public sector to live up to a social contract that distributed the benefits of growth. Given that Detroit has long symbolized the promise and failure of this American dream, it is unsurprising that it emerged as a key site for rumination on the end times of industrial capitalism, the dangers of financialization, and the sustainability of our collective future.

Debates over post-Fordist and postindustrial futures have long conjured nostalgia, resentments, hopes, and worries over the future of work. Deep anxieties animate discussions of what should become of cities once booming with industry in the wake of factory closures, union busting, free-trade agreements, outmigration, and the rise of the information economy. In the 1960s, the concept of *postindustrial society* named societal transformations taking place because of cybernation and automation. The term captured concerns about impending economic obsolescence, on the one hand, and a rising leisure class, on the other.[6] By the 2010s, debates over the future of postindustrial cities continued to turn on concerns about technology and work. As Detroit illustrates, however, these debates were also bound up with questions about how and for whom to repurpose urban land and infrastructure, as cities reorganized in response to the logics of finance capital and the uncertainties wrought by climate change.

After the precipitous stock market collapse of September 2008, Detroit began to generate headlines as a cautionary tale of where other cities might be headed. As the executives of the Big Three automakers groveled in Washington for a relief package and General Motors declared bankruptcy, one longtime Detroit-based journalist explained, "I began to get calls from reporters around the world wondering if the Rust Belt cancer had metastasized and was creeping to Los Angeles and London and Barcelona. Was Detroit an outlier or an epicenter?"[7]

Analysts struggled to make sense of the economic fallout and late capitalism's malfunctions. Consider the former Federal Reserve chair Alan Greenspan's bewildered concession that the global financial crisis had revealed a "flaw" in free-market ideology. In this context, the fixation on Detroit is best understood as dissociative.[8] This is to say, the blank beauty of the city's expansive ruins and narratives of decline were nonreferential to reality. They represented capital while disappearing it, engaging in a form of obfuscation that mirrored that of global finance capital's own detachments and abstract violence.

The media maelstrom fed on itself, invigorating global interest in postindustrial cities as sites from which to reconceptualize urbanization and the economy. The ascendant notion that distressed cities built to support larger populations and bygone industries—like Flint, Leipzig, Turin, and Osaka—could be productively shrunk was not new. It rehabilitated old, largely discredited ideas of "planned shrinkage" from the 1970s, when ill-conceived efforts to clear urban neighborhoods led to the relocation of residents in the name of renewal.[9] The idea was expressed most fully as policy by New York City housing commissioner Roger Starr. There, planned shrinkage led to the reduction in fire services, much of the South Bronx going up in flames (as well as other parts of the city), and the subsequent withdrawal of services from "sick" neighborhoods that were poor and nonwhite.[10]

If shrinkage was a qualified disaster forty years earlier, the theory had newfound luster in the early 2000s. Shrinking cities—cities that faced a mismatch between their spatial footprints and populations because of processes of deindustrialization and demographic transition—had long been written off by planners and policy makers. But by the early 2010s, they'd begun to embrace them as exciting opportunities to radically reimagine the urban form, particularly leaner, greener templates for an era of planning defined by the dual mandates of austerity and sustainability. The green city, once a fringe idea that conveyed alternative visions for society, began to blossom in the sunshine of a neoliberal economic order.[11]

The demands of growth had long dominated American urban planning. Planned shrinkage was, ironically, no different. Its corollaries were models of corporate restructuring and downsizing. Cast in this light, shrinkage was an opportunity to experiment with unbuilding, retrofitting, reuse, and repair as a means of capitalist urban growth.[12] The public's fascination with shrinking cities has been tempered somewhat since the Great Recession; however, efforts to reimagine the urban form continue to shape old industrial communities—through plans, policies, and projects—in ways that remain poorly understood.

Rethinking Abandonment with Detroiters

Many books have been written about Detroit. The city has been a key case for studies of industrial capitalism, unions, Black politics, the Black Power movement, Black theology, and whiteness and racial identity.[13] Urban studies scholars, in particular, have turned to Detroit to investigate the racialization of housing and urban development.[14] Few works, though, have attended to how property and land politics have evolved in the context of increased financialization, planned shrinkage, and sustainability mandates. Abandonment too has remained undertheorized, particularly given its prominence in narratives of postindustrial decline.[15]

When I began studying Detroit, it seemed necessary to both reread abandonment narratives and center land and property relations in the story. *The City after Property* forwards three arguments related to these concerns. First, I argue that to more fully address the politics of disposability that pervades urban life, neoliberal urbanism must be analyzed as part of a longer evolution of racial capitalism, settler colonialism, and slavery. Second, I argue for greater attention to how discourses of abandonment shape urban planning and governance decisions. Finally, I argue that land struggles should be taken as important sites of scholarly inquiry because they illuminate how modern property organizes abandonment as well as alternative ways of conceiving of personhood, rights, nature, and sovereignty. I'll return to these three areas. Before I do so, I explain how conversations with Detroiters made me realize that both property and abandonment needed more analytical attention in urban studies.

Urban studies scholars often explain Rust Belt places in terms of postindustrialism—and the cognate processes it denotes, deindustrialization and suburbanization. Scholars of political economy have offered associated analytics—from urban metabolism to global flows, the spatial fix, networked urbanism, and planetary urbanization—to illuminate how, for example, capital flows through the built environment to realize surplus value and how infrastructural networks constitute the material and social fabric of the city. Meanwhile, scholars have drawn attention to shifts in the mode of capitalism from a system based primarily on deriving profit from the discipline of labor (e.g., through automation in Detroit's factories) to one based on deriving profit from debt and rent (e.g., through subprime mortgages, the fringe economy, and the rentier economy).[16]

Such political-economic analyses are critical for making sense of urban change and pressing societal challenges. Indeed, the unprecedented financialization of real estate markets illuminates the speculative, predatory, and parasitic nature of late capitalism and helps explain why gentrification has become a household term. Yet, crucially, the land and property struggles I encountered on the ground in Detroit often exceeded the explanatory power of such categories, analytics, and temporalities.

Political-economic analyses of postindustrial decline tend to take twentieth-century industry and its absence as a baseline reference point. In doing so, they elide the longer histories of imperialism and colonialism that condition distributions of power and forces of exclusion and appropriation in both the industrial and the postindustrial eras. Put another way, they foreclose a deeper interrogation of abandonment, failing to see it for what it is—a social relationship and racialized project bound up with property—and, thus, are unable to adequately address either the worldviews and systems that hold it in place or the movements that emerge to counter it. These dynamics begged a question of how I might better account for tense and tender struggles taking place over Detroit's "abandoned" lands.

As mentioned above, the notion that Detroit was abandoned—read almost exclusively as empty—pervaded popular and academic narratives. Yet when longtime Detroit residents of different backgrounds talked with me about the city, they described a landscape that was not empty but densely "storied," to use Mishuana Goeman's term.[17] They emphasized what Detroit had once been and the hopes that people invested in the city. They described a place where one could find work and join the middle class, a bastion of Black homeownership, Motown, America's largest Black city, a key center for Black radical and labor movements.

Residents and community activists talked about abandonment in ways that were qualitatively different from planners' landscape typologies. Crucially, they were more likely to foreground loss than emptiness. As sociologist

Alesia Montgomery has observed, through sounds, scents, tastes, and feelings, they conjured a place that once was and that could still be.[18] They continually made the claim that Detroit's crisis was less about abandoned lots than about the abandonment of *people*, casting light on the profound distortions of Blackness and Black aspatiality on which popular representations of the city rested.

In contrast to popular narratives that blamed Detroit's decline on corruption, irresponsible actors, and faceless political-economic forces, residents were quick to explain that it was more local and systematic. It was state-sanctioned violence and racist housing policies. It was planning. It was urban renewal. Relentless policing. These ongoing processes—rooted in an apartheid past—had taken on new formations like subprime mortgage foreclosures, urban shrinkage, "rightsizing," strategic renewal, and green redevelopment that linked Detroit's predicament to other places.

Indeed, by the early 2010s, post-Katrina New Orleans had become a key analog for Detroit. Planners and policy makers likened Detroit's half-century-long process of depopulation to a "slow motion Katrina."[19] The juxtaposition of the shock of natural disaster with Detroit's slow industrial decline—accelerated by the jolt of the recession—painted a picture of two cities struck by the vagaries of nature. This framing masked how predicaments facing New Orleans and Detroit were caused not by the exceptional forces of nature but by human decisions. As Andy Horowitz writes in a history of Katrina, "Somebody had to build the levees before they could break."[20]

The comparison between Detroit and New Orleans was more than metaphorical.[21] Planners, researchers, and policy makers traveled between the two cities. They exchanged ideas about how to manage problems associated with shrinkage and compared data. Notably, the variables they deemed comparable—number of blighted structures and vacancy rates—registered abandonment in terms of surplus property, land, and buildings, not residents.[22] The centrality of property in framing shared problems and solutions was striking. Meanwhile, other shared factors—histories of French colonialism, structural racism, and neoliberal governance—were elided.[23]

In both cities, plans to address abandonment became blueprints for a future that forgot its past.[24] Planners and politicians cast urban abandonment as a technocratic issue rooted in vacancy and depopulation, which could be solved through smarter land use, greening, public-private partnerships, entrepreneurship, volunteerism, and above all, shoring up property values. Before property values in Detroit could be bolstered, though, the breakdown in the property regime had to be addressed.

What is a property regime? I use the term property regime to refer to the logics, ideologies, and regulatory and juridical infrastructures that enable ownership by specifying relationships among people and between people and things. These specifications delineate what kinds of things count as property (such as land, ideas, objects, genetic material, people), who can own them, in what ways, and how they should be valued. All these decisions presuppose and reproduce forms of personhood and the norms and power relations of a society.

Places like Detroit are useful for thinking about the modern property form because they upend its presumed fixity. Science and technology studies scholars have observed that when systems are working, they are often taken for granted, particularly by those whom they benefit. During moments of breakdown, however, when users are unable to reap the benefits of the systems, they are more likely to question, transgress, work around, and enact alternatives to them. Moments of breakdown can, thus, provide insights into how systems are assembled, how they work, and for whom. This truism—often observed in studies of infrastructure (e.g., power grids, water pipes, bridges, dams)—is also useful for thinking about property regimes.[25]

Indeed, when property regimes are challenged or destabilized—be it through popular protest, war, disaster, political transition, or economic change—the process of stabilizing them or transitioning to a new regime can be a violent and complex affair. In the 2010s, the question of what to do with the Detroit's so-called abandoned lands dominated the political sphere and posed a logistical nightmare for government. Land acquisition and disposition policies led to lengthy and confusing procedures rife with political maneuvering. As government officials made efforts to streamline processes, passions flared among residents and in planning meetings about who was to blame for Detroit's predicament and what should be done.

Moments like these brought to the fore the political nature of property and the tremendous normative, material, legal, and discursive work involved in its stabilization.[26] They also suggested that those tasked with planning and land management were ill prepared to confront the problem at hand. Ironically, while contestations laid bare the fictitious nature of property itself and its oppressive history and function, bureaucrats doubled down on reifying it, approaching it as a technical issue of value or, at best, a political-economic issue of use and access. Missing, however, was an understanding of how urban land and property struggles reflect epistemological and ontological questions about how to live. How might more theoretical and empirical attention to the history and changing nature of modern property formations help us understand the stakes of such questions?

The Political Life of Property

Before property becomes a formation or a regime, it is an idea. But what kind of idea? Legal scholars generally approach property as a "bundle of rights" or set of "jural relations." Economists have often understood property as the best way to allocate scarce resources.[27] For example, utilitarian theorists have argued that property rights incite humans' self-interest to improve that which they own and encourage trade. Meanwhile, neoclassical economists have similarly argued that the privatization of common land is necessary to induce improvements and hard work (ignoring that common pool resources are often successfully managed). Indeed, as anthropologists have demonstrated, property regimes are cultural. There is nothing absolute about property, which is to say, modern property formations are not given.[28]

Modern private property rose in tandem with racial capitalism. Indeed, it is a precondition for capitalism, one that emerged through prolonged and violent historical struggle to control land and human beings. From the dispossession of smallholder European peasants to the conquest of the Americas, the transatlantic slave trade, and marriage under coverture, the rise of modern property created new ways of relating to the self, others, and the world. To understand redevelopment struggles in Detroit—as well as land and housing struggles in other cities—we must account for how this history shapes the present.

It's impossible to talk about liberal imaginaries of freedom in the United States without talking about property. Indeed, a hallmark of liberal justice is the right to real property. It is articulated as the right to acquire, possess, use, and dispose of land and physical resources; the right of first possession; and the right of contract and transfer of alienable property rights. While the right to property is often upheld as an entitlement of citizenship, this universal discourse is betrayed by the raced, classed, and gendered history of property itself, which continues to evolve to shape the material and psychosocial space of the American metropolis.

John Locke's assertion that every man had property in his person and that the labor of his body on the land and its resources made them *his property* is foundational to American jurisprudence.[29] This assured a certain freedom for the self-owning subject so long as he could materialize possession. Many could not. Large segments of the population in Europe were, in Eva von Redecker's words, "bereft of property." In the early nineteenth century, settler colonialism served as a "partial resolution to this conundrum," as Redecker writes. "Europe's surplus population could seek 'despotic dominion' in the

New World, replicating the dynamics of dispossession by propertization, this time by dispossessing indigenous people."[30] For example, the Treaty of Detroit codified the theft of Ottawa, Chippewa, Wyandot, and Potawatomi lands in what is now southeast Michigan. Its signing in 1807 underscores the relative newness of a system that also barred enslaved people and married women from owning property because they were not considered legal persons. This is to say, though Locke understood property as inherent in and an extension of the human subject, it was not just any subject but one who was an Anglo European, male, able bodied, and of a particular class.

On the colonial frontier, property making was state making. Indeed, the protection of property was the raison d'être of government.[31] The US Constitution linked the ideal of liberty to the sanctity of private property, first by summoning a liberal subject, and then by endowing this new citizen with the right to bear arms under the Second Amendment to protect *his* person, home, and property. In practice, the modern property form necessitated and continues to necessitate extensive social institutions that grant entitlement and securitization. This is apparent in efforts to shore up Detroit's property regime.

In the modern city, the form and function of property remain bound with the creation of racialized subjects, political subjectivities, and ideas about whose lives are valuable and whose are not. Indeed, liberalism and modern legal subjectivity have long been adjudicated on "one's capacity to appropriate."[32] Brenna Bhandar demonstrates how modern property laws and rationalities for private property were conjoined with emerging racial schemas, which together determined who was—and was not—fit to own land. Status, as Bhandar shows, was conferred based on colonial rationalities of improvement and justified by emerging "scientific" and legal conceptions of race that served the explicit purpose of delimiting entitlement, use, and enjoyment of land and other immovable property.[33]

Patterns of land ownership and wealth disparities in the Detroit metropolitan region exemplify how white people have been endowed with a vastly greater capacity than other racial groups to own property, establishing what legal scholar Cheryl Harris calls an enduring "property interest in whiteness."[34] This is a financial interest and a cultural identity that many whites fiercely cling to today, whether in overt demonstrations like brandishing guns or in quieter ways like moving to neighborhoods with "good" schools. Such racial and spatial ordering, as critical geographers have long argued, serves to naturalize the inequalities produced by capitalism to the benefit of elites.[35] It has also served to naturalize the self-possessive individual as the ideal citizen.

As this suggests, if we want to understand the politics of abandonment in contemporary Detroit, we must go beyond deindustrialization and suburbanization to illuminate how they are symptomatic of the structuring logics on which racial capitalist property regimes rest as well as exemplary of how historical power blocs secure their dominance. This is to say, abandonment must be interrogated not simply as a state or condition of being left behind but as intrinsic to the ownership model itself.

Modern property functions not merely through dispossession, as Grace Kuyoungown Hong reminds us, but by occluding and criminalizing other ways of relating to land, nature, and one another.[36] A proliferation of important early twenty-first-century work in urban geography, influenced by the rise of Black, Indigenous, and Latinx geographies, has recast urban land questions in North America and beyond by uplifting the ways oppressed communities have preserved relationships to space and place outside of dominion.[37] Detroit—a settler city steeped in Black radicalism and labor movement politics—has much to teach us about the role alternative geographical imaginaries and placemaking practices play in countering abandonment and realizing liberation.

The Politics of Abandonment

It's safe to say that the term *abandonment* is most often associated in popular consciousness with individual-level psychological theories, such as those that seek to explain fear of rejection, advocate for attachment, and treat trauma. Meanwhile, urban studies scholars have studied the grief associated with displacement due to urban renewal, arguing that when people's attachments to place are severed, communities commonly experience what Peter Read calls "place bereavement" and what Mindi Fullilove describes as "root shock."[38]

The approach to urban abandonment developed in this book traces a related but different genealogy through the structuring logics of property relations. An examination of the etymology of the word *abandonment* helps illustrate some of these connections. Notably, the term's development shows how the social norms and meanings often ascribed to abandonment are bound up with the historical emergence of Western regimes of private property, coincident processes of racialization, and the rise of the liberal state as described in the previous section. The term *abandonment* is traced to the eleventh and thirteenth centuries in Middle French. At that time, *mettre à bandon* meant to put under anyone's jurisdiction or domain, to proscribe, to release from proscription, to banish. *Ban* referred to a restriction or obligation under feudal or church law. "There is a close association between a*ban*donment and other derivatives of ban, such as French *au ban*, meaning to outlaw, or the English 'band' meaning something that binds, fetters, or restricts; or bandit—one who is outside the law, unrestricted," writes sociologist Roger Salerno.[39] Thus, in its earliest uses, abandonment described submission to the authority, control, or jurisdiction of another. It denoted servitude and complete and utter surrender, for example, the submission of the serf to the master or the priest to the church.

By the fourteenth century, abandonment was also used to describe disregard for social obligation or "an abdication of one's rights or obligations to another person, place, value, or thing."[40] With the rise of agrarian capitalism, and as the enclosure movement in England forced tens of thousands of peasants from common farmland, the word's use expanded to refer to the severing of feudal ties, alienation of property, homelessness, and loss of a fixed place in the world. These new meanings signified a global rupture in relationality.

The rise of free-market capitalism, the Reformation, the Enlightenment, and the degeneration of medieval fealty and familial and patrimonial loyalties were not isolated European events. They were shaped by colonialism, the transatlantic slave trade, and new spatialized racial and gender divisions that denoted who was capable of ruling and who was not.

Under liberalism, abandonment started to connote something new— *freedom*. But it was a contingent freedom. Indeed, as philosopher Sylvia Wynter argues, the emergence of secular Man as a political subject, outside the church hierarchy, was realized only on the basis of the "'coloniality of power' and racism."[41] Within the context of colonialism and slavery, abandonment took on a new meaning. It came to denote, Salerno writes, "at one's own discretion," "at one's own will," and "without interference."[42] Abandonment, in this sense, was anchored by its opposite—slavery and servitude, that is, by those who lacked free will and, crucially, by those denied ownership of themselves and land. These meanings were eventually joined by others: "unrestricted freedom" and "free without responsibility."[43]

Thus, abandonment came to hold a double meaning, referring to both individual freedom and freedom from responsibility to others and place.[44] Abandonment, in short, denoted severalty—or the denial of mutuality and accountability—but it was also the foundation of liberal personhood. The unfreedom of some became the foundation of the freedom of others.[45]

This etymology underscores how the politics of urban abandonment are rooted in the conjoined histories of modern property and racial capitalism.

David Harvey has used the term "organized abandonment" to describe how the global financial system's drive to accumulate profit overdetermines how diverse actors—property owners, developers, the state, and residents—produce, use, transform, and *abandon* the built environment.[46] Elizabeth Povinelli uses the term "economies of abandonment" to name the ways that neoliberalism and late liberalism kill off social projects that do not produce market forms of life.[47] Likewise, Ruth Wilson Gilmore explains "organized abandonment" or "planned abandonment" as a strategy of racial capitalist state formation, tightly wedded to "organized violence," that exploits and treats vulnerable communities as surplus.[48] My approach extends these conversations by emphasizing the foundational role modern property plays in the politics of abandonment.

Throughout the book, I use the phrase the *politics of abandonment* to flag three interventions: First, rather than seeing capital as simply having moved on, leaving so-called abandoned cities in its wake, I aim to elucidate how racial capitalism is produced and reproduced through the conjoining of race and property, as well as through the state's role in capacitating the factors of production that enable its mobility.[49] Since the 2008 subprime mortgage crisis, racial capitalism has reemerged as an analytic and method to understand how race, colonialism, and capitalism intersect to shape the world.[50] Processes like the tax-foreclosure auction (the focus of chapter 3) and the corporate land giveaways under emergency management and bankruptcy (discussed in chapter 5) demonstrate how capitalism is secured through *ongoing* racialized primitive accumulation facilitated by the state and direct much needed attention to the central role that land, property, and debt play therein. Seen in this way, Detroit's abandonment is not merely an outcome of flight. Rather, it is an active state strategy and racialized mode of governance.

This formulation makes clear that capital, as Adam Bledsoe and Willie Wright argue, does not simply leave poor Black and Brown people and communities of color behind but rather targets them as a fix for value extraction and accumulation.[51] Put another way, abandonment is "a strategic exercise of power," to draw on the words of Leslie Gross-Wyrtzen, and an old social problem refashioned as a condition of racial state retrenchment.[52] Not only does it subtend the neoliberal regulation of life. It is also its organized outcome, Gilmore reminds us.[53] This active, relational, and, crucially, racialized understanding of abandonment is important to emphasize precisely because postindustrial cities are so often taken to be sites of absence—places absent capital, absent government, absent people. This book aims to disabuse us of this myth.

This brings us to the second way I use the phrase the *politics of abandonment*—to signal a political field in which interest groups deploy abandonment as a category toward different ends. When abandonment is reduced to vacant housing, buildings, lots, or blocks, as it often is in scholarship on postindustrial cities, the historical production of abandonment as a category and political field itself is obscured. To understand the conditions of possibility that allow categories of abandonment to emerge in specific times and places, we need to attend to how abandonment discourses circulate and are enacted through property regimes. For example, I examine how discourses of marginal and wasted land rooted in Eurocentric notions of personhood and improvement work to devalue entire groups of people and their lifeways.[54]

Analyzing continuities and shifts in the assignation of "abandoned" and "wasted" lands—from the doctrines of discovery to planners' and city officials' contemporary classifications—underscores how such political categorization functions as a mechanism of resource transfer. It also suggests how categories of abandonment, vacancy, and waste—and the mythologies they conjure—are deeply embedded in Western conceptions of the human. Such discourses act as powerful material, cultural, and symbolic forces in the production of white belonging and resettlement. They also subtend neoliberal calculations of risk that justify austerity and moral indifference as viable public policy. The stakes of this categorical work, as activists' critiques make clear, is not simply revanchist urbanism but also the negation of alternative ways of ordering society developed by communities who reside in what sociologist Avery Gordon names as "in-difference" to forces of capital and power.[55]

Thus, a third way I use the term the *politics of abandonment* is to direct attention to the struggles over places commonly seen as "left behind" by people and capital. My interest here is in what these struggles reveal about how people organize "social projects" that run "diagonal to hegemonic ways of life," in Povinelli's words, or in Gilmore's words, at "novel resolutions" in an effort to establish more democratic forms of urbanism.[56] There is an urgency, I believe, in understanding how people who lack resources but not, as Gilmore writes, "'resourcefulness' develop the capacity to combine themselves into extraordinary forces and form the kinds of organizations that are the foundation of liberatory social movements."[57] This urgency is felt acutely when it comes to rethinking and reorganizing land and property relations.

If liberal property formations organize abandonment, then we ought to learn from those who have sought to break with the propertied logics that structure racial capitalism and the racial state. Indeed, struggles over the making and unmaking of property regimes in Detroit bring into stark relief the centrality of land—in its material, psychic, and spiritual realms—to liberation. The epistemological and ontological breaks forged through such struggles open possibilities for imagining more just urban futures *after property*, in which a sense of collective identity supersedes the ideal of self-ownership and land is held in sacred relationship to the broader web of life rather than abstracted as a commodity.

Overview of the Book

The following chapters offer a recent history of land and property politics in Detroit. Chapter 2 (On Our Own Ground) rereads Detroit's postwar decline from the vantage point of radical activists who staked claims to urban space. The 1967 rebellion in Detroit—which erupted in a geopolitical context of Cold War anxiety and global movements for decolonization—ushered in a new phase of political struggle in which questions of land and territory became central. I demonstrate how the uprising presaged the rise of the Black political class in Detroit as well as a neoliberal assault on progressive politics that continues to this day.

This is, perhaps, nowhere more evident than in continued struggles over the right to stay put. By the 2010s, Detroit had gone from a bastion of middle-class Black homeownership to a foreclosure, eviction, and speculation hotspot, where a new class of land barons reigned. Chapter 3 (Stealing Home) tells the story of how one of the world's largest tax-foreclosure auctions functioned as a technology of wealth transfer. The auction wreaked havoc on the city. It deepened racial disparities, fueled speculation, and unmade the long-standing American dream of homeownership. The chapter traces the origins of the auction to a well-organized US property and states' rights movement that aimed to privatize public land, discipline the poor, and preserve ruling elite entitlements.

I also examine how the auction contributed to huge agglomerations of de facto public land. The glut of state land raised critical questions about how tax-reverted lands should be used, cared for, owned, and transferred. Chapter 4 (White Picket Fences) analyzes the stakes of new formations of authority, citizenship, and care that became central to state efforts to stabilize property markets.

State efforts to manage and dispose of property were complicated by the fact that land was not empty. Residents had long staked claims to land in various ways, from invoking historical loss and racial injustice to establishing gardens and community centers, mowing fields, and squatting in houses. These community caretaking practices on interstitial lands illuminate a reworked vision of the urban commons and land ethic rooted in Black urban life and spatial politics. Such insurgent forms of sociality underscore the tremendous capacity for self-organization that resides in communities. They also suggest that reimagining ownership is critical to countering planned abandonment.

State plans to privatize de facto public land were indelibly shaped by the Great Recession. Throughout my fieldwork, Detroit was mired in debates over debt and indebtedness. In chapter 5 (Accounting for Unpayable Debt), I examine how efforts by the state of Michigan to impose emergency management coincided with the launch of the Detroit Metropolitan Truth and Reconciliation Commission, which was charged with investigating race-based inequities in the region. On the face of it, they were distinct processes. One focused on reconciling fiscal debt; the other, moral debt. Yet their proximity in time and space—and the related tensions that surrounded both—suggest the importance of thinking about how the politics of accounting and collective memory work have become a key facet of twenty-first-century urbanism.

In the second half of the twentieth century, anti-Black dystopian images of Detroit as an urban jungle and place to fear dominated the media. By the twenty-first century, Detroit was more commonly conjured as an urban wilderness and new American frontier. In this new era, struggles over the future of Detroit were indelibly shaped by pervasive mythmaking manifest in cultural events like parades, photographic representations, ruin tourism, and general discourse. Chapter 6 (Conjuring Terra Nullius) tells the story of the revival of the legend of *nain rouge*—an impish red dwarf that haunts Detroit—to explore the integral role of terra nullius in the territorialization of whiteness. I also analyze efforts by residents to counter vacancy discourses by illuminating the importance of geography and geographical imaginaries to social justice struggles.

I extend this line of thinking in chapter 7 (Political Ecologies of Austerity) to consider how the discursive and technical treatment of land as empty and of private property as a civilizing mechanism on the frontier extend through contemporary urban planning practices in ways that facilitate large-scale green redevelopment schemes. I analyze how vacancy is categorically and strategically deployed within a racialized assemblage of interests, forms of expertise, and governmental techniques to revalue urban space under late capitalism. Specifically, I tell the story of a proprietary assessment called the Market Value Analysis (MVA), which city officials in Detroit and across the country have used to make critical decisions about which neighborhoods to target for investment, disinvestment, and public-service upgrades or disconnections. If industrial labor defined Detroit's economy and land-use planning decisions in the twentieth century, the MVA illuminates the extent to which real estate markets and finance capital do so in a new age of austerity and the stakes thereof for urban futures.

Efforts to reimagine Detroit turned on encouraging new land uses. As I explore in chapter 8 (The Garden Is a Weapon in the War), a diverse range of actors—from activists to planners, financiers, and foundations—began to herald postindustrial Detroit for its agrarian potential. I tell the story of financier John Hantz's controversial proposal to build the world's largest urban forest in the center of the city. I contrast the aspirations of Hantz Woodlands' with those of Black radical farmers in Detroit, who have sought to respond to racial capitalism and political abandonment by establishing community infrastructures and institutions that support Black life.

I conclude with an epilogue (Reconstructing the World) that considers the rash of protests against the water shutoffs in Detroit in 2014 to reflect on what the key arguments regarding property and abandonment made in the preceding chapters might offer for making sense of urgent land and housing questions facing other cities. Here I consider what the visions and aspirations of those organizing to fight against the water shutoffs suggest for the possibilities of untethering urban governance and planning from the protection of capitalist interests, property rights, and property values.

Collectively, these chapters reveal that the paradox of a city with too much land but not enough to go around is not a paradox at all but rather a reflection of the constitutive relationship between property and abandonment. They show how racial capitalism expands, literally on the ground, through new assemblages aimed at repairing and maintaining private property regimes in postindustrial and shrinking cities. They demonstrate how the lived implications of a "new Detroit" for longtime residents, especially for those who are poor, Black, and marginalized, turn on the ways property rights and land use are negotiated and enacted across racial and economic difference. Ultimately, *The City after Property* invites readers to think with Detroit activists, residents, and scholars about the role of land and property in bringing about more ethical forms of societal organization.

Where Is Our Land?

OUR LAND IS IN TWO AREAS.

First, scattered across America, our land is sections of the Northern cities where our people now live and have lived, in some, for two hundred years.

Second, lying in a great black belt across the South, our land is the counties of the South where we have lived and worked the land and clung to it for 300 years, despite the most brutal oppression the world has known.

ALL OF THIS LAND IS ILLEGALLY HELD IN CAPTIVITY, AS A COLONY, BY THE UNITED STATES GOVERNMENT.

Figure 2.1 | An undated illustration from the *New Afrikan: Voice of the Provisional Government of New Afrika. Source:* Robert Williams Papers, 1959–1997, Bentley Historical Library, Ann Arbor, MI. Image courtesy of the Bentley Historical Library.

on our own ground

In retrospect, I'm not quite sure what I expected when I drove to Twelfth and Clairmount. A memorial, a sculpture, a mural, perhaps. Something to let me know that this was where the events that some called the "1967 riots" and others called the "Detroit rebellion" erupted.

In many ways, no marker was needed. The uprisings were etched into the demography, economy, geography, and politics of the metropolitan region, as well as burrowed deeply in the collective conscience and psyches of residents.

I parked and got out of my car. The corner was quiet save a few passing cars. Wide swaths of grass ran parallel to the road where buildings used to be. The intersection was largely indistinguishable from any other. I looked around, trying to reconcile the scene with historical photos.

In 1967, the area had recently changed from a Jewish enclave to a predominantly African American neighborhood. A bustling, dense strip of more than two hundred businesses, many of them still owned by former Jewish residents, lined the street: barbershops, drug stores, supermarkets, bars, laundromats, clothing stores (figure 2.2).

This was before the early morning of July 23. Before the police raided the *blind pig*, an (after-hours, unlicensed) bar located in a second-floor apartment where a party was being held for two returning servicemen from the Vietnam War, before plainclothed white police officers forced guests down a narrow stairwell and into paddy wagons packed so tight that it was hard to breathe.

The commotion roused people in nearby apartments who were sleeping lightly in the summer heat. They spilled forth onto the streets by the hundreds.

Figure 2.2 | Twelfth Street, one month before the July 1967 rebellion. *Source:* Photo by Ira Rosenberg, *Detroit Free Press*, reprinted in Bill McGraw, "Before '67 Riot, Detroit Thought It Could Avoid Civil Unrest," *Detroit Free Press*, July 15, 2017.

As rage filled the air and dawn neared, thousands more joined. By morning, those who knew nothing of the nighttime strife awoke to the stench of smoke, a hazy sky, stores looted and burned, broken glass, and tanks rolling through their neighborhoods. For days, residents heard the constant blare of sirens and rata-tat-tat of snipers. Parents warned their children to stay away from windows because of gun fire. When all was quiet, the sense of loss settled and, for some, resolve.

I suppose I went to Twelfth and Clairmount that day hoping to see something that would help me grapple with the historical import of 1967; the conditions that led to it and the politics of memory that surrounded it.

After my visit, on the fiftieth anniversary of the uprisings, the state historical commission finally placed a marker at the site. The green plaque, embossed with gold-painted letters, quantified the damage caused by the unrest, which lasted for more than four days: 1,600 buildings were destroyed; more than seven thousand people were arrested, hundreds were injured, and forty-three people died. The marker also explained how President Lyndon B. Johnson ordered the Kerner Commission to conduct an investigation of the unrest. It determined that while the unrest was not coordinated, it was a response to "poverty, segregation, racism, unemployment, 'frustrations of powerlessness' and police actions that enforced a double standard for how people of different races were treated."

Conspicuously missing from the plaque was any mention of the state's militant response. Within a week, the Michigan State Police, the National Guard, and the 103rd Airborne descended on the city, seventeen thousand strong. Most of the more than seven thousand arrested were African American, many brought in for no other reason than being young and Black. Of the people who died, thirty-three were Black, ten were white. Nearly three-fourths of them were killed by law enforcement personnel.[1]

The plaque used the neutral language of "civil unrest" to describe what had transpired. I'd not been in Detroit long before I was schooled on the differences between riots and rebellions. While many people used the term *riots*, activists eschewed it. Riots signaled an irrational response that elided the inequities that had led to 1967.[2] By contrast, the term *rebellion* signaled a response to the political and economic abandonment that made life in the Black community increasingly untenable. The police force, which was 95 percent white, was so fascist and brutal, it was frequently referred to in Black communities as an occupation army.[3]

By 1967, key leaders of the freedom struggle, including Malcolm X, had been murdered. The promise of the Great Society era and urban renewal had crumbled, making poor housing conditions worse. There was increasing unemployment as car companies that had sustained the regional economy embraced automation, outsourcing and relocating their operations. Calling the events of 1967 a rebellion tethered them to a lineage of Black struggle and to a historical consciousness of resistance. Such competing frames—unrest, riots, and rebellions—underscore the complex politics of history and remembrance.

When I began this project, two popular narratives dominated explanations of Detroit's decline. One privileged deindustrialization as the key explanatory factor. Another blamed the ineptitude and corruption of Black elected officials. In both, 1967 played a pivotal role in accelerating white and capital flight. Yet both narratives ignored the state's role in sponsoring flight through racist housing policies. They also both overlooked how white and capital flight emerged as reactionary responses to the growing power of the Black radical and labor movements, which were increasingly staking claims to urban land, resources, and political power.

To make sense of land and property politics in the 2010s, it is essential to account for the complex forces that led to the rupture of 1967 and the realignment of power that ensued in its aftermath.

A Segregated Promised Land

Let's begin, then, by considering the racial and class dynamics that animated early twentieth-century Detroit and the role of state and capital interests in fomenting division among social groups.

The city, which fanned out, low and wide, from the banks of the Detroit River, had become an industrial powerhouse, not least because it served as a crucial transportation hub connecting the Great Lakes to the Erie Canal. Detroit was the world's largest producer of cast-iron stoves. It was also known for a number of other products including ships, rail cars, foundry and machinery parts, and pharmaceuticals. By the late 1890s, Michigan capitalists, confronting natural resource exhaustion in timber, began channeling money into the emerging auto industry.

Migrants—from Appalachia, the Black Belt, which stretched from Alabama to Mississippi, and other places—streamed to Detroit looking for opportunity. Drawn by the rapid expansion of American industrial capitalism, between 1820 and 1930, the city's population increased a thousandfold.

Behind these big shifts were individual stories. I was often struck in interviews by how residents' affective attachments to the city were intimately bound to their arrival stories or those of their ancestors. "We called it the 'Promised Land' because you could come here and change your life," said Shelia Porter, who described how her grandfather arrived in 1920 to work for Ford. "Everybody that I've ever talked with in Detroit, and I do this, I talk to everybody, right, came from somewhere where they didn't want to be servants or slaves or hopeless and they knew they'd have a chance. It's a whole city with an entire history of people that said, 'I'm going to go there. I'm going to try that.'"[4]

Porter's family story speaks to the hopes and dreams that drew many migrants. By the time her grandfather arrived, a dozen firms dominated the formerly decentralized US auto industry. Henry Ford's "low cost, high volume" assembly lines, which opened in 1908, introduced not only a new system of production but also a model for social discipline and economic development—Fordism. The model was manifest at Ford's River Rouge plant in nearby Dearborn, which employed an astounding 100,000 laborers under one roof. Word spread throughout the South of Ford's Five-Dollar-a-Day Plan;

factory workers could sometimes make more in a day than in a whole week back home.[5]

For Black people who lived in the South, Detroit promised not only gainful employment and upward mobility but also an escape from the failures of Reconstruction. It promised an escape from sharecropping and declining opportunities in manufacturing. It promised an escape from the fear of lynching; from the courts in Alabama, Arkansas, Georgia, Mississippi, South Carolina, and Texas, which continued to sell Black people into chain gangs; and from the general racial strictures of Jim Crow.[6]

While many Black migrants fled the South to Detroit of their own volition, they were also actively recruited. Northern capitalists seeking to ameliorate the scarcity of European labor caused by the onset of World War I advertised jobs in Black newspapers, touting unprecedented wages. They sent labor agents to rural outposts to enlist migrants, and they encouraged them to caravan northward together. Railroad companies even sponsored free passage. Meanwhile, real estate companies ran campaigns hyping Michigan as a place "Where You Will Enjoy Splendid Schools, No Segregation, No Lynching, Good Roads, Civil and Political Rights, Peace and Plenty."[7]

Approximately two million African Americans left the South during the First Great Migration (1910–1940). More than 100,000 arrived in a Detroit where Polish, Hungarian, Jewish, and Italian enclaves had begun to splinter, giving way to neighborhoods increasingly organized by class.[8] And yet, despite the promise of "no segregation," African Americans across the class spectrum were forced to live together, many in crowded tenements on Detroit's East Side.[9]

Neighborhood segregation was reinforced on the shop floor. Despite promises of racial parity and higher wages, management often exploited racial differences in their hiring and promotion practices with the aim of thwarting cross-class solidarity among laborers.[10] The twinning of racist regimes of labor and property conferred new forms of status among diverse populations of European immigrants, to which they fiercely clung, particularly when facing economic precarity.

Indeed, racial animus ebbed and flowed with economic crisis. As unemployment grew after World War I, African American periodicals warned that antagonisms in industrial cities were nearing a breaking point. "There is trouble brewing in Detroit," reported the *Messenger* in 1921, describing how Black laborers were "forced to work for a meagre wage" and how the Ku Klux Klan was "stirring up race prejudice, trying to get Negroes to return South" by offering to pay their railroad fare.[11]

The Klan exerted a tremendous political force on politics in Detroit, particularly regarding the preservation of segregated housing.[12] But it wasn't just the Klan or local officials. The federal government also compounded racial tensions. As part of an effort to thwart the development of domestic communist tendencies in the wake of the 1917 Russian Revolution, the government, in collaboration with the National Association of Real Estate Boards, began promoting homeownership as a "patriotic duty."

As part of its Own-Your-Own-Home campaign, the Department of Labor ran advertisements in newspapers and distributed more than two million posters to hang in factories and businesses across the country that featured white couples or families with slogans like "The man who owns his own home is a better worker, husband, father, citizen, and a real American."

The campaign was brilliant in many ways. Property ownership, after all, ensconces people in the capitalist system. The Own-Your-Own-Home campaign suggested how state and capital could use homeownership to pacify the masses by melding nationalism and consumer culture and suppressing cross-racial solidarity.[13] A 1929 advertisement for Bloomfield Village, touting it as a place where "exclusiveness endures," exemplifies how these dynamics over homeownership played out in Detroit (figure 2.3). Even so, it would be some time before such tendencies quelled the labor movement.

By the 1930s, Detroit had become a central hub of the growing US and international labor movement. Autoworkers' willingness to support the socialist presidential alternative to Roosevelt in 1932 suggested rising levels of class consciousness nationally. Such sentiments were only further galvanized by the Great Depression, drawing support for the passage of the Wagner Act in 1935, which guaranteed the right of private sector employees to form trade unions, engage in collective bargaining, and organize collective actions like strikes.

In response to widespread discontent among the working classes, state and capital interests again turned to housing to quell the social upheaval.[14] In 1933, the federal government established the Home Owners' Loan Corporation (HOLC). Mandated to protect urban homeowners from foreclosure, the HOLC issued long-term self-amortizing mortgages, growing US homeownership exponentially among working-class and middle-class whites. It also established the first countrywide appraisal system, making property values commensurable across distance.[15]

Commensurability necessitates standardized measures and rubrics of value. To this end, the HOLC hired appraisers to assess the "quality" of neighborhoods in American cities with at least forty thousand residents. In Detroit,

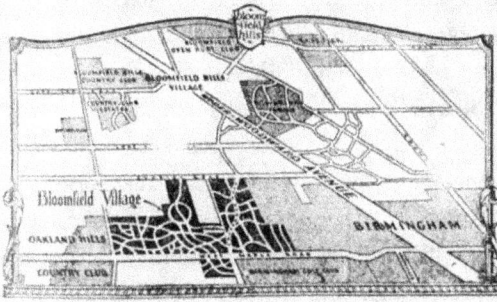

Figure 2.3 | A 1929 advertisement for Bloomfield Village, a subdivision of Bloomfield Hills, where "exclusiveness endures." The ad reads: "City neighborhoods change rapidly! So do neighbors! An intermingling of mixed creeds, nationalities—even races—inevitably follows spreading commercial areas into once desirable city neighborhoods. There is one answer to this 'neighborhood' problem—Bloomfield Village." According to the write-up, the community would be "protected forever by Hudson Bradway's 'Building and Use Agreement.'" Similar advertisements for Bloomfield Village published in other newspapers mention that the agreement, which would be mailed upon request, provides "a uniformly good neighborhood protected for all time against the invasion of undesirable neighbors." *Source:* Advertisements in *Detroit Free Press*, January 13, 1929; and *Birmingham (Mich.) Eccentric*, August 29, 1929, part 1, p. 4.

as well as in 238 other cities, appraisers assigned every block a rating from A to D. A-rated areas were considered "hotspots" that showed room for growth, whereas D-rated areas were considered high-risk zones characterized by "lower homeownership rates, poor housing conditions, 'detrimental influences in a pronounced degree,' and 'undesirable population or an infiltration of it.'"[16] The assessments were translated into a series of color-coded risk assessment maps, with A ratings coded in green, B in blue, C in yellow, and D in red, that real estate brokers, bankers, and the federal government used to make decisions about home sales, loan amounts and rates, and mortgage insurance.[17]

As racist property practices excluded African Americans from most of Detroit's neighborhoods, a Black metropolis formed within the city proper with its own robust social and economic infrastructure. Black Bottom and its central business district, Paradise Valley, were to the Motor City what Harlem was to New York, and what the South Side Black Belt was to Chicago. Paradise Valley, which boasted more than three hundred Black-owned businesses and many nightclubs, was a place where teachers, middle-class professionals, and very poor people all lived together. As Black workers accumulated wages, gained financial footing, and pursued philanthropic ventures, the neighborhood grew.[18] It had a hospital with a library in it, houses on every lot, access to public transportation, cooperative living in housing projects, churches with full congregations, cleaners, beauty shops, clothing stores, butchers, furniture stores, pawn shops, and nightclubs and theaters like Paradise Theater, where jazz greats like Duke Ellington, Dizzy Gillespie, Billie Holiday, and Louis Armstrong played.

As Black Detroit expanded economically, so too did it politically. By the late 1930s, it roiled with class interests and various political impulses, from liberals who supported integration and held capitalist ambitions to those who harbored more social democratic, communitarian, and separatist tendencies. These commitments—often overlapping and at other times in tension—brought forth new Black political organizations, such as local branches of the National Association for the Advancement of Colored People (NAACP), the United Negro Improvement Association, the Communist Party, and the Brotherhood of Sleeping Car Porters and Maids. On the brink of World War II, Black political organizations were poised to support liberation struggles on numerous fronts, including against wage discrimination, against segregation in the military and National Guard, and for labor union integration and open housing.

Detroit's factories retooled for war production. Ironically, the transformation of Detroit into the so-called Arsenal of Democracy opened opportunities for advancing civil rights. With almost a million Black men enlisted in the armed services, the Double V campaign, first championed by the *Pittsburgh Courier* in 1942, spotlighted the hypocrisy of the war era by calling for a double victory against fascism abroad and at home. Using the rhetoric of freedom and democracy, women and Black people—newly hired in retrofitted factories—demanded civil rights and better labor conditions and wages.[19]

Political education within the auto factories was a defining feature of the time. With labor and leftist organizers, including the Congress of Industrial Organizations, the Socialist Workers Party, the Workers Party, the Industrial Workers of the World, and the Communist Party, circulating radical literature within the plants, laborers became steeped in Marxist and other revolutionary theory. Such collective study among workers on and off the job

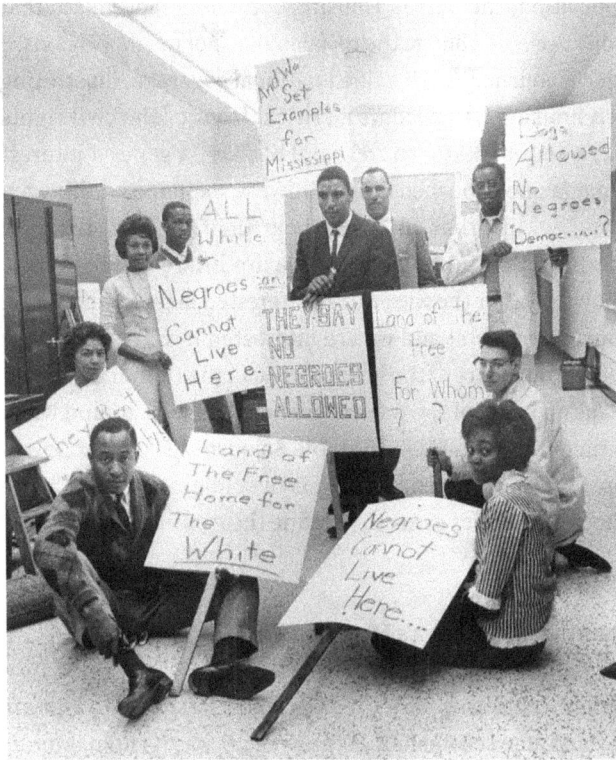

Figure 2.4 | Members of the NAACP's Housing Committee create signs in the offices of the Detroit branch for use in a future demonstration, 1962. *Source:* Image courtesy Archives of Labor and Urban Affairs, Walter P. Reuther Library, Wayne State University. Photo ID 24841.

strengthened the Black political base. Black workers joined the United Auto Workers (UAW) and the NAACP by the tens of thousands, pushing both union leadership and Black liberals toward a more radical civil rights agenda around job rights, law enforcement, voting, and, notably, housing (figure 2.4).[20]

Some civil rights gains were made during the war, but efforts to expand victory and government housing continued to be met by white anxieties and violence.[21] Take, for example, the infamous battle over the Sojourner Truth Housing Project in Detroit. Public housing was still segregated in 1941. Yet local housing officials thought a new Black public housing project in the Seven Mile–Fenelon neighborhood would be uncontroversial because Black residents already lived nearby. They were wrong. White residents launched a massive organizing campaign against the project. After civil rights groups, leftist labor organizers, and defenders of public housing pushed back, the project eventually proceeded as planned. But when Black families moved into the complex in February 1942, fighting erupted among the more than one thousand supporters and opponents who had gathered. In a regressive turn, aimed at placating the opposition, the Detroit Housing Commission promised that no new housing projects would change the racial makeup of neighborhoods.[22]

The struggle over Sojourner Truth gained national coverage, illustrating the extent to which housing had become a critical front of the civil rights struggle.[23] In 1944, a commentator in *Negro: A Review*, a general interest African American magazine published in the Midwest, explained it this way: "The subject of housing, like that of jobs and our fighting men strikes at something close and meaningful to all of us. We are interested in homes, homes of our own now and after the war; we are interested in the continuation of Government housing projects; and we are interested in wartime victory housing. Are we getting our share of the housing, or can the Detroit Sojourner Truth riot be taken as an index of the way we are being pushed around when it comes to Government housing?"[24] Indeed, the Sojourner Truth battle was a bellwether of tensions to come when millions of soldiers returned home after the war and housing politics came to redefine the American landscape.

The Postwar Unmaking of America's Heartland

If the first half of the twentieth century transformed Detroit into America's industrial heartland, the second half of the century was its unmaking.[25] Suburbanization spurred by federal housing policy, combined with the capital restructuring of Detroit's automobile sector, dealt a massive blow to working-class solidarity and trade unionism.

Factory management in Detroit responded to labor militancy and growing global competition by restructuring and automating production. One after another, Detroit's auto plants closed—the Packard plant, the Hudson plant, the United States Rubber plant, the Studebaker plant. Massive layoffs ensued. While some factories retooled, many companies found it easier to construct new facilities in the Midwestern suburbs, where there was ample space, and in the South and internationally, where unions and labor laws were weaker. From 1947 to 1955, the Big Three—General Motors, Chrysler, and Ford— constructed twenty new plants in the Detroit suburbs. Metal and machinery industries clustered around them, followed by residential growth, services, and major shopping areas.[26] Capital restructuring was aided and abetted by both the 1947 Taft-Hartley Act, which restricted labor organizing, as well as by the Red Scare, which fostered fear and paranoia about communism.

Meanwhile, growing economic precarity continued to fuel a white backlash around the housing question. For many white workers, homeownership was both a material marker of wealth and a symbolic marker of achievement that provided a sense of self-worth. If meeting monthly mortgage payments was often a struggle, it was also a point of pride. For these reasons, it didn't take much for fears of job loss to spark fears of home loss, particularly given painful memories of foreclosures during the Great Depression.

White workers struggling to retain their place in the diversifying postwar economy clung to exclusionary property regimes and only more so, as the open-housing movement gained power. When *Shelley v. Kraemer* (1948) outlawed restrictive covenants, white residents joined community associations in droves, intent of defending the racial "purity" of their neighborhoods.[27] At the same time, opportunistic real estate brokers used concerns over the transmutation of the color line to their advantage. Brokers—Black and white alike—engaged in *block busting*, a profit-making strategy that exploited white racial animus to their advantage. It worked like this: First, brokers would sell a home to a Black family in a white neighborhood. Then, preying on white residents' racial fears and their anxieties over property devaluation, brokers offered to buy their homes. Eager to salvage equity, white property owners were often quick to sell at below market value. The same brokers would then turn around and resell their homes to Black buyers at higher prices, profiting doubly.[28]

White homeowners' insecurity about property devaluation was not simply a bigoted myth. It was driven, in no small part, by the federal government and the HOLC's codification of racist logics into housing markets. As mentioned earlier, federal housing programs discriminated at the scale of individual mortgages, but the Federal Housing Administration's (FHA) financing of racially exclusive subdivisions had a much larger effect. An infamous example is Detroit's so-called Wailing Wall, also known as the Birwood Wall—built by a developer seeking a loan to build an all-white subdivision on Detroit's northwest side. After World War II, the developer applied to the FHA for financing. The FHA, which mandated racial homogeneity in housing developments, denied mortgage insurance in mixed-race neighborhoods as a matter of course. While the FHA determined the planned subdivision too risky an investment because it was adjacent to a Black neighborhood, they offered a workaround. If the developer built a wall to separate future white residents from their Black neighbors, the FHA would guarantee financing and insurance.[29] The one-foot-thick, six-foot-high, and half-mile-long wall, which remains standing today, serves as a reminder of the inextricability of racial and spatial demarcations.

The Birwood Wall is but one example of how the state racially managed postwar streams of finance. Another is the Veterans Administration (VA).

Following World War II, the VA worked with the FHA to provide insured mortgage financing and housing subsidies for returning veterans, fueling new geographies of racial segregation. Approved mortgage applicants could purchase new single-family detached units on private lots with low monthly payments in metro Detroit's expanding suburbs, which made up most of the postwar construction. Before the war, most white families could not afford to move out of the city. Afterward, thanks in no small part to the federal government, most white families could and did. Yet, Black families were systematically denied credit and, thus, excluded from new housing markets.[30] Put simply, federal housing interventions manufactured both a new housing market and a new property regime that induced complacency.

By 1968, when the Fair Housing Act made redlining illegal, sixteen of Detroit's richest suburbs had no Black homeowners, and most of the others had very small Black populations.[31] As residents and businesses relocated to

Figures 2.5 and 2.6 | *Left:* a 1959 photograph of Hastings Street, which ran through Black Bottom. Photo by Art Greenway. *Right:* The same aerial view in 1961, now of the Chrysler Freeway. Photographer unknown. *Source:* Both images courtesy of the Detroit Historical Society, cat. 2014.036.043 and cat. 2014.036.047.

the suburban fringe, Detroit's central city neighborhoods faced underdevelopment and poverty. Meanwhile, the federal government exacerbated it. In Detroit, as elsewhere, the Federal Aid Highway Act of 1956, along with the Housing Acts of 1949 and 1954, gave cities substantial urban renewal dollars for highway construction and so-called slum clearance. African American communities were often the first to be razed. In Detroit, Chrysler Freeway and Edsel Ford Freeway cut through Black Bottom and Paradise Valley (see figures 2.5 and 2.6). The violations were extensive. Black businesses, community spaces, places of worship, homes, and schools were obliterated overnight and replaced by new developments including Lafayette Park and Gratiot Redevelopment Project.

To this day, Paradise Valley and Black Bottom occupy a formative place in former residents' memories. In interviews, they often recalled brick streets, the oak, apple, and cherry trees that lined the neighborhood streets, kids playing, and Black businesses that met residents' needs. "We did not people Woodward Avenue. We had no reason to go there," recalled former Black Bottom resident Dr. Tommie Johnson. "We had a black YMCA, and we had a black YWCA.... We had Lark Grill which was a wonderful eating place.... And they got rid of the Pittsburg Courier office, that was right down there on Adams. They just tore up a whole area. And it distributed my church . . . it was all very disturbing because you had the feeling that wait a minute, they're trying to get rid of everything that's Black around here."[32]

By this time, African Americans were able to move to other parts of the city, and Black homeownership was on the rise, but the material, social, and economic infrastructure developed over decades to support the Black community suffered a dramatic setback. Residents like Johnson remembered well what is too often elided in popular narratives of Detroit's industrial decline: how a series of well-defined public policies gave rise to the "Black ghetto" and then demolished it, while at the same time incentivizing whites to flee the city for the suburbs.

A striking and visible color line started to emerge between the city and its suburbs. Meanwhile, despite worsening job prospects, African American migrants continued to arrive from the South. Between 1940 and 1960, the city's Black population tripled. In 1940, Black residents made up 9.2 percent of the city population. By 1960, they made up 28.9 percent. Yet with automation and factory closures, employment opportunities were few and far between. It was common for Black workers to be the last hired and the first fired. Indeed, by the 1960s, Black unemployment rates were double those of whites.[33]

As whites justified their relocation in terms of property values, many remained willfully ignorant of the role that racist federal housing policy and finance played in driving metropolitan transformation. The counterrevolutionary tendencies of the Own-Your-Own-Home campaign and the Better Homes in America campaign a half century prior seemed to have finally reached their fruition with suburbanization, which effectively stifled class consciousness, pacified the middle class, and buttressed McCarthyism, sowing the seeds for the rise of the New Right. Meanwhile liberal reformers increasingly turned to cultural explanations of poverty, developing band-aid programs that left unchanged the structural conditions that created racial disparities in the first place. Suburbanization and the expansion of homeownership for white metro Detroiters led to a new regional racial and class structure, and with it, new contests over space and political power.[34]

The Geopolitics of Urban Rebellion

To understand contemporary debates over the historical remembrance of the 1967 uprising, one must understand the Black radical movement's claims to urban space in the larger geopolitical context of Cold War anxieties and anti-colonial movements. By the 1960s, established organizations like the NAACP, the Urban League, and the Trade Union Leadership Council found themselves increasingly out of touch with a generation of activists frustrated by calls for integration. The younger generation, who tended to organize through affinity groups rather than through traditional political channels, increasingly began to demand spatial and economic control over their communities.[34] Their efforts included the formation of the city-wide Citizens Action Committee, which aimed to foster Black-owned businesses; the Freedom Now Party; and radical study groups like the revolutionary Black nationalist/socialist action cadre Uhuru (meaning "freedom" in Swahili). Meanwhile, a number of activists studied with Black Marxist C. L. R. James, who made Detroit his base in the 1950s. Two of his comrades, Grace Lee Boggs and James Boggs, would go on to become important political activists and lifelong Detroiters.[35]

In November 1963, Malcolm X delivered his famous speech "Message to the Grassroots" at the Grassroots Leadership Conference in Detroit. The speech called for Black people to put aside their differences and unite against a common enemy (whites). He also emphasized the importance of land to liberation struggles: "Revolution is based on land. Land is the basis of all independence. Land is the basis of freedom, justice, and equality." That same year, on August 28, 1963, at the March on Washington, as part of his "I Have a Dream Speech," Martin Luther King Jr. suggested that the United States still owed financial compensation for slavery. In 1865, Union general William T. Sherman had promised to redistribute roughly 400,000 acres of land to newly freed Black people under Special Field Order No. 15 but failed to do so. King asserted, "America has given the Negro people a bad check, a check which has come back marked 'insufficient' funds."

Three years later, in 1966, at a rally in Detroit, Stokely Carmichael argued that community control was a necessary response to the spatial politics of racial capitalism, which created extractive economies in the Black community. "We don't have to move into white suburbs to get a better house. All they need to do is stop exploiting and oppressing our communities, and we going to care for our communities. . . . It's only because we don't own and control our communities that they are the way they are."[36]

Meanwhile, James and Grace Lee Boggs went a step further that same year when they published a revision of the Communist Party's controversial Black Belt Nation thesis, "The City Is the Black Man's Land."[37] Since 1928, the Communist Party had approached Black liberation by advocating for an African American Southern nation.[38] By contrast, the Boggses observed that many of country's largest cities would soon be dominated by African Americans, and they argued that Black movements should focus on urban political power. In the wake of liberal failures, they argued that Black people should claim control of cities and reorganize life from top to bottom.

"The war is not only *in* America's cities," they argued. "It is *for* these cities."[39] Cities, they argued, should be organized like factories in the 1930s, with cadres that could function like labor organizers to mobilize the masses to expropriate and redistribute resources. Their vision was sweeping. It included the development of "a new Constitution that establishes a new relationship of government to people and to property, as well as new relationships between the national government, the states, and the cities, and new relationships between nation-states."[40] As African American studies scholar Stephen Ward writes, "The essay [was] an attempt to deepen the movement's theoretical basis by formulating a revolutionary theory of Black urban struggle that would reorganize not just Black communities but American society."[41]

As Black liberation and allied movements contended with the limits of integration and voting rights, uprisings engulfed urban America. During the 1960s, every major central city in the United States with a sizable Black population experienced civil disorders. From 1964 to 1967, 257 different cities had 329 major rebellions. After Martin Luther King Jr.'s assassination on April 4, 1968, there were another 200 uprisings in 172 cities.[42] Inner cities across the country were on fire, literally and figuratively (see figure 2.7). The violence reached a new level in the summer of 1967, after unrest in Omaha in March, and in Nashville in April. By June, violence had erupted in Cincinnati, Buffalo, Boston, Atlanta, and Tampa. And by mid-July, rebellions had spread to Newark and then, days later, to Detroit.[43] Policy makers and local officials seemed to have been largely caught off guard, even though African American intellectuals and activists had predicted the riot storm for some time.

In 1963, for example, James Baldwin had argued that rebellions would soon "spread to every metropolitan center in the nation which has a significant Negro population." If dramatic steps were not taken to "end the racial

Figure 2.7 | Fires from burning buildings on Detroit's West Side light up the early morning sky on July 24, 1967. Spectators watch from a distance despite the late hour. *Source:* Image courtesy of Detroit News Collection, Archives of Labor and Urban Affairs, Walter P. Reuther Library, Wayne State University. Photo ID 25990.

nightmare," he wrote, "the fulfillment of that prophecy, recreated from the Bible in song by a slave, is upon us: God gave Noah the rainbow sign. No more water, the fire next time!"[44]

The following year, Black radical Robert Williams, a former Detroit autoworker and US Marine who became famous in 1957 for forming armed self-defense groups in Monroe, North Carolina, before being exiled to Cuba, echoed Baldwin. In a prophetic essay that circulated widely in the *Crusader*, a pan-African journal, he warned, "This year, 1964, is going to be a violent one, the storm will reach hurricane proportions by 1965 and the eye of the hurricane will hover over America by 1966. America is a house on fire—FREEDOM NOW!—or let it burn, let it burn. Praise the Lord and pass the ammunition!!"[45]

The nationwide rebellions signaled what historian Brenda Plummer has called a "crisis of governability" in urban communities that was shaped by a geopolitical context in which decolonial movements and Cold War anxieties were on the rise.[46] Racial tensions had become a source of embarrassment for the Kennedy and Johnson administrations because they threatened the credibility of the United States as an international arbiter of democracy.[47] Policy makers felt increasing pressure to deal with civil rights abuses and persistent inequality at home. They were also concerned that nonviolent direct action, used as a strategy in the South, would become less appealing as the civil rights movement turned northward, and that its leadership would be unable to quell urban unrest.

Indeed, the freedom movement in Detroit and beyond was increasingly guided by a growing commitment to international solidarity, decolonialization, and fighting for a reordering of the capitalist imperialist world system.[48] This internationalist orientation and solidarity networks had been decades in the making. For example, shortly after the United Nations formed in 1945, the Civil Rights Congress, under the leadership of William Patterson and Paul Robeson, filed a petition (1951) charging the US government with Black genocide under the Geneva Convention.[49] A few years later, the nonaligned movement was initiated in Bandung, Indonesia (1955), the Afro-Asian People's Solidarity Organization was formed in China (1957), and the Revolutionary Action Movement (RAM)—the first Maoist-influenced organization in the United States—was founded in Cleveland (1961). During the March on Washington in 1963, Mao issued a statement against American racism, characterizing the African American freedom struggle as part of global struggles against imperialism.[50] Rising internationalism and the Cold War geopolitical context had major, if often overlooked, implications for domestic urban policy.

Policy makers went on the offensive. When the passage of the Civil Rights Act (1964) and Voting Rights Act (1965) did not quell protest, *community* became a new terrain of the liberal state and urban governance, as national leaders attempted to realign civil rights with liberalism rather than radicalism. This effort was embodied most fully in the Community Action Program, which launched in 1964 and became the centerpiece of the War on Poverty. Through the establishment of community action agencies, the Community Action Program sought to "empower the poor," remedy poverty, and contain protest by devolving political power to the neighborhood level.[51]

Detroit's community action agency was named Total Action Against Poverty; it received the nation's largest allocations of federal funds, though most went to Head Start, leaving a diversity of other programs underfunded. Meanwhile, Detroit sought to alleviate poverty with its own Community Renewal Program, which aimed to close the gap between physical and social planning. Detroit was also a demonstration site for the federal Model Cities Program, which aimed to develop strong citizen participation in target areas. They all failed, however, to address deep systemic issues that caused urban poverty. For example, the Community Renewal Program suffered from what planning scholar June Manning Thomas has called a "mechanistic faith" in social scientific data collection, and the Model Cities program faced chronic underfunding.[52] As historian Daniel Immerwahr argues, the anti-poverty programs like the Community Action Program and Model Cities drew inspiration from participatory models of community development that US policy makers had deployed abroad to steer former colonies away from communism by means of rural development and counterinsurgency. At home, however, such strategies led to unforeseen outcomes.[53]

With the uprisings, the country witnessed, as historian Russell Rickford writes, "'maximum feasible participation of the poor'—the watchword of the antipoverty programs—become kinetic reality in the streets."[54] Despite the rash of rebellions in other US cities—forty in 1966 alone—policy makers in Detroit were caught off guard: "'67 was not expected," the Community Action Program training director for Detroit later recalled. "We had a plan."[55] Their plan, however, underestimated both the hardships residents were facing and their ability to be placated.[56]

When the 1967 rebellion erupted in Detroit, frustrations over the lack of economic and political self-determination were channeled into an assault on those who controlled housing and commerce. Rioters targeted "the most visible symbols of capitalism and racism: first, property, and second, the firefighters and policeman who protected it," as historian Ahmad Rahman explains.[57] Property—in both landed buildings and commercial goods—embodied unequal power relations, urban segregation, and the spatial isolation of African Americans.

Federal investigators found no evidence of premeditation by Black militants or clear racial patterns of property destruction, but they did find some evidence of low-level organization of arson and looting that suggested protestors may have targeted businesses perceived to be extorting residents. Whites, Chaldeans, and Jews, who dominated store ownership, suffered more losses than Blacks. Moreover, properties with the words "Soul Brother" painted on them were conspicuously spared. The signage signaled that the stores should not be looted because they were Black-owned businesses (or non-Black business owners in solidarity).[58]

The uprisings radically altered the racial demography and wealth distribution in the metropolitan region. To be sure, white flight and capital flight were underway before 1967. Approximately twenty-two thousand residents left the city between 1964 and 1966. But the exodus after the uprisings dwarfed this figure. In 1967 alone, forty-seven thousand residents (mostly white) left the city. In 1968, eighty thousand residents departed. And in 1969, another forty-six thousand left.[59] One author described the changing landscape this way: "For sale signs sprung up in every white neighborhood, seemingly in front of every house. There had always been a lot of vacant land outside the city, and Detroit's suburbs had been expanding slowly since the fifties; now developers threw up houses, schools, and shopping malls beyond Eight Mile Road. Some people were so panicked they spent the winter of 1967–68 sleeping on their relatives' couches or shivered in half-completed tract homes."[60]

Racial hysteria set in. Many whites in the suburbs imagined the city to be a threatening place. Some bought guns, hired private guards, and cut economic and social ties with the city. Residents of the nearby city of Warren went as far as forming a militia. A right-wing white organization called Breakthrough emerged with the explicit mandate of arming white residents and encouraging them to remain in the city. Its founder argued that police had failed to protect whites, and if Detroit became majority Black, "guerrilla warfare" would ensue in the suburbs. The John Birch Society made similar claims through a front organization called Truth About City Turmoil.[61] Detroit's change from a predominantly white city to a majority Black one was the fastest and most complete of any other American city.

Making Sense of the Uprisings

The uprisings might not have been planned or coordinated, but the sense making that happened in their wake was deliberate. As contemporary debates over the terminology *riots* and *rebellion* suggest, it mattered tremendously how the uprisings were understood. Different narratives, after all, portend different responses.

After the uprisings, white analysts sought to explain the disorder by turning to social science explanations like agitator theory, the frustration-aggression hypothesis, and blocked-opportunity models. There was widespread consensus that the uprisings were unplanned but not irrational or meaningless. Most agreed that they were a form of "Negro protest," a claim so banal as to reveal nothing.[62]

President Johnson moved quickly to appoint the National Advisory Commission on Civil Disorders to investigate the uprisings nationwide and make recommendations on how to "prevent or contain such disasters in the future." The commission issued the Kerner Report (named after the commission's chair Otto Kerner). The report stated that the United States "was moving toward two societies, one black, one white—separate and unequal. . . . White institutions create it, white institutions maintain it, and white society condones it."[63]

While the Kerner Report was celebrated for its condemnation of racial injustice, many of its findings—though not its ultimate takeaways—came from a little-known, controversial 167-page draft report. The report, *The Harvest of American Racism: The Political Meaning of the Violence in the Summer of 1967*, prepared by a team of young social scientists, warned that radical—not moderate—changes were imperative if the growing urban rebellions were to be contained. The Harvest Report "exploded the political tensions within the Kerner Commission," writes historian Malcolm McLaughlin, and "exposed a growing rift within liberalism."[64] Whereas the Kerner Report called for expanding public programs, the Harvest Report called for radically restructuring existing power structures; it saw the "business of compromise and coalition building that governed White House politics" as woefully inadequate.[65]

The Harvest Report's assessment reflected Black Detroiters' sense of the racial and class inequities that spurred the uprisings. Black Detroiters preferred to call the uprisings a *riot* by a four-to-one margin (48 percent to 13 percent) in their immediate aftermath. Within a few months, however, the numbers reversed, and the majority—56 percent (compared to 19 percent)—preferred *rebellion*.[66] Interviews with Black residents after the uprisings revealed a shared sense that the unrest was about claiming space in a city that had largely been closed off to them. One man put it this way: "I work in Detroit [and] live in Detroit but I don't Feel Free. . . . There are so many places closed to me."[67] The growing centrality of space, place, and geography within the freedom struggle was reflected in a survey conducted after the rebellion, which found that 75 percent of adult Black residents expected to have more autonomy in their neighborhood because of the uprising.[68]

In a sermon, Jaramogi Ageyman, formerly Albert Cleage Jr., of the Shrine of the Black Madonna, argued that the uprisings were a "logical" outgrowth of the Black Power movement, not "orgies of criminality."

> There is a difference between a riot and a rebellion. A riot is a little group perhaps more interested in looting than in freedom. But a rebellion is a community that has decided that it will no longer tolerate the kind of racial oppression that it has been forced to tolerate. . . .

People look around and say, we are tired of these slums. We are tired of all the conditions that we have to put up with. We are tired of the whole situation and we are not going to tolerate it any longer. And then a whole community erupts. . . . That is a rebellion.[69]

The "first gunshots of the rebellion," Ageyman argued, were fired decades before, with court cases to outlaw segregation in the South, the bus boycotts, and freedom riders, among other forms of resistance. Ageyman's speech reflected how the rebellions were analytically being put to work to advance the liberation struggle. It also suggested the ascendance of Black Power as a strategy and an umbrella term for several different movements and causes.

Geographies of Black Power

The uprisings and Black Power movement radically reshaped the material terrain of urban social struggle and its theoretical basis. Debates over integration versus separatism—and how to meaningfully break from white supremacy and racial capitalism—became more acute after 1967.

Ageyman's arguments echoed resolutions passed at the Newark Black Power Conference.[70] The Newark conference attracted a broad base of supporters: the attendees' reframing of the uprisings as revolutionary and necessary proved influential. One journalist wrote, "[It] was clearly not just a small, secret meeting of burning eyed radicals, but a gathering of over 1,000 registered delegates from 38 states, representing a cross-section of Black America. There were old women from Rochester on welfare, Mississippi cotton pickers, municipal judges, Black Muslims, Black Catholics, broken down ex-boxers, Black Republicans, and a police captain from Harlem. Every major Black organization in the U.S. was represented."[71]

On the first day of the conference, a mere three days after the rebellions in Newark—where 26 people were killed, 725 injured, and 1,500 arrested—and three days before the violence in Detroit broke out, the delegates adopted a resolution that the nationwide rebellions were necessary for the freedom movement to advance.[72] On the afternoon of July 20, the young program director of the Student Nonviolent Coordinating Committee, Ralph Featherstone, took the floor.

"In order that our Black brothers in Newark have not died in vain," he said, "I have a resolution I want to read." The resolution called for "the nation of

Black people which lives in the United States" to "join the endless legion of Freedom Fighters by the fighting and dying for their freedom." "Be it resolved," Featherstone proclaimed, "that this National Conference on Black Power on July 20, 1967, hereby goes on record as strongly endorsing the black revolution. Further, that it proclaims its approval of the rebellions in cities from Watts to Newark as necessary to achieve nationhood."[73]

The resolution—while not officially adopted—was approved "in spirit" on the spot amid cheers and shouts. Officially, the conference delegates adopted only one resolution, the Black Power Manifesto, which "condemned 'neocolonialist control' of Black populations worldwide and called for the circulation of a 'philosophy of Blackness' that would unite and direct the oppressed in common cause."[74]

Condemning neocolonialist control meant grappling with matters of sovereignty and nationhood, which in turn meant dealing with foundational questions of land and territorial control. Stokely Carmichael and Charles Hamilton's *Black Power: The Politics of Liberation in America* (1968) extended Frantz Fanon's assertion in *The Wretched of the Earth* that institutional racism in the United States was colonialism. Carmichael and Hamilton argued, "There is no 'American dilemma' because black people in this country form a colony, and it is not in the interest of the colonial power to liberate them."[75] Eldridge Cleaver, the first information minister for the Black Panther Party (BPP), echoed these sentiments in a widely circulated essay, "The Land Question" (1970): "Black people are a stolen people held in a colonial status on stolen land, and any analysis which does not acknowledge the colonial status of black people cannot hope to deal with the real problem."[76]

By the late 1960s and 1970s, the question of how, where, and on what land a political base should be built became a defining debate among Black radicals. Black agrarian movements argued that unemployment in the industrial North made a Southern land strategy more urgent. Meanwhile, the rebellions had put the urban on the revolutionary agenda in a new way, as activists turned toward the city as a site for land reclamation and as the domain of Black politics.[77] In the ghetto, where underdevelopment and violence were rampant, the "the teleological narrative of black uplift through citizenship" was not reassuring, writes Nikhil Singh. Instead, activists began "embrac[ing] black urban space as the basis of a renewed and very different kind of radical vision: the site of a radically dispersed black nation and the model of the internal colonization of America's black people."[78]

That most Black Detroiters claimed the uprising as a rebellion suggests that such sentiments were widespread. It is notable, then, that urban studies accounts of postindustrial decline tend to leave aside such analyses, engaging the 1960s uprisings as solely a driver of white and capital flight, not a political claim to space. This elision has stakes for the present, particularly as historical placemaking and memory projects become an integral part of the urban growth machine.

The desire for territory that defined this period was "a matter of finding free space," as Robin D. G. Kelley argues. "Land is space," Kelley writes, "territory on which people can begin to construct their lives. The dream, after all, is to create a new society free of the overseer's watchful eye."[79] In this context, power was conceptualized as coming from land—land for raising food, land for freedom and dignity, and land for "owning the job."[80] Thus, while land was not the end goal, as Detroit illustrates, it was seen as a means because decolonization was understood as requiring a spatial reorganization of colonial geographies.[81]

In the wake of the rebellion, Detroit emerged as a key site for Black nationalism and as a battleground for the reparations movement. One influential movement that began in Detroit was the Republic of New Afrika (RNA). In 1968, five hundred radicals at the Black Government Conference at the Shrine of the Black Madonna church in Detroit signed a Declaration of Independence with the aim of creating an independent Black nation that would occupy five Southern states (Alabama, Georgia, Louisiana, Mississippi, and South Carolina).[82] The RNA rearticulated the Back to Afrika movement—rerouting the desire to escape to Africa into a project that aimed to reconfigure US territory so that a New Afrikan citizenship could be realized.[83]

The main goal of the RNA was to establish an independent sovereign nation for Black people in the rural South—to operationalize Amiri Baraka's assertion "Black is a country." But they also sought, at least rhetorically, to claim land in "the Northern cities where our people now live and have lived, in some, for two hundred years."[84] Detroit remained the RNA's base until 1970.[85]

The BPP also established a chapter in Detroit in 1968, the same year the RNA declared independence. Like the RNA, they saw the reconfiguration of spatial relations as essential to achieving liberation, though, they were intercommunal in their orientation, not nationalist. Drawing on the ideas of Malcolm X, Frantz Fanon, Che Guevara, and Mao Tse-tung, they deployed a territorial strategy that sought to develop solidarity networks and power centers that were global in reach but locally dispersed. The Detroit chapter was one of forty chapters, including international chapters in England, Israel, Australia, and India.

The Detroit chapter was founded in response to the conditions of deprivation and racism that caused the uprisings. In a symbolic move, they established their first headquarters two blocks from the epicenter of the rebellion at Twelfth and Euclid.[86] The Detroit Panthers, like other branches, instituted survival programs, including programs to feed children, clothe families, and provide for medical needs. The survival programs responded to the failures of the Keynesian welfare state by creatively reorienting flows of capital to the needs of the people. They were envisioned as a way to escape the oppression of US empire through everyday social reproduction, mutual aid, and the establishment of a political base of resistance.[87]

In their Ten Point program, the BPP called for the overdue debt of "forty acres and two mules," for "land, bread, housing, education, clothing, justice, and peace," and for a United Nations–supervised referendum for "black colonial subjects" to determine their "national destiny." Instead of seeking to establish a national land base like the RNA, the BPP focused on reclaiming institutional spaces—for example, housing projects, schools, community centers, and prisons—and developing city-center communes with the goal of making liberated territories.[88]

The BPP's approach was based on a recognition that the spatial scales of world capitalism had changed. In prescient analysis of neoliberal globalization, Huey P. Newton, party founder and theoretician, argued that this fundamental change in imperialism, in which nations were now integrated into one community through capitalist production and consumption, would lead to a shift in interclass relations. He predicted that increased precarity for all races would give rise to a reactionary white working class that would fail to see the "objective enemy." New forms of constituent power and cross-racial alliances were thus necessary to capacitate new forms of life, politics, and institutions capable of liberating communities. For these reasons, Newton argued that the globalization of capital made Black claims to national sovereignty obsolete.[89] "Blacks in the U.S.," he wrote, "have a special duty to give up any claim to nationhood now more than ever. The U.S. has never been our country; and realistically there's no territory for us to claim. Of all the oppressed people in the world, we are in the best position to inspire global revolution."[90]

The BPP's focus on theorizing the new global terrain of capital resonated with Marxist labor alliances that formed in Detroit, like the Dodge Revolutionary Union Movement (DRUM), which promoted solidarity among Black workers. DRUM precipitated the formation of revolutionary union movements (RUMs) at other plants—Ford, Cadillac, General Motors—and at nonautomotive facilities in Detroit and beyond, like the US Postal Service. Eventually the various RUMs incorporated as the League of Revolutionary Black Workers (LRBW). They sought to overthrow capitalism, reform the corporate management structure of the UAW, and bring about racial equity by organizing workers at the point of production—the shop floor. Although the league was short lived, it made an indelible mark on radical organizing within the labor movement and beyond the factory.[91]

One example of their involvement in organizing beyond the factory was on April 26, 1969, when members of the LRBW, in collaboration with other activists, including James Forman of the Student Nonviolent Coordinating Committee (SNCC), took over the National Black Economic Development Conference (NBEDC). The conference, which was being held in Detroit, had been organized by social justice advocates in collaboration with Black clergy and the Black business community. There Forman issued the Black Manifesto (distinct from the Black Power Manifesto mentioned earlier) to the approximately six hundred to eight hundred attendees. While demands for reparations had been longstanding, dating to the crimes themselves, the Black Manifesto was distinct in its approach. It had two parts. It began by describing African Americans as a "colonized people" and argued that such oppression could be overcome only by a global revolution against capitalism. They called for Black socialism and $500 million in reparations (a demand that later grew to $3 billion) from white churches to be used to strengthen Black political and economic institutions. Land topped the list for funding as drafters of the manifesto earmarked $200 million for a Southern Land Bank, which aimed to help "people who want to establish cooperative farms but who have no funds."[92]

In many ways, the manifesto's demands and concerns with land rearticulated those already made by the RNA, the BPP, Cleage, and the Nation of Islam, but Forman's tactics differed. In the subsequent months, advocates of the manifesto began interrupting church services in the Detroit area and beyond to demand reparations.[93] For example, on June 1, 1969, Forman, along with NBEDC leaders Mike Hamlin and John Watson, who were also members of Detroit's LRBW, interrupted an Episcopalian parish in Bloomfield Hills. They demanded ten thousand dollars from the 2,300-member congregation. The church's response was similar to others: they expressed sympathy but chose not to give at an organizational level. While the Black Manifesto fell short of its goals, it motivated other organizations and movements to continue demanding reparations, including in the form of land.[94]

Black activists were not alone in debating the land question nor in demanding sovereignty and reparations. Indeed, allied movements like the American Indian Movement (AIM), the Chicano group Crusade for Justice, and the Chicano Mexicano and Puerto Rican group Movimiento de Liberación Nacional saw land as the necessary material grounds for liberation and self-determination. Their shared understanding that the United States functioned as a capitalist imperialist system that exploited people of color at home and abroad suggested that freedom required a fundamental reorganization of property relations.[95]

The threat posed by these revolutionary ideas did not go unnoticed by the prevailing power structure. If the rebellions—and the struggles for land and territory in their aftermath—were an attempt to violate the capitalist racist spatial order, then the reconfiguration of domestic urban policy that followed was decidedly as an effort to defend that order.

State Repression and the Rise of Neoliberal Urbanism

The Detroit rebellion became a linchpin in congressional debates over the efficacy of urban poverty programs. Desperate to quell unrest, policy makers shifted tactics. Whereas Johnson's Great Society programs previously focused on "maximum feasibility participation," after 1967, urban policy was increasingly defined by crime control, surveillance, punitive policies, and mass incarceration, in short, race and class warfare. Meanwhile, politicians engaged in fear mongering, pitting the suburbs against inner cities. As Richard Nixon said in 1968 as a presidential candidate, "If we allow [the crime wave] to happen, then the city jungle will cease to be a metaphor. It will become a barbaric reality and the brutal society that now flourishes in core cities . . . will annex the affluent suburbs."[96]

In Detroit, the law-and-order approach meant a rise in policing and a militant crackdown on movement leaders. By the late 1960s and early 1970s, the Detroit Police Department (DPD) Criminal Intelligence Bureau had begun working in concert with the Michigan State Police and the FBI's COINTELPRO program, which targeted and sought to neutralize "subversive" civil rights, labor, Black Power, and New Left groups. Their surveillance program was extensive. The DPD and the Michigan State Police kept dossiers on up to 150,000 "subversives," the majority of whom lived in Detroit, including members of the LRBW, the RNA, and the BPP.[97]

As the neoliberal carceral state formed, many activists faced incarceration and surveillance. Meanwhile, others were recruited into electoral politics. The rebellions countrywide presaged the election of African Americans to political office from Newark to Detroit. Diverse coalitions came together to build a Black electoral base and political class that promised to expand the ideals of social democracy and legal battles for racial equality. Between 1969 and 1974, the number of Black elected officials rose to sixteen congressional representatives and 104 mayors.[98] Among them was Coleman Young, who, in 1973, was elected mayor of Detroit, a position he would hold for twenty years.

Young was elected on a platform to abolish the city's controversial plain-clothed police squads, which he called "execution squads," and establish instead a "people's police department."[99] Once in office, he sought to integrate the 5,500-member police force, which was 85 percent white, and create a more "citizen-friendly" organization.[100] As the federal government dismantled Great Society initiatives like the Model Cities Program for urban development, Young sought to fill the gaps. Building on voter enthusiasm, he continued former mayor Jerome Cavanagh's local Great Society programs with more attention to racial equality. He built new parks, recreation centers, and low-income housing. He also facilitated the hiring of African Americans to head and staff numerous agencies. By his second term in office, 40 percent of his appointees and senior management were Black, causing white leadership to accuse him of launching a "divisive racist campaign" that would make "rebuilding and revitalization under him impossible."[101]

While many Black Detroiters celebrated the Young administration's focus on social welfare and racial discrimination, conservative whites' disdain grew over time.[102] After his election, many white residents who had the financial means left the city. In 1969, 891,000 white residents remained. By the time Young began a second term in 1976, 348,000 of them had left. Meanwhile, between 1970 and 1990, the percentage of Black residents in Detroit increased from 44.5 percent to 78.4 percent.[103] The mass departure of white residents decimated the tax base and threw Detroit into economic turmoil, which was compounded by an economic recession.

For these reasons, many residents argued that even though the 1967 uprisings led to widespread physical destruction, the major destruction came *after* the rebellion. The outcomes were devastating. Commercial firms and department stores went bankrupt or abandoned their Detroit sites. During the 1970s, Detroit lost almost a quarter-million jobs, leading to harrowing conditions in Black communities. Fiscal crisis, poverty, and unemployment became chronic. One-third of residents lacked any earned income. Sixty percent received some public assistance. Public services were reduced, and many municipal employees were laid off. Public schools faltered and gun violence intensified.[104] Meanwhile, the Supreme Court's regressive and enormously significant decision in *Milliken v. Bradley* (1974)—known as the Detroit school busing case—allowed for the de facto segregation of school districts in metropolitan Detroit, contributing to a separate and unequal educational landscape that only drove more families from the city.[105]

As Detroit's economy plummeted, the suburbs boomed, an indication that capital had taken flight from Detroit but not from the entire region. Real estate values starkly illustrated these disparities. In 1960, Detroit contained half of the region's property wealth. By 1980, the city's share had shrunk to 16.5 percent. During these decades, property values in nearby Oakland and Macomb County rose tenfold. By 1983, the Detroit region had the widest household income gap of any large metropolitan area in the United States.[106] It only worsened as the crack epidemic swept urban communities and welfare retrenchment continued unabated.

Meanwhile, steep declines in jobs heightened tensions within the labor movement. As union leaders sought to discredit Black revolutionaries and auto companies attacked the bargaining power of the UAW, union membership declined sharply. As historian Heather Ann Thompson reports, in 1969, 1,530,870 union members worked for the Big Three. By 1979, membership was reduced to 840,000, and by 1983, to a mere 477,000 workers. The declining membership of the UAW mirrored the nation. In the 1960s, approximately 30 percent of all US workers (public and private) were in unions. By 1983, this figure had fallen to 20 percent, and by 2010, to a mere 11.9 percent.[107] Workers paid dearly. So did progressive politics more broadly. Reductions in the bargaining power of workers had a deleterious effect on progressive social justice organizing across the city because unions had functioned as a critical infrastructure.

The confluence of such forces—the corporate repression of labor militancy, the professionalization of radical activists, and the expansion of federal housing programs that guaranteed nominal property ownership and led to suburbanization—diminished counterrevolutionary tendencies and laid the grounds for a new landscape of American urban governance, defined, on the one hand, by hypersurveillance and mass incarceration, and on the other, by the proliferation of philanthropies, nonprofits, and public-private partnerships that filled the gaps created by retrenchment.

At the beginning of his tenure, Young represented an effort by Black politicians to expand liberal social provisions. By its end in the eighties and early nineties, however, his administration embraced a neoliberal growth agenda at the expense of social and economic democracy. Like other Black mayors across the country, Young ascended to power at a time of municipal fiscal crisis and was forced to contend with an anemic tax base. This was not a situation of Young's making, yet his use of tax abatements, federal development grants, and austerity measures more often benefited private capital than residents (exemplified, perhaps most famously, by the demolition of the Poletown neighborhood in 1981 for General Motors). Young's focus on downtown and riverfront development and pragmatic alliances with corporate and suburban power brokers led many progressives who had helped put him in office to feel that their more radical visions for social change had been jettisoned.

Despite corporate and state efforts to contain radical movements, activists continued to seek more just configurations for social life. As they faced the dual challenges of state warfare on their movements and the demise of the industrial class, long thought to be the vanguard of the revolution, new projects and coalitions emerged. In the late 1970s, for instance, the Detroit Alliance for a Rational Economy (DARE) organized against Young's approach to the city's economic development. They argued against tax breaks for the wealthy and called for "rational reindustrialization" and the development of a "public enterprise sector" that was rooted in "community and municipal rights to industrial property." Historian Austin McCoy writes, "DARE activists . . . advocated for a mix of measures including worker ownership and special zones for communally-owned firms to operate with the hopes of fertilizing the ground for the development of a socialist economy in the city."[108]

In 1979, they organized the "City Life in the 80's Conference" to redefine the contours of radical struggles for a new decade. That the conference, which was held on September 29 at Sacred Heart Seminary on West Chicago at Linwood, drew a crowd of five hundred people from a range of block clubs, religious groups, and community organizations suggests widespread concerns among residents over social justice and the trajectory of urban development. Ken Cockrel, a member of both city council and DARE addressed the issue of Detroit's so-called renaissance: "People are led to believe that the unprecedented coalition of public and private sector elements have saved Detroit," he said. "But there is a Detroit which doesn't receive much attention from the multi-millionaire 'renaissance-builders,' and that is the Detroit of the people, of neighborhoods and communities. . . . It's time that these people sat down at the Detroit table and received their share of the City's renaissance pie!"[109]

Throughout the eighties, DARE and other groups put forth robust visions for alternative urban development plans, but with the restructured auto sector, they found themselves lacking the support of a strong organized labor force. They also faced a political firewall, according to McCoy, in the form of Young's capitalist growth coalition and his broad base of African American supporters.[110]

Meanwhile, other groups engaged in grassroots community development, representing a shift in strategy from organizing in factories at the point of production and against the racist growth machine to organizing the neighborhood. For example, James Boggs and Grace Lee Boggs, who had been involved with a group called National Organization for American Revolution in the 1970s and 1980s, began to shift their attention to local issues. Increasingly distressed by the violence and drugs pillaging their communities, they along with other comrades launched We the People Reclaim Our Streets. Every Friday night for five years, they marched through Detroit's neighborhoods promoting an ethos of care and organization. Others similarly sought to reclaim neighborhoods from drugs and gang violence, including Clementine Barfield, who founded Save Our Sons and Daughters (SOSAD) in 1987, after her son Derek Barfield was killed the previous year. SOSAD organized against gun violence and developed programs aimed at reducing youth homicides. Then in 1996, after police violence killed nine Detroiters alone in one year, the Detroit Coalition Against Police Brutality formed to address police brutality, repression, and criminalization by promoting community-led public safety, conflict mediation, and peace in neighborhoods. Meanwhile, other groups focused on building grassroots power through housing rehabilitation, the arts, place-based education, job creation, and environmental justice. In so doing, they grappled with the question of what kind of society should be built in the ravishes of racial capitalism and what it would take to realize their visions.[111]

Tensions between these alternative visions for development and those of the neoliberal growth machine persisted into the 1990s and 2000s. Compounding matters was the fact that Young and subsequent administrations increasingly relied on bonds and notes sold on capital markets to fund both long- and short-term operating costs. With deregulation and the neutralization of union power, finance capital and credit-rating agencies had come to wield tremendous power over local decision-making, effectively repurposing urban public policy toward the needs of finance capital rather than the social needs of local communities.[112]

These dynamics are illustrated by Detroit's credit-rating debacle in 1992, when Moody's downgraded the city's debt from investment to speculative grade (Ba1), significantly raising interest rates on borrowing. The city's finance director argued it was unfair because they had spent the last two years responding to Moody's concerns by exacting "fiscal surgery" on the city; but, he said, they were committed to keeping "a scalpel in hand" if that was what it took.[113] This deference to market interests continued in subsequent mayoral regimes. For example, when Dennis Archer, a successful Black lawyer and Michigan Supreme Court justice, became mayor in 1994, after Young's two-decade reign, he immediately met with Standard and Poor's managing director to make sure he was incorporating their concerns into his strategic plan. By the end of his second term, Archer's neoliberal development ideology had transformed Detroit's downtown landscape with the construction of Comerica Park (baseball stadium), Ford Field (football stadium), three casinos, the Compuware corporate headquarters, Campus Martius downtown park, the GM takeover and $500 million redevelopment of Detroit's Renaissance Center, and several new downtown condominium developments. Signaling bolstered corporate confidence in the city, credit ratings rose from junk to investment-grade levels.[114]

When Kwame Kilpatrick, a thirty-one-year-old state congressman, became Detroit's youngest mayor ever in 2002, the centerpiece of his campaign platform was demolition as urban redevelopment. His successor David Bing, a former NBA basketball star who was elected in 2008, also ran on a campaign to demolish thousands of buildings. Large-scale demolitions—like those done for the Walter P. Chrysler Expressway and the Gratiot Redevelopment Project, which displaced thousands of Black families and businesses—had largely fallen out of favor. Public dissent following urban renewal had made the blanket bulldozer approach largely unviable as an urban redevelopment strategy. Demolitions happened but on a more distributed scale. Indeed, by the aughts, house-by-house demolitions were a mainstay of urban governance.[115]

State-led demolitions underscore how capital accumulation is dependent upon local actors creating the conditions for its mobility and how this often includes major modification to the built landscape. Demolitions also illuminate the changing function of property in the new economic conjuncture. As suggested earlier, industrial Detroit once epitomized labor as the predominant mode of capitalist extraction. Recall Ford's River Rouge plant where more than one hundred thousand workers labored under one roof. By the 2010s, Detroit found itself increasingly beholden to the interests of speculative finance and reliant on nonprofits and foundations to support social services. Detroit administrators, like those in many other cities, turned to real estate as a primary mode of development.

Under neoliberalism, urban planning as a field had become largely beholden to what geographer Samuel Stein has termed the "real estate state," in which planners themselves played complex and contradictory roles.[116] In cities across the country, officials and planners adopted a development model that turned on boosting real estate values in a variety of ways, including offering tax breaks to incentivize development, demolishing public housing, slashing affordability requirements, and privatizing public spaces. It was a suite of well-developed policies but in Detroit where there was a high level of informality in landed property relations, the path was less clear-cut and more chaotic, rendering visible the contingent and ongoing work of property making as a resolution to racial capitalist crisis.

✳

David Bing had just assumed office when I began research for this project. He served only one term—before being succeeded by the city's first white mayor in thirty years—but it was a pivotal four years. At the start of his tenure, Bing launched a master planning process that would come to territorially and politically reconfigure Detroit. New money for demolitions flooded the city under the Neighborhood Stabilization Program and the 2010 Hardest Hit Funds, which aimed to provide relief for communities most affected by the subprime mortgage crisis. Meanwhile, polarization between the state's conservative base and its Black cities was at an all-time high. A Republican-controlled state legislature and newly appointed Republican governor Rick Snyder's deployment of bold authoritarian forms of government that targeted Black majority cities in the name of fiscal crisis only exacerbated tensions.

As Detroit took center stage in the struggle to stave off emergency management and capital interests returned for a piece of the pie, land questions took center stage in political debate. Huge agglomerations of land had moved from private to de facto public ownership, yet lacked a mandate for redistribution or a shared vision for what to do with the thousands of properties that overspilled the city's coffers. Debates over Detroit's future reflected housing concerns nationally in the wake of the subprime crisis, but they were articulated in place-specific ways. Detroit's land and housing crisis, as I discuss in the next chapter, was compounded by a state-mandated tax-foreclosure auction that played a large role in transforming a city once renowned for Black middle-class land and homeownership to one with bountiful land but landless people.

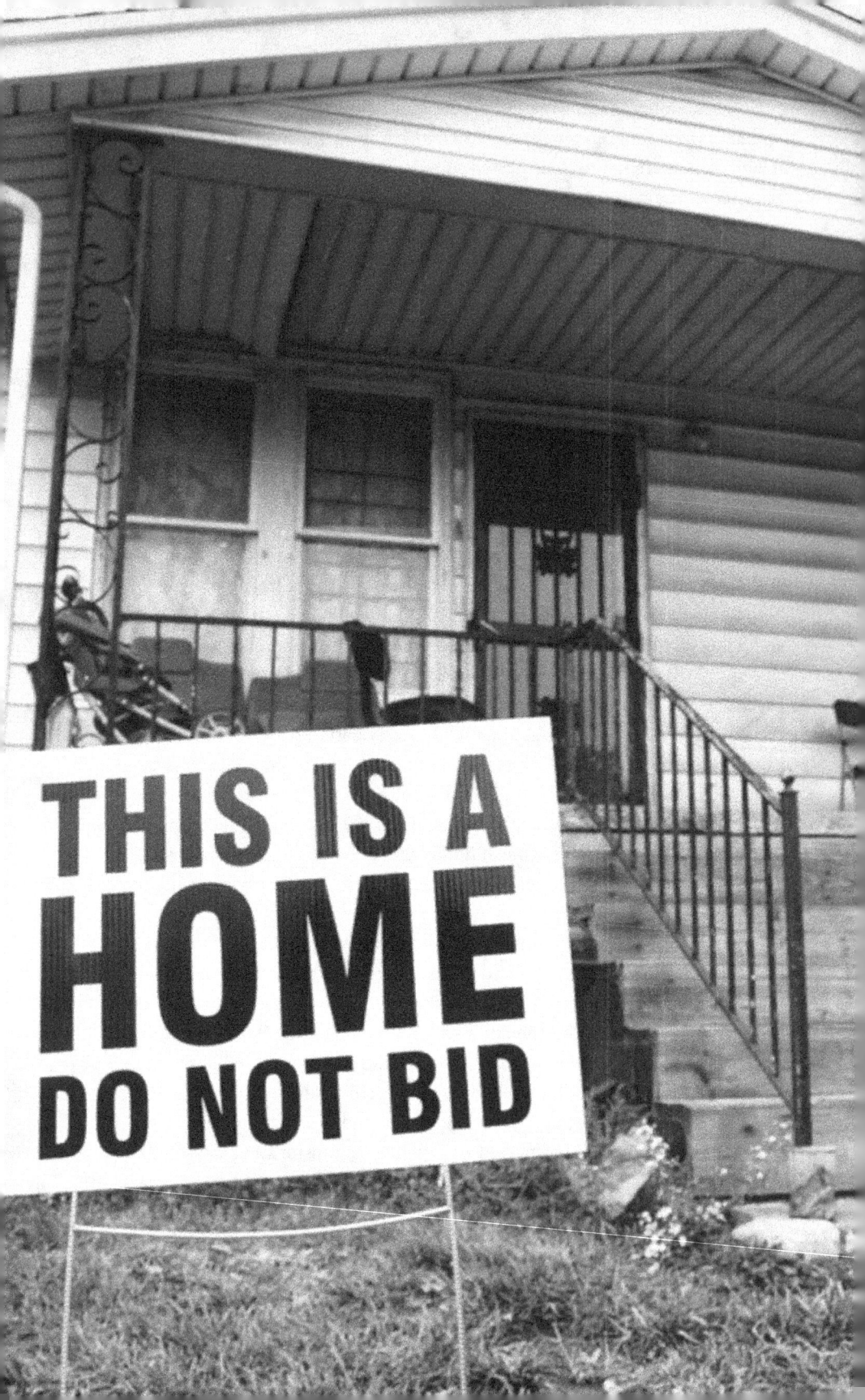

stealing home

3

"It's the last day to pay," the man said to a passerby marveling at the line of homeowners spilling out of the Wayne County Treasurer's Office building in downtown Detroit. The gray winter day in March 2015 seemed to match the mood of those clutching envelopes and folders stuffed with legal paperwork as they waited for hours in hopes of keeping their homes from being auctioned. Once they entered the building, a police officer directed the homeowners, most of whom were African American, where to go to "make arrangements." "When you get to the eighth floor, you will get a number," the officer yelled. "Keep that number! Then go to the fifth floor." There, residents filed into lines where they waited for cashiers to settle their debts or arrange payment plans to spare their homes from foreclosure.

Each October, Wayne County, which encompasses Detroit, holds the country's largest tax-foreclosure auction. Houses have been sold for as little as $500. In 2015, as many as one hundred thousand residents faced eviction as investors snatched up properties at rock-bottom prices.[1]

Figure 3.1 (opposite) | A sign that reads "THIS IS A HOME. DO NOT BID." These signs were distributed as part of a campaign by the Tricycle Collective to intervene in the Wayne County tax-foreclosure auction. The Tricycle Collective, which existed from 2014 to 2019, raised money to keep Detroiters in their homes. *Source:* Photo by Garret MacLean, reprinted in Michele Oberholtzer, "Myth-Busting the Detroit Tax Foreclosure Crisis," *Detroit Metro Times*, September 13, 2017.

The line outside the Treasurer's Office signaled the end of the process of fighting the loss of one's home before it landed on the auction block. This process began with the appearance of one's property in the *Detroit Legal News*. Each December, the daily print newspaper published a supplement that listed the tax-delinquent properties in Wayne County subject to foreclosure. Over three inches thick, comparable to a substantial Sunday newspaper, the supplement was a gauge of the city's housing crisis. At first glance, the supplement's heft seemed to confirm popular perceptions of Detroit as a sink of dead capital and surplus land. Yet, a closer analysis reveals a more complex story about how ownership has shifted under neoliberalism and the ways Detroiters' homes were caught up in interscalar governmental politics, long circuits of finance capital, and Black indebtedness.

I didn't set out to study the auction. But I quickly realized I could not tell a story about the redevelopment of Detroit without trying to explain why the state was foreclosing on tens of thousands of homes annually when the city desperately needed residents. Many foreclosed homes were owned outright and had been in families for generations. The auction, thus, suggested that the city's so-called renaissance was more complex than speculative capital taking advantage of the national housing market fallout. It depended on a local but systematic state-led process of unmaking Black homeownership. If homeownership is a proxy for economic advancement in the United States, the Wayne County tax-foreclosure auction signified a significant rollback of the economic gains that African Americans had made in the late twentieth century and a reversal of homeownership more generally as a stable form of equity.[2]

To be clear, Detroit was hard hit by the subprime foreclosure crisis. Between 2005 and 2015, more than sixty-five thousand homes had underwater mortgages. But the larger problem was tax foreclosures.[3] Whereas mortgage foreclosures resulted from a failure to make mortgage payments, tax foreclosures resulted from the failure of a property owner, be it a speculator, bank, or homeowner, to pay their property taxes. In the former, the bank seizes the property, whereas in the latter, the state seizes the property and puts it up for auction.

Tax-foreclosure auctions are not unique to Detroit. Within the United States, all states endow lower-level governmental entities with the capacity to collect delinquent taxes through auctions. But the scale of the Wayne County tax-foreclosure auction was unusual, owing, in no small part, to Detroit's success as a bastion of middle-class homeownership. During the 1960s and 1970s, Detroit was lauded for its Black homeownership rates. After fair housing legislation passed in 1968, rates increased for thirty years. By 1990, almost half of all African Americans in Detroit owned their own homes.[4]

Homeownership was the foundation for a way of life. Longtime resident and educator Michelle Morris recalled her impression of Detroit in 1966, when her family relocated there:

> When we were coming here on the bus, on the Greyhound bus, we did not know what we were coming to. But we were coming from Chicago, and everybody on the bus was just so enthusiastic to be coming back to Detroit; they were saying, "That's Detroit. That's my town." We could not figure out why. As we drove into the city, the bus passed Oakman Boulevard, went past Outer Drive, and people were pointing, saying, "That's my auntie's house; that's my grandma's house," and I'm thinking all of these big and beautiful homes belong to Black people. That was really astounding because I had come from Buffalo, New York, and Chicago. In Buffalo, Black people did not own houses like these, and in Chicago, everyone was living in apartment buildings, so that was really different.[5]

Homeownership, as Morris suggests, was a point of pride for Black Detroiters. But it was also more than that. Given that a home is often a family's biggest asset, the growth of homeownership that struck Morris as unique was instrumental in building Black wealth and the city's Black middle class. But since the late aughts, Black homeownership rates in Detroit had steadily fallen.[6] Another resident and community activist, Claude Faye, echoed Morris's concerns: "A lot of retirees, homeowners . . . are dying off and are leaving their property to the kids. The kids don't have a job, so they're losing the property."[7]

Lack of employment was part of the problem, but the auction represented something more insidious—how a complex history of supposedly race-neutral mandates to curtail blight and revitalize real estate markets led to a massive state effort to dispossess the city's most vulnerable. Such mandates, as we will see, were part and parcel of reactionary efforts by the US property rights and states' rights movements to privatize public housing and discipline the poor. The auction demonstrates how they have taken on new sinister formations: the state takes property, homes no less, from the poor and then facilitates their transfer to those with more means, often the investor class.

The Magnitude of Recurring Loss

The woman who first told me about the auction was named Glenda. It was October 2010. I bumped into her in the lobby of a community center called the Commons. In her midforties, Glenda was a local activist.[8] She approached me with a welcoming familiarity even though we'd not met. She was agitated after a meeting at the Wayne County Treasurer. It seemed like she needed someone to listen. We sat down at a table, and she launched into a story about how her house, where she lived with seven family members, had been mistakenly put up for auction.

As Glenda talked, she rummaged through her purse, pulling out a slightly tattered bill that showed she owed $6,000 in back taxes. Shaking it, she explained that her house had been wrongly assigned a *flipper tax*—the rate for an investment property, not the rate for one's primary residence. I learned this was not an uncommon error.

Historically, property tax receipts have played an important role in laying claim to property entitlement and, crucially, to citizenship. Within the context of civil rights struggles, Black homeowners commonly presented tax receipts when demanding their right to public space and amenities like swimming pools, parks, and beaches.[9] "In Jim Crow America, the right to speak for others, or simply to speak for oneself, remained bound to property," historian N. D. B. Connolly writes. "Owning land or buildings gave the otherwise disempowered or disenfranchised certain political entitlements. . . . It made one a symbol of what 'the Negro' was worth in an otherwise white world. The affirmative power of property created important political space for black people to shape the state."[10] As I listened to Glenda, I wondered how the affirmative power of property differed in an age of financialization and unpayable debt.

The Wayne County tax-foreclosure auction took place every fall. It comprised two bidding sessions. During the first session, held in September, the opening bid was the sum of the delinquent taxes and fees. Properties that didn't sell during this first round would go up for auction again in a second session held in October, in which opening bids started at a mere $500. Glenda's plan was to buy back her house through the second auction because it would be cheaper to bid on her house than pay the back taxes, which she could not afford. That she would consider bidding on her house underscored how the auction gave rise to perverse calculations of risk and reward.

Glenda made certain I understood that her situation was not anomalous. Scores of families faced similar predicaments. "Five thousand people will be out of their homes in the wintertime," she said on the verge of tears. She described the heightened sense of anxiety around her neighborhood as prospective buyers cruised by to photograph homes listed on the auction roster.

That night, I did a search online. "Mass Foreclosure Auction Represents Economic Fallout," read a headline in the *Detroit News*, one of the city's daily papers. I began hearing about the auction from others. A few days after chatting with Glenda, I met Fernando when we were volunteering in the same community garden. As we pulled weeds, Fernando told me how he'd come to Detroit from Mexico. He farmed several lots in the city, where he raised chickens and vegetables for market. He had recently acquired two houses through the auction that he planned to rent. He was excited for the extra income, but he struggled with the ethics of potentially displacing the tenants still residing in the houses. He aimed to keep them on.

Taken together, Glenda's and Fernando's stories illuminate the contradictory nature of the auction: the aspirations it conjured and the losses it generated. For people like Fernando, who were not wealthy but had cash on hand, the auction was an opportunity for economic advancement and financial security. For middle-class newcomers, it was an unparalleled opportunity to own a home without a mortgage. For speculators and developers, it was a lucrative opportunity to snatch up properties in a city poised for a "comeback."

For longtime residents, like Glenda, however, the auction was the cause of tremendous stress and grief. Losing a house is an excruciatingly traumatic experience because people's relationships to home and attachments to place far exceed the logic of the commodity form. Many foreclosed homes, as mentioned above, had been in Black families for generations. When wages and welfare benefits are not enough to get by on, family property has long served as a safety net, providing a sense of financial security and economic independence. The auction upended the notion that once one's home was paid off, it was a relatively secure asset that could be passed down for generations.

The loss of a home at the auction, thus, represented a significant material and financial loss but also the loss of things less tangible, such as the well-being that comes from having a place of refuge. A home is where babies are born, where children are raised, where friendships are formed, where meals are shared, where people die, where families are made over generations, where ancestors rest. A home roots you in relationship to a community. When families lose their homes, there is the physical displacement and financial precarity that comes with the loss, but there is also the loss of the place that stores those memories as well as dreams. Neighborhoods are also fractured by these losses.

Foreclosure becomes publicly visible only at certain moments. The posting of an eviction notice. A crowd of protestors gathering. Movers arriving backed by police. Much of the work of wresting property away from families happens behind the scenes, before a home is turned inside out. The crafting of laws.

The signing of contracts. The exchange of bills and paperwork. The rejection of pleas at legal hearings. And before any of this, it begins with the mundane and procedural bureaucratic work of fashioning the ideal propertied subject. The sorting of those who are considered worthy of liberal personhood and its entitlements (i.e., homeownership) from the unworthy. The incentivizing and disciplining of the citizenry to ensure responsibility and compliance with the property regime.

The historical roots of the words *foreclosure* and *eviction* reveal their base violence. In Old French, *foreclos* and *forclore* meant "exclude, shut out; shun; drive away." In Middle English, *forjuggen* meant to "condemn, convict, banish."[11] Similarly, the etymological root of *eviction* stems from *evictionem*, meaning to "overcome, conquer." From the 1580s, eviction denoted "dispossession by judicial sentence, the recovery of land or tenements from another's possession by due course of law."[12] This stands in contrast to earlier English common law, which left it up to landlords to decide how best to regain their properties; they often resorted to force.[13]

In the 2010s, Wayne County foreclosed on homes like a treadmill with no off switch. Between 2011 and 2015, 1 in 4 properties were foreclosed on for unpaid taxes. Between 2009 and 2017, Detroit's 36th District Court averaged thirty-five thousand evictions a year. Once the redundancy of multiple evictions at the same address is accounted for, 20 percent of renting families (or 26,400 residences) still faced eviction every year.[14] To be clear, not all these evictions were the result of the auction, but they suggest the sweeping extent of the city's housing crisis. According to the American Community Survey (2011–2015), Detroit's average household size was 2.55 people. This means, that 26,400 evictions translated to 67,320 people. That's approximately 1 in 10 Detroiters.

To better grasp these numbers, imagine that each dot in figure 3.2 represents one person. The figure contains 420 dots. Now picture a book with 160 pages filled with dots like this one. This would represent the number of Detroiters affected by eviction annually.

This simple math hints at the magnitude of the crisis. Yet the distance between the numbers and the human experiences of the suffering feels vast. The arithmetic of loss can turn into an accounting exercise that conveys the scope of contemporary urban crisis while leaving uninterrogated the uneven ways it is experienced across gendered race and class lines. Such arithmetic is also insufficient for understanding the political processes, parties, and individuals responsible for such excessive devaluation of human life. The biggest

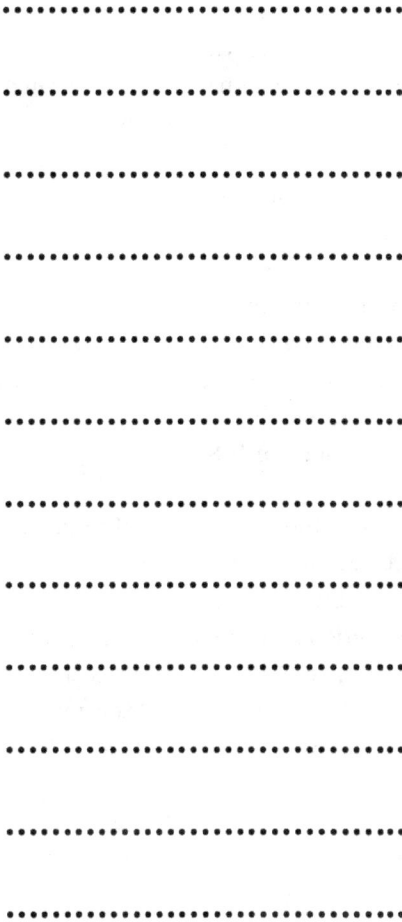

Figure 3.2 | The image contains 420 dots. It would need to be replicated 160 times to represent the number of Detroiters affected annually by evictions. *Source:* Created by author.

risk, however, is an overemphasis on violence and dispossession, which can background the lives, desires, and world making of those who live its effects. The risk of becoming an "academic coroner," in Clyde Woods's words, is real.[15] But, in the case of the auction, there is also a danger in moving too quickly past the magnitude of loss and the associated questions about how state and capital forces come together to organize such human rights violations, not to mention how communities fight back.

In a poem entitled "Big Numbers," the poet Ajmer Rode writes, "The human mind / is essentially qualitative. . . . / quantitative analyses rarely touch our souls."[16] Rode goes on to play with big numbers. He imagines sitting in a gravel pit counting one billion pebbles, which he estimates would take approximately fourteen years. He then imagines counting the amount of money African countries owe to rich foreigners ($200 billion). To count this high would require being born forty times over and counting continually for twenty-four hours per day. If we think like Rode with big numbers, the sixty-seven thousand-plus residents affected by evictions translates into the size of the entire city of Muncie, Indiana. If a person counted at the rate of one number per second, it would take eighteen hours of nonstop counting to reach this high.

Rode then considers the five million children who die annually because of this debt. Their combined daily cries of more than a trillion a day, he writes, float into the atmosphere. Once soundwaves are generated, they may change form, as Rode reminds us, but they never leave the atmosphere. One day, these cries might hit you and shatter your soul, or they might hit you and nothing happens.[17]

I think about the line stretching outside the Treasurer's Office, homeowners waiting, folders stuffed with receipts, to plead their cases. Some will be successful. Many won't. City officials were generally quick to admit the process was problematic. Yet this recognition failed to unleash a collective reckoning. In Rode's terms, there were cries, and they hit people's souls, but the treadmill continued to churn. How? Why? And what did this modern form of dispossession reveal about current ownership regimes, democracy, and societal accountability?

In 2014, the *New York Times* published an online visualization tool designed to illustrate the extent of the auction. It was a mosaic of 43,634 images from Google Maps Street View, each depicting a foreclosed property on the brink of being auctioned (notably, the spread did not include the tens of thousands more that risked mortgage foreclosure). Square photographs of the fronts of homes appeared in a grid, their distribution fluctuating based on the size of one's computer screen. One could scroll through rows of houses organized by neighborhoods. For example, Bagley neighborhood had 989 foreclosed properties listed; Brightmoor, 1,482; Brooks, 1,899; Chadsey, 717; Conner, 1,375; and the list went on (figure 3.3).

Some of the properties were vacant lots, but the majority were not. If you looked closely, you could see human life. Cars in driveways. Chairs on porches. Children's bicycles. Grills. Hanging plants. Trimmed hedges. Flower gardens in bloom. Trash cans awaiting pickup.

The mosaic included background information on select properties, highlighting that many were multigenerational, well-loved homes and that their homeowners faced significant challenges in keeping them despite being em-

Figure 3.3 | Online mosaic entitled "Here Are the 43,634 Properties in Detroit That Were on the Brink of Foreclosure in 2014." Author screenshot. *Source:* Matthew Bloch and Haeyoun Park, *New York Times*, June 26, 2014.

ployed. A woman named Patricia Adams, for example, lived on Portlance Avenue. A mother of two who ran a childcare business from her home, Adams did not have enough money for property taxes. She owed more than twenty thousand dollars and hoped to get her house back at the auction.

Such hardships were echoed by Renata Lewis, a mother of three who lived on Balfour Road. She had bought her house from a family acquaintance only to learn after she moved in that the property was behind on taxes. She owed nearly ten thousand dollars, which she could not afford.

On Lenox Street, Ronald Ford Jr. was behind seven thousand dollars in property taxes for a home his family had bought in 1969. His mother had paid off the mortgage years before. Ford had a hard time finding work. When his mother grew ill and moved into a nursing home, he could no longer afford the taxes.

James Calloway lived on Westbrook Street. He used his disability payments and food stamps to support himself and his three children but could not afford his property taxes. He owed more than ten thousand dollars, according to county officials.[18] It would take more than thirty-four weeks of full-time work at a minimum wage job to make this much money. For someone on disability, who makes an average of $1,277 per month, it would take approximately 65 percent of their annual payout.[19]

Herein lies the absurdity: Adams, Lewis, Ford, and Calloway all owed taxes, but they all also owned their homes. They had paid them off or inherited them from family members who had spent years making mortgage payments. It is worth repeating that it was this possibility of achieving homeownership that had distinguished Detroit in the mid-twentieth century. "We were known for our houses," said longtime resident Alana Davis in an interview. "We had beautiful, beautiful homes. . . . That is gone."[20] But why?

Scrolling past row upon row of houses, viewers of the mosaic got the sense that something had gone terribly wrong but learned little about why Detroit had gone from a model city of homeownership to one of property-less residents amid abundant land and houses. How did such a vast dispossessory system come to be? What justifications, power blocs, pedestrian bureaucratic work, and forms of complicity enabled it? What allowed it to continue?

A Brief History of the Auction

In March 2012, I joined activists from across the country for a national gathering hosted by the Moratorium NOW! Coalition to Stop Foreclosures, Evictions, and Utility Shutoffs to demand a two-year national moratorium on foreclosures. Moratorium NOW! is a coalition of grassroots activists and organizations, union and religious leaders, farmers, politicians, and concerned citizens from across Michigan. They formed in 2008 to fight for the passage of Senate Bill 1309, which would have stopped all mortgage foreclosures and evictions, including through direct actions and legal proceedings. The conference built on the momentum that had been gaining nationally as the Occupy movement, unions, and community organizations came together to fight for housing justice in the wake of the subprime crisis.

I was eager to learn about the strategies that people were using to fight foreclosures. Efforts like Moratorium NOW! were making strides by challenging the moral values associated with making good on debt obligations (and the shame of not). They also advocated for homeowners to confront the state and creditors as a collective body rather than as individual debtors.[21] The call for a moratorium drew inspiration from antieviction campaigns during the Great Depression. With nearly a quarter of the labor force unemployed in 1933, a wave of evictions swept the country. In response, unemployed councils formed to advocate for workers, including the Detroit Unemployed Council.[22] Chief among the demands of the unemployed councils was a moratorium on evictions. Widespread worker and community organizing, including rent strikes and eviction resistance, resulted in twenty-five states enacting moratoriums on foreclosures, including the Michigan Moratorium Act of 1938.[23]

Nearly seventy-five years later, the Moratorium NOW! Conference, which was held at the Central United Methodist Church in downtown Detroit, a hub for activist organizing in the city, kicked off with a series of rousing speeches. They painted a stark picture of the housing crisis while celebrating the victories of homeowners who had successfully renegotiated mortgages after activists staged home defenses. With the room energized, participants got to work. I huddled with five housing activists who shared their experiences fighting foreclosures and evictions through direct actions and legal tactics. "It's impossible to fight this one house at a time through eviction defense," one participant argued. "Neighborhoods need to band together to fight for those being foreclosed upon." The group went on to discuss strategies for securing a moratorium to keep people in their homes, stabilize communities, and develop long-term solutions to the housing crisis.

Crisis moments elucidate distributions of power. Full of contingency, they are often moments of structural change for good and for ill. The Moratorium NOW! campaign illustrates how a crisis had galvanized people to advocate for more progressive urban land and housing policies. Likewise, its historical precursor—the antieviction campaigns during the Great Depression—had successfully amassed widespread support for the idea of public housing and affordability mandates, leading to the passage of the formative Housing Act of 1937. Revolutionary tendencies linked these histories as did revolutionary backlash.

The establishment of a public housing program under the US Housing Authority (the precursor to the Department of Housing and Urban Development, or HUD) was a watershed moment.[24] In Detroit, Brewster Homes was constructed north of the city's center for Black residents, while Parkside Homes on the far East Side was reserved for whites. By the 1950s and 1960s, housing desegregation had become a key pillar of the civil rights movement in the North, eventually compelling governments at all levels to ban racial discrimination in housing and to expand public housing.

The Wayne County tax-foreclosure auction emerges from the efforts of a longstanding well-organized reactionary movement focused on countering such successes. "If the civil rights movement's greatest victories came with claiming public authority to pry open the private sector—the housing market, the job market," historian Elizabeth Blackmar writes, "[then] the political reaction against democratization focused in on the public sector."[25]

Public housing became a key site of political contestation. Even though it was explicitly for working families—not for the poorest of the poor— opponents, including real estate trade groups, builders and suppliers, and property owners' associations, maligned it as socialist, arguing that it would discourage hard work and encourage dependence on the state.[26] As a result, it became racially coded as Black and shrouded by negative public sentiments, even though whites had long benefited from federal mortgage subsidies, tax breaks, and state-sponsored low-cost housing. The conservative taxpayer revolt of the seventies and eighties only fueled such attitudes with calls growing in intensity to end housing assistance and dismantle "the projects"—many of them built just a decade earlier.[27] These sentiments helped sustain the conservative push in the nineties to privatize public housing, out of which emerged Public Act 123 (PA 123), which mandated the auction. The act revised Michigan's tax-reversion law by accelerating the state's residential tax-foreclosure process. Tax reversion is a process that allows the state to legally seize property for nonpayment of taxes. Before the law passed, it took seven years to foreclose on a property. Afterward, it took only three.

On its face, PA 123 seemed like public interest legislation—a way for public officials to address problems of tax evasion and community blight more efficiently. The impetus, however, had less to do with helping distressed neighborhoods in Detroit than with using the city as a test case for legislation supported by the property rights and states' rights movements to privatize public property and discipline the poor. Put another way, the justification for fast-tracking foreclosures in Michigan was intimately tied to debates over— and the backlash against—the state's role in public housing provision.[28]

Public Act 123 went into effect in 1999 during the administration of Republican John Engler, who served as a three-term governor of Michigan from 1991 to 2003. As geographer Joshua Akers has shown in a history of the auction, PA 123 was one of numerous bills crafted for the Michigan legislature between 1997 and 1999 by a network of conservatives circulating between government and free-market think tanks, like the Washington, DC-based Hudson Institute. Public Act 123 was bundled with the Michigan Urban Homestead Act. Imagined as inseparable and complementary, the auction would target "blighted" properties and generate stability by increasing market demand for housing in the city. Meanwhile, the Urban Homestead Act would enable the state to give vacant houses to the poor to homestead (shorthand for fixing up and improving). Seen as a win-win, public housing would be dismantled, state dependents would become propertied citizens, and land in the public coffers would be privatized. If successful, it would be a model that could be replicated in other states.[29] A team of four out-of-state Hudson fellows researched and drafted the PA 123 legislation with funding from the W. K. Kellogg Foundation, the Mott Foundation, the Rollin M. Gerstacker Foundation, and the Kinship Corporation of Chicago. As Akers's research uncovered, they argued that the seven-year-foreclosure process needed to be fast-tracked because by that point most of the houses would need too many repairs and thus be unsuitable for homesteading.[30]

At the helm of the effort was John C. Weicher, a University of Chicago–trained economist who had spent decades moving between HUD and free-market think tanks, where he pushed for the privatization of public housing. As Akers writes, Weicher had long argued that HUD interfered with the private housing market and that public housing should be eliminated and replaced with a voucher system. Notably, his proposal became instrumental in the early nineties as part of the Home Ownership Opportunities for People Everywhere (HOPE) legislation, when he worked under HUD Secretary Jack Kemp, a fiscal conservative (and former NFL quarterback) who was developing an urban homesteading plan to privatize public housing complexes and sell them to their former residents.[31]

Weicher's vision inched closer to reality in late 1992, when as part of Kemp's HOPE program, Congress passed the Urban Revitalization Demonstration (URD), which authorized capital funds for the removal and replacement of blighted public housing. Under the Clinton administration, URD continued as HOPE VI, marking a pivotal shift in US housing policy toward vouchers, lower-density housing projects, and the federally funded demolition of notorious "projects" like Cabrini-Green in Chicago and the Brewster-Douglass Housing Projects in Detroit, among hundreds of others (a trend started in 1972 with the demolition of Pruitt-Igoe in St. Louis, Missouri). Most of them have not been replaced.

As public housing was strategically dismantled, conservative think tanks and government officials promoted urban homesteading as public interest legislation to uplift the urban poor. When the Michigan Urban Homestead Act was presented to the state legislature in 1999, it was celebrated, Akers writes, as a "fresh take" on the federal Homestead Acts aimed at settling the American West beginning in 1862. Republican politician Bill Schuette (then a Michigan state senator and a sponsor of the 1999 act, later state attorney general) argued that whereas the "challenge" in the nineteenth century was "a wild and lawless West; today it is Cabrini Green and South Central Los Angeles."[32] The Michigan Urban Homestead Act, like its racist antecedent, prescribed private property ownership to remedy social ills (violence, poverty, blight, disrepair) and "build real neighborhoods" in the inner city.[33] On the nineteenth-century frontier, would-be settlers could apply for a homestead, which formally included 160 acres, at little or no cost by simply filing an application for land, improving it, and registering a deed. Although the Homestead Act was widely celebrated as the so-called great equalizer in land relations, not everyone was eligible. After all, it was the 1830 Indian Removal Act that made 270 million acres, or 10 percent of US land by area, available for the Homestead Acts. While nonwhites could technically apply for a homestead, eligibility required citizenship, which African Americans did not gain until the passage of the Fourteenth Amendment in 1866, and Native Americans, not until 1924. Even then, comparatively few nonwhites became homesteaders because of the initial outlay of capital needed.[34]

Like the act's forebearer, the new one sought to deploy the regulatory power of the state to create private property and responsible propertied subjects. Thus, the bureaucratic work ensued of discerning who was worthy of ownership and who was not. New homesteaders not only needed capital but would have to meet certain moral requirements. Senator Schuette explained it this way: "Just as Lincoln's homesteaders were required to fulfill certain minimal conditions, Michigan's Urban Homestead Act has a similar message tailored to the problems of a new era: keep your kids in school, make sure that they learn to read by the fourth grade, stay crime- and drug-free, and make a good-faith effort to improve your public housing unit. A homesteader invests courage and commitment and receives a home and a chance to break the cycle of despair."[35] Potential homesteaders were to be subject to strict reviews on these conditions, as Akers reports: "Convicted felons and parolees were excluded. Drug tests were required. Proof of school attendance was to be provided each term. Credit counseling would be mandated for some participants. In addition, tenants were expected to pay 80% and 90% of the market rate for rent while homesteading and bring houses up to code within 18 months."[36] Schuette summed up the program: "If staying off drugs is a hardship, if continual employment is not your bag, or if you don't care if your kids stay in school, this isn't for you."[37] The guidelines and Schuette's comments smacked of anxieties about Black indolence and dependence that, since Emancipation, as Saidiya Hartman has argued, have led to racist state policies aimed at fashioning Black people into responsible rights-bearing liberal individuals, forcing them again and again to prove their worthiness.[38]

The Urban Homestead Act became law but was never implemented in Detroit. That said, its history matters for understanding the auction, because legislation has afterlives even when it is never enacted. The Urban Homestead Act was bundled with Public Act 123, which accelerated the foreclosure process and went on to play an important role in shaping a speculative and exploitative landscape of property ownership in Detroit. By the 2010s, the auction had become both a driver of dispossession and a major obstacle to city officials' ability to curb speculation. Local officials often claimed they had little power to stop the auction and were forced to work around it because the laws governing it operated at the state level. While the foregoing history of foreclosure law in Michigan helps explain the roots and rationales for the auction, it does not explain how local officials navigated the bureaucratic and moral dilemmas that came with it.

A New Era of Debt Relations

Looking for answers to these questions, I went to interview Mark Schmidt, an official who worked in the Wayne County Treasurer's Office, in December 2012.[39] We met in his office in the monumental county building in downtown Detroit. Schmidt was wearing a pale blue button-down shirt with a red tie. We began with small talk about how the city had changed over the course of his fifty-eight years of life. Schmidt grew up on the East Side of Detroit but lived three blocks outside the city in the wealthy and largely white enclave of Grosse Point Park.

"Into the sixties, the strength of Detroit was always in its neighborhoods. We had vibrant neighborhoods. People knew their neighbors. The family unit was strong and nowhere stronger than in the African American community," said Schmidt. "I think if you looked at statistics, individual home ownership in Detroit in the sixties was enormous, probably well beyond any other city in the United States. I think if you tracked the numbers, you'd see that trend reversed."

He explained how it was not only white flight that was a problem in the late sixties and seventies but also redevelopment efforts that concentrated resources downtown to the detriment of neighborhoods. I gazed out a three-bay window that overlooked Old St. Mary's Catholic Church and the Greektown Casino. The casino was a legacy of this history, born in the shift from production-centered to entertainment- and consumption-centered models of development.[40]

Below the window was a long ledge lined with holiday cards, a *Comparative Bible Study* book with gold embossed print, some scraggly plants, and family photos. My gaze landed on a wooden gavel. Schmidt explained that he had worked a number of odd jobs—manufacturing, construction, demolition, teaching—before he became a probate judge. After being a judge for twenty years, Schmidt was ready for a change. He knew Ray Wojtowicz, the longtime treasurer of Wayne County, a post he had held for thirty-six years. Their families were both Polish. When it came time for a change, Schmidt talked with Wojtowicz and got the job.

The *Legal News* supplement—the public foreclosure listing—sat on Schmidt's desk. When I asked about it, he joked about its heft. "I'm always worried about lawsuits from paper boys," he said. "Don't break your back."

Ostensibly, the purpose of the ledger was to inform the public of foreclosures, allowing a period for liens to be claimed against the property. But it also served another function. Schmidt explained, "Publication goes back to the days when you'd go down to the town square, give notice, tack it up on a board, and people would say, 'Oh my goodness, John Deer didn't pay his taxes, shame, shame.' And then he'd run in and pay his taxes. Eventually, they went to newspapers, and it continues to this day."

The relationship between shame, blame, and poverty is complicated. Schmidt's historical example insinuated that the errant taxpayer had the ability to pay but chose not to. Indeed, Detroit's tax-delinquent residents were often blamed for the city's poorly functioning public services and fiscal crisis. Yet the material weight of the ledger suggested something more structural and endemic than mere negligence or delinquency.

In 2011, Wayne County foreclosed on twenty-four thousand properties. In 2012, it foreclosed on forty-two thousand properties, and in 2013, the county would foreclose on another forty-two thousand. In a two-year period, 10 percent of all the properties in Wayne County had gone through tax foreclosure. The sharp increase could be explained, in part, by an ailing economy, but it was also the result of county-level decisions. Though the state mandated the auction, officials did have some discretion. According to Schmidt, after 2011, county leaders decided that they were "not doing anyone any favors" by holding off on foreclosures. "The earlier you can get the taxpayer's attention, the more likely they will pay their taxes, stay in their homes, and stabilize the community," he said.

Opening the paper, Schmidt walked me through how the foreclosure listings were organized by township. Properties appeared in a three-column ledger that included property number, address, and interested parties. The third column, "interested parties," referred to creditors who had taken out liens on a property, meaning that the property owner owed more money than just back taxes.

My eyes landed on a property that had more than a dozen interested parties listed: Trinity Chapel Funeral Home; State Farm Automobile Insurance Company; numerous individuals; Bobson Construction Company; Mr B's Carpet Cleaning. It was not just that Detroiters didn't have money to pay property taxes; they didn't have money to pay for a lot of things. Phone bills. Loan payments. Window repair bills. Funeral expenses. Federal taxes. Even water bills.[41] In 2006, the Detroit Water and Sewerage Department started placing delinquent water bills on residential tax notices, meaning that if you fell behind on your water bill, your house could be seized. The Detroit-based research collective We the People estimated in 2014 that between 12 and 26 percent of tax foreclosures were a result of overdue water bills.[42]

The ledger represented the deepening crisis of social reproduction and the complex forms of indebtedness that had come to define late capitalism. It was more than a record of the tattered security that homeownership was supposed to yield. Its sprawling listings indexed the scope, urgency, and kinds of indebtedness that precipitate foreclosure, even as they obscured the struggles that people go through to try to keep their homes. It brought into stark relief how most families could not get by without taking on substantial debt to cover basic expenses, such as health care, food, clothing, and utilities.

To be sure, the ledger included some speculators who gambled and chose not to pay their taxes. It also included banks that had repossessed properties in the wake of the mortgage crisis and failed to pay taxes. But a large number of the listings were homeowners on the losing end of decades of neoliberal policies that had attacked the power of organized labor, depressed wages, raised unemployment, and allowed for the unchecked expansion of fictitious capital and debt with little regulation—all in an attempt to recoup corporate profits. Put another way, the ledger illuminated the extent to which debt (massive amounts of it) had come to sustain daily life.[43]

As Schmidt flipped through page after page of listings, I thought about how bureaucracies use what anthropologist Matthew Hull calls "graphic artifacts" to govern, such as files, reports, maps, and petitions, which, in turn, become constitutive of the form and function of government.[44] In the case of the ledger, it mediated discourses and practices of foreclosure and also helped to fabricate state authority. By positioning debt as a central technology of governance, the ledger precipitated new arrangements of property and state power.

"Our laws on foreclosure were written back when we were told if you have money invested in property, it will never lose its value," Schmidt told me. "When they drew up the law, they thought, the worst thing that happens is someone doesn't pay their taxes. The idea back then was that's the hammer to get people to pay their taxes. However, the economy declined so powerfully, and people just couldn't pay."

It was not that just *some* people could not afford to pay their property taxes. In 2012, almost half of Detroit's property owners did not pay.

Such extreme tax-delinquency underscores the linkages between the labor and housing sectors. In the first half of 2009, Michigan lost thirty-two thousand jobs per month. The Michigan Labor Department attributed more than half of these losses to the automobile sector. As the Big Three's workforce ballooned abroad, their domestic workforce shrunk. By 2010, they employed only 171,200 US workers, a more than twofold decrease in just ten years.[45] In places like Detroit that still depended heavily on the automobile sector, the economic distress was overwhelming. Plant closures reverberated widely, resulting in the dramatic loss of trade for companies that supplied materials to them, a massive decline in patronage to local businesses, associated drops in tax revenue, and, significantly, home losses. After Chrysler and General Motors declared bankruptcy in 2009, the federal government bailed them out to the tune of $15.6 billion. Assistance, though, to underwater and tax-delinquent homeowners—whose distress was intimately linked to the auto-industry restructuring—was slow to materialize. The effects were devastating.

"Credit became really difficult," Schmidt recalled. "We became the only bank in town. People had to make a choice between feeding their family and paying their taxes." Elsewhere Schmidt had opined that if residents could not afford their taxes, then they couldn't afford to own a home. He suggested they should become renters instead.

It was a well-trodden argument, one that on the face of it comes across as imminently practical: houses take maintenance, maintenance takes money, which many people don't have, and if this is the case, homeownership is not for them. Yet, it's a reasoning that presumes, first, that landlords care for the buildings they own; second, that they pay their taxes; and third, perhaps most critically, that the poor, rather than capital interests and the state itself, are culpable. Political theorist and philosopher Vafa Ghazavi, in an essay called "Ethics at a Distance," writes, "We do a distinct kind of wrong when we refuse to notice social structures that co-opt us in elevating some while subordinating others. We mistakenly substitute a focus on individual blame for what should be a concern for the common good."[46]

Schmidt wanted me to know that he didn't condone the auction and that there were practices in place to help homeowners, however imperfect. He emphasized that the county and city were merely carrying out state policy, reminding me of a point made by Jill Stauffer that often "what causes harm and destroys worlds is not (or not only) individual people who set out to do harm, but also whole ideologies rallied around supporting that harm, supported actively or passively by large populations—nearby or distant, sometimes even the whole world—standing by and doing nothing to resist them."[47]

Deference to rules, orders, and chains of command is a practiced strategy of neutralizing political agency. Sometimes it serves as an outright justification for a collective wrongdoing. What it is not, though, is an appeal to ethical principles. Or, perhaps, in Schmidt's case it was, but it was an appeal limited by the ethical norms that held taxation to be foundational to good citizenship and the state's ability to carry out its care duties.

My point is not to indict any one individual. Intention is not required for there to be harm. Rather, following Ghazavi and Stauffer, my aim is to direct attention to the ideologies of property and social structures that lead to dispossession, displacement, and disregard for human life—and, ultimately, the urgent question of what it takes to break from them. It is an effort to reveal the increasingly complex set of ownership relations that have created what Brenna Bhandar has aptly named an "anti-accountability structure."[48]

Blaming and disciplining poor homeowners—rather than capital and the state—shrouded the business of debt. As Schmidt explained, after two years of nonpayment, the interest rates on resident's tax bills went from 1 percent to 1.5 percent monthly, or 18 percent annually. It was "usurious," he said, "other than the fact that the government was involved and it wasn't a crime."

What Schmidt didn't say was that the auction had become a vital revenue stream for Wayne County. Every year Detroit, like other cities and townships, sold uncollected taxes to their home county to recoup costs. To buy the debt, the county borrowed money at a low interest rate. It then set about collecting the taxes, making money in the process through interest, fees, and auction sales. As one local paper reported, "It appears the county now relies on property owners' misfortune to balance its budget."[49] Since the financial crisis of 2008–2009, high-interest rates on back taxes had redirected hundreds of millions of dollars from Detroit residents to Wayne County's coffers. In 2013 alone, Wayne County made a surplus of $64 million from tax collection, a figure that was wildly out of step with the tax surplus of more affluent adjacent counties, raising significant questions about the morality—or rather immorality—of payments.[50]

The Auction as a Site of Transfer

We typically think about taxation as the mechanism by which states fund themselves and redistribute resources among their citizenries, benefiting those with less means. But the auction did something decidedly different. Not only was the state taking money from the poor to balance its budget, but it was also acting as a site of transfer: taking what was often a poor family's largest asset and transferring it to the rich.

This was not a new story. Throughout US history, taxation has been wielded as an instrument of white supremacy and intergenerational wealth accumulation among white elites.[51] As sociologists Kasey Henricks and Louise Seamster write, "Often presumed as arcane and dreary, the tax system's complexity, along with its lack of transparency, work to conceal its discriminatory nature. Taxation is insulated within layers of bureaucracy, lending its corrosive effects and slow devastation to communities of color a certain 'killing them softly' quality."[52]

Indeed, white resentment about civil rights gains has been articulated nowhere more forcefully than around the property tax.[53] As more and more Black people became landowners in the post-Emancipation era, discriminatory taxation became common. For example, local tax collectors routinely neglected to record tax payments made by Black people, leading to fines, higher tax rates, and, for some, delinquency and property loss. Meanwhile, property assessments were also discriminatory. Homes in predominantly African American neighborhoods were worth less on the market than those in white neighborhoods, but they were frequently assessed at a higher rate, meaning owners paid a disproportionate amount of their income in taxes.[54]

Another example of how the burden of taxation rests on the poor is that lower-income cities often have higher tax rates than their surrounding suburbs. Since the property tax revolt in the early 1980s—solidified by Proposition 13 in California, Reagan-era tax cuts, and other state-level tax-limitation measures—the burden of taxation has increasingly shifted onto low-income and middle-income families, particularly families of color. As discussed in the previous chapter, suburbanization allowed wealthy families to effectively withdraw their tax money from cities.

Detroit is a prime example of these dynamics. Complaints about excessive taxation, particularly given the lack of public services in some neighborhoods, was a common theme in conversations with residents. Resident Yvonne Jones explained,

> We pay more taxes than anybody in the United States of America and do not receive the type of service, just everyday regular service. . . . The fact that the lights are out, the fact that they don't pick up the trash in a timely fashion, the fact that they don't cut the grass, all of these things that we've paid for over and over and through the nose. . . . We see them constantly and steadily building up downtown and neglecting the community and the neighborhoods. And we the people, we have to suffer.

Jones was right. In the early 2010s, the city's property tax rate, or millage rate, was among the highest in the nation for large cities, even though its median household income was the lowest.[55] A property tax rate, or millage rate, is the tax levied on the assessed value of a property by a governing authority of the jurisdiction in which the property is located. Detroit's millage rate in 2012 was 67.74, meaning that a residential owner of a house assessed at $60,000 would owe $4,064 annually in property taxes.[56] Likewise, if a house were assessed at $150,000, taxes would be $10,161. By comparison, Portland, Oregon, which, at the time, was roughly the same size as Detroit by area (133 square miles versus 139 square miles) and had fewer residents (584,000 compared to Detroit's 714,000) had a millage rate of 16.40, meaning that the homeowner of the $60,000 house would pay only $942 annually, and the owner of the house assessed at $150,000 would pay $2,460 annually.[57] Atlanta, also comparable in area to Detroit, with a population of 420,000, had a millage rate of 33.634, half the rate of Detroit's. The 2012 median household incomes in Portland ($51,238), Atlanta ($49,605), and Detroit ($26,955) underscore how the outmigration of white and upwardly mobile residents of all races creates a situation in which the tax burden falls on fewer, poorer residents, leading to higher taxes.[58]

A high millage rate wasn't the only problem. In the wake of the 2008 subprime crisis, property assessments frequently exceeded their sales value because the city had failed to downwardly adjust their assessed value to reflect the market plunge. Schmidt estimated that an average home sold in Detroit on the open market was assessed at eighteen times its sales value. He pointed to an even more dire devaluation, however: the assessed value of tax-foreclosed homes sold on the auction were sometimes assessed at more than 120 times the amount for which they ultimately sold.[59]

"We have seen property values decline 90 to 95 percent in some homes," he said. "We have some that are still assessed by the city at $60,000 to $70,000, but I can't sell them for $500."

Schmidt's casual acknowledgment of overassessment was later confirmed by legal scholar Bernadette Atuahene and urban economist Tim Hodge, who found that in 2010 alone, almost 85 percent of properties in Detroit were overassessed.[60] To be clear, assessed values and market values are often not the same. They do not need to be the same by law. A tax assessor should, however, ensure that all properties maintain the same assessed value relative to their market values regardless of the racial or economic makeup of the community. In 2016, the American Civil Liberties Union (ACLU) of Michigan, NAACP Legal Defense Fund, and the Covington and Burling law firm filed a lawsuit asserting that the city of Detroit's failure to reduce tax assessments in concert with the plunging values that followed the Great Recession violated the Fair Housing Act and due process. A reappraisal found that of 173,000 homes reviewed, more than 92 percent were overassessed between 2010 and 2016 by an average of $3,800.[61]

If the subprime mortgage crisis signified the ascendance of finance capital and the burdening of large swaths of the population with unpayable debt, then the tax-foreclosure auction represented another side of this story—that homes were not being lost from serpentine loans or spending beyond one's means (they were, after all, owned outright) but because of the failure of the city and the state to develop municipal taxation and monetary policies that adequately responded to the growing crisis of social reproduction. To put it another way, the state's solution was disciplinary, punitive, and repressive. It was also corrupt. It sought to hold individuals responsible for their poverty as a personal failing of citizenship obligations while defaulting on its own responsibility to uphold the social contract and serve the people. What was lacking—as the Moratorium NOW! Coalition underscored—was an ethical confrontation with the conditions that led to the crisis in the first place. A confrontation with the fact that in the country's largest Black city, the hard-won rights to Black homeownership were now conditional on homeowners' ability to repay unpayable debts.

Confronting the Abstraction of Violence

In 2009, the same year that both Chrysler and General Motors underwent bankruptcy proceedings, almost nine thousand homes went up for auction, a leap from past years. "Taken together, the properties seized by tax collectors for arrears and put up for sale . . . represented an area the size of New York's Central Park," one journalist reported.[62]

That October, prospective buyers crowded into the noisy ballroom of 400 Monroe, the county building, to cast their bids. Bidders were instructed to bring a valid license or state ID, a Social Security number, and a one-thousand-dollar cashier's check, which functioned as a deposit. "What's your bid?" called the auctioneer. His staccato delivery goaded bidders to up their offers. After five hours of calling out properties, the auctioneer repeated "no bid" like a chant. "Okay," he said. "We only have 300 more pages to go."[63]

Nine thousand homes. The number exceeded the housing stock of many small towns. The figure, however, would pale in comparison to those in the years that followed. In 2010, thirteen thousand homes went up for auction.[64] Unable to deal with the sheer number of foreclosed properties, the county moved the auction online, creating new opportunities for speculators to profit off the distress of poor families. Properties then sold at a heated pace. In 2014, during phase two of the auction, when opening bids started at five hundred dollars, closing bids rushed in at a rate of approximately one hundred every fifteen minutes.[65]

The pillage was anonymized in the virtual realm. In contrast to the in-person auction, bidders were affectively shielded from the anxieties of home-owners. They no longer had to face people like Glenda who sought to buy back their homes or the anguish they expressed when they were outbid.

To be clear, advocacy groups like the United Community Housing Coalition (UCHC) tried to intervene on residents' behalf. A nonprofit organization that provided housing assistance to Detroit's low-income residents, UCHC started trying to help homeowners save their properties from the auction in 2010. That year, they purchased 147 homes for mostly homeowner occupants by covering the two-thousand-dollar deposit required to enter the auction and by acting as the bidding agent, but it was still an incredibly risky proposition.

The most desirable houses on the auction block—and the first to go— were often those that had been lived in and cared for by homeowners. To combat the anonymity of the auction, some homeowners turned their homes into canvases for public messages. In 2012, Kelly Parker, an unemployed cancer patient who owed twelve thousand dollars in back taxes and whose two-bedroom home was for sale through the foreclosure auction, covered its outside in graffiti. In red, she spray-painted, "We will keep our house," "We will NOT be moved," and "THIS IS OUR HOME." A sign in the yard scrawled in black marker read: "Sick, Single Mother's Home."[66]

Stories like Parker's underscore the burdens and invisibility of household debt. Her signage brought the individuality of debt into public view. The subprime mortgage crisis had called into question the morality of Wall Street firms and purveyors of subprime loans. By contrast, the tax-foreclosure auction directed renewed attention to the morality/immorality of the accounting practices of the state and state accountability more broadly. It also reframed the moral dimension of repayment. Indebtedness, under modernity, is bound to moral personhood. The repayment of debts tends to increase one's social standing, while lapsed debt signals irresponsibility and deviance. Parker's signage challenged the social stigma of tax delinquency and prevailing assumptions that one ought to repay debts.

Public signage and buying back one's home were only a few of the strategies that homeowners deployed. Others engaged in less public forms of "fiscal disobedience," such as property defacement.[67] It was not uncommon for property owners to strip foreclosed homes of metal piping, doors, hot water heaters, and other valuables. Others channeled their pain and rage into sabotage: pouring concrete down drains, bashing out support beams, tearing down interior walls, and sealing doors shut with superglue and bolts. Landlords facing foreclosure sometimes stripped houses of their valuables without informing their tenants that the property had sold.

If the property owners didn't do it themselves, scrappers were quick to identify recently vacant houses. One person in an interview described the process this way: "You know, so the house was immediately vacant, and then two days later somebody would come in and steal the furnace. . . . People would drive around and look for moving vans. They marked the house when the moving van was there. The next day, they'd come in, break in, and steal all the copper out of the basement. . . . It just devastates our community. The shell of the house is still there. The quality of the house is still there. But you need somebody living in it. We need neighbors."

Dispossessed homeowners and locals looking for deals at the auction represented just a fraction of the sales. Most of the homes went to real estate speculators, contract sellers, and slum lords who bought in "bulk" (meaning they purchased more than one hundred properties). Some investors sought to gloss over the moral depravity of the auction by touting auctioned homes as an ethical investment. Several UK-based firms developed "turnkey" programs in which they would list the property, oversee its refurbishment, source tenants, deal with managing the rental, and pay its property taxes. They advertised these programs as an opportunity to make a great return on investment while simultaneously helping the "underprivileged" and the city at large by curtailing the encroachment of blight.

Brazenly, they also hyped them as a low-risk investments because many landlords received Section 8 subsidies to rent to poor families. As one company, Detroit Property UK, stated, it's "a perfect win, win for everyone [because] investments are backed by the US government who pays up to 70–90 percent of rent."[68] Recall that the auction originated from a broader push to privatize public housing, which also resulted in the Housing Choice Voucher Program. The irony, though, ran even deeper: the voucher program subsidized rentals, but it did not require landlords to stay up to date on their taxes, creating a cyclical problem in which auctioned housing purchased for rentals often ended up back on the auction block.

The auction played a large role in tipping Detroit from a majority home-ownership city to one where landlords reigned. By 2015, for the first time in fifty years, more than half of Detroiters were renters. Former homeowners found themselves renting their own homes sold at auction or living under exploitative land installment contracts.[69] To make matters worse, many landlords failed to do even basic upkeep. Tenants were left with no heat in the winter, broken windows, mold, rodents, dangerous electrical systems, and even sewage-filled basements.[70]

To say that speculators preyed on Detroit is an understatement. They ravaged the city. To blame them alone for the plunder, however, obscures the state's role in facilitating it. The state not only transferred public housing dollars into the hands of speculators. It also delivered them homes and a new class of propertyless tenants.

✳

The losses associated with evictions and foreclosures rippled across the community, for example, in Southwest Detroit where Alba lived.[71] Considered one of Detroit's most vibrant neighborhoods, Mexicantown, as some called it, had been home to generations of Latinx communities. Today, it is celebrated for its small businesses, low vacancy rates, colorful murals, and the vibrant Clark Park. Unlike most of Detroit, it has seen a resurgence of settlement over the past decade, in no small part due to the 1994 North American Free Trade Agreement, which displaced families from Mexico and Central America. The strength of Southwest Detroit's neighborhood economy and the strong sense of solidarity among its residents created a cultural cradle for new immigrants.

At the same time, the area faced challenges, including pollution from toxic industrial plants to the west, gentrification to the east, surveillance from

Immigration and Customs Enforcement (ICE) at the riverfront, especially since 9/11, and an increase in racial profiling by county and state police, which were not bound by Detroit's sanctuary city ordinance. The challenges contributed to precarity and foreclosures, as Alba's block showed. Alba explained how a Latinx family owned the house on the corner. They had been renovating it, little by little. An elderly woman lived next to them until she lost her home through tax foreclosure. After her house became vacant, it burned down. It charred the side of the house the Latinx family had been renovating as well as the house on the opposite side. All three houses were now vacant because of a single foreclosure.

The next house down the block belonged to another Latinx family. After the father was deported, they moved out. "All the children on that block have been displaced which is a really hard, a sad thing."

Before the family left, Alba and her neighbors gardened together on a lot owned by a speculator. "The kids were really into it. They were planting and sowing seeds. Growing and eating all the produce," Alba said. "When the children went away there was a loss of impetus, almost completely, because there's nobody to grow for in the same way that children get excited about it."

Alba continued to go house by house, narrating the changes on her block. There was the house whose roof was covered by a tarp. Its family was struggling to get enough money to fix it.

There were also new people on the block. A young white man had purchased a foreclosed home, previously owned by another Latinx family. After he moved in, he put up a fence around his house and the side lot, which neighbors had collectively maintained for decades. The enclosure created tension. Meanwhile, the neighbors in the next house down moved after the father lost his job. They had rented. After they left, the landlord was foreclosed on.

"Every single house on this block has a very specific story and is a story of struggle," Alba said. "A lot of the stories on this block are a microcosm of what's happening all over Detroit. It's the displacement. It's the violence. It's the gentrification. It's the loss of property because of finances."

Other residents had similar stories to Alba's. Jameelah explained how Highland Park, an enclave city surrounded by Detroit, had changed.[72] Home to the Highland Park Ford Plant, the neighborhood had been a vibrant community with many Black businesses. The plant was demolished in the 1950s and most of the businesses were now shuttered. From 2001 to 2009, Highland park was under emergency management.

"We don't have no fire station. We don't have no police station. . . . It just no longer exists," Jameelah explained. "The schools are closed. You know where there used to be five or ten schools within that little community, . . . [now] you barely have one or two."

In 2011, DTE Energy repossessed the bulk of Highland Park's streetlights—some 1,400 poles, lights and all—because of the city's inability to pay a bill for four million dollars.[73]

When Jameelah was a little girl, she was inspired by a Black woman who owned an alteration shop. She imagined she'd start her own business. "I look back now, and there's so many abandoned buildings and so many burned up houses. I was like, how does the economy allow a live community like this to die and not have a restitution plan to bring it back?"

A restitution plan would hold the state and county government accountable for restoring and supporting neighborhood life—keeping people in housing, keeping schools, parks, and libraries open, keeping lighting on. A restitution plan would also involve returning land and housing that was stolen.

The auction led to huge agglomerations of tax-inverted public land. Seized properties were offered first to the city and state before they were resold to private owners. The mass transfer presented officials with pressing political questions about how to manage, or even dispose of, all the properties to which the city now held title. At the same time, as I examine in the next chapter, it presented a potential opportunity, if yet unrealized, to radically reconceptualize and democratize urban property regimes, to right wrongs, to compensate for losses, and to engage, as Jameelah put it, in some form of reparation and redress.

Figure 4.1 | Paul Strand, untitled photographic print, 1917. *Source:* Image courtesy Library of Congress, Prints and Photographs Division, TR1.C5 1916/1917 (Case X) [P&P].

white picket fences 4

Detroit's property regime came undone, slowly, over years. As I write this, I'm not sure *undone* is the word I'm looking for to describe the liminal and contested state of ownership of much of the city's land—the cloudy property titles, squatting, anti-eviction defenses, and widespread caretaking that happened at the neighborhood level. *Undone* means not tied or fastened, like a shoelace. It also means not finished. A person, I am reminded, can also come undone. None of these seem quite right.

I sometimes use the term *breakdown* to describe the status of Detroit's property regime. I'm unsure if *breakdown* adequately captures how racial capitalism, by design, thrives on failure—and the role property plays therein. But I do think moments of break down—when things fall apart—expose the normal order for what it is. They can also render visible the ways people collectively try to take control to better their lives.

When landed property regimes are working, it's easy to take them for granted, a ready-to-hand backdrop for modern life. By contrast, when property regimes break down, like in Detroit, societies are forced to confront numerous political and ethical questions about how to put them back together: Who or what should be able to own property? How should it be transferred? What kind of rights does property ownership bestow? How should such entitlements be protected and by whom? How should land be valued, used, and cared for? Is re-privatization the best course of action? And the list goes on.

One could imagine such deeply moral questions leading to more progressive land and housing policies. In Detroit, for example, vacant houses could be rehabilitated and redistributed to those in need. Neighborhoods could control land for community-development projects. Land could be de-commodified. Residents, after all, were already collectively organizing themselves to care for the land and one another.

Such caretaking took a variety of forms. It looked like grassroots efforts to transform lots into community spaces for theater, movie nights, and festivals. It looked like establishing pocket parks, constructing trail systems, gardening, planting orchards, and transforming buildings into canvases for artwork. It also looked like routine maintenance: picking up trash, mowing, boarding up vacant houses, and organizing home tours to showcase the quality of housing stock. These forms of bottom-up urbanism illustrate the extent to which new social worlds had taken root, and in some cases flourished, on devalued land. At the same time, they created a sense of collective investment in the city's so-called abandoned land, giving rise to competing claims, some formal and others informal.[1]

The chaos on the ground was mirrored administratively. Foreclosures had wreaked havoc for homeowners and tenants. They also presented a Sisyphean challenge for city officials for which they were largely unprepared. Huge agglomerations of de facto state land in Detroit's municipal coffers tested the limits of the city codes and charter. Why? How? The disposition of de facto public land in Detroit involved the development of new laws, policies, and governmental assemblages that would transfer property titles and rights from the state to individuals, businesses, or corporations. But no playbook existed on how exactly to proceed.

The challenges were myriad. They were not merely about the need for more efficient measures to retitle deeds and transfer rights. Rather, the transfer of rights required new forms of political authority.[2] It also required that those tasked with overseeing the land problem imagine the kinds of propertied persons who would bear the new rights as well as the risks and debts that came with them.

Given that neoliberal state power coalesces, in no small part, through the production of property and citizenship, such decisions mattered greatly.[3] In the twenty-first century, it is a truism that finance capital impinges on local political autonomy. The disciplining of urban public policy through credit ratings is one way. Another is the intrusion of economic logics on the imagination, on desire, on the sense of self. But it is not always clear how exactly it happens. Nor is it a forgone conclusion.

Surplus Land and an Overwhelmed State

The municipality's regulation of land use, distribution, and access happened primarily through two departments, the City Planning Commission (overseen by city council) and the Planning and Development Department (controlled by the executive branch). The latter was responsible for the acquisition and disposition of most of the city's tax-reverted land. The department had the right of first refusal on properties that didn't sell in the auction. If they accepted them, the city received them for free. They were "not really 'free,'" however, one city official pointed out to me, because the city had already lost the taxes on them.

In 2011, the Planning and Development Department sat on fifty-two thousand surplus properties. Nearly all of them were residential homes that came through the tax-foreclosure process.[4] While some of these properties were from speculators, many came from dispossessed homeowners.

The city lacked the capacity to maintain all the properties—in terms of both people power and policies. They also lacked the capacity to dispose of them efficiently. The city was the largest landholder and seller in the region, but only seven city real estate agents were responsible for selling all its properties.

"We have hundreds of people waiting to buy land," said Ben Price over lunch one day in August 2012.[5] Price worked in the Planning and Development Department. He was among the dozens of city workers and planners I interviewed during my fieldwork who worked within the city's land governance assemblage, which consisted of the city's planning departments, public-private institutions like the Detroit Land Bank Authority, the Blight Removal Task Force, and a bevy of nonprofits. The decentralized nature of the assemblage had resulted in a patchwork of recommendations, laws, and regulations that determined legitimate and illegitimate ownership and use of vacant, abandoned, and tax-foreclosed land.

Detroit was often described to me as a planners' paradise because of the opportunities to try new things. But, as Price made clear, the daunting logistics of accepting, managing, and selling so much land tended to dash any romanticism.

Once a buyer expressed interest in a property, the transfer involved no fewer than eight approvals and signatures for each of the thousands of properties. First, the city council had to sign off on the sale of all parcels except for those adjacent to property that a buyer already owned. Then the council signed off on the sale, after which the property deed needed to be signed by the director or deputy director of the Planning and Development Department.

Additionally, it had to be signed off on by the head of finance, a top official of the corporate council, the assessor, an engineer, and two witnesses.

Each signature could take a day or two.

If someone was out of town, it could take up to a week.

Disposing of de facto state land was not the only problem; the city also had upward of three thousand properties tied up with inquiries and defunct development agreements. Real estate brokers faced challenges when trying to show city properties because there was no easy-access database.

The dispositions process was a source of frustration for residents and community groups seeking more secure tenure over land that they already cared for and managed. The city ran an Adjacent Lot Program, but it was available only to homeowners. Residents described filing for ownership rights only to have the city lose their applications multiple times. Another program, called Farm-A-Lot, allowed people to farm on empty land, but tenure was temporary, in part because the city had no urban agricultural ordinance.[6] By city officials' own admissions, the dispositions process was an organizational nightmare.

"Our procedures are ridiculous," said Price. "It is almost impossible to negotiate. We need to be able to just move this stuff through the system quickly." Price, who was new to the job, argued that the city needed to change its "mindset." He took cues from the bestseller *Good to Great: Why Some Companies Make the Leap and Others Don't*, which argued that it is not the latest technology or a high-profile CEO that makes companies successful but a corporate culture that encourages discipline.[7] Price sought to shift the organizational culture of the municipal government and what he saw as an endemic mentality of fear. Many city officials were afraid to sell land, he said, because "we might need it someday." For Price, the priority was to increase the flow of properties through the Planning and Development Department. Good government depended on it.

Price's quest to bring efficiency and strategic decision-making to the local government was common among those working to shore up the city's collapsing property regime. For example, much anticipation surrounded the Detroit Works Project, as I discuss in chapter 7, with the hopes that it would deliver a long-term strategic framework for decision-making. Streamlining disposition procedures was a necessary first step in fostering favorable conditions for investment.

A key task of the city government was to develop new institutions and regulatory oversight to carry out this work. This involved the governance of land and people. Property, after all, is a not a thing but a bundle of rights that defines people's relationships with one another and with respect to things. If, for Price, successful government depended on changing workplace culture, it also turned on incentivizing and disciplining property owners in the creation of market value. Put simply, the question of how to build real estate markets dominated the state's unwieldy efforts to stabilize the city's property regime.

The Planning and Development Department's creation of the White Picket Fence Program—designed to dispose of surplus city land—illustrates how city officials tasked with building real estate markets faced a series of questions about who should (and who should not) have rights to make land into property, not to mention, who had (or did not have) the ability to add value to it. These were moral decisions, though, they were rarely framed in such terms.

Caretaking as Politics by Other Means

The White Picket Fence Program was developed to incentivize property owners to buy adjacent lots in areas of the city where planners aimed to spur development (figure 4.2).[8] The lots were sold for two hundred dollars. After the purchase, the city gave buyers a two-hundred-dollar gift card to be used for fencing and beautification. On its face, it was a win-win situation. The city wanted to reduce its land holdings. People wanted to buy lots. But if our analysis stops here, then we miss how neoliberal notions of care and value shaped the state's imagined solutions to the city's land crisis.

To understand the implications of the White Picket Fence Program, we have to understand how it leveraged the informal practices through which residents claimed and maintained vacant lots. The most prolific care happened at the neighborhood level, where residents self-organized to collectively maintain and protect vacant properties in their neighborhoods. One of the most extensive systems of this kind that I encountered was in the historic Grandmont Rosedale neighborhood on Detroit's West Side.

First developed in the 1920s, Grandmont Rosedale boasted Tudor, colonial, and craftsman-style homes. It had long been considered one of the city's most desirable residential communities. Over the decades, as other neighborhoods lost residents, Grandmont Rosedale remained relatively stable. Then, the foreclosure crisis hit, and neighborhood home values plummeted.

I first heard about Grandmont Rosedale's neighborhood caretaking in the fall of 2011. Community Legal Resources (CLR), a nonprofit organization that led a collective initiative called the Detroit Vacant Property Campaign, had

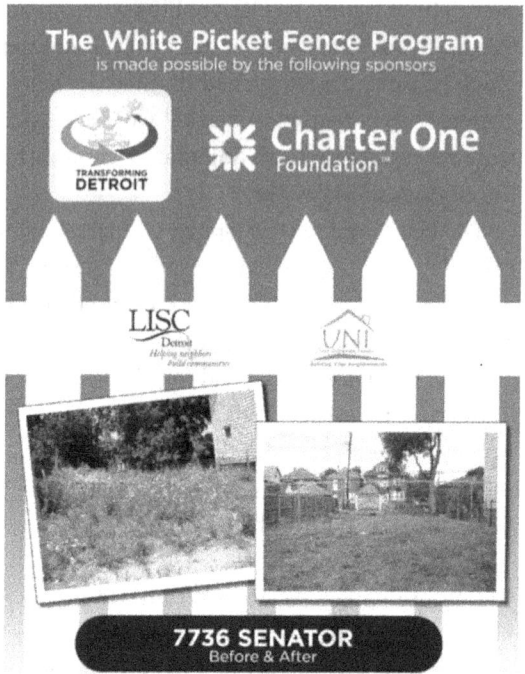

Figure 4.2 | Flier advertising the White Picket Fence Program.

been hosting a series of public meetings about vacant land. The Grandmont Rosedale Neighborhood Association was one of a number of organizations to which CLR had awarded small grants for property maintenance and security patrol. A representative of Grandmont Rosedale named Shirley was there to share tips on how to fight vacancy and blight.

A tall woman with graying hair, Shirley explained how they started by surveying the neighborhood, using Google maps to indicate vacant homes. A neighborhood "patrol team" would then use the maps to organize work teams. The teams tried to make the vacant houses look inhabited. They planted flowers, drove up and down driveways when it was snowing, and mowed lawns. They boarded up windows and doors to deter illegal dumpers, squatters, and scrappers who stripped vacant houses.[9] They also designated point people to do surveillance. This involved watching houses for suspicious activity and fostering relationships with the police, in case they needed to call on them to deal with squatters.

In addition to physical maintenance and surveillance—or what in practice was more like camouflage and disguise—the neighborhood association designed systems to hold absentee property owners responsible. The association's members made calls, asking property owners to cut their grass and deal with abandoned cars. If it was a bank-owned property, a manager would typically send someone for maintenance. But most property owners did not respond to their phone calls. Neighborhood association members followed up with letters, documenting blight violations and listing fines associated with the maintenance they'd done. The letters stated that if an owner did not pay, the association would report them to the authorities. No one ever repaid them for upkeep.

I was struck by how ideas of improvement structured their carework. They hoped improved lots would lead to higher property values, a proxy, as Shirley explained, for the quality of neighborhood life. When homes fell into disrepair, it could be devastating for the neighborhood. Once two or three houses were stripped, a block could be formally designated as blighted. Then, demolition could begin. Improving lots, thus, was important because it suggested not only neighborhood inhabitancy but market value, and, thus, viability.[10]

Grandmont Rosedale was one example, among many, of programs that encouraged and incentivized residents to maintain and improve Detroit's vacant lands. In the face of public-sector rollbacks, residents' voluntaristic investments of time and energy often elicited a feel-good politics. But as geographer Kimberly Kinder argues, one should be wary of romanticizing such trends.[11] They were clearly not a panacea for austerity. Indeed, volunteerism as democratic reconstruction aligns surprisingly well with the neoliberal agenda. Indeed, many nonprofits, philanthropies, and volunteer-based projects are symptomatic of the state devolution of care. The entrepreneurial citizen was, after all, the imagined ideal of neoliberal ideology. And residential caretaking on its own did little to stop the privatization and destruction of public goods.

That said, caretaking in Detroit was far from homogenous. Some forms of neighborhood caretaking functioned as political participation, mutual aid, and as a means of building grassroots power. It would, thus, be a mistake to dismiss all caretaking as concessionary to the antiwelfare state. Take, for instance, the Riverfront East Congregation Initiative (RECI), a collaboration of seventeen diverse faith communities with twenty-six thousand congregants, which formed in 2010 to shape the future of Detroit's East Side, an area of the city that had some of the highest foreclosure rates. RECI's approach to reimagining the politics of place illustrates the possibilities of how community carework can function as democratic transformation in the face of political abandonment and austerity.[12]

RECI engaged in what they called "place-based ministry." They aimed to ignite residents' imaginations surrounding their congregations. One way they did this was by practicing common governance and collective decision-making. Respect across difference was a core value. It guided them as they developed a shared understanding about who they were and what they wanted for themselves.

As part of this discernment process, they engaged in participatory, asset-based organizing. For instance, shortly after RECI formed, representatives from each congregation gathered to research and take stock of community resources. A congregant named Ada explained how she was surprised when others came back with photos of abandoned houses. "The photographs were not like those you'd see in the news but [like] this house can be rebuilt or rejuvenated in some way," she said, explaining how the process cast the neighborhood where she had lived for forty-eight years in a new light.

Fostering hope was central to RECI's work. "Oftentimes I am with people who don't spend very much time in places of hope in the city," an organizer named Rosalind said. "There's enough negativity, and the reality is that there's some pretty serious challenges about living in the city. One of the big things I keep reminding myself is that . . . you really have to put yourself in a position of being in those spaces of energy and positive work. Because if you don't spend your time there, I think it can really get debilitating."

I appreciated Rosalind's insights. I'd long felt that hope has the power to galvanize the masses, but it can also be naïve. Brazilian educator and philosopher Paulo Freire argued that naïve hope—by which he meant hope that lacks a critical edge, hope that lacks a foundation in political struggle—can ironically cause hopelessness. "Without a minimum of hope, we cannot so much as start the struggle," argues Freire. "But without the struggle, hope, as an ontological need, dissipates, loses its bearings, and turns into hopelessness. And hopelessness can become tragic despair." For these reasons, he advocated for "a kind of education in hope."[13]

Similarly, RECI sought to deepen hope through relationship building and experiential education. After taking stock of community assets, representatives from each congregation began meeting one Saturday every month to plan ten-week intensive "academies" for congregation members in which they would learn about community assets on the East Side, including an organization that helped citizens returning from prison, a group that focused on teaching young people trades, community gardens, restaurants, bookstores, and other businesses that gave back to the city and did so "humbly." They also formed working groups, which held educational forums to arm congregants with knowledge of the city's land-use policies and processes, as well as development proposals, sending liaisons out to attend community planning meetings and report back. They worked to hold public officials accountable. When developers came to them with proposals, they asked, "Do they have our community's best interest at heart?"

When the state made welfare cuts, RECI made a resource guide—"a list of folks who were providing resources to the community"—and encouraged congregation members to support them. They included On the Rise Bakery, Korash Florist, Swanson Funeral, They Say Restaurant, Gardella Furniture, and True Value Hardware. The map also marked fresh food assets and the congregations that constituted RECI. They were trying to cultivate what they called an "economy of the community." This entailed building social relationships, which, in turn, would empower the community to take responsibility for changing political conditions. They buttressed this work through the development of community infrastructures that provided life-sustaining resources. For example, they hosted a food pantry, a clothes closet, a free community meal and movie program, a book club, and community gardens.

To idealize such place-based ministry would misrepresent the hardship residents faced and the perils of antiwelfarism. Yet to dismiss it as apolitical or as merely a stopgap measure does a disservice to the political theorizations, alternative ways of living, and structures of affect that people develop when relegated to the underside of liberal democracy. Recognizing RECI's neighborhood caretaking as politics by other means opens analytical space to inquire into how the tremendous capacity for self-organization and horizontal mobilization that exists in communities can manifest in oppositional and propositional politics. Both are necessary for building alternatives to neoliberal forms of planned abandonment. If the outcomes are never guaranteed, it behooves us to get curious about what moves people to come together and how they do so.

Geographer Deborah Cowen writes, "One-off protests and petitions do not threaten the status quo, but sustained alternatives that open up both the imaginative and practical possibilities for other ways of life certainly do, and these are anchored in infrastructure."[14] They are also, as RECI demonstrated, anchored in place, on the land. For this reason, it mattered greatly which forms of neighborhood care and stewardship the state recognized and sanctified via property entitlements and which it overlooked. With this in mind, let's return to the White Picket Fence Program and consider the politics of recognition and the forms of propertied citizenship that animated it.

Good Fences Make Good Citizens

The White Picket Fence Program was one of the many programs that emerged in the early 2010s to deal with ambiguous land tenure by returning "abandoned" land and housing to the private market and incentivizing community care. On its face, it was a seemingly benign, practical attempt to make vacant land productive, but its embedded assumptions were far from neutral. It revealed how deeply entrenched norms and exclusions associated with American propertied citizenship undergirded new land governance policies.[15]

The White Picket Fence Program leveraged the existing Adjacent Lot Program in neighborhoods selected by the Detroit Works Project as demonstration areas. Many people were already tending adjacent lots, as one of the program's developers, Gary, explained to me, but they didn't formally own them. Officials hoped the offer for a white picket fence would encourage homeowners to make formal property claims. The fence, however, was more than just an incentive. Officials hoped it would deter illegal dumping and reduce the work of the maintenance department by communicating that land was being privately cared for.

"It's almost like the tragedy of the commons: when no one owns it, no one feels responsible for it," Gary said. "When someone owns it, that person is calling the police when someone dumps on it."

The fence, in short, would signal ownership and promote the kinds of responsibility and oversight that came with it. Residents were not required to put up white pickets. The construction cost of a picket fence, notably, exceeded the amount of the gift card. They could instead opt for a chain link fence. But the image of the white picket fence was important. As Robbie Davis and Ed Williams write, "The way we define ourselves as individuals and as a nation becomes concrete in how we build fences."[16]

Fences foundationally shape perceptions of space, notions of public and private, and ideas of improvement. As Nicholas Blomley writes, fence building is a "performance of property" that is both citational, in that it references numerous other performances, and iterative, in that it re-performs this history.[17] In this sense, the designers of the White Picket Fence Program were onto something. Named to conjure the American dream, the White Picket Fence Program played on strong cultural symbolism.[18]

In the postwar United States, the white picket fence denoted the "good life." It was a marker of status and of a racial boundary. Popular culture cast white picket fence neighborhoods as serene communities in which white families lived in suburban dream houses and fulfilled heteronormative domestic roles. Black and other people of color were entirely absent or brought in to perform stereotypical work as maids and landscapers. "For mainstream white [TV] viewers, this universe was a sweet return to normalcy, balance, and calm torn asunder by the wartime upheaval in gender roles and family norms," argues writer Sikivu Hutchinson. "For viewers of color, it was an insidious erasure of the terrorism they continued to experience under American apartheid. Mother, Father, Dick, Jane, and Spot were the perfect alibi for the burning streets of the deep Jim Crow South and the teeming slums of the deceitful North, black America's Promised Land."

This postwar TV fantasy wasn't just problematic for its racial exclusion. White picket fence domesticity served as anti-civil-rights propaganda, as Hutchinson argues. It drew white families into a consumptive culture that sedated and sheltered them from politics and revolutions underway in gender and racial norms.[19] The White Picket Fence Program was rooted in this history regardless of the stated intention of its developers, one of whom explained the name as trying to be "cute."

The White Picket Fence Program illustrates how state securitization entails, as urban studies scholar Ananya Roy writes, "determin[ing] which forms of informality will thrive and disappear."[20] The White Picket Fence Program, for example, restricted applications for side lots to *existing* property owners. Thus, renters, unhoused people, and collectives were effectively excluded from gaining legal rights to tax-reverted land through the program. Moreover, as mentioned, the program only operated in select areas deemed promising for future development. The White Picket Fence Program is an example of how bureaucratic efforts to reimagine Detroit's property regime hinged on officials making judgments about the kinds of subjects and places that were likely—or unlikely—to produce speculative economic value. As one of many governmental efforts to constitute a new property regime in the early 2010s, it raised a critical set of questions, such as, who was being included and excluded from these efforts? Who got to decide the metrics of improvement and productive labor? How did the capacities of individuals and groups to make land into property vary? What kinds of people and property practices were considered legitimate within existing governmental and economic structures, and which were deemed illegitimate?

There is a deep irony in how the White Picket Fence Program worked to conjure the American dream at a time when so many residents were being dispossessed of it. If the tax foreclosure auction (discussed in chapter 3) sought to discipline irresponsible property owners, the White Picket Fence Program, by contrast, sought to incentivize responsible ones through promoting enclosure and improvement.

Neoutilitarian ideology insists, as property theorist Carol Rose writes, that "property is supposed to *do* something, and what it is supposed to do is to tap individual energies in order to make us all more prosperous." From this vantage, property rights are seen as fundamentally good because they inspire people to improve the things they own.[21] But what does it mean to improve? Improvement for who? Improvement for what?

The notion that enclosure induces improvement—you care for what you fence—echoes the famous line in Robert Frost's poem "Mending Wall" that "good fences make good neighbors."[22] While this line is often invoked, the poem is an anxious mediation on enclosure and the yearly mending of a wall that separates the narrator's and his neighbor's property. As they engage in the rite of repair, and ironically find mutuality in doing so, the narrator remains ambivalent about what is being walled in and walled out.

Might the absence of a fence make good neighbors, I wondered? Moreover, what kind of land policy might be imagined if an ethic of care was taken to be primary rather than iterative of the fence itself?

Alternative Ethics of Place and Property

"There are vacant lots. There are vacant houses. However, nobody's burning anything down in my neighborhood. The neighbors cut the grass," said Kathleen. "They board up different properties. For all intents and purposes, they keep the fronts looking like people still frequent them."[23]

Kathleen, who worked in public housing advocacy and with RECI, lived around the corner from the old Packard plant that sprawled along Mt. Elliot Road and East Grand Boulevard. "You know, you almost have to see it to believe it. Although the neighborhood has changed in the way of the population, the life has not gone out of [it]."

People walked dogs. They gardened and shared vegetables. Newcomers lived side by side with African American families like Kathleen's, who had been there for generations. She had known many of her neighbors since they were all kids. They were now raising their own children.

She grew animated talking about the hours she spent in her yard at all times of day and night. She painted, gardened, listened to music. "I just love it there," she said. "And we don't even have a fence between my yard and my neighbor's yard, so we cut each other's grass. I have a deck, we share that. . . . When people are so down on what's going on with them, I'm like, 'well, gosh, where do you live?' I don't feel like that."

It was a fleeting comment but it stayed with me. The White Picket Fence Program had been on my mind. Kathleen's sense of mutuality and joy interested me because it hinted at the potentials of unmaking liberal property and suggested a tradition of property relations absent walls and fences. If liberal property law interpolates the self-possessed individual, by contrast, Kathleen's conscious decision not to build a fence—and to take pleasure in that choice—offered a different logic of property and personhood.

Kathleen's comment also stood out to me because it encapsulated the myriad ways that Detroiters were inhabiting the breakdown of the private property system though sharing, stewardship, and solidarity. What might these practices reveal, I wondered, about unwedding property systems from the self-owning person?

Anthropologist Sarah Pinto argues that rather than focusing on rebuilding or rehabilitation as a response to breakdown, "there might be an ethic to be found in and by way of dissolution." Pinto writes, "I find it useful to pause in dissolution, to imagine it less as an aberration from which people seek to recover than as a condition in its own right, incipient or realized, to focus on the habitation of breakdown as much as (or more than) on making anew (or remaking)."[24]

When land loses market value, geographer Rachel Goffe observes, it becomes the grounds for alternative forms of meaning making, autonomy, refusal, pleasure, and community.[25] Goffe is writing about rural Jamaica, but her insights are useful for thinking about property breakdown in places like Detroit too because they direct attention to how the quotidian practices of repurposing devalued land for community needs—from maintaining lots to fighting evictions, growing and preparing food, blocking water shutoffs, sharing electricity, and so on—gave rise to alternative ways of knowing, imagining, and being in relationship to land and one another outside of capitalist logics.

To take these experiences seriously is not to gloss over Detroiters' complex relationships to American ideals of property and homeownership, nor to minimize their diversity of viewpoints about what should be done with the city's land. But rather it is to insist that if we want to decommodify property—and enact systems that reject degradation, extraction, and accumulation—then learning from the grounded practices of mutuality at play in communities like Detroit is a good place to start. From there, we can consider what nurtures such practices and how they might be normed at institutional and legal levels.

When you begin naming something, it changes the way you see the world. Given this, it is important but insufficient to just name the mechanisms—conceptual and material—that need to be abolished to realize more just socio-ecological property relations. It is also critical to name and chart the values, practices, ideas, and traditions that support the work of democratic reconstruction.

In our Uniting Detroiters project interviews, land control emerged as a major area of concern. Participants' reflections on their personal relationships to land and practices of community stewardship revealed a shared set of political and moral commitments in relationship to land—a land ethic, if you will, that was at once deeply historical and emerged from communities of practice. The existence of such a land ethic suggests some lines along which a decommodified property praxis may be nurtured.[26]

The first theme was placemaking and challenging displacement. Residents often began their reflections on land by connecting their own familial histories of loss and migration to ongoing displacement caused by urban renewal and foreclosures. They talked about dispossession as more than the loss of land. It was an assault on a whole way of life that was rooted in place-based relationships. Cecily McClellan, a longtime Detroiter and *People's Atlas of Detroit* contributor, explained how her extended and close-knit family network was forced to move from Black Bottom because of urban renewal. "Everybody knew everybody," she said. "Within a few-block radius, my grandmother and my mother's sisters lived—my mother had eight living siblings for a period in Black Bottom. Therefore, it meant I could go literally a few blocks over to my grandparents' home or my mother's sister or see my uncles on Joseph Campau Avenue or Chene Street in the business areas." McClellan now lived on Calvert Street where she had been working to rebuild the sense of community that she experienced in Black Bottom.[27]

Other residents also reflected on the violence of urban renewal to argue for the collective remembrance of resistance. Another *Atlas* contributor Michelle Martinez, who is an environmental justice activist from Southwest Detroit, discussed how her family's land was taken for the Ambassador Bridge and the Gateway Project: "My grandfather owned a store that no longer exists. My grandmother's house that she grew up in is the service drive. My great-grandfather's house in which he raised nine kids, that's now the service drive for the highway. So, we have had land and now it's gone because of that transportation infrastructure, like many in Detroit. We don't have a material history of what that multigenerational landownership looked like. I wish that I could still walk into my grandfather's house or my great-grandfather's house and see what that life was like."[28] Martinez urged Detroiters to look to traditions of resistance for models of collective land ownership. She offered the example of *palenques* in Latin America, later called maroons in the United States, where runaway slaves first took flight to Indigenous settlements and then grew numerous enough to form their own autonomous communities. As Cedric Robinson documents in *Black Marxism*, the networks of *palenques*, *mocambos*, *quilombos*, and maroons were extensive. The Spanish referred to the "fugitives" as *cimarrones*. Hundreds of thousands of fugitive slaves formed their own communities, including in Mexico, Brazil, and Jamaica, which were then replicated throughout the Spanish territories and newer colonies.[29]

Some of them were permanent, many were fleeting, but as Martinez reminds us, like Robinson, the remembrance of such radical traditions stretches the imagination. The importance of marronage was not only physical survival, Martinez explained, but its sustenance of community relationships. Despite colonial masters trying to pay enslaved Africans and Indigenous people to disclose where runaway slaves had gone, they refused. "People refused that financial incentive or incentive of 'freedom' from slavery from their slave master in favor of an alternative idea of their own control, their own autonomy," Martinez argued. "Those skills of resistance . . . were transferred to the children."[30]

The history of marronage disavows the self-possessed individual and preserves alternative epistemologies and ontologies of land, property, and personhood. Maroons, writes anthropologist Justin Hosbey and geographer J. T. Roane, "articulated 'something akin to freedom,' realized within the ecologies that the colonial order could not 'tame.' Inhabiting these ecologies and keeping them 'untamed' demanded alternative ways of thinking about land use, stewardship, accumulation, and the environment."[31] Notably, marronage is not just a historical example of resistance. Nor is it confined only to swamps, mountains, or other undesirable rural landscapes. As geographers Celeste Winston and Willie Wright have both argued, marronage is a possibility in the contemporary city, too, as evidenced by collective forms of Black placemaking.[32]

Another way that Detroiters conveyed a land ethic was by suggesting that the struggle against dispossession would not be solved by mere possession of land. Solving the land crisis, many observed, was not as simple as redistribution or the transfer of rights to individuals, because other entitlements had been stripped away as well. If households had no source of regular income, land rights would not necessarily benefit them in an immediate sense. To be clear, many people did want secure individual tenure, but they also wanted some measure of self-determination and community control. Collective control required dispersing power and reimagining the function of the state and citizenship at a time when neoliberal political rationalities were perfecting the ideal citizen-subject as an entrepreneurial self-possessive individual. "The land question is really a question of our civic mind," as a local activist named Alice put it. "We need more agency, more self-determination, and more standing."[33]

Residents argued that the land should be put back into productive use in ways that would serve the community. They emphasized the hypocrisy of dominant narratives that Detroiters failed to care for the city when it was actually speculators, banks, and out-of-towners who owned large swaths of the city but took little responsibility. *Atlas* contributors Kezia Curtis and Jessi Quizar underscore this point when they write, "it is . . . precisely outside investors' remove from the city, their lack of personal investments, such as relationships with neighbors, that make it seem financially logical and beneficial to neglect the land that they own. This kind of impersonal monetary investment arguably *causes* blight in Detroit."[34]

Indeed, others pointed out how austerity was self-fulfilling. Cutbacks in city maintenance contributed to a discourse that a profit motive was required to get things done. For these reasons, residents argued that it was important to go beyond critiquing local government to demanding property laws and governance that served the common good. One strategy they used was to claim the public sphere as a commons. This framing stemmed from a recognition that programs of self-help and self-sufficiency sometimes risked ceding too much power to neoliberal forces, a particularly salient critique given the looming state takeover and bankruptcy.

People often asserted that the land they cared for belonged to them. Yet others cautioned that the notion of belonging was complicated by the raced and classed history of European property law. The concept of private property, after all, comes from *privatus*, which means depriving other people of access and use of what you've enclosed. Belonging ought not be thought about as possession but a recognition of the larger whole of which land and people were a part. Land governance could honor such values by privileging care and stewardship.

The psychic, community, and ecological value of land, they argued, needed to be recentered. Such conversations tended to be deeply philosophical and historical, underscoring the clash of values between European notions that you can own the earth versus Indigenous and African traditions in which land is a living entity and the site of ancestral life. Getting into a right relationship to land thus meant grappling not only with historical dispossession but also with ecological exploitation, nature-culture binaries, and the sentience of nonhumans. "I was thinking about this term 'abandoned'—I just hate the terms 'abandoned' and 'vacant,'" a participant named Richard said in one of our community conversations. "I think about who has not abandoned the land . . . the chickaree and sweet clovers . . . acknowledging the people who lived here before. . . . We need to acknowledge the care that has been given by those who have no voice, or a voice we chose not to listen to."

Such an ethical and relational orientation toward "nonownership of land" was expressed by another *Atlas* contributor Lee Gaddies, who argued for the importance of remembering the "historic mandate" of African American stewardship. He explained how his "family came off of land in the South and retired back to that land, never letting it go. . . . That has become indoctrinated in our family, that you are not the owners of the land, you are stewards of that land for the next generation. I think that we have allowed somebody else's vision of success to cloud that historic mandate to us. Once upon a time it was 'Don't sell the farm,' right?, Never sell the farm. Never ever, ever, ever!'"[35] Gaddies's insistence to "never sell" was a strong rebuke of financial markets, capitalist rationalities, and the mechanisms—compounded over generations—that have allowed large corporate owners to seize large swaths of urban land. Scaled up, such remembrance could serve—and ought to serve—as a powerful antidote to the racial-spatial violence of capitalism. This required, as many pointed out, sustained education and dialogue that could shift consciousness and create social transformation. If old paradigms of propertied citizenship were not shed, as one group member put it, "we are going to invariably end up right back with what we have now." Constructive dialogue was not a given but rather a capacity that could be cultivated and a necessary counterstep to the absence of relationality at the heart of dominion.[36]

*

Before planners started deploying caretaking as a land governance tool and placemaking as an economic development strategy, they already existed in communities.[37] They often emerged in ways that were improvised and elemental but also coordinated. For example, caretaking looked like developing new systems of stewardship, such as neighbors who came together to keep the grass of vacant houses mowed and to make them looked lived in. It looked like reclaiming basic services and public utilities by reconnecting disconnected infrastructural networks, such as rigging electrical wires or turning water back on. At other times it meant hustling to make a buck, like the repair shop set up in a parking lot or the hair salon in a basement.

Caretaking scaled up to community placemaking. It took the form of people developing and supporting new social infrastructures like Black bookshops, community gardens, clinics, social centers, and art and music programs. It took the form of rehabbing houses and churches and building new schools and media outlets. These collective spaces for health, education, and cultural production were rooted in theories of empowerment and collective emancipation. They were places where people engaged in practices of collective governance and decision-making, collective study and resource sharing.

These experiments in living, which were about meeting basic needs and fostering the conditions for Black life, contributed to what many have named as Detroit's resilience. In interviews, residents often outlined a distinct fabric of social relations on so-called surplus land that marked the coordinates of a fugitive city in which all people could live dignified lives beyond the logics of capitalism, racism, and exploitation. In this way, the practices of neighborhood care functioned not simply as stopgap measures. They were efforts to prefigure a more just city. As Detroit faced fiscal crisis and economic structuring, it was this vision and city that residents sought to defend.

accounting
for unpayable debt

"Gil Scott-Heron wrote a song, 'We Almost Lost Detroit.'" The woman paused. She was addressing members of the state review team who had been appointed by the governor of Michigan to investigate Detroit's finances.

"Well, I'm here to say, we're not gonna lose Detroit." Her voice resounded throughout the meeting room at Cadillac Place, a marble-laden neoclassical building in the New Center area of Detroit, which was originally designed as the headquarters of General Motors.

It was March 26, 2012. The public sphere had been dominated since the previous fall by declarations of Detroit's fiscal crisis. I started going to meetings after Mayor Bing warned that cash shortfalls might require an emergency manager to save the city from financial ruin. The review team was required to hold their meeting publicly. I'd expected them to be dull bureaucratic affairs. I was wrong. They offered a window onto the deeply moral politics of accounting and debt that surrounded the fabrication of crisis and the structural adjustment of the public sector.

In the wake of the Great Recession, Detroit was among dozens of municipalities—from Scranton, Pennsylvania, to San Bernardino, California—that faced market-oriented structural adjustment in response to insolvency. In majority-minority cities like Detroit, the American dream turned American nightmare underscored how the racial inequities of the real estate market were intimately tied to the fiscal crisis.

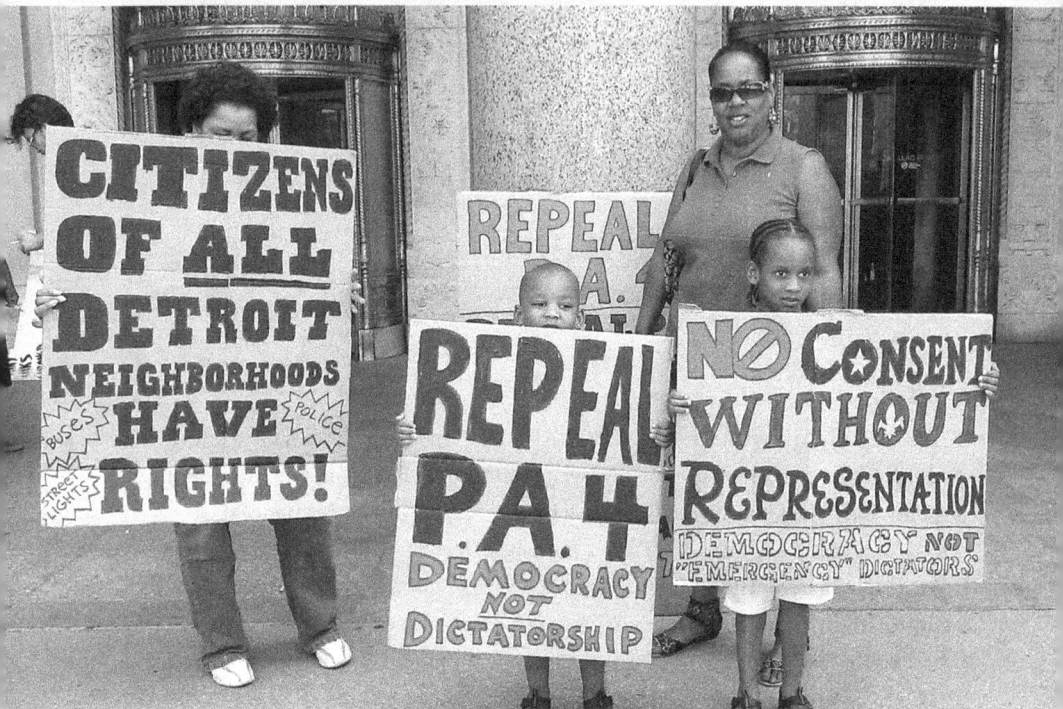

Figure 5.1 | Protestors calling for the repeal of Public Act 4—the Emergency Manager Law—on July 11, 2012, at the Michigan Court of Appeals, District 1, located at the Cadillac Building in New Center Detroit. *Source:* Photograph by Stephen Boyle.

Across the country, dire warnings rung out about the economic fallout. A report from the Pew Charitable Trust estimated that property tax receipts would not return to 2009 levels until 2039. Local governments, particularly poor cities, would bear the brunt of these losses. Absent debt forgiveness, the report's authors argued, municipalities would likely have to slash their budgets for decades to come. Services would be reduced to the bare minimum of police and fire protection.[1] Such predictions seemed to be unfolding fast in Detroit.

The state financial review team was charged with determining if the city was in an official crisis. Their findings mattered immensely. A declaration of crisis would vest the governor with the authority to appoint an emergency manager to balance the city's budget.

In Michigan, emergency managers were tantamount to mini-dictators. They were endowed with sweeping decision-making powers over a city's finances and operations, superseding those of locally elected representatives. They had the authority to negotiate and terminate labor contracts; impose pay cuts; hire and fire employees; privatize assets; change budgets without legislative approval; and initiate municipal bankruptcy proceedings.

I didn't catch the woman's name and was unsure if she was there to represent an organization or to just speak her own truth to power, but I was moved by her words. They boomed throughout the room, which was crowded with approximately a hundred people, including welfare rights activists, reporters, union members, and concerned citizens. I was surprised by the turnout given that it was midday and that the meeting had been both rescheduled and moved. The review team had canceled their two previous meetings, last minute and with little explanation, leading to an elevated level of frustration for those in attendance. The room felt thick with righteous indignation.

The prospect of a takeover had incensed many residents and activists, who saw it as an attempt to loot the collective Black legacy of Detroit. Their rebuttals recalled the historic debts dating to conquest and slavery, on which the financial system owed its existence. They also served as a reminder of how racial differentiation was a well-worn mechanism of financial innovation.

The financial review team's investigation coincided with that of another commission that was engaged in a radically different kind of accounting. Four months earlier, in November 2011, the Metropolitan Detroit Truth and Reconciliation Commission on Racial Inequality (MDTRC) was established to investigate the historical roots of race-based unequal opportunity in the Detroit metropolitan area and to foster a shared understanding of the regional legacies of segregation and housing discrimination.

The financial review team and the MDTRC were distinct processes, but their proximity in time and space suggested to me the importance of reflecting on the politics of unpayable debt. I was interested in the differences between and premises upon which fiscal and moral reconciliation rested. As residents' outrage made clear, unpayable debt was much more than money owed. It was a debated terrain on which new regimes of governance were launched and on which residents and activists demanded redress and articulated new visions for society.[2]

The Racialized Geography of Debt

The threat of fiscal crisis hovered over Detroit like a blimp—bloated and a bit unwieldy. Dissonant news headlines announced its arrival in the form of grave predictions that Detroit would run out of money by April 2012 alongside headlines heralding its comeback. The city's cash-flow issues weren't new. Officials had worried about a potential takeover by the state of Michigan ever since budget deficits and junk bond ratings plagued Mayor Kwame Kilpatrick's administration in the early 2000s. The city had borrowed extensively to sustain its operations. As time went on, it continued to do so, eventually borrowing to service its debt obligations. When David Bing campaigned for mayor in 2008, he did so on his business acumen, pledging to restore order to the city's finances. Then the Great Recession hit and the city was forced to borrow even more.

The looming cash crunch led to vociferous debates over who was to blame for the debt burden. One of the more popular stances—steeped in racism—blamed the city's fiscal crisis on decades of Black governance, which had supposedly enabled a culture of corruption and misrule and fostered a racially hostile environment for investment capital.

Others argued that unions had forced municipal leaders to make impossible pension promises, sinking the city's budget and destroying the auto industry. In addition to blaming the unions and city government, commentators also reproached "delinquent" property taxpayers for draining Detroit's finances and called for new tax collection systems.

More nuanced positions drew attention to the global political economy and structural drivers, arguing that big business, corporate tax incentives, and corporate trade pacts were responsible, not unions or poor homeowners who made for easy scapegoats. Some called for the federal government to bail out the city, like they had done for the banks and the automakers.

Less discussed, however, was how decades of reductions in federal and state aid to cities had led to a brutal cycle of deficit spending, particularly in majority-minority cities like Detroit. The racialized geography of debt in the United States, which had driven subprime mortgage creditors to prey on Detroiters, was also obscured. Creditors' profitability model, after all, as Paula Chakravartty and Denise Ferreira da Silva argue, strategically targeted racial difference or, put another way, debtors who had an inability to pay.[3] To be clear, debtors' inability to pay was not for want of the moral attributes associated with responsible economic subjects like productivity, accountability, and independence, as prevailing discourse suggested. Rather unpayability was baked into the system itself. It is how financial gain under racial capitalism works.

Historically, white debt has generated white wealth, while Black debt has generated more Black debt, as sociologist Louise Seamster argues. Black debt is also what has guaranteed white wealth. There is a damning throughline from enslaved people being forced to purchase their own freedom to sharecropping to high-interest loans to the racialized geographies of debt that precipitated the application of emergency management in Michigan.[4] If the financial review team found Detroit to be in crisis, it would become the sixth city in Michigan to fall under emergency management. Notably, all these cities, except one, had majority Black populations, and this was in a state where a fraction of the population identified as Black or African American.[5] The racial inequity was deeply troubling.

The issue was larger than poor urban residents bearing the brunt of austerity. It was also a matter of constitutional rights to equal protection. If the governor appointed an emergency manager to Detroit, the city's elected officials would be stripped of their decision-making authority, essentially nullifying the local voting rights of more than half of the African Americans who lived in the state.

Thus, forty-seven years after the Voting Rights Act prohibited racial discrimination in voting, the long and ugly history of white efforts to suppress the Black vote—from murder to poll taxes and gerrymandering—was manifesting in new ways that had nothing to do with the ballot box per se but rather with the power of finance capital to define the terms of debt. Put simply, debt served as a pretense to dismantle the social contract, to facilitate new enclosures, and to gut any vestiges of the welfare state. It also served as a pretense to undermine Black home rule.

Debt is typically understood as a fiscal matter. Yet residents' outrage at the possibility of the city losing political autonomy made it abundantly clear that debt was a historical and racial matter too. It was not lost on them that new strategies of capital accumulation that had emerged under neoliberalism were iterative of earlier forms of racial and colonial subjugation.[6] Put simply, the game had been rigged since the beginning.

Any honorable audit of the city's supposed fiscal crisis, therefore, would need to start by asking, who owed who what? It would seek to account for the inheritance of Detroit's debt. This inheritance, after all, explained why it was mostly Michigan's majority Black cities that were in crisis. Many of them, like Detroit, had been left to shoulder the fiscal burden of deindustrialization and suburbanization. Their reduced tax bases were used to pay not only for city services but also, ironically, for pensions for suburbanites who were no longer residents. When state and federal governments slashed revenue sharing, their debts soared and a vicious cycle ensued.

Reconciling Shared History

Several months before the financial review team meeting at Cadillac Place, on November 5, I attended the inaugural event of the MDTRC. Curious about the commission's work and how they framed reconciliation in a tense political landscape, I joined a crowd of approximately three hundred people, including residents, community activists, nonprofit leaders, and academics, among others, inside a large ballroom of the cavernous Cobo Hall Convention Center in downtown Detroit.

A feeling of hopeful anticipation hung in the air as Naomi Tutu gave a keynote address. Tutu is a human rights activist and daughter of Desmond Tutu, who chaired the South African Truth and Reconciliation Commission following apartheid. "A shared history is needed to claim and accept truths," she said.

Proponents of truth and reconciliation believe that in situations where violence has divided communities, giving voice to past harms can lead to healing by creating a more comprehensive understanding of what transpired, thus liberating victims and, ultimately, enabling communities to advance toward a better future.

The philosopher Jill Stauffer writes, "Proponents of truth commissions argue that, in a setting where many long-standing harms come not (or not only) from discrete criminal action but the effects of violence, poverty, oppression, or silence, the stories collected by truth commissions can build a more comprehensive narrative of harms."[7] Another foundational notion of truth and reconciliation is that if victims are given a voice—"that *does not rely on*—that is set free from—perpetrators and legal institutions"—they can be liberated from the past.[8]

As Tutu spoke, I wondered what it meant exactly to "share" history? To be liberated from the past when the past was not past? *Shared history* felt like a tricky proposition. It presupposes that communities or whole societies might agree on what elements of the past should be remembered as well as those that should be forgotten, not to mention a shared understanding of the importance of remembrance.

Remembrance—or the act of remembering—is about more than revisiting past events. It is also about deciding how the narrative relationship among events is established.[9] "Collective memory is not an inert and passive thing," literary theorist and Palestinian advocate Edward Said has observed, "but a field of activity in which past events are selected, reconstructed, maintained, modified, and endowed with political meaning."[10] As this suggests, individual and collective memory are intimately entangled.

After World War I, French philosopher and sociologist Maurice Halbwachs developed the concept of collective memory in his book by the same name. *La memoire collective* (*On Collective Memory*), which was published after he was deported to and died in the Buchenwald concentration camp, has become a foundational text on how human memory is shaped in relation to collectives.[11] "I have shown that memory is a collective function," Halbwachs argued. "If recollections reappear, this is because at each moment society possesses the necessary means to reproduce them."[12] Truth and reconciliation commissions, in this sense, can be understood as efforts to intervene in the process of memory production.

After Tutu's keynote, a series of speakers talked about their involvement in truth and reconciliation work from developing reparations for the Residential School Program in Canada to investigations of Liberia's tumultuous history of conflict. I sat with other attendees, who clustered at round tables, sipping coffee and nibbling at breakfast.

One of the panelists shared a story about how the state of Maine took her from her home on the Wabanaki reservation when she was a child. They put her into foster homes, where she was raped, beaten, starved, and tortured, but the state neglected to take her out.[13] "Some of us may never achieve a level of peace and a dignity of peace," she concluded over tears. The intimacy of her testimonial—her pain and aspirations—punctured the procedural formality of the event. Her grief drew in the spaciousness of the room, giving people pause as they shuffled to the buffet line.

How do we account for moments like this one that are fleeting yet powerful?

Moments when indictments of the past collapse into hopes for the present and the future.

Moments when words hang in the air, when time expands to hold the brokenness.

Moments in which harm and violence and weariness rest alongside wisdom, perseverance, and desire.[14]

Such moments change the contours of absence.

As I listened to the speakers, I thought about how the politics of memory stand in as shorthand for struggles over whose and which histories prevail.[15] For Halbwachs, the past is a social construction shaped mainly, if not totally, by contemporary concerns. This is to say, present-day interests, beliefs, and aspirations fundamentally shape how the past is viewed.[16] I wondered what it would take for individual recollections gathered by the truth commission to become collective memory, that is, to become powerful—or shared enough—to do the work of repair. At the same time, I wondered how competing visions for the city's future would give rise to competing narrations of its fractured past.

Such moments of grief and grievance—and the reparative demands that emanated from them—were not unique to the inaugural event of the truth and reconciliation commission. They were also regular features of public meetings about fiscal debt. As the speaker's assertions at the start of this chapter suggest, moments like these interrupted conventions by challenging propriety. They gave voice to historical struggles and unrealized alternatives. They made moral claims on those in charge as well as on anyone else who was listening.

At the same time, fidelity to protocols—from the gavel pounding dissent into silence to the two-minute limit for public comments—narrowed engagement with the lived experience and wisdom such moments contained. Still, they played an important role in shaping political discourse. If memory, as Halbwachs argued, has a collective function, then these moments exposed a counter-history of the city's fiscal crisis, one capable of illuminating not only the trappings but also the transformative possibilities of debt.

The Politics of Reparative Accounting

The MDTRC was only the second-ever truth commission established in the United States (the first was in Greensboro, North Carolina). Truth commissions originated in Latin America, where in the seventies and eighties, they were used in the wake of authoritarian regime-led atrocities and "disappearances" of political dissidents. They didn't become popular globally, though, until the establishment of the South African Truth and Reconciliation Commission in 1994, which set off what scholars Barry Schwartz and Horst-Alfred Heinrich have called a "swelling wave of repentance."[17] The world became caught up in a "fever of atonement," observed the Nigerian writer Wole Soyinka.[18]

Repentance and atonement took different forms, including apologies, memorials, and the expansion of truth commissions, particularly in countries undergoing political transitions. By the early 2000s, truth commissions began to be used in places where there was no formal transition of power but rather a rising tide of multicultural politics. For example, in the high-profile cases of Australia and Canada, the TRC process was used to try to ease tense relationships between the colonial state and Indigenous communities. Notably, in the United States, no federally mandated counterpart existed.

The Detroit commission, like the one in Greensboro, was community led. It was not tied to any state or juridical process, but was an independent effort initiated by a nonprofit called Michigan Roundtable for Diversity and Inclusion. The commission began in late 2009 and early 2010 as part of the organization's Race to Equity Project, which included a series of mock trials and workshops that examined the history of institutional racism and federal housing discrimination in the metropolitan region. Project leaders initially chose to focus on housing because it was a major driver of racial wealth disparities. The MDTRC was the second phase of the project. Imagined as a two-year undertaking, it was to be guided by the Housing Project Partnership, which included representatives from local universities, government agencies, banks, and nonprofits. The MDTRC's nine-member volunteer commission was charged with investigating the history of regional racial segregation and preparing a final report with the aim of easing racial antagonisms.[19]

It was a formidable undertaking that entailed, as the commission's charter suggested, addressing not just the racist history of housing but the legacies of settler colonialism and slavery, including Native displacement; how regional enslavers exploited loopholes in the Northwest Ordinance of 1787, which prohibited slavery; how, despite Detroit being an infamous stop on the Underground Railroad, authorities enforced the federal Fugitive Slave Act; and how free African Americans were forced to pay a five-hundred-dollar bond to remain in the Territory of Michigan.[20]

The charter asserted that while the civil rights movement had made advances, structural racism and inequities persisted. Its authors argued that when racial injustice is unaddressed, it "festers, like a dream deferred, creating pain, anger and despair. . . . It can and has undermined the very fabric of our communities." At the same time, they wrote, "It can and has led to righteous action to build a more just and equal society." The 1967 rebellion, they suggested, was a good example of both.[21]

Outmigration from Detroit happened in waves, over decades. But Detroiters often remarked on what felt like the suddenness of panic-stricken white flight after 1967. Properties were abandoned all over town as federal housing policies, combined with a torrent of fear, that drew whites to the suburbs. Classrooms flipped from white to Black seemingly overnight.

The writer Marsha Music recalls in her essay "The Kidnapped Children of Detroit" how as a child, she'd be playing in the street with a group of friends—Black, Brown, white—in her integrated middle-class Highland Park neighborhood, and the next day, her white friends would be gone. According to Music, the trauma of it was so great that a "false narrative" arose that "all the white people left after sixty-seven."[22]

> And so, I say, my friends were kidnapped, snatched away from their homes, often under cover of night or in rushed moves that split friends apart for a lifetime. I watched Mary Martin fly as Peter Pan on TV, and it seemed my friends too had been lured to a Neverland. Did they cry when they were taken, missing their old friends? Did they think of what they'd left behind when they woke in homes with no deep porches or rich oaken banisters? On streets with no lush, ancient trees? Where it took a car—or two—to get anywhere, with lawns so new that grass had yet to grow?[23]

Music's remembrance gives texture to the lived experience of Detroit becoming "one of the most racially segregated and fractured Metropolitan Areas in the Country," as the commission's charter statement claimed.

The fault line between Detroit and its suburbs was, for me, first indexed by differential state maintenance as I drove into the city. On one side, the pavement was pockmarked, on the other side, smooth. On one side, the grass in public spaces was uncut and wild, on the other side, neatly manicured. This uneven landscape suggested a border, if one did not immediately grasp "the fatal couplings of power and difference," to invoke an oft-quoted phrase from Ruth Wilson Gilmore, that gave rise to it and the differential life chances on either side of it.[24]

At the MDTRC inaugural event, after the plenary on truth commissions, local scholars and researchers shared statistics and maps about outmigration and inequality in the metro area. In 2011, over half of working-age residents in Detroit could not find jobs. The child poverty rate in the city stood at 60 percent. Wayne County, which was made up mostly of Detroit, had the lowest life expectancy rate in the state. Meanwhile, the median household income in the surrounding suburbs was double that in Detroit. The income gap grew even larger when Detroit was compared to its third- and fourth-ring suburbs, underscoring the fact that the city's myriad crises were largely due to racism and regional isolation.[25]

The metropolitan area is a case study in how under racial capitalism, as Seamstress reminds us, white wealth—particularly when it is homogenized—compounds to create more white wealth and how Black debt too—particularly when it is homogenized—compounds to create more Black debt. This is how racism functions. It pushes disproportionate costs of participating in the capitalist system, as Gilmore argues, onto those most distant from levers of power.[26] The retrenchment of redistributive forces worked the same way. Fiscal cuts at the federal level had dramatic impacts on local governments, which, having few places to turn for new revenue streams, ended up punishing those places and people most in need of support.

Detroit is a "city of loss," said Gloria House in another keynote at the inaugural event. A longtime civil rights activist and literature professor at University of Michigan–Dearborn, House talked of the loss of population, the loss of the city's tax base, the loss of city services, public education, homes, grocery stores, parks, medical services, jobs, and lives. These losses—and those that loomed on the horizon—were an indictment, in her words, of the "corporate racist lawlessness" that sustained centuries-old practices of dispossession. Thus, appeals to the law alone, House argued, would not "hold back the assault against our humanity." Rather, the work, as she put it, was in the "imagining and building of new forms of community that our children and grandchildren will continue to develop. That is our calling in this time and this place: resistance to oppressive forces on the one hand; conceiving and building of a new society on the other."[27]

Local austerity measures were only the most recent round in the long-standing conservative project to gut the welfare state, which, as Chakravartty and Ferreira da Silva argue, should be understood as a project of gutting the "mechanisms of redress."[28] Detroit, in this sense, signaled how a rising tide of revanchism nationally was articulating in locally specific ways.[29]

In interviews, residents frequently pointed out that the state's threat of emergency management was a continuation of unresolved racial antagonisms between Blacks and whites and that there were "interests" who wanted the city back. "I feel like the auto industry got bailed out, the banks got bailed out, Wall Street . . . multimillionaire derivative traders got bailed out," said one local activist. "You can bail out a municipal authority. . . . I think it comes from a profound sense of—really hatred. I think people in this state hate Detroit. It is beyond even racism. . . . There is this emotional tone of hate that's exhibited in the legislature. Even reading the comments of the news. . . . It's painful. It is painful how Detroit is derided and abused."

These sentiments carried over into public meetings like the review board, with which I opened this chapter. As the women delivered her public comments, the ten-member team, headed by Michigan treasurer Andy Dillon and other state political and business elite, sat poised, poker-faced at the front of the room.

"We're not gonna lose Detroit. We're not going to give in," she said forcefully. "We're not gonna let you come in and take Detroit. And some of you think this is a joke about money. We're talking about people's lives. We been giving, giving, giving in Detroit. We ain't got nothing more to give. But we ain't gonna let you come in and take the little bit that we have left away from us because somebody wants Detroit."

Her denunciation of the board was not a call for more racial democracy or racial representation. The review board, after all, was majority Black, as was the city government. Rather, it was an invitation to anyone listening to continue the struggle for radical social democracy; a reminder that the only reason Detroit had become a beacon of union power and Black power was because people had fought and died making it so.

The blame, thus, fell not only at the feet of Michigan's conservative base but also at the feet of Detroit's Black political class. In an op-ed Detroit activist and writer Yusef Shakur underscored this betrayal and the hypocrisy of the truth and reconciliation process amid the state takeover. "In order for a Truth and Reconciliation process to grow within Metro Detroit," Shakur wrote, "we need to take a deeper look at the historical patterns of racism that are perpetuated today. We have witnessed a tragedy of Black politicians openly betraying the people they were elected to serve by going out for self and selling Detroit out to the highest white bidders."[30]

If great hope surrounded the formation of the MDTRC, the process, as Shakur suggested, was also rife with skepticism. Many grassroots activists participated in the inaugural event. But others suggested to me in casual conversation that the commission's emphasis on *studying* the causes and legacies of segregation didn't go far enough. A few expressed concerns that the commission's mandate was too broad and unworkable. Still others cautioned that the commission would try to move too quickly toward unity, without addressing how historical racialized violence was connected to new modes of governance and urban investment that were leading to widespread dispossession and hardship for residents.[31]

The ambivalence that surrounded the truth and reconciliation commission was not unique to Detroit. It reflected concerns expressed globally about the outsized promises of truth and reconciliation and how reconciliation, unwittingly, can become another manifestation of colonial violence.[32] Adam Sitze, a scholar of law, jurisprudence, and social thought, writing about the South African TRC, refers to it as an "impossible machine" because it did not produce reconciliation; it overpromised itself. The flaw, he argues, was that the crime of apartheid was not the subject of the commission, which focused on what was already legally characterized as abuse, thus leading to a focus on individuals and perpetrators at the expense of institutions and structures of governance.[33]

The entangled temporalities of the truth commission and the financial review team recall scholar Mahmood Mamdani's warning of the dangers of individualizing reconciliation and attempting it without redistributive justice and redress.[34] Indeed, reconciliation and redress have distinct meanings with different assumptions about accountability and responsibility. To *reconcile* means "to restore to friendship or harmony"; "settle, resolve." By contrast, *redress*, as a noun, means a "remedy or compensation for a wrong or grievance." As a verb it means "to set right: remedy," "to make up for: compensate"; "to remove the cause of (a grievance or complaint)"; "to exact reparation for: avenge."[35] Reparation, as a subset of redress, suggests that one can amend wrongdoing through financial compensation or helping one's victims.

In short, reconciliation seeks to resolve harm without necessarily taking material actions, whereas redress (and by extension reparation) is about identifying accountable parties or structures and instituting mechanisms of responsibility and change. In this sense, state redress would imply that the state would facilitate or be held accountable and compensate for wrongs and losses. In Detroit, this was far from reality. As mentioned earlier, the Detroit commission was not sanctioned by any state bodies, nor was it linked to any promises of state redress. If, as geographer Joshua Inwood writes, "state authority is unprepared and unwilling to engage in serious reflection that is necessary to understand the reproduction of uneven life chances," then how can the historical and ongoing assault on the humanity of Black people, Brown people, and poor people be held back?[36]

Almost Lost Detroit

In Gil Scott-Heron's famous song "We Almost Lost Detroit" (the name of a book by John G. Fuller), he was reflecting on the 1966 partial meltdown of Enrico Fermi Nuclear Generating Station, located on the shore of Lake Erie, but its broader message was that

> when it comes to people's safety
> Money wins out every time.
> And we almost lost Detroit.
> This time, this time.
> How would we ever get over
> Over losing our minds?
> You see, we almost lost Detroit
> That time.
> Almost lost Detroit
> That time.
> And how would we ever get over . . .
> 'Cause odds are,
> We gonna lose somewhere, one time.
> Odds are
> We gonna lose somewhere sometime.[37]

The speaker's invocation of the song captured the trauma and mania that come with loss. But it was also a demand. A demand to maintain Detroit's Black home rule. A demand to live out the dream of freedom that made Detroit Detroit.[38]

As one resident named Jo Ann said in an interview, the city was invested with Detroiters' blood, sweat, and tears. "We are entitled to this," as she put it. "We have paid a lot of dues here. We've lived through incredible, incredible humiliation and degradation." For public workers and retirees, their financial futures were also indelibly tied to those of the city.

"We not gonna lose Detroit," the speaker said to the members of the review board who seemed to be trying hard to keep their composure amid the audience's chorus of um-hums. "We can sit around this table, but we not gonna go away."

"That's the slogan, 'no justice, no peace.' You're not going to have peace. We'll be outside your door. You'll be laying in your bed. We'll be marching outside your door." A member of the review team rose and indicated that her two minutes were up. The audience muttered in disdain.

"They trying to tell her she's out of time," said the woman next to me, shaking her head, disapprovingly.

The speaker was undeterred. "You think you can make rules up," she concluded. "Well, we gonna make rules up."

The crowd followed her lead, rising from their seats to chant, "No justice, no peace. No justice, no peace. No justice, no peace."

After several spoken rounds, they erupted in song, drowning out the meeting proceedings with a soulful and lilting rendition of the gospel hymn turned civil rights anthem "We Shall Overcome."

Unfinished struggles for liberation overdetermined the structure of feeling in public meetings about the state takeover. There was nothing particularly unique about this one. Like others, its rhythm was syncopated. Team members moved haltingly from agenda item to agenda item as they sought to conduct business as usual amid a rising tide of discontent. Their determined attempts to call the room to order grew increasingly halfhearted, as did their assurances that they had a plan that could put the city back together. It seemed as though they were trying to convince themselves as much as the crowd. Calls of protest and outrage deafened their ability to discuss what kind of recommendation to make to the governor.

A few weeks after the financial review team meeting, on April 4, 2012, the city council held a meeting on the thirteenth floor of the Coleman A. Young municipal building in downtown Detroit. The nine-member all-Black city council had assembled to vote on a financial stability agreement, better known as the consent agreement, which had been approved by the financial review team earlier in the day. Having been hammered out through a series of contentious meetings the previous fall and winter, the agreement was an attempt to avoid a state-imposed emergency manager. If approved, the agreement would create a nine-member financial advisory board that would be charged with monitoring and evaluating the city's debts, expenditures, and payments in a wide variety of areas from the constitution of individual city departments to contracts and deals with creditors and bondholders. The advisory board would be made up of a medley of partisan appointees, including three individuals appointed by the governor, one by the state treasurer, two by the mayor, and two by the city council. A ninth member (likely to be a tiebreaker in any deadlock) was to be appointed jointly by the governor and mayor and subject to confirmation by the city council. Under the agreement, the mayor and city council would still hold formal powers, but state oversight was widely viewed by many residents and elected officials as an unwelcome concession that the city of Detroit was being forced to make.

The meeting room brimmed with protestors, reporters, and security guards. That it was the forty-fourth anniversary of the assassination of Martin Luther King Jr. made it an especially poignant day. Someone passed me a paper sign with "NO" stenciled in black. After the room reached capacity, the security guards ushered attendees to a separate spillover "listening" room. The city council had refused to hold the meeting in a larger room to accommodate the scores of concerned residents eager to have their voices heard, from African American church leaders to union representatives, seasoned organizers active during the civil rights and Black power era, and a younger generation of community activists who worked on a range of issues from foreclosures to water shutoffs. After quieting the room, the city council president, Charles Pugh, invited public comment, stressing that speakers were limited to two minutes each.

They went one by one. Some speakers seemed like they were waging a war against forgetting the past as much as demonstrating against policies in the present. Others emphasized the threat the takeover posed to Black self-determination. Older activists invoked the names of local Black freedom fighters who faced impossible odds and considerable violence in their struggle for liberation. Every two minutes, the gavel pounded, interrupting individual testimonies, but they'd already been entered into a river of affirmations of collective heartache, frustration, and defiance. I couldn't help but think of their testimonials like truth and reconciliation in real time, but they refused reconciliation—economic and otherwise.

Speakers compared emergency management to slavery. They shamed city council members, arguing that the Black political class had forgotten where they came from.[39] A historian named Paul Lee used his two minutes to remind them. He came bearing a 1966 photo of Stokely Carmichael, who was then chair of the Student Nonviolent Coordinating Committee. The photo showed Carmichael delivering an address at a campaign rally in support of two Black candidates running for Detroit city council. At the time, only two members of the council were Black, despite the city having a nearly 50 percent African American population. Lee argued that whereas much of the civil rights movement had focused on voting registration drives in the South, Carmichael recognized a need for Black power in Northern urban centers like Detroit. Both candidates lost in the election; however, Lee's point was about how in the wake of 1967, a broad coalition from Black nationalists to Black moderates came together to wrest political control from the "white power structure," creating the conditions of possibility for those on the city council to hold their positions today.

Another speaker shared Lee's sentiments: "It is obvious that we have completely forgotten our history. My heart really is aching. I think just about everybody in the room can feel what's about to happen. . . . It is a disgrace, and it is an outrage. In signing this, you are forever changing the city of Detroit. I pray that God will forgive you all. It's certainly going to be hard for the people to forgive you." On occasion, demonstrators threatened to burn the city down again, referencing 1967. Others argued that the state's violence should be met "by any means necessary," echoing Malcolm X's famous phrase. But instead of calling for residents to arm themselves to defend their communities, they urged them to "hit the streets" to fight for their jobs, pensions, homes, and schools.

Housing rights activists condemned fraudulent bank practices and racist, predatory mortgages that resulted in foreclosures. An attorney, who was a tireless housing advocate, became increasingly worked up as he spoke, bellowing with his fist pumping in the air that the ratings from the subprime mortgage crisis had devastated the city. Others critiqued tax breaks and state property giveaways to developers. "Land and water mean wealth and power for the people," one person said.

Allies joined them from nearby cities. "It's not going to be easy for you," said a middle-aged white woman from Pontiac, which had been under emergency management since 2009.[40] She spoke haltingly through tears: "People are going to have to be cut, cut, cut. No one person should have this much power. . . . You're going to have to issue bonds, loans . . . that's going to make you deeper. We need to stand tough. . . . You are going to have depression, oppression; you are going to have jobs taken away."

After an hour of public comment, during which speakers unilaterally opposed the consent agreement, the council approved it by a five-to-four vote. The vote—an outright rebuke to the will of the people—gave the state of Michigan sweeping power over the city's budget and finances.

The approval of the consent agreement that day was the prelude to a massive structural adjustment of Detroit's government that would transform the city. The austerity measures that followed intermingled with plans underway to rightsize and transform Detroit into a new lean, green city. And, on March 14, 2013, less than a year after its approval, Detroit entered emergency management at the behest of Governor Rick Snyder, who appointed an African American bankruptcy lawyer, Kevyn Orr, to the post.[41] Less than four months later, Orr recommended that the city file for bankruptcy. Governor

Snyder approved Orr's recommendation on July 18, 2013, making Detroit the largest US city to ever declare bankruptcy. The city's debt—an estimated $18 to $20 billion—was, in short, unpayable.[42] It was reconciled via a massive transfer of city land and assets to creditors.

Meanwhile, the truth and reconciliation commission's efforts to reconcile the region's moral debts floundered. During the first year, three commissioners resigned from their positions. By the end of the third year, only one African American remained on the commission. Three years out, the MDTRC had largely disintegrated. In 2018, a Facebook page remained, but nobody had posted on it since 2013. The Michigan Roundtable kept a page on its website for the commission, but the link was broken.

Failed reconciliation projects reveal the challenge of repair, perhaps even more so than those declared apparent successes. The tensions and ambivalences regarding the truth and reconciliation commission underscore how, in some situations, resentment and resistance might actually be more restorative than forgiveness. Forgiveness, as geographer LaToya Eaves has argued, risks "being used as a pacifier rather than for addressing the larger structural problems of white supremacy, racism, and (cis-hetero) patriarchy." Similarly, Stauffer argues that forgiveness might not be a goal worth reaching. She quotes Indigenous studies scholar Glen Coulthard (Yellowknives Déné), who argues, "Under certain conditions, a disciplined maintenance of resentment in the wake of historical injustice can signify 'the reflex expression of a moral protest' that is as 'permissible and admirable as the posture of forgiveness.'"[43] Resentment, in this sense, is not an inability to get over the past. Nor is it an end unto itself. Resentment as moral protest illuminates structures of oppression that cause harm and suggests that breaking from them requires more than reconciliation.

*

I came to think about the residents' two minutes of public commentary as a process of truth telling sans reconciliation. Put differently, it was a practice of reparative witnessing that was as much about resistance as it was giving voice to the radical imagination and the possibility of another world. Paula Ioanide, a scholar of comparative race and ethnicity studies, argues that "legacies of ethical witnessing" bequeath to us different epistemologies and ontologies that align with justice—different ways of being, thinking, and knowing that foreground collective responsibility and that are visionary and generative.[44]

The speakers persuasively engaged in such ethical witnessing by inverting the political meaning of the city's indebtedness. Rather than the city being indebted to the banks or the state, they argued instead that the suburbs had a debt to the city and that Black city officials had a historical obligation to their ancestors to carry on the liberation struggle. This inversion exposed, first, how the city's fiscal crisis and its unpayable debt—as conceived of by the state—was rooted in a longer history of racial capitalism and looting. It exposed, second, the inadequacy of how care and moral obligation function within liberal democracy. And finally, it exposed dreams passed from one generation to the next that went beyond "limited emancipation," to use Saidiya Hartman's phrase.[45] This inheritance had a debt, but it could never be repaid, only honored by carrying forth the liberation struggle.

The cacophony of public testimonials, the harmonizing, the reminders of the aspirations of freedom were the legacy of these dreams. They resounded loudest when the room was the quietest.

When the gavel pounded repeatedly, eventually yielding a lull but not consent.

When the elderly Black woman rose and devoted her two minutes to a mostly silent prayer. Eyes closed, body swaying.

"Do not let them take away our home rule, our dignity," she implored. "Let us stand on our own ground."

conjuring terra nullius 6

The predominantly white crowd advanced down Woodward Avenue, Detroit's main throughfare, singing and dancing in pursuit of the *nain rouge*—an impish red figure with a sharp-toothed grin—that they sought to banish from the city. Many of the revelers donned colonial garb.

It was March 10, 2011, and the second occurrence of what would become the annual Marche du Nain Rouge (March of the Red Dwarf). The parade began with a rousing battle cry outside the newly revamped Third Street Bar. Led by a marching band, the crowd wound through Cass Corridor. Once the epicenter of counterculture and radical politics in Detroit, the neighborhood had recently been rebranded as Midtown, a sign of how private redevelopment and philanthropic investment dollars were flowing into select areas. The procession ended in a very different part of town, Cass Park, a meeting place for the city's homeless population. There, revelers set about destroying effigies of the *nain rouge*, while cheering for a new Detroit.[1]

From its outset, the event generated tension between the participants, mostly new arrivals and suburbanites, and longtime residents and activists, who called it a "march of gentrification." The professed aim of the march was to foster creative placemaking and urban regeneration. Its founder described it as simply "a sort of Mardi Gras tradition, a chance for catharsis after a long

Figure 6.1 (opposite) | The Red Dwarf speaks at the Marche du Nain Rouge, 2015. *Sources:* Courtesy of Marche du Nain Rouge and *Detroit Metro Times*, Lee DeVito, "The Legend of the Legend of Detroit's Nain Rouge," *Detroit Metro Times*, March 16, 2016.

winter," a way to mark "new beginnings" and "celebrate whatever is good and working in the city."[2] Critics pointed out that such good intentions were complicated by the racial and classed dimensions of the procession itself, which culminated in the banishment of one of the few people of color at the event—the red dwarf. The myth upon which the festival turned also raised questions about the meaning of "new beginnings." New for whom? And for what?

The Marche du Nain Rouge revived a colonial-era frontier myth in which the red dwarf is a harbinger of doom. The abbreviated version goes something like this: On March 10, 1701, a party was held in St. Louis, Quebec, in honor of the French explorer Antoine de la Moth Cadillac, who'd just returned from France, where he'd traveled to convince Count Pontchartrain, Louis XIV's chief minister, to invest in the development of a fort and settlement on "le Détroit." At the gathering, a fortune teller, gazing at Cadillac's palm, predicts he will establish a great city with more inhabitants than New France. The fortune teller's good news, however, is tempered by predictions of battles and bloodshed with the "treacherous" Indians and the "hated English" over possession of the city. When Cadillac asks if the city and his new fortune would be passed to his children, the fortune teller responds that his future and theirs lay in his hands. She instructs him to "beware of undue ambition" and to make sure he "appeases the Nain Rouge." Laughing off the warning, the next day, Cadillac sets off on his expedition.[3]

A few months later, he founds Fort Pontchartrain du Détroit, on the banks of the river. French soldiers build a new fort with a storehouse, barracks, and houses. Time passes. The settlement grows with more soldiers, farmers, merchants, and eventually families. Native bands settle on the outskirts, far outnumbering the French. Then, on March 10, 1707, exactly six years after Cadillac's meeting with the fortune teller, he issues the first land grant of Fort Pontchartrain du Détroit to his interpreter. To mark the transfer of feudal rights, the villagers hold a ceremony.[4]

After the party, Cadillac takes an evening walk with his wife. Strolling in the King's Garden, he comes upon the prophesied dwarf: a red-faced "uncouth figure" with a "bright, glistening eye" and "sharp, pointed teeth." Rather than heeding the fortune teller's warning to appease the dwarf, he strikes him with a stick. "Get out of my way, you red imp!" he yells. Cadillac's luck immediately takes a turn for the worse. He is arrested in Montreal, forced to give up his seignory in Detroit, and transferred to the French colony in Louisiana as governor; he dies in France leaving no inheritance to his children.[5]

The legend doesn't end there. According to folklore, French, British, and US settlers continue to spot the red dwarf in Detroit, particularly when threats loom: in 1763, before the Battle of Bloody Run; in 1805, before a fire burned most of the city to the ground; during the War of 1812, before American general William Hill surrendered Detroit to the British army; and, then, after a long lapse, before the uprisings of 1967.

I didn't expect to write about eighteenth-century myths or early colonial history when I arrived in Detroit. I'm neither a folklorist nor a historian. But I kept returning to the legend of the *nain rouge*—and the history from which it emerged—because I sensed that it might reveal something important about the cultural and philosophical work entailed in the appropriation and reappropriation of space. "Just as none of us is outside or beyond geography," Edward Said wrote, "none of us is free from the struggle over geography. That struggle is complex and interesting because it is not only about soldiers and cannons but also about ideas, about forms, about images and imaginings."[6]

When I first heard about the Marche du Nain Rouge, I thought about historian Patricia Seed's argument that "ceremonies of possession" played a key role in the conquest of the New World. Colonialism was advanced through militarism and physical occupation, but Seed makes the point that ceremonies, discourses, and cultural practices were also critical to establishing authority and ownership. For example, the Spanish made grave declarations of intent to claim land and remain, and, importantly, they recorded their solemn utterances; the English planted gardens; and the French staged processions.[7]

The parade struck me as some sort of odd ceremony of *re*possession. Recall that by the 2010s, national and international fascination with Detroit had yielded a dizzying array of books and documentaries, thousands of articles, a tourism industry, and journalistic exposés. *Time* magazine bought an old house for its journalists to live in for a year; CNN Money established a downtown office to showcase hopeful profiles and investment opportunities. Television shows toured the city's majestic ruins and abandoned landscapes. The intensity and symbolic violence of these forms of cultural production are hard to overemphasize.

The revival of the legend of the *nain rouge* brought the historical continuum of colonial appropriation into stark relief. As such, it opens a window onto how the cultural production of a new Detroit happened through the reenactment of colonial myths as well as through forms of erasure and distancing in the photographic, journalistic, and cartographic realms.[8]

Settler Anxieties and Ceremonies of Repossession

Myths play a fundamental role in the cultural production and reproduction of societies and nation-states. They carry values, customs, worldviews, and ideologies. They arouse memories and fantasies. They contain conflicts, questions, and anxieties from the original mythmaker. But they also change over time, some parts kept, some reworked.[9]

The myth of the *nain rouge* was first transmitted orally. It did not appear in written form until local folklorist Marie Caroline Watson Hamlin documented it in her 1883 *Legends of Le Détroit*, described as a book of "weird tales, quaint customs, and beautiful traditions" passed down by French settlers.[10] The book's cover is adorned with a gold embossment of a soldier planting the French flag and cross into a patch of earth. It includes more than thirty folk stories along with genealogies and narratives of the "early French families," of which Hamlin was a descendant. The book suggests how French culture before and during Hamlin's life (1850–85) navigated and mythologized the brutal violence and dispossession on which their settlement was predicated.[11]

The first legend, "The Cross and the Manitou," recounts the seventeenth-century travels of two Breton Sulpician priests—François Dollier de Casson, an ex-soldier, and René de Brehant de Galinée, an amateur surveyor—who were on a mission to convert Indian tribes who lived along the fur trade routes of the Great Lakes. The priests' travelogue—published as *Journey of Dollier and Galinée (1669–1670)*—is the earliest European written account of Detroit, and it thus provides a contrast to its interpretation two centuries later. At the time, the region was sparsely populated by Europeans. The French Crown had just sent an influx of settlers to New France and instructions to explorers and missionaries, like Dollier and Galinée, to secure trade routes around the Great Lakes by establishing outposts and making alliances with Indigenous tribes, who had long inhabited the fluvial hinterlands.

By the time Dollier and Galinée laid eyes on the region surrounding the narrow strait between the two Great Lakes, they'd had a long and trying journey. A storm struck as they camped on the banks of Lake Erie, washing away their baggage—including guns, ammunition, and other provisions—and their altar service, which they took as an act of the devil. The portable consecrated stone altar service likely included a complex assortment of vessels and vestments required for Mass, and its destruction would have been a considerable loss, not only for them personally but also for their mission to the Ottawa, Potawatomi, and western tribes.[12] After some debate, they decided to return to Montreal for a replacement. They plotted a passage from the end of Lake

Erie to the "Fresh Water Sea of the Huron," which would then lead them to the Georgian Bay–Ottawa River route to Montreal.[13] First, though, they had to pass through le détroit, the narrow strait that the Algonquian called Yondotiga (The Great Village) and Waweatunong (The Crooked Way); the Huron, Karotaen (Coast of the Straits); and the Iroquois, Toghsaghrondie, or the more modern pronunciation Teuschsa Grondie (Place of Many Beavers).[14] Here, they docked.

They wrote in their travelogue that it was a "remarkable" place, "held in great veneration by all the Indians of these countries, because of a stone idol that nature has formed."[15] Their description of what happened next underscores the extreme physical and cultural violence through which European aspirations for salvation and territory turned. Surmising that the Indians worshipped the stone carving as a manitou, the priests, along with their crew, avenged the loss of their chapel and their dearth of provisions by pounding it with an ax and breaking it into pieces, which they flung into the river. "There was not a man of us who was not filled with hatred against this false deity," Galinée wrote. Later that day, the crew killed a bear and a deer, which the priests interpreted as a reward from God for their good actions.[16]

In Hamlin's retelling of the incident, she writes that after they destroyed the idol, they planted a cross affixed with the coat of arms of France and a placard with an inscription that claimed the "unoccupied" region as New France (the image is replicated on her volume's cover).[17] By the time of the priests' journey, ideas of Manifest Destiny would have been codified into the doctrine of discovery, which held that European nations were entitled to lands that were deemed terra nullius, a logic that laid the theological and legal framework for colonizing much of the world.[18]

The term terra nullius has a range of meanings, including empty, uninhabited, unoccupied, deserted, idle, and wasted land. Its most literal translation is "land belonging to no one" (terra meaning "earth," and nullius deriving from nullus, "no one").[19] But as Dollier and Galinée's travelogue suggests, terra nullius was a legal fiction and ex post facto justification. The European political theorists who developed the legal justification for terra nullius, as well as the explorers and colonists who voyaged to new lands, knew they were inhabited.[20] Given the recognition of occupancy, Europeans could not technically claim to have discovered the region, though doctrine would have allowed them to claim discovery and stake territorial rights if they asserted that the land was empty, underutilized, or misused. According to doctrine, land occupied by those deemed to be pagan idolators and Enemies of Christ—including the Indigenous peoples whom Dollier and Galinée sought to convert—could be legitimately expropriated for the purposes of spreading Christianity.[21]

When Cadillac arrived at the same site in 1701, it was some thirty years after Dollier and Galinée. He had recently convinced Count Pontchartrain, Louis XIV's chief minister, that development of a fort and settlement in the region would help France gain the upper hand in the fur trade because it would extend their control of trade routes and their ability to establish economic and political alliances with Indigenous people.[22] For years after its establishment, as historian Tiya Miles argues, Fort Pontchartrain du Détroit was a geographical and cultural borderland, isolated from other colonial settlements and thus a fragile enterprise. Odawa, Ojibwe, Potawatomi, and Wyandot lived side by side along the banks of the Detroit River and adjacent to the fort residents. Efforts to maintain peace between Native tribes and colonists took constant diplomatic negotiations and alliance building, which was greased by the exchange of gifts and supplies, intermarriage, and treaties.[23]

In the hundred years between the establishment of Fort Pontchartrain and Hamlin's publication of *Legend of Le Détroit*, competing territorial claims among the French, British, Indigenous nations, and aspiring US republic resulted in numerous treaties. The treaties established a new geopolitical and legal sense of space. They also led to confusion because of different conceptualizations of law, jurisdiction, and tenure, not to mention different epistemologies and ontologies of land.

By the turn of the nineteenth century, Native sovereignty had been greatly reduced, but Indigenous people still controlled significant amounts of territory, which stretched for hundreds of miles between Euro-American settlements.[24] The lives of early French families documented by Hamlin would have been foundationally shaped by state efforts to expand colonial settlement and neutralize threats to it. Hamlin's volume of legends, in general, and the story of the *nain rouge*, in particular, underscore how colonial security was haunted by the conditions of its own violent production. The *nain*, a seeming composite of shapeshifting creatures in both French and Indigenous traditions, exemplifies these dynamics. In the folklore of Normandy, the *lutin* is a type of hobgoblin, gnome, or sprite. A similar spirit trickster called the Nanabozho, or Nanabush, figures prominently in Anishinaabe traditional storytelling myths, particularly among the Ojibwe.[25] Given the perpetual sense of threat, it is likely not incidental that the dwarf, understood to be a menace, is red, as colonists referred to Indigenous people as the "red man" or "red-skinned."[26]

Legends like the *nain rouge* suggest how colonists obfuscated and sought to rationalize the reign of terror and dehumanization of life that enabled their settlement. Historians have filled volumes detailing the horrors of American expansionism, its inseparability from anti-Indigenous and anti-Black racism, and its reliance on the dis/possession and monetization of land and people.[27] The logics and abstractions that justified genocide, slavery, and the seizure of Native land gave rise to complex legal and juridical structures that redistributed land to white settlers, white farmers, railroad companies, and other capitalist enterprises. Such legislated dispossession is the foundation of the American republic. In the region that became Michigan, it looked like the 1795 Treaty of Greenville, which vastly reduced Indigenous land holdings in the Northwest region. It looked like the 1807 Treaty of Detroit, which marked the boundaries of an area of land to which sachems, chiefs, and warriors of the Ottawa, Chippewa, Wyandotte, and Potawatomi Nations agreed "to cede and forever quit claim," and like the 1842 La Point Treaty, which left Indigenous peoples in Michigan with only thirty-two square miles of reservation land, less than 1 percent of the state's landed area.[28] A decade later, it looked like the 1851 Indian Appropriation Act, which established the reservation system, followed by the Homestead Act of 1862, which incentivized westward expansion, and the Pacific Railway Act of that same year, which granted vast tracts of land for the construction of the transcontinental railroad.

All this bears repeating—and more—because it is what has secured white supremacy and capitalist accumulation over generations. And it bears repeating here and now because it is the period in which Hamlin is writing. Hamlin was born in 1850, a year before Congress passed the Indian Appropriation Act, and died, at the age of thirty-five, two years before the enactment of the Dawes Severalty Act, which made tribal lands alienable as private property. Five years after her death, in 1890, newspapers in Detroit, a bustling industrial powerhouse with more than 200,000 residents, reported on the massacre at Wounded Knee in which US soldiers killed over one hundred Lakota to stop the Ghost Dance. If Wounded Knee underscores how American expansion rested not only on legislated expropriation and redistribution but also on genocide in the name of calming settler anxieties, Hamlin's text reminds us of the myths that followed.

According to the founder of the Marche du Nain Rouge, the festival was supposed to mark new beginnings. Indeed, in Cadillac's time, settler celebrations of feudal land transfers also marked new beginnings, though for others, they marked the end of worlds. From the seventeenth through the nineteenth centuries, when the Anishinaabe leaders of the Great Lakes were asked by colonial officials to sign treaties and land sale agreements, they did so with pictographs representing their *nindoodem* (clan) identity. The pictographs depicted the region's flora and fauna, such as eagles, cranes, and herons; woodland caribou; bears, otters, and beavers; turtles and snakes; and fish, including poke, sturgeon, whitefish, and channel catfish. They also included flora—birch, oak, and white pine—and merman images.[29]

Members of the same *nindoodem* regarded one another as siblings, even when they'd never met and came from different communities, thus preserving kin networks and lateral alliances that were at the center of the Anishinaabe's worldview, knowledge system, and political geography. Delegatory pictographs functioned like seals on treaties. Whereas the seals of colonial governments impressed in wax the Crown's coat of arms, signaling heraldic kin connections, *nindoodem* pictographs represented kindred connections to other humans as well as to flora and fauna, suggesting a more expansive relationship to land than property and territory.[30]

Many of the pictographs on the treaties depicted animals expressing danger.

Eagles with wings swept back, poised to catch prey.

Cranes in an attack posture known as the "ruffle charge."

Caribou in what biologists call an "excitation leap."

These images give new meaning to "predatory value"—a term that Jodi Byrd, Alyosha Goldstein, Jodi Melamed, and Chandan Reddy use to capture how capitalism, colonialism, and liberal property relationships come into being through forms of racialized dispossession, subjection, appropriation, and the formation of whiteness as an identity.[31]

Indeed, in Hamlin's lifetime, the question of how to establish a collective sense of citizenship and belonging among new European immigrants remained a vexing political problem. Locally, legends like the *nain rouge* would have served to promote traditional French culture and its place in the emergence of new national lore. Twelve years after the publication of Hamlin's book, the legend of the *nain rouge* reappears in the folklorist Charles Skinner's *Myths and Legends of Our Own Land* (1896). Skinner, a member of the recently established American Folklore Society, sought to combine Indigenous folklore and diverse settler legends into a new national lore, or "American folklore."[32] It was a mission enthusiastically supported by President Theodore Roosevelt (1901–9), who saw folklore as providing a potential common ground, national symbolism, and a founding mythology for the rapidly expanding republic.[33] These political motivations and this context may help explain why the figure of the *nain*, derived from Indigenous *and* European myth, was incorporated into European-white folklore.

After a spate of nineteenth-century sightings (the last being 1812), the *nain rouge* was reportedly not spotted again until 1967. This period of nonappearance aligns with an era of vast seizures of Native land, and thus, perhaps, a sense of diminished threat among colonists. It also coincides with the rise of another myth, that of the vanishing Indian, and the absenting of Indigenous presence in regional folklore and urban histories.[34] Indeed, by the twentieth century, Detroit's history becomes largely narrated in terms of Black-white relations, despite persistent Indigenous presence.[35]

It is perhaps unsurprising, then, that when the *nain rouge* makes an alleged reappearance before the 1967 rebellion, it seems to indicate a Black (rather than red) threat. This shift is illustrated by a bizarre informational video produced in 1968 called "Know Your Nain." The video—which features an entirely white cast—reframes the *nain rouge* from a harbinger of doom to an aid in identifying threats to the city. Depicted as a red cartoonish imp, the 1960s *nain* is used to model right behavior. It instructs viewers to pick up litter, keep their homes up to date and beautiful, and, finally, watch out for their fellow citizens by identifying threats. The last scene features a group of urban administrators and planners gesturing to a large map on the wall and pointing to shaded areas, presumably those where threats lurk. Though the sequence argues for embracing the *nain*, the red dwarf is still a palimpsest of the structuring logics of racialized banishment and ontological negation at the heart of settler colonial urbanism. In the late 1960s, these structuring logics were reflected in the deepening regional divisions between the city and the suburbs and the physic space of threat that prevailed between them.

The revitalization of the legend of the *nain rouge* in the 2010s reflects another geographical shift. It suggests how urban redevelopment and recapitalization required assuaging deep-seated anxieties and fostering a sense of white belonging in a new generation of suburban Detroiters returning to the city. The Marche du Nain Rouge can thus be understood as one small part of efforts to normalize white repossession—to mark "new beginnings." Meanwhile, other efforts lay in shifting popular imaginaries of the city—which since 1967 had been rooted in fear and paranoia—toward a sense of fascination with decline.

Race, Nature, and the Politics of Erasure

Detroit has had many monikers. D-Town. Paris of the West. Motor City. Motown. Arsenal of Democracy. The Most American of American Cities. Each of these nicknames represents different cultural constructions of space and forms of nostalgia.

After 1967, dystopian nicknames, like Murder City and America's First Third-World City, often crowded out more laudatory ones. Public commentators began to portray Detroit as a war-torn landscape. The August after the rebellion, the cover of *Life* magazine featured an orange sky aglow from a burning building, silhouetted by soldiers in combat uniform, rifles erect. The headline read "Negro Revolt: The Flames Spread."

Popular news articles, steeped in anti-Blackness, suggested that the city's central business district was engaged in an ongoing battle with physical and moral decrepitude.[36] The decaying city risked sucking downtown into it. What was needed, one reporter wrote, was a "defensive enclave behind streets and cleared areas [that could serve as] fields of fire."[37] The war terminology *fields of fire* refers to cleared areas that make it impossible for approaching enemies to hide from gun fire. Given the militarization of the city, the war analogy was not far off.

The racial rebranding also drew on medical and psychological metaphors. Journalists personified Detroit as sick, disfigured, troubled, dying, unhappy, distant, remote, unfeeling, ugly, violent, and depressing. It was a place that had, in the words of reporters, lost its muscle, carried symptoms of disease, and was marred by ugly scars.

At a time of guerrilla warfare in Vietnam, jungle metaphors merged with battle imagery. A journalist at the *Los Angeles Times* observed, "Detroit has shown us how close we are to the jungle."[38] And, in the wake of the 1967 rebellion, seeking to reestablish law and order, the vice president of the United States, Hubert Humphrey, declared, "the rule of the jungle must not and will not prevail."[39]

The use of natural metaphors to explain urban change was not new. Since at least the late 1920s, commentators had used the lexicon of blight (borrowed from plant science) to explain the spread of urban decay.[40] But the jungle comparison, long a motif in travel and colonial writing, did something different. It represented the city as a whole (not just parts of it) as a wild place only fit for savages, providing justification for white and capital flight as well as for discriminatory and punitive public policy.[41]

The cultural production of Detroit as a place to fear became further entrenched as the crack-cocaine epidemic ravished the city in the eighties. With half of Black men out of work and the drug economy thriving, images of Detroit as a battleground persisted. The war on drugs and the war on crime perpetuated media portrayals of the majority Black city as dangerous, recursively justifying the rise of mass incarceration and punitive urban policy.

They also contributed to the entrenchment of a material and cognitive racial boundary that divided Detroit from its surrounding suburbs.

For these reasons, when public perceptions of Detroit underwent a shift in the 2010s, it was notable. The media continued to cast Detroit as a space of Black deviance, lawlessness, criminality, and pathology but increasingly mixed in representations that evoked the sublime of fantastical ruination and romantic wilderness, a spatial trope long integral to the territorialization of whiteness.[42]

My first exposure to the genre that locals called "ruin porn" were Yves Marchand and Romain Meffree's haunting photographs of exteriors of iconic buildings, like the Packard Automotive Plant and the Grande Ballroom, in a slow state of collapse. The photographs are collected in a book called *The Ruins of Detroit* but I first encountered them on the internet, where they'd gone viral. That family and friends who knew little about Detroit sent them to me suggested a rising interest in and collective fascination with the city. The photograph of the empty Michigan Central Station (figure 6.2), designed by the architects of Grand Central Station in New York in the same Beaux-Arts style, suggested the grandeur of a previous era. The image caption notes Michigan Central Station's relatively recent closure in 1988, when Amtrack cut services, but it does little to contextualize the forces, like real estate mogul Manuel "Matty" Maroun's controversial ownership, that caused it to sit in a state of abandonment for more than twenty years. Marchand and Meffree also photographed the interiors of buildings—a former police station with a cascading pile of Polaroid mugshots dating from the 1970s, a dentist office with a dusty pink reclining chair and overstuffed filing cabinets, and a biology classroom in the historic 1922 Cass Technical High School (figure 6.3). In 2008, when the photograph was taken, paint peeled from the walls, broken beakers lay like crushed ice on the floor, while others still neatly lined shelves alongside flasks, scales, funnels, and test tubes. Like this image, many of the captured interiors suggested a city that had faced a quick collapse and rapid exodus, though, as Marchand and Meffree themselves note in the caption of another photograph of Cass, the school had not been abandoned but was relocated to new premises.

Other books followed *The Ruins of Detroit*, like *Detroit Disassembled* (2010), *Detroit: 138 Square Miles* (2011), *Lost Detroit* (2013), and *Abandoned Detroit* (2019), to name just a few. Like *The Ruins of Detroit*, their photographs were arresting and conjured a nostalgia for the heyday of industrial capitalism. Wide-angled photographs, for example, like those of the sprawling River Rouge plant, as shown in Andrew Moore's photograph *The Rouge, Dearborn, Michigan* (figure 6.4), bore witness to the ephemerality of capital and the

Figure 6.2 | Yves Marchand and Romain Meffree, *Michigan Central Station*, 2007. The train station was built in 1913, designed by the same architects who built New York City's Grand Central Station. Michigan Central has been closed since 1988, when Amtrak shut down lines across the countrys. *Source:* From Marchand and Meffree, *The Ruins of Detroit* (2010).

exhausted dreams of modernity, but in a way that seemed to suspend the city within the end of the industrial era.

Another motif in the ruin genre was disaster. In addition to post-Katrina New Orleans, commentators likened Detroit to Chernobyl, Stalingrad, and Pompei. It was as if Fordist collapse had spelled the end of history for Detroit and Detroiters. Such comparisons to places consumed by rapid disaster in which residents were killed en masse and had to flee turned on what anthropologist Johannes Fabian has called a "denial of co-evalness," which is to say, a disavowal that the other occupies the same historical epoch as the observer, in this case, the more than 700,000 residents who remained in Detroit.[43]

Such sensational renderings of decline contributed to a voyeurism in which the spectacle of decline became something to contemplate and experience.[44]

Figure 6.3 | Yves Marchand and Romain Meffree, *Biology Classroom, Cass Technical High School*, 2008. Cass Tech opened in 1922 and is a leading technology school in Detroit. The school relocated to a new building in 2005. The old facilities were demolished in 2011. *Source:* From Marchand and Meffree, *The Ruins of Detroit* (2010).

Take, for instance, ruin exploration, which sometimes happened through paid tours and urban safaris like the Gritty Tour offered by Segways2u. As geographer Emma Slager observes, ruin tourism is a mechanism by which the postindustrial city becomes a site of consumption rather than production. The prototypical example of this shift is the replacement of factories with lofts. Slager encourages reflection on the ways in which ruined and abandoned landscapes themselves become objects of consumption.[45] In Detroit, ruin-centered urban exploration can involve critical history but more often it gives rise to fetishization and ends up creating spaces of visibility and invisibility that become symbolically and affectively affixed to the city with material consequences.[46] As a 2012 *National Geographic* article exclaimed, "Even outsiders have started arriving, drawn by a sense of adventure. . . . If you visit Detroit, you're an explorer."[47]

Figure 6.4 | Andrew Moore, *The Rouge, Dearborn, Michigan*, 2008. *Source:* Part of Moore's Detroit series, published in *Detroit Disassembled* (2010).

A New American Frontier

Detroit is often heralded as the place where the twentieth-century American dream was born. It is also lamented as the place where it died, giving rise to the question, could it be reborn? Overtures to the city as a new frontier, a place with vacant pristine land waiting to be claimed and tamed, suggested as much. As one journalist wrote, "Millennials can join the fight for a just and sustainable future and demonstrate America's character once more."[48]

Another wrote, "Detroit, for all its problems—or perhaps because of them—has become nothing less than a new American frontier. Once, easterners heeded the call to 'Go West, young man,' to leave behind the comforts and sophistication of the established citadels in search of adventure and fortune and to tame this great continent. Now, that same whisper is starting to build around Detroit."[49] Proclamations like these suggest that by the 2010s, the thrill of venturing into an imagined lawless Wild West tempered white and corporate fears of venturing into and investing in the majority Black city.

Frontier mythology has long been used pave to the way for capital investment and urban development. Geographer Neil Smith argued decades ago that frontier discourse and imagery capture the aspirations of "economic progress and economic destiny, rugged individualism and the romance of danger, national optimism, race and class superiority," and, in so doing, "rationalize and legitimate a process of conquest" on which capitalism depends.[50]

Building on Smith, Rebecca Kinney, in a deep analysis of the cultural narratives and popular culture that produce the "new" Detroit, argues that the concept of the frontier functions as a "marker of anticipation of the city's ascent. . . . The underlying assumption is that space is being 'underutilized' but that with the right new people, or new ideas, or new infusion of cash, the city can be returned to its former productivity." Kinney shows how the remaking of Detroit as a market and site for extractive capital is entangled with cultural narratives like the frontier that condition places for death and rebirth.[51]

Frontiers—and the affirmations of racial belonging they generate—gain their power through reenactment over generations. Frontier narratives are a method of claiming land and a way of being in relationship to land. They are imaginative projects that erase history and geography. Frontiers, as anthropologist Anna Tsing argues, "ask participants to see a landscape that doesn't exist, at least not yet. It must continually erase old residents' rights to create its wild and empty landscapes where *discovering* resources, not stealing them, is possible. To do so, too, it must cover up the conditions of its own production."[52]

The cultural production of Detroit as a new American frontier happened not only through the reenactment of colonial legends like the *nain rouge* and the romanticization of ruins but also, crucially, through narratives that invited investors and new settlers to discover and stake a claim to Detroit's wild and empty lands. In the popular media, images of resurgent nature supplanted representations of the urban jungle, such as photographs of houses ensnared in vines (what some called "feral houses," as depicted in figure 6.5), skyscrapers with saplings growing on their roofs, groves of invasive Chinese "ghetto palms," and wildlife sightings. These images exaggerated nature's resurgence through visual and discursive circumscription, that is, by cropping or editing what appeared in or beyond the frame. Take, for example, this 2011 blog post, typical of rewilding discourses:

Figure 6.5 | An image from photographer James Griffioen's Feral Houses series, 2006–2009. *Source:* http://www.sweet-juniper.com/2009/07/feral-houses.html.

Detroit is turning into an urban prairie, with grass overtaking sidewalks, sapling trees towering over fences, and utility lines competing with tree branches. Old alleys resemble hiking trails, and empty lots are thick with wildflowers. In the summer, plant growth overtakes many abandoned houses. Giant trees are growing on the roofs of skyscrapers. Abandoned buildings are full of pigeon roosts and feral cats that keep the rat population in check. Wild dog packs roam neighborhoods, hunting the pheasants, turkeys, opossums, roosters and raccoons that have returned to the city. *Ailanthus altissima*—also known as the "ghetto palm" or the tree of heaven—has spread throughout the city. Over time the remaining homes will become crushed by these trees planted by homeowners decades ago. The plaster walls will eventually fade into dust.[53]

The passage underscores both the political stakes of nature metaphors and the different kinds of cultural work that they can do. In the 1960s and 1970s, jungle and battle imagery signaled the city's descent into darkness (or Blackness). By contrast, the return of nature suggested here is its salvation. In American myth, the prairie conjures the pioneering spirit, nation building, and settler land rushes. Repurposed in the urban context, it recycles a settler colonial trope that has long pacified the violence of Indigenous genocide and land theft to make the resettlement of Black spaces seem heroic.[54]

Like representations of ruins, rewilding narratives deemphasized the ongoing struggles of hundreds of thousands of the city's human inhabitants or, in many cases, omitted them altogether. Geographer Nate Millington has drawn attention to how such representations become particularly problematic when resurgent nature is celebrated as cleansing, a discourse with racial connotations.[55] Consider, for example, comments like this one, cited in Millington, which was posted on a blog about Detroit's feral houses: "I am pulling for mother nature to take back that which was used and abused. . . . Consume it and keep marching forward."[56] Or this one: "Who can complain when vast tracts of downtown Detroit are being reclaimed by nature[?] Like the ancient temples of Cambodia, the earth always wins against the will of men. The city's asphalt is cracking open and reverting back to prairie; foxes and deer are making malls and parking lots their new hunting grounds."[57]

Appeals to the transcendental qualities of sublime wilderness have long been a motif in Euro-American environmentalism, deployed by well-to-do city folks in the nineteenth century to promote an escape from industrializing cities.[58] Images of nature's benevolent resurgence in Detroit should therefore be understood as culturally signaling a spatial distance from the threat of Blackness and poverty and, thus, providing symbolic and psychological grounds for the city's capital rejuvenation.[59]

These kinds of representations and discourses occurred with a sort of frenzy that drew people to the city and evinced a powerful grip within it. Put simply, they rendered a space, predominantly inhabited by Black residents, as empty, valueless, and available for appropriation and new modes of capital accumulation. Such trends are larger than Detroit. As geographers Adam Bledsoe and Willie Wright argue, global capital accumulation is made possible, in part, by society's "continued . . . insistence on Black inhumanity and a Black lack of cartography, which casts Black spaces as empty."[60] It is no surprise, then, that the representations of emptiness were mirrored in the cartographic realm.

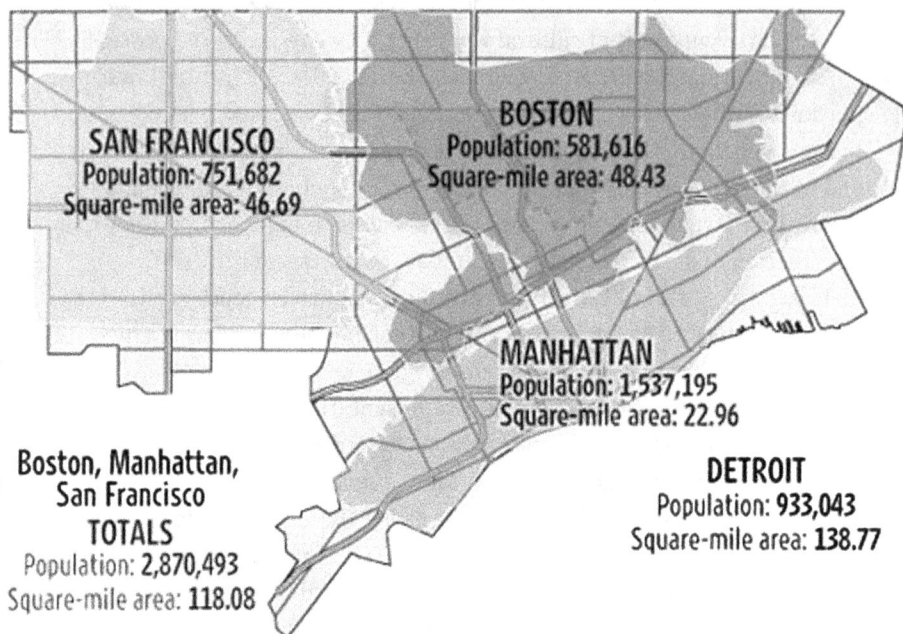

SAN FRANCISCO
Population: 751,682
Square-mile area: 46.69

BOSTON
Population: 581,616
Square-mile area: 48.43

MANHATTAN
Population: 1,537,195
Square-mile area: 22.96

Boston, Manhattan, San Francisco TOTALS
Population: 2,870,493
Square-mile area: 118.08

DETROIT
Population: 933,043
Square-mile area: 138.77

Figure 6.6 | Map comparing the size of Detroit to Boston, Manhattan, and San Francisco. It shows that the square mileage of Detroit is more than all three cities combined. *Source:* University of Detroit Mercy and *Detroit Free Press*.

It's hard to overemphasize the significant proliferation of maps in the 2010s depicting dispossession and vacancy. Like battle and jungle metaphors of earlier decades, visualizations of vacancy had policy implications. In practical terms, they extended discourses of emptiness by making the city legible to potential investors. They were the spatial foreplay to a massive round of new enclosures, privatization, wealth extraction, and capital accumulation. By suggesting that the existing population lacked the capacity to improve the land but also the ability to govern effectively, they positioned new settlers, entrepreneurs, and finance capitalists as agent in making Detroit great again.

Maps, as geographers have long argued, are not merely representations of reality but arguments about the way the world works or should work. If maps, in the words of geographer Denis Wood, "blossom in the springtime of the state," then the remapping of Detroit did not merely reflect a new urban order defined by state emergency power, hypersurveillance, market totalitarianism, and austerity but was also instrumental in its making.[61]

There were the parcel surveys that took stock of vacant and "improved" properties. There were the market value analysis maps, which I discuss further in the next chapter, that divided the city into discrete market types. There were placemaking maps like the one focused on "inchvesting," created by an organization called Why Don't We Own This?, which sought to sell one-square-inch microplots of land with the aim of spurring so-called Good Samaritan speculation.[62]

There was the widely circulating map that appeared in the *Detroit Free Press* in 2009 comparing Detroit to three other major cities (figure 6.6). The first layer of the map shows the municipal outline of Detroit inside a blank white square, decontextualized from the adjacent suburbs and Michigan more broadly. Whereas representations of ruins tended to depict a Detroit out of time, vacancy maps like this one isolate the city in space. The second layer of the map contains the areal and population sizes of San Francisco and Boston superimposed inside Detroit, suggesting that there was ample space for their combined populations of 2.8 million.[63]

Finally, there were the blight maps like the one produced by the Detroit Blight Removal Task Force (DBRTF), which found 84,641 properties to be blighted (figure 6.7). This number represented 22 percent of the properties surveyed, yet the map appeared as a smattering of color, giving the impression that the entire city should be razed. The DBRTF's assessment report added to this storyline and was itself a testament to the enduring power of blight discourse:

> Blight is a cancer. Blight sucks the soul out of anyone who gets near it. . . . Blight is radioactive. It is contagious. . . . Blight is also a symbol . . . of all that is wrong and has gone wrong for too many decades in the once thriving world-class city of Detroit. . . . Just like removing only part of a malignant cancerous tumor is not a real solution, removing only part of incremental amounts of blight from neighborhoods and the city as a whole is also no real solution. Because, like cancer, unless you remove the entire tumor, blight grows back.[64]

The DBRTF report predicted that removing all the blighted structures would take a mere three years. Blank slate representations of Detroit, it seemed, were set to become a material reality.[65]

"For probably the first time in Western civilization in a major metro area, you're going to have large parcels of *vacant pristine land* that have paved streets, utilities of sorts, cable, phone, water, sewer—everything at affordable

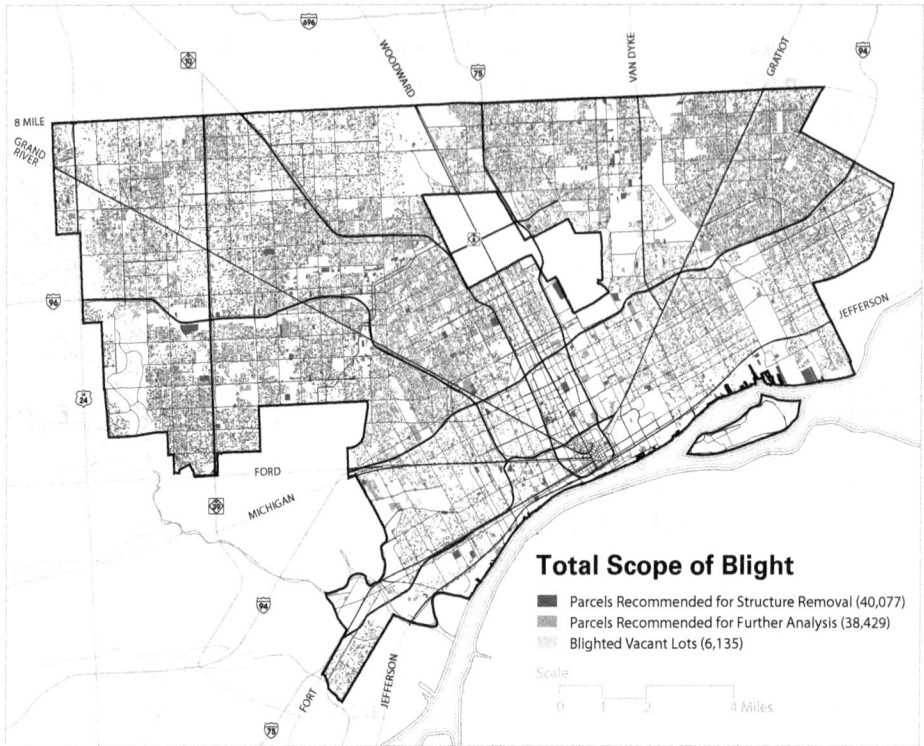

Total Scope of Blight

■ Parcels Recommended for Structure Removal (40,077)
▦ Parcels Recommended for Further Analysis (38,429)
▨ Blighted Vacant Lots (6,135)

Scale

0   1   2   4 Miles

Figure 6.7 | A map that appeared in the 2014 Detroit Blight Removal Task Force Plan, which recommends 40,077 parcels for removal and 38,429 for further analysis. *Source: Every Neighborhood Has a Future . . . And It Doesn't Include Blight,* Detroit Blight Removal Task Force Plan, May 2014.

land prices," piped the real estate titan Dan Gilbert.[66] The celebration of this imagined future required a spatial remove unavailable to most residents. It is hard, after all, to see ruined buildings romantically, vacant land opportunistically, or people as nonexistent when you make your home among them.

To Be Held in Common

"The word 'vacant' or 'derelict' is pejorative. We say, 'open space.'" Regina rose from her chair, speaking to a group of seven others who nodded in agreement. "I would like to tender that the land that is open space is held in the commons, held by the people."

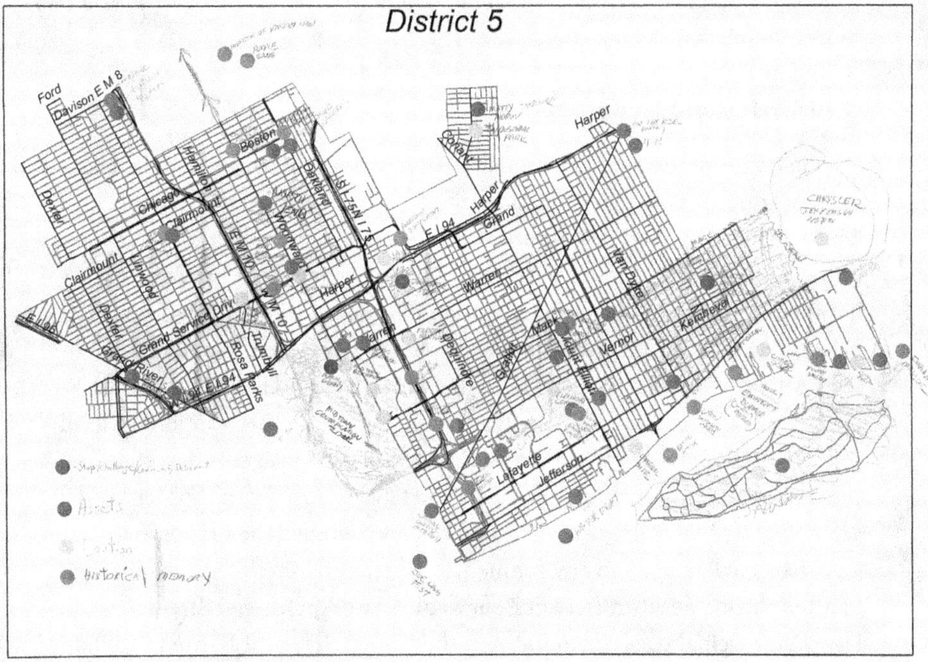

Figure 6.8 | Community map of District 5 produced as part of a Uniting Detroiters project workshop, August 2012. Participants created their own legend. The color-coded dots stand for stop/challenge/community detriment; assets; caution; and historical memory.

It was August 2012. About fifty activists and residents had gathered at the Solanus Casey Center on Detroit's East Side as part of a Uniting Detroiters workshop to talk about the city's redevelopment agenda and how land use figured into it.[67] The meeting was intended to bring together groups from across the city to discuss Detroit's land questions: How should land be held, by whom, for whom, and by what processes? We also hoped the gathering would help build capacity to democratize such decision-making. As part of the workshop, participants made their own maps in small groups; it was an attempt to counter vacancy discourses, recenter residents' own theorizations and sense of place, and to stimulate conversations about what they wanted for the future of the city.

Regina's group pinned their work-in-progress map on the wall (figure 6.8). It was a large printout of District 5, a council district that bordered Grosse Pointe and extended northwest from the Detroit River near Belle Isle toward Hamtramck. The group of six huddled together, discussing which sites to include, what was worth remembering, what was worth honoring, and why. They developed their own color-coded legend.

Red = Stop/challenge/community detriment
Green = Assets
Yellow = Caution
Blue = Historical memory

Their map key was simultaneously commemorative, strategic, and visionary. Red dots denoted sites of danger and harm that were of local concern. There was one for Matty Maroun, the notorious land speculator and owner of the Ambassador Bridge, which was the most trafficked border crossing between the United States and Canada and the only one privately owned. The bridge's narrow design and poor access points meant that it generated constant smog. The conditions only became worse after 9/11, when policy makers deemed the bridge a vital and vulnerable infrastructure. National Guard soldiers, police units, and US customs and immigration agents descended on the transit hub, conducting surveillance on trucks crossing the border as well as on the largely Latinx neighborhood that surrounded the bridge.[68]

Other red dots marked environmental hazards and sites of extraction. One marked the incinerator. Detroit Renewable Power on Russell Street was the largest municipal trash incinerator in the United States. It burned a million tons of solid waste from thirteen nearby counties, most of which were whiter and more affluent than Detroit. Asthma and lung problems were rampant in the neighborhoods that surrounded the incinerator. For decades, activists had been battling for it to be shut down.[69] Another red spot marked Hantz Farms, which, as I discuss in chapter 8, was an audacious proposal by a financier to build the world's biggest farm on the city's East Side.

The yellow dots—threats—included the city's renowned Belle Isle Park, whose management the state was considering taking over as part of broader fiscal austerity measures; the site of a controversial plan to build a light rail that would do little to remedy severe public transportation gaps; and the so-called Midtown Gentrification Zone, a T-shaped area that stretched from downtown to midtown. The zone was emblematic of the return of corporate capital and private investment and the displacement of longtime residents. Companies like Compuware, Twitter, the high-end watchmaker Shinola, and Blue Cross Blue Shield, to name just a few, had recently built offices.

Meanwhile, billionaire Dan Gilbert was on a spending spree, buying up more than two million square feet of downtown real estate, which he monitored from a control room with hundreds of surveillance cameras and a private security force. His Bedrock realty company had launched a downtown advertising campaign that featured window posters of a mostly white crowd and the words "See Detroit Like We Do." It was evidence of how, as Rebecca Kinney argues, private investment in Detroit hinged on the symbolic and physical disappearance of the city's Black population and the visibility of white (or multiracial) newcomers.[70]

As longtime residents faced eviction, resettlement incentive programs (sponsored by corporations, medical and educational institutions, and foundations) targeted the zone, offering entrepreneurs and the professional class $20,000 forgivable loans for home purchases and $2,500 annual rental allowances.[71] The Midtown Gentrification Zone—along with the group's other red and yellow dots—foregrounded how race, class, and historical power blocs worked together to facilitated "socio-spatial enclosures," to use Clyde Woods's term.[72]

At the same time, the group's blue and green dots drew attention to cartographies of liberation and the recuperative role of place. They marked sites of resistance and critical consciousness that were being written out of Detroit's history. They also brought sites of Indigenous and Black struggle into the same frame, suggesting their linked history and the importance of allied work.

The oldest historical site that the group marked was that of the Fox Indian Massacre in Grosse Point Park. Historians have written about how the massacre occurred when Fox (Meskwaki), Kickapoo, and Mascouten tribes, seeking to align themselves with the English in territorial struggles over trade routes, besieged Fort Pontchartrain in 1712. In a five-day struggle, the French killed more than a thousand Fox Indians.

The second-oldest historical site was Bloody Run Creek, where the Battle of Bloody Run was fought on July 31, 1763. British troops had planned a surprise attack on Pontiac's forces, which were holding a siege of Fort Detroit. Pontiac's warriors eventually defeated the British; the creek was said to have run red from the blood of wounded and dead soldiers.

Other blue dots included the blind pig on Twelfth Street, where the 1967 rebellion began; Black Bottom, known as the heart and soul of Detroit's African American community, which was bulldozed during the urban renewal years; and Northern High School, where in 1966 students staged a three-week civil rights walkout. In 1969, students staged another walkout and started a Freedom School at St. Matthew's and St. Joseph's church, a few blocks from the school. The walkouts signaled the disarray of Detroit's public schools after the rebellion and a sense of empowerment among Black Detroiters to take community control. Several groups organized the walkouts, including Citizens for Community Control of Schools, West Central Organization, and Students for Justice later renamed All-African People's Union, which argued that community control alone was not enough. They wanted curricula overhauled so that students could garner skills they needed to engage in the radical transformation of society rather than be trained for disappearing jobs.[73]

In addition to historical events, blue dots denoted sites of cultural significance like the site of Motown Records. The company, which had deep roots in Detroit's Black community, produced the likes of Marvin Gaye, Martha Reeves and the Vandellas, Diana Ross and the Supremes, Lionel Richie, the Temptations, Stevie Wonder, Smokey Robinson and the Miracles, Michael Jackson and the Jackson 5, and many more. Motown grew into a music industry giant that helped create a Black commercial culture, which, in turn, shaped the struggle for civil rights.[74]

These historical points plotted by Regina's group illustrate how events that might seem temporally distant are implicated in the here and now. Dipesh Chakrabarty uses the term *time-knots* to name "a plurality of times existing together, a disjuncture of the present with itself."[75] The map made clear how time-knots are spatialized; how space, in the words of Doreen Massey, is a "constellation of on-going trajectories." When we travel across space, she argued, we are traveling not across a surface but across "geometries of power" and "stories so far."[76] The map illuminated how alternative spatial histories and liberatory futures knot the past and the present.

Katherine McKittrick argues that "geographies of domination" hold within them different social orders. The counter-cartographies of the Black diaspora population "can incite new, or different, and perhaps more just, geographic stories," she writes.[77] The group's mapping of "sites/citations of struggle," to use McKittrick's phrase, illustrates the limits of conventional geographies and returns us to Ruth Wilson Gilmore's oft-quoted line: "A geographical imperative lies at the heart of all struggles for social justice."[78]

The map included more green dots ("assets," according to the legend) than any other color, calling attention to Black geographies, or as Alex A. Moulton puts it, "the ways in which Black people have made spaces in which they could flourish and pursue liberatory dreams."[79]

There were dots for community gardens, like the North End Gardens, where neighbors grew kale, collards, beets, lettuce, sweet potatoes, and much more on six acres. They also ran a job center, offered cooking classes, and delivered food to folks in elder-care facilities. Jerry Hebron, who started the project, was motivated by a desire to restore the neighborhood of her youth and combat gentrification.[80] Other green dots marked cultural centers that sought to uplift Black culture and democratize the arts, like the Dabls Mbad

African Bead Museum and the Detroit Repertory Theater on the West Side, Michigan's oldest professional theater, known for its progressive mission to democratize the arts and portray the lives of neighbors on stage.

Dots marked places of worship, community development organizations, public parks and libraries, and schools like the new James and Grace Lee Boggs School on Goethe Street, which offered education for kindergarten through eighth graders and sought to carry on the Boggsian tradition by humanizing education, supporting the transfer of multigenerational wisdom, and nurturing creative and critical thinkers who contribute to the well-being of their communties.[81]

The constellation of blue and green dots uplifted a spatial logic rooted in abundance, relationships, and mutuality rather than scarcity and partition. It pointed to the tremendous power that is held in communities.[82] It suggested, as Regina argued, that the land was not vacant. It was not empty. It was not without memory. It was not surplus. It was not property. It was not capital. Rather, the land was held in common, by the people, as sacred space, as memory, as life over generations.

*

The specter of abandonment hung over Detroit, obscuring this radical underside. It lurked in photographs of sunken mansions and wild landscapes. It expressed itself in suburban nostalgia. It conjured processions and betrayed itself in the figure of the *nain rouge*.

When I first started writing about the *nain rouge* and the cultural production of abandoned Detroit, I wanted to account for how claims to the city were being made in the present. But the critique also felt insufficient for informing more just geographies.

Avery Gordon writes about haunting as one way that abusive systems of the past are felt in the present. Haunting, she argues, happens in those moments when the familiar becomes unfamiliar, when "the over-and-done-with comes alive, when what's been in your blind spot comes into view."[83] "Haunting raises specters," Gordon continues, "and it alters the experiences of being in time, the ways we separate the past, the present, and the future."[84]

It calls attention to what is at once a "seething presence" but hard to grasp.[85] It raises the question of how things could be otherwise. Thinking with Gordon, I realized the story of the *nain rouge* functioned not only as a colonial reenactment of possession but as a parable of an abandoned Detroit that contained within it a different future.[86]

Recall the fortune teller's instructions to Cadillac: appease the *nain*. This call for *conciliation* (rather than *banishment)* resonates with Indigenous conceptualizations of a spirit, trickster, and teacher called Nanabozho, or Nanabush, who figures prominently in Native storytelling. As Ridie Wilson Ghezzi writes about Ojibwe traditions, stories about the Nanabush were not just entertaining but about "keeping the tribe alive."[87] Likewise, according to Leanne Betasamosake Simpson, within Nishnaabeg thought, the Nanabush is an important teacher who reflects human behavior and models how to know and not know by demonstrating what happens if we don't take responsibility for "our own baggage or trauma or emotional responses." The Nanabush, as Simpson writes, "stories the land with a sharp criticality necessary for moving through the realm of the colonized into the dreamed reality of the decolonized, and for navigating the lived reality of having to engage with both at the same time."[88]

Storying the land, no doubt, means different things for Indigenous and non-Indigenous people. For those who are non-Indigenous, it entails learning about our own ancestral legacies in relationships to the land. It involves grappling with the afterlives of colonial conquest and slavery. And it involves learning from efforts to organize land and life otherwise. Put another way, it means facing—rather than banishing—what haunts us. This is the parable of the *nain rouge*.

political ecologies of austerity

I didn't notice the map until Marla Lewis pointed it out to me. I was sitting in her office overlooking the Detroit River. The lights from the casinos in Windsor flashed in the distance. It was June 2012, almost two months after the passage of the consent agreement that put Detroit's budgetary decisions under the control of a financial advisory board. I had gone to interview Lewis about the Detroit Works Project (DWP), a major foundation-funded initiative to create a new citywide plan. Lewis worked within the executive office of the Bing administration and oversaw the project. I had been following the DWP process since I had arrived in Detroit, going to public meetings, reviewing planning documents, and interviewing planners and city officials. I was eager to talk with Lewis to glean an insider's perspective on the challenges and tensions that surrounded the project.[1]

The DWP was no easy undertaking. The city presented a conundrum for planners. Planning theory had long espoused models that assumed linear growth trajectories: places went from small to big, rural to urban, agrarian to consumptive, preindustrial to industrial. Many rapidly growing cities, especially in the global South, sought to follow this model but struggled to expand infrastructural services at a pace that matched the influx of new residents. Detroit, by contrast, faced the opposite problem: too much infrastructure for too few residents. From a planning perspective, the city's challenge was how to grow economically while shrinking its physical footprint. Yet there

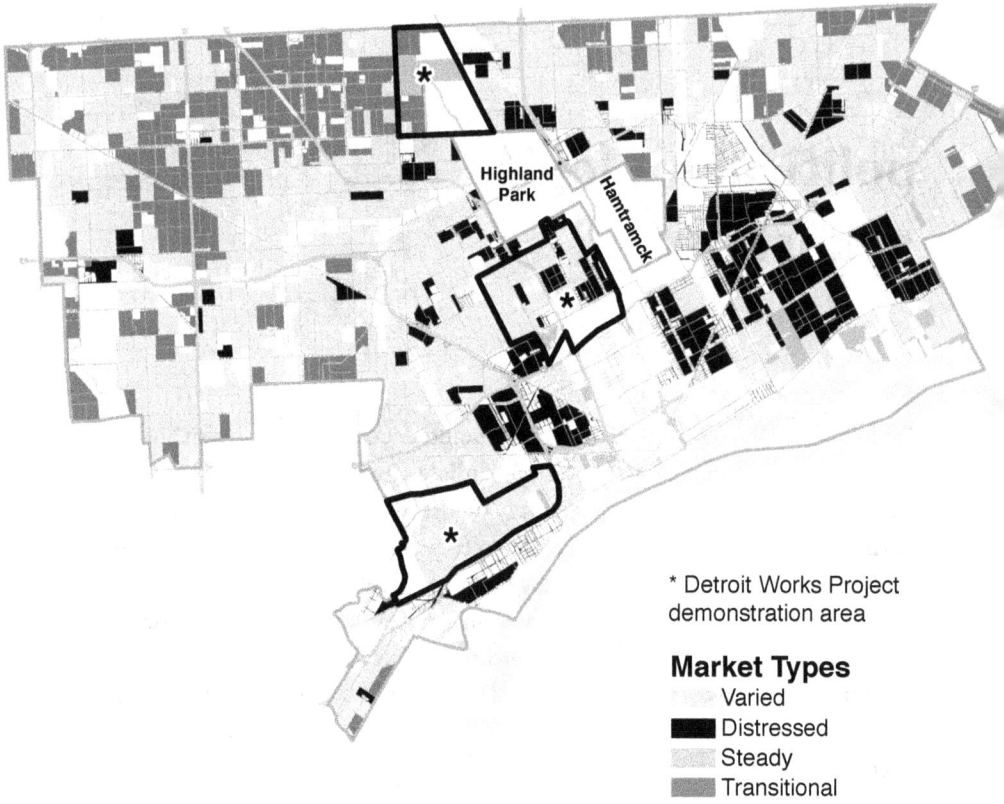

Figure 7.1 | A reproduction of the 2012 combined Residential Physical Condition Analysis plus the Market Value Analysis for Detroit in gray tones. *Source:* Hamilton Anderson Associates/Reinvestment Fund/Tim Stallmann.

was little planning theory that modeled this, nor was there much precedent for dealing with the thorny technical and political questions planners faced. Should residents be moved? How should roads and utilities be rerouted? Should police and firefighting districts be reconfigured? Should maintenance services be discontinued?

The idea of shrinking Detroit was not new. A 1990 vacant land survey had recommended demolishing and decommissioning parts of the city. A few years later, in 1993, Detroit's former auditor issued a report, *Management by Common Sense*, that called for the city to be downsized and for large parts to be reverted to nature.[2] But these proposals were so incendiary that they were shelved for nearly twenty years—that is, until the DWP.

When the DWP project launched in the fall of 2010, it was to great fanfare. It was heralded for its scale, ambition, and proposed innovative uses of urban greening. A team of skilled planners were at the helm. The well-chosen name—Detroit Works—signaled optimism amid economic volatility. It intimated that labor, which had defined Detroit's past, might also define its future. It also conjured an image of functional public works and infrastructure. Given that residents were desperate for both jobs and city services, the planning process was highly anticipated, but it had gotten off to a troubled start, rife with skepticism and pushback.

Lewis welcomed me with a warm smile and weathered enthusiasm for her charge. We had been talking about the rocky start to the planning process when she abruptly turned and pointed to the brightly colored map on the wall. "That's the city's development plan," she said.

I was confused, but not by Lewis showing me a map. After all, hundreds of maps had been produced as part of the planning process. But I was surprised at her assertion that such a simple-looking map could be *the* city's development plan, particularly given that an extensive participatory planning process was still underway.

The map, called the Market Value Analysis, or MVA, segmented the city into market-based zones, each associated with a color. Lewis explained that it was both diagnostic and prescriptive. Each color corresponded to a set of strategies for investment and disinvestment and for the allocation of municipal funds and services. Purple indicated a steady market zone, green meant transitional, and orange distressed. Blue areas had too much heterogeneity at the block level to assign a category. (Map 7.1 shows the MVA restyled in gray tones.)

That most of the map was blue—uncategorizable—signaled that its color coding was less a reflection of actually existing market boundaries than an attempt to produce them.[3] Green areas/transitional markets tended toward the outer edges of the city, whereas orange/distressed areas surrounded downtown and stretched eastward to the border with Grosse Pointe. The map contained very few purple/steady zones, aside from the Palmer Park area, the villages on the East Side, and the marina.

According to Lewis, the administration would focus on encouraging development and investment in middle market zones. By contrast, federal, state, and local dollars were to be withheld from orange areas, where upward of ninety thousand people lived, until the market "ripened," meaning that it exhibited the capacity to generate a return on investments.

I found the map's uncanny resemblance to twentieth-century redlining maps to be jarring. Lewis' disclosure that a community development financial institution (CDFI) had made the map only further confounded me. From what I understood, CDFIs were largely created to mitigate the effects of redlining. They offered lending to Black and other people of color in communities where credit was difficult to access. Why, I wondered, was an organization founded to reverse discrimination producing a map that seemed destined to discriminate?

The map became a puzzle for me. I set out to understand where it came from, why and how it was made, and its stakes. I interviewed planners, city officials, and government workers. I pored over planning documents. The story of the map, I learned, was larger than Detroit. It was a story about urbanism under financialization and how austerity melded in new ways with sustainability mandates. It was a story about how value was conceived and measured, the social orders that were prioritized in those definitions, and the role that planners and planning theory played therein. And it was a story about the algorithmic mutation of property markets and the power of data-driven analytics to depoliticize contentious planning processes.

Planning Future Cities for Late Capitalism

The challenges the DWP faced early on had everything to do with the messy politics of value creation. Value is an elusive concept. Dictionary definitions often emphasize the regard in which something is held, or its importance, worth, or use. Anthropologist Arjun Appadurai has argued that "valuation regimes" shape the priorities around which social orders are organized and give meaning to life. But what makes things—land, clothing, stones, or neighborhoods—valuable or not and why?[4]

When the DWP launched, data-driven urbanism and algorithmic planning were ascendant. To be clear, data-driven analytics were not new. Urban researchers and planners had long analyzed extensive data sets in urban design, even if, historically, most have been derived from small-scale surveys and coarse aggregate statistics.[5] What was new, however, was the scope and scale of the research enabled by information technology, big data, advances in sensor and mobility technologies, state-sponsored surveillance, and predictive algorithms.[6]

Lewis and her colleagues hired a bevy of experts to conduct policy and neighborhood audits. They gathered a dizzying array of data—data about foreclosed homes, vacancies, roads, water lines, sewer lines, bus routes—that they hoped would illuminate neighborhood conditions and inform the planning process. They were excited to share their findings and seek input from residents. The inaugural DWP meeting was planned for September 14, 2010. It was the first of a series of meetings to be held and was thus highly anticipated by planners and residents alike. More than a thousand residents packed the pews of the Greater Grace Temple on the city's northwest side.

Lewis and her colleagues were pleased with the turnout, but the meeting quickly went sideways. Residents had arrived anxious and expecting answers. They were aghast that Mayor Bing was not in attendance. As one resident put it, "I didn't come here for a breakout session. I came here to hear from the mayor."[7] Lewis and other officials promised he'd be dropping by, but whispers spread that there was a hidden plan. Mayhem ensued. Small-group breakout sessions devolved into shouting matches. By the time the mayor arrived to close the event with a short speech, scores of residents had stormed out, calling the meeting a sham. Bing's efforts to assuage the crowd largely fell flat. Subsequent meetings were less raucous, but residents remained wary.

The DWP meeting underscored how planning is rarely immediate. It is more often the result of prolonged struggle and negotiation in which people tend to express a deeply held sense of place and desires for the future.[8] Contestations over the DWP turned on old questions of race and power. Yet the political terrain had shifted. The Great Recession overshadowed the planning process. Thousands of residents came out to voice concerns about rampant school closures, lack of jobs, and industrial contamination. Some people expressed fears that the DWP would lead to their eviction and relocation. Debates over the potential shuttering of neighborhoods became broader debates over austerity, entrepreneurial urban governance, and who had the power to make decisions about the day-to-day functioning of the city and its future.

Throughout the fall, tensions continued to run high, with residents furious over what they perceived as the inaction of government officials and the lack of transparency surrounding the DWP. Then, on December 9, 2010, almost three months after the inaugural meeting, in an effort to reassure residents, Bing held an ill-planned press conference. According to Lewis, Bing wanted Detroiters to know that the DWP wasn't all talk and that there would be a plan by March. She cringed as she recounted how Bing, borrowing language from corporate America, announced that Detroit would be "rightsized."

In business vernacular, rightsizing refers to cutting costs and maximizing profits by reorganizing management and shrinking the workforce for absolute efficiency. Applied to cities, the parallel is a reduction in public services and the geographical reach of infrastructure. As Bing put it, the municipal government would eventually "shut off public services to roughly a third of the city's geographic footprint." Residents would be incentivized to relocate to one of seven to nine yet-to-be-identified "population centers." No one would be forced to move, Bing said, but those who remained in areas slated for underdevelopment "need to understand that they're not going to get the kind of services they require." These residents, he concluded, would be better off in parts of Detroit where they'd receive "water, sewer, lighting, public safety—all of that."[9]

Bing's statement was a public-relations nightmare. People were furious that the city planned to pull the plug on neighborhoods where thousands still lived. Social justice groups responded by holding their own people's movement assembly and demanding a more equitable and inclusive planning process. "The Detroit Works Project is something being done to us, not with us or for us," a local activist named Jay Hammond said at the time. "The whole thing is about shutting down utilities that taxpaying citizens pay for, to force them out of neighborhoods. What is that if it's not . . . urban renewal; it's negro removal, right?"[10]

Another resident, Jorge Rees, talked about the moral complexity of closing neighborhoods. While it may sound ideal on paper, the implications—as had been shown with Black Bottom and Poletown—were massive. "When you uproot someone, I don't care if it's a shack, it's their shack. You might be moving them to something different, but you're upsetting their whole way of life."[11] In response to the uproar, the planning team had no choice but to pause and regroup. Activists told me later that they thought they'd succeeded in shutting down the process.

Yet quietly behind the scenes, the planning team was reconfiguring their strategy. They needed a "course correction," said Lewis, to win back people's trust and follow through on Bing's promise of a plan. They made several adjustments: First, the Bing administration publicly disavowed the contentious language of rightsizing. Second, they split the DWP into short-term actions, which would remain under the executive branch, and a participatory, long-term engagement process run by foundations. This change would show Detroiters that while the DWP valued participation, it was not all talk. The short-term team then set to work coming up with a plan, which included hiring the CDFI Reinvestment Fund (RF) to conduct a market value analysis, the outcome of which was the colorful map tacked to Lewis' office wall.

It didn't take me long to discover that Detroit was not the only city with such a map. By 2018, RF had made proprietary MVA maps for more than forty US cities, including New Orleans, San Antonio, Camden, Newark, Pittsburgh, Philadelphia, Baltimore, St. Louis, Milwaukee, Houston, and Dallas. The proliferation of the MVA raised a number of questions: Why was it emerging now? What went into its production? And what did it reveal about the function of property values under late capitalism?

Inscribing Valuation Regimes

Reinvestment Fund didn't get its start as an MVA mapmaker. To understand its odd trajectory from antidiscrimination financing to making maps that look like redlining maps, it's important to entertain a brief history of the 1977 Community Reinvestment Act (CRA) and CDFIs. This is story about how deregulation and financialization have impacted community development, the work that goes into developing valuation regimes, and the contingent, if not arbitrary, ways that places are disciplined by the logics of capitalist economic value.

Reinvestment Fund was founded in 1985 in Philadelphia by a small group of community developers, activists, and businesspeople as a community loan fund; it later became a certified CDFI.[12] Recall that when CDFIs emerged in the seventies, owing to the CRA, their purpose was to ameliorate the effects of racist housing practices.

The CRA was landmark legislation. It prohibited banks from discriminating in lending and required that they address the credit needs of their entire service area. For decades, however, its mandate went largely unenforced, that is, until the disintermediation of local financial markets led nonbank lending to significantly outpace bank lending.[13] Banking disintermediation, which emerged in the United States in the 1980s, refers to a trend in which banks sell rather than hold the loans they originate, and the loans eventually become tradable securities. Additionally, *disintermediation* references a shift in which borrowers seek credit from capital markets rather than from banks, and investors put their money into bonds, securities, and stocks rather than into savings accounts.

Notably, this period is also marked by massive federal cuts to social programs and assistance to cities. As philanthropies and nonprofits scrambled to fill the gaps created by state retrenchment, municipalities were also increasingly forced to rely on bonds and notes sold on the capital market to fund both long-term operating costs and day-to-day functioning.[14] The growing power of finance capital and credit ratings over municipal governance contributed to the repurposing of urban public policy toward the needs of finance rather than toward the social needs of local communities.[15]

This shift opened niches for CDFIs to offer new forms of financing for poor people and for poor neighborhoods to develop community businesses, nonprofits, commercial real estate, affordable housing, and institutions that served local needs and also investors' pocketbooks.[16] It is for this reason that CDFIs are often referred to as "activists as well as financial pipelines"; their mandate of poverty alleviation comes by way of connecting low-income communities to finance capital.[17] By the early 2000s, 550 CDFIs across the United States managed $6.5 billion in investments, and some, like RF, which had become major financial players in urban planning and development, even sought their own credit ratings.[18]

Reinvestment Fund described itself as a "socially responsible community investment group" that aimed to make a difference for "low-wealth people and places" by delivering the capital, analytics, and expertise necessary for the development of equitable communities. It focused on "America's distressed towns and cities," helping municipal governments direct their spending of "scarce" public resources with the expressed aim of boosting real estate markets. It offered a host of services, including real-estate development financing, social impact bond financing, and increasingly data analysis and warehousing to help determine how to intervene in global markets.[19] Reinvestment Fund had, in short, become more than a financial lender. It was a data banker and an assessor of investment risk in the name of the public good.

As a data warehouse, RF was small. It did not, for example, bank data on the scale of Amazon. Reinvestment Fund's embrace of data banking and analysis is noteworthy, however, for the way it extended—or arguably, negated—the traditional mandate of CDFIs. In its new role as a go-to consultant for municipalities, RF was not simply making decisions about where to offer or deny individual credit but reshaping the geography of municipal and private-developer spending in cities across the United States.

The MVA was one of RF's policy-solution initiatives. In RF's words, the MVA "creates an innovative data-driven framework for restoring market viability and wealth in distressed urban real estate markets."[20] While the color-coded zones on the MVA were attention grabbing and clearly delineated, its framework for restoring market viability was not. The algorithms from which the maps were generated were proprietary, though the firm did reveal that it relied on property-value indicators (such as residential sale prices, the presence of subsidized housing, properties with building-code violations, housing vacancy, credit scores, and ratios of prime to subprime loans) and social indicators (including race, ethnicity, employment, education, area incomes, crime data, public-school performance, and building conditions) to identify areas with similar market characteristics. The weights given to these variables were not made public, obscuring the exact mix of factors that distinguished a "steady" area from a "distressed" one.

After conducting statistical analysis of census tract and block-group data-sets, RF staff worked with "local market experts" to "ground truth" their market type categorizations. Ground truthing is a social scientific term used to verify quantitative analysis through direct observation and measurement. Reinvestment Fund's ground truthing involved driving city streets with MVA drafts and GPS locators to verify that the block groups that fell into different market types were significantly different.[21] When necessary, according to RF's director of policy solutions, Ira Goldstein, they made adjustments based on "fieldwork" findings. Yet it's worth pointing out that their so-called ground truthing was still constrained by the way the algorithm delimited value.[22]

To be clear, the MVA's algorithm defined value and market potential from the perspective of financial gain. Goldstein explained that the indicators used in the MVA were selected "because they reflect the conditions that any developer might observe when evaluating areas for investment or intervention."[23] Indeed, the MVA's property-value indicators—real estate, crime data, public-school performance, and other business-formation indicators—were all related to exchange values and estimated returns on investment. As a result, it was impossible for the model to account for and represent the diverse and complex ways residents valued the places where they lived. For example, it had no way of accounting for the inordinate amount of time Detroiters spent collectively tending land and buildings they did not own. Nor could it account for noneconomic values like care, interdependence, and self-determination that were for many Detroiters of paramount importance. These valuations were illegible within the MVA's coding scheme. If value, as David Graeber has argued, brings universes into being, then, we could say, values like mutuality and solidarity occupied a universe—or city—distinct from the one that the MVA was attempting to conjure.[24]

Rendering the Political Technical

As I continued my research, it seemed like the MVA was everywhere. I saw it on the office walls of planners and government bureaucrats. City workers took it out to explain important service-delivery changes, for example, where the city would continue and discontinue mowing, do street maintenance, and repair senior housing. A number of people expressed relief that they had a tool for decision-making based on verifiable data because it helped depoliticize and smooth over contentious planning decisions.

At a time when finance capital was reorganizing the form and function of municipal governance, this ability to claim neutrality was particularly important. One of RF's selling points for the MVA was that it was an apolitical, data-driven, user-friendly, and objective representation of market value. RF promised that it would take the "subjectivity out of decision making" and guide city officials on where and how to direct "scarce" public resources to "leverage or clear the path for private investment" so that city residents, who were "consumers," could receive quality services. Like other algorithmic-planning approaches that had increased in popularity, the MVA's discourse of objectivity hid the moral and technical choices that surrounded its data collection, design, and prescriptive outcomes.[25]

That Detroit was one among more than a dozen cities that had hired RF to conduct MVAs, underscored the tool's appeal to officials facing deeply political and divisive decisions. In New Orleans, for instance, city officials used the MVA to help decide where to offer homes for auction and where they should be saved until the "market ripen[ed]."[26] In St. Louis, as in Detroit, the MVA guided municipal decisions regarding where to distribute public money and incentivize private investment.[27] In Newark, the MVA helped administrators "drill down" and understand foreclosures. In Baltimore, it was used to develop a Community Development Block Grant Comprehensive Plan, guide the capital budget plan for the city, and decide which projects to support with local, state, and federal incentives.[28] In Detroit, the MVA helped coordinate the use of governmental and philanthropic funds. It was also used to target code enforcement.

Indeed, one governmental priority that extended across the MVAs for all cities was "Quality of Life Code Enforcement (broken window syndrome)." The focus on increased security and policing was not surprising, given that a key feature of the entrepreneurial city is the defense of real estate values.[29] Yet the standardization of policing by a CDFI, according to the market viability, represented a new phenomenon. In Detroit, code enforcement was a priority in steady, transitional, and distressed market clusters, whereas in high-value areas, only "some activity" was recommended. That *quality of life code enforcement* was the intervention for broken windows syndrome recalls Fred Moten's argument that broken windows policing takes Black life as the "broken window," as a "threat to the normative order." Before Emancipation, the enslaved were protected property, but they also constituted a threat to the idea of property, as Moten argues. They could flee. When they were no longer property, new forms of control emerged, like lynch laws and, decades later, broken windows policing. "To fix a broken window," as Moten puts it, "is to fix another way of imagining the world."[30] Under the framework of the MVA, to fix a broken window is to enforce through surveillance, citation, and punitive practices a new quality of life. Put another way, it is to discipline people and places to behave in ways that yield a return on capital investment.

Appeals to objective risk calculations seemed to give bureaucrats a feeling of security amid austerity. In a 2012 interview, a Detroit city planner told me, "As resources get limited and we look for greater impact, everyone is moving to a targeted strategy. You can't have targeting be a political decision." She showed me a document of service-delivery changes associated with the MVA zones. "It has to be driven by empirical data. That is our reality here. I have to imagine colleagues in other cities feel the same way. You can't have people saying, well, you just picked these areas because . . ."

Her comment made clear to me how the MVA served a dual function: it was the state's resolution to a crisis in public trust. At the same time, it was an attempt by the state to resolve its fiscal crisis through data-driven territorial reorganization.

Two years later, the chief of staff to the mayor of St. Louis similarly praised the MVA for enabling city officials to rely on "data" rather than on "experience, intuition, and hunches."[31]

Such sentiments suggest how algorithms become "stabilizers of trust, practical and symbolic assurances that their evaluations are fair and accurate, free from subjectivity, error, or attempted influence," as communication studies scholar Tarleton Gillespie writes.[32] They are taken to have "calculative objectivity."[33] Algorithmic prescriptions, though, still required some public relations finesse, at least in the realm of planning.

Recall that when the DWP went on pause, it split into two arms—the short-term planning team, which had produced the MVA, and the long-term participatory planning team. In the spring of 2012, I attended a series of community conversations hosted by the long-term team, which had been engaged in an aggressive regime of participation. Their strategies included acknowledging past mistakes, assuring residents they were now listening, hosting gamified planning charettes, and traveling around town with a fold-up "roaming table," from which they disseminated information and stimulated playful rather than contentious conversations. At public meetings, the long-term planning team routinely began by sharing participation figures, for example, that over eight months, they had reached thirty thousand people and had four thousand meaningful conversations. Yet it was never clear how this scale of engagement translated (or not) into developing a long-term plan, leading to the sense that planners were more invested in the quantification and performance of engagement than in meaningfully including residents in the process.

After I learned about the MVA, I was eager to understand the long-term planning team's position on it. Given their extensive outreach, I expected them to view the MVA as problematic. I quickly realized my assumption was naïve. According to Matthew Stinton, one of the team's lead consultants, the long-term planning team not only knew about the MVA but were using it as the basis for a new land-use typology that would guide their development recommendations with one small—but important—change.[34] Eschewing the language of *markets*, they opted instead for *vacancy*. According to the new typology, "distressed" markets—or rather "high vacancy" areas—were to be slated for greening. Stinton emphasized that this shift in terminology—from distressed to vacant—was important because for Detroiters the language of vacancy was less political.

"Everyone is looking at language," Stinton said. "It's highly scrutinized. We finally found something that is accessible to the public. It's high vacancy. It's low vacancy. Even though what we're talking about is more than vacancy, it's easy."

Other planners I interviewed explained the rhetorical shift from "distressed" to "vacant" in similar ways. One said that when the typology, which described some neighborhoods as "distressed," was released to the public, residents were, in her words, "immediately offended." They felt it suggested that they had a "distressed reality," even though planners assured them that they were talking not about the people, but about the market conditions, as she put it, which are either strong or weak. "A lot of this data was using terminology that [the people] weren't used to," she told me. "But we've been talking about vacancy in this city for a long time, so someone talking about low vacancy versus moderate vacancy versus high vacancy, they are not going to debate that. It's just what it is."

By emphasizing vacancy, Detroit's planners deemphasized debates over residential relocation and state disconnection, rendering a political process technical. The presumed objectivity of and comfort in naming vacancy also concealed the historical, racialized logics of value and risk that the MVA reiterated as a mode of governance. Put another way, the MVA indexed the long-standing and deeply embedded links between race and property values while masquerading as an objective assessment of public and private investment risk.[35]

From the Science of Risk Mapping to Municipal Redlining

Though planners upheld the MVA as an ahistorical performance assessment of which neighborhoods were doing the "best" in market terms, it is better understood as part of a continuum of the racialized history of risk mapping.

Like advocates of the MVA, the creators of the early risk-rating systems that preceded redlining saw themselves as pioneering a much-needed scientific, apolitical, objective assessment that would promote wise investment and economic growth.[36] In the early 1930s, the National Association of Real Estate Boards (NAREB) in Chicago, one of the key progenitors of real estate science—known as *realology*—was obsessed with developing standard scientific methods for ascertaining and measuring value and risk. Some local standards existed in land-value atlases, but the real estate community lacked a standard appraisal practice across the field. The NAREB set out to create one. Association members worked with Homer Hoyt and Robert Park at the University of Chicago, who codified the idea that race and ethnicity were important to the rise and decline of property values. Specifically, Hoyt argued that the influx of Black people to neighborhoods would lead property values to fall precipitously. The NAREB's campaign for realology got a boost in 1934 when the FHA was created. Following the stock market crash, the FHA, seeking to stabilize the US housing market, turned to Chicago professionals engaged in developing real estate science and technology to help them design uniform approaches to valuation, risk rating, and racial appraisal. The FHA's *Underwriting Manual* and the infamous residential security maps (also known as redlining maps, as discussed in chapter 2) produced by the Home Owners' Loan Corporation (HOLC) linked the value of property to the differential values of racialized groups.[37] While redlining has been illegal for more than fifty years, its legacy persists in mortgage lending patterns as well as in the ways racialized judgments about value and risk become baked into urban-development models.[38]

That the MVA bore similarities to a redlining map was not lost on its developer. Consider his reflection on the MVA's potentially thorny activity of shading block groups:

> Although labels are only meant to serve as shorthand, clients may be reluctant to label a market "distressed," for example. Similarly, color can evoke emotion rooted in the history of many US cities (for example, red may be associated with the practice of redlining and coloring an area red may give the impression that resources will not flow to the area). We have dealt with these issues by having the recipients and stakeholders choose labels and colors that minimize potential discomfort. In the end, although clients or other stakeholders may contest the name or the color of a market on a map, they do not contest the way the data describe their area. As John Adams once declared, "Facts are stubborn things."[39]

Yet, if facts are stubborn, they often are so not because they are right but because of the structures and systems that accrete around them. Economic facts, after all, as Anna Julia Cooper observed long ago, are abstractions infected by racism. The problem of value is not an issue of fact but of politics.[40]

The MVA, like earlier risk assessments, worked to recast dense relationships among people and places in terms of separate market types, partitioning urban space and populations for the purpose of standardizing the production of market values. In the 1930s, the security maps created new frontiers for capital accumulation by rendering places commensurable across distance and difference and legible for investment and disinvestment. Decades later, the MVA was also creating new frontiers.

As a one-size-fits-all solution that remained relatively constant from city to city, the MVA appeared to be setting new development standards. Standards are powerful, as Geoff Bowker and Susan Leigh Star write, because they have a temporal and spatial reach across time and distance. They format material worlds that have "significant inertia and can be very difficult and expensive to change."[41]

To be clear, while the MVA bears similarities with earlier forms of risk mapping, they are not the same. In the twentieth century, a racist housing market emerged from the systematic denial of credit and investment. By contrast, in the twenty-first century, the MVA did not withhold credit or even operate through the extension of subprime mortgages (reverse redlining). Instead, it proffered a novel mode of city planning and governance in which entire neighborhoods could be deemed too risky for private investment and, in some cases, too risky for the delivery of public services based on their perceived "market strength." In this sense, the MVA risked functioning as a new kind of *municipal* redlining by promoting a mode of racialized governance that operated through calculations of which areas and people promised a good return on investment.

On the whole, areas slated for investment in Detroit were significantly whiter and richer than distressed areas set for "replace, repurpose, and decommission." The Blacker and poorer the neighborhood, the more likely it was to face a reduction of or disconnection from public services.[42] These dynamics underscore how the value of whiteness is predicated on the devaluation of Blackness, or, as Katharyne Mitchell has argued, how whiteness is constituted by one's ability to manage future risk, whereas Blackness is demarcated as high risk or, in the lexicon of the MVA, distressed markets.[43] They also recall how, as Asha Best and Margaret M. Ramírez write, "property, as a racial capitalist social construct, extracts value from the continually 'reorganizing' of Black life." This happens through practices like urban renewal and forced displacement as well as quieter mechanisms like the MVA's alteration of resource flows.[44]

While the MVA is ostensibly an evaluation of markets, strategies developed from its classification schema run the danger of positioning neighborhoods deemed distressed to be unworthy of economic investment. By extension, then, the people living in them risk being cast as improper economic subjects and, thus, as expendable or, at best, improvable. In short, the MVA acts as a sorting mechanism: it sorts out which neighborhoods (and the people living in them) are too risky for private investment and public works and which are a worthwhile risk. What happens when a neighborhood is not a worthwhile risk?

When a Reading (Misreading) of the Landscape
Becomes the Landscape

In 2012, I met with Angie Mead, who was then the manager of Detroit's General Service Department, in her office on Belle Isle, an island park often referred to as Detroit's crown jewel.[45] Amid seeds, tools, and equipment, she explained how keeping nature at bay in the city was a constant battle for residents and city workers.

When Mead began working for the department in 2009, the city coordinated the mowing of approximately 50,000 lots. Over three years, the number increased to 120,000. It was a logistical nightmare to keep track of which lots were public and private. Whereas the city used to mow only public lots, they had decided for the sake of expediency to cut all unmowed grass regardless of ownership. This was good in theory but bad in practice. They worked with private contractors who were suddenly cutting three times as many lots as before. They couldn't keep up. The situation became unmanageable.

At this point, Mead pulled out a large copy of the MVA map. In comparison to the map that I'd seen on the walls of government officials, this one was well used. It was laminated, streaked with fingerprints, and crinkled at the edges. She explained that the map had been distributed to all city departments with a mandate to modify service delivery based on the new market zones. The map helped her prioritize where to mow. In "distressed" and "varied" market areas, contractors had scaled back to windowpane cuts, which at a minimum gave cars visibility. A windowpane cut entailed trimming only street corners by one tractor width. It could be done quickly. By contrast, in "steady" and "transitional" market areas, contractors continued mowing in full. A full cut differed from the typical mowed lawns. It reduced the grass to a jagged stubble but did not prepare it for residential or social use, a task that fell on residents.

Mead suggested we drive around so I could see the effects of the mowing changes. She narrated the landscape as she drove, pointing out where the factories used to be, how some houses were clearly empty, but others, it was uncertain. As we maneuvered slowly through East Side neighborhoods, I thought about how shifts in state maintenance served as a proxy for changes in global capitalism. Mead was in effect narrating the political ecological outcomes of the MVA.[46]

Mead had been relieved to receive the MVA. Like others whom I interviewed, she said it made her job easier because it gave her a decision-making protocol. But it also made her anxious for the people who lived in the neighborhoods deemed "distressed" markets. They still needed services.

"Distressed" areas, she wanted me to know, were by no means vacant, a fact evidence by the public outcry when the General Services Department sent a letter to residents to alert them to changes in mowing services. The city set up a call center to make residents feel heard, but their complaints would have no bearing on public policy. Over a hundred calls came in each week, with more directed to the mayor's office and the General Services Department office. "The calls were overwhelming," Mead said. "It would take up to two months to return the calls, if they [were] returned at all." Many were not. The state's lack of responsiveness troubled Mead.

Driving within an area designated distressed by the MVA, we passed rows of seemingly inhabited and well-cared-for houses, demonstrating how the heterogenous conditions on the ground exceeded the simplicity of the map. One block over, Mead stopped the truck on a particularly deserted street and gestured to the expanse. "On some blocks there will just be one house, . . . but people don't want to move. Some of them do, but others don't—and others can't. You can't move a ninety-year-old; she'll die," she said matter-of-factly. "But if the ninety-year-old who is living on a block by herself went out and yelled, no one would hear her."

Landscape maintenance, in its presence and absence, indexed the top-down, market-driven political priorities and values that were reshaping Detroit's urban landscape and the lives of the people who occupied it. Mead explained how, over the course of a season, brush can grow so high that it obscures houses. "If a lot is unattended, there will be weeds up to your knees in three months. After five or six months, saplings will have started to take over."

The tree of heaven, *Ailanthus altissima*, known locally by the derisive nicknames "ghetto palm" and "stink tree" (for its smell) was particularly destructive. It was brought to the United States in the 1700s from China and Taiwan and planted extensively for shade in cities, including Detroit, only to be identified later as invasive. It now thrived in rubble areas and vacant lots, where its aggressive root system damaged pavement, sewers, pipes, and building foundations. If *Ailanthus altissima* had had such an unintended effect on the built environment, I wondered, what might be the effects generations from now of landscape maintenance decisions made under the logics of the MVA?

Before my tour with Mead, I understood that the MVA had the potential to radically reshape the distribution of services in Detroit. I had not realized, however, how the new mowing regime was, in effect, a decision to cede "distressed" areas to nature, even though they were still inhabited. As much as these decisions were about keeping the brush down, they were also long-term decisions about where to support settlement and what areas to "let go"—or abandon.

Displacement is often understood as people being pushed out of place. The case of the MVA elucidated a new kind of infrastructural displacement at work in the twenty-first-century city. Rather than residents being pushed out of place, entire neighborhoods—and their inhabitants—risked being disconnected from public works and services in the name of making other areas stronger. In this scenario, people were not being forced to move—or compensated—but were being left behind.[47] This did not happen all at once. In Detroit, it was a gradual and organized process that the MVA helped facilitate.

Mowing—or the lack of mowing—signaled this new kind of displacement. The city's decision not to mow certain areas, like a large swath of the East Side, marked the first stage of abandonment and withdrawal of care from neighborhoods deemed not to carry the promise of future market value. In a material sense, then, the decision not to mow reproduced the MVA map on the ground, fragmenting the city into developed and underdeveloped areas. Put simply, the map's reading (or misreading) of the landscape became the landscape.

*

As plans for Detroit's future progressed, the MVA became the foundation for the territorial reordering of the city. While bureaucrats were careful to distance themselves from the language of rightsizing, city officials used the MVA to rationalize investment and disinvestment in technical rather than political terms and to allocate scarce resources with more geographical precision. The MVA also came to dramatically shape the Detroit Future City (DFC) Strategic Framework plan that resulted from the participatory arm of the DWP.

The fifty-year citywide plan, which was released in December 2012, aimed to solve the city's spatial mismatch through urban greening. If past proposals to revert large swaths of the urban landscape to nature had been controversial, the DWP presented it in a new green veneer. Rightsizing was no longer simply downsizing. It was also sustainability.[48]

The land-use typology promised a "new garden (and blue) city identity" that would reshape perceptions of Detroit. Residents of the "future city" would be connected to jobs and services across a "canvas of green" that included "stately boulevards, open green space, urban woodlands, ponds and streams, and new uses of natural landscape to clean the air, restore ecological habitats, and produce locally sourced food."[49] The plan's ecological vision was laudable and appealing; however, it elided the significant redistributive politics associated with the attendant retraction of public works and service delivery that the MVA made clear.[50]

This elision was particularly ironic given that the three-hundred-plus-page DFC plan revolved around a reconceptualization of the urban landscape as infrastructure. The plan reflected an emerging urban mandate to replace monofunctional traditional "gray" infrastructures with polyfunctional "green" and "blue" infrastructures that were intended to work with nature to achieve multiple benefits.[51] For example, an urban green space might be designed to manage storm water, sequester carbon, provide a space for recreation, reduce crime, and, notably, raise property values.[52]

As this definition makes clear, green infrastructure was about more than ecological sustainability. In market terms, it created the conditions of possibility for previously devalued spaces to become valuable. It also functioned as a biopolitical and territorializing project through which the city's population and economy could be managed in a new era of austerity. But, as we will see in the next chapter, it wasn't just rolled out carte blanche. It came into conflict with how communities had been repurposing landscapes for decades to serve their needs and as the basis for another politics.

the garden is
a weapon in the war

The July sunlight filtered into the dim room through pale pink blinds on the windows facing Field Street. It made geometric patterns on the burgundy-colored carpet and glinted against the framed artwork and portraits that hung from muted blue walls. Grace Lee Boggs sat slightly hunched in a worn armchair, eyeglasses dangling from her neck. A notepad was balanced on the armrest. Shelves overflowing with books, vinyl records, and stacks of papers lined the room, serving as a testament to James and Grace Lee Boggs's lifetime of organizing and to the central place that their living room held for the local activist community.

At ninety-seven, Grace was still sharp. She continued to write and organize. After James (known to many as Jimmy) passed away in 1993, she had achieved a minor celebrity status in activist circles, which, as much as she relished it, she described as taking her by surprise.[1]

I sat with ten others in a semicircle around Grace. We had come to have a conversation as part of a two-week-long gathering called Detroit 2012, organized by the James and Grace Lee Boggs Center to Nurture Community Leadership. The gathering aimed to engage several big questions: What kind of society do we want? What kind of economy can we build? What sort

Figure 8.1 (opposite) | Photograph of an urban garden, 2012. *Source:* Author photo.

of education do we need? These questions, the organizers argued, required thought, conversation, and reflection on practice.

"Most people don't associate transformation with revolutions. They make them seem different," said Grace. "It's not only about being against, but about transforming institutions and ourselves. Transformation needs to be integral to revolution." Grace grew animated as she explained how the rebellions of the 1960s forced her to begin thinking about the distinction between rebellion and revolution, referring us to a chapter on dialectics in her and Jimmy's book *Revolution and Evolution in the Twentieth Century*.

Published in 1974, the book was a sweeping indictment of US imperialism, neocolonialism, multinational capitalism, and the military industrial complex. They argued that economic development would not solve society's most pressing problems, nor would labor unions, which too often capitulated to management. Instead, they implored readers to think both internationally about revolution and historically about the relative newness of the United States as a political experiment. The kind of revolution needed, they argued, required a "revolutionary political apparatus" that would allow the people to make decisions about land control and reorganize state institutions.[2] It also required that people have a vision of what to do with such power.

An excerpt from *Revolution and Evolution in the Twentieth Century* had been in the precirculated pamphlet that we were supposed to have read prior to our conversation with Grace. The pamphlet, *(R)evolution in the 21st Century*, included a selection of essays by Grace and older pieces she had coauthored with Jimmy. Organizers of Detroit 2012 hoped the pamphlet would spark discussion about the kind of social change demanded by a new century.

"It's difficult to do anything different than protest unless you project an alternative. Not everyone will grab on, but some will. We're responsible for the American Revolution," Grace said, before pausing to do introductions and take questions. The first one came from a student named Hannah, who was considering relocating to Detroit to become involved in activism. She asked Grace her thoughts about urban farming and what it might look like to reclaim the city for the people.

By 2012, Detroit had become a mecca for urban farming—a city transitioning from Motown to Growtown, as headlines put it. Urban farming occupied an outsized place in the national and international media. A diverse range of actors—from activists to planners and financiers to foundations—touted its potential. The city boasted more than a thousand registered community gardens and thousands of unregistered family, school, and church gardens. A widely cited study from 2010 estimated that the city, county, and state governments owned more than 4,800 acres that could potentially be cultivated, just a fraction of which would be necessary to meet residents' fresh vegetable and fruit needs.[3]

As the American Institute of Architects put it, Detroit was "particularly well suited to become a pioneer in urban agriculture at a commercial scale."[4] The excitement around postindustrial agrarianism ignited debate over whether it might save Detroit and other declining cities.[5]

In contrast to the city's "ruins," gardens served as potent symbols of rebirth, as illustrated by the pervasiveness of images in the media of sunflowers poking through rubble, vegetable patches becoming oases in food deserts, horses grazing on urban prairie grass, and tractors idling on empty city streets. I'd been trying to understand what lay beneath the surface of this postindustrial pastoral sublime, so I was interested in Grace's thoughts on Hannah's question.

Grace responded emphatically: "We are bringing the country back into the city in Detroit. . . . When people can feed themselves, they can free themselves. *How* we bring the country back into the city is the question we need to ask."

I agreed. The question of *how* was crucial. Not all urban agriculture projects were alike. For old-timers in low-income communities, urban gardens had long been a form of sustenance. By the aughts, however, particularly for a younger generation skeptical of institutional and state reform beyond the local, urban gardens had become a form of place-based political action. Meanwhile, dozens of foundations and nonprofit organizations had begun to support food production and greening in the city, raising concerns about philanthropic accountability and long-term sustainability. In the absence of a broader class-based political response, it seemed clear that urban agriculture initiatives—and sustainability initiatives more broadly—would pave the road for new waves of privatization and gentrification.[6]

Most of the gardens in Detroit were still small. But hype over the city's agricultural potential was beginning to attract new actors who ranged from young (mostly white) idealistic farmers from outside the city interested in farming a few lots to entrepreneur-investors envisioning larger projects. Among them was financier John Hantz, a former American Express financial manager and owner of Hantz Financial Services, who in 2009 caused a stir when he proposed to build the world's largest urban farm on Detroit's East Side, not far from the Boggses' home.

The proposal to establish a large-scale farm in the symbolic center of industrial capitalism was, in many ways, exceptional. For one, the racial optics of the project were jarring: a wealthy white financier raising a large farm in the nation's largest Black city. For another, it suggested a radically different kind of urban future than its industrial past. Finally, the amount of land that Hantz proposed to buy—so close to the city center at a rock bottom price—was unprecedented.

The proposed farm, which aimed to redefine urban growth, recalled the aspirations of the garden city movement. In the nineteenth century Ebenezer Howard—in a short book, *To-morrow: A Peaceful Path to Real Reform* (1898)—had proposed the development of self-contained company towns outside the city. Howard applied utopian ideas prevalent in late nineteenth- and early twentieth-century literature to planning and architecture: country cottages, schools, and factories, circled by agricultural estates would provide local produce, open space, and fresh air. Voluntary cooperation among villagers would negate the need for a strong state.[7]

Howard's ideas were seductive. They inspired Henry Ford's Village Industries experiment, which aimed to integrate factory and agrarian life, as well as his creation of Greenfield Village, which replicated a small Midwestern town, in an effort to preserve a preindustrial way of life that ironically had largely disappeared in no small part due to Fordism. Both projects reflected Ford's lifelong questioning about what it meant to live right and his own ambivalences about industrial modernity.[8]

Decades later, Hantz's proposal was reminiscent of Howard's garden city. Yet born in the wreckage of Fordism, it was a response to a different era and problem. At the turn of the twentieth century, Howard sought to alleviate the entwined crises of rural depopulation and urban overcrowding. By contrast, at the outset of the twenty-first, Hantz sought an antidote to deindustrialization, urban depopulation, and depressed real estate markets.

Advocates of the garden city embraced it as a "spatial palliative"—a way to curb labor discontentment and restore the health of the urban working class, seen as at risk for physical and social degeneration due to industrial overcrowding.[9] At the same time, an investor-backed community trust would buy land for new garden cities. Inspired by both socialist ideas and also the radical economist Henry George, who argued for the single tax, Howard proposed that rents fund public works, services, improvement, and, eventually, residential ownership of the land.[10] More than a century later, Hantz's proposal echoed Howard's ambition, but it turned on a radically different philosophy of land ownership. For Hantz, farming was a strategy to privatize land (not, as Howard had proposed, to turn it into common property). It was also a way to circumvent the inefficiencies of local government and, in so doing, make Detroit more "livable."

Hantz's proposal struck a chord in the region, eliciting hope, anticipation, promise, anxiety, bewilderment, and resistance. Some saw it as a creative and benevolent effort to deal with vacant land. Others worried that a large farm would attract rodents. Some argued that Detroit needed industry, not urban farming. Reverend Jesse Jackson called it "cute but foolish."[11] Meanwhile, activists charged Hantz with orchestrating a land grab that capitalized on grassroots agrarian projects decades in the making.

On its face, the Hantz Farms debate appeared to be an issue of land access and resource distribution. But it stood for much more. If in the 1960s, racialized labor regimes and the residential color line were key sites of contestation, the controversy over Hantz—and postindustrial agriculture more generally—suggested that urban land and nature had become new sites of social struggle. Indeed, the question of *how* the country was to be brought back into the city, as Grace framed it, was, above all, a deeply political and spiritual question of how to live and organize society.

Postindustrial Agrarianism and the Question of How to Organize Society

I first read about the Hantz Farms project in a glossy 2009 *Fortune* magazine article entitled "Can Farming Save Detroit?" The image that accompanied the piece was an architectural rendering for the age of ecomodernism: white high rises with hard angles were adorned with solar panels and hanging vegetation. Hydroponic geodesic domes. Sleek windmills. Garden pods. Enclosed walkways, but no people. A red tram—a replica of the city's People Mover—circled above monocrop fields.[12]

The origin myth of Hantz Farms, as told by its founder, went like this: Every morning, the middle-aged white financier drove through the city to the planning and investment firm he owned in the suburbs. One morning, he realized that the mismatch between Detroit's population size and spatial footprint was a problem of supply and demand. With almost thirty thousand acres of abandoned land in Detroit, he thought, there is no incentive to buy real estate, because every year it became cheaper. He then pledged $30 million to build "the world's largest urban farm." Reducing the supply of land on the market, he reasoned, would drive up real estate prices, which would, in turn, give buyers a reason to act, promote development, and make the city more livable.

After reading the *Fortune* piece, I Googled the project and encountered a different aesthetic. Hantz's website featured a photograph of a verdant monocrop cornfield that looked like it could have been Iowa with the title, "Introducing Hantz Farms: Detroit is about to redefine urban growth."

It reminded me of cultural historian Leo Marx's trope of the "machine in the garden," an image that captured tensions between the pastoral ideal and nineteenth-century industrialization and debates over which version would win out. What did its transposition—the garden in the machine—suggest about the changing nature of postindustrial land?[13]

These thoughts about global capitalism and altered landscapes were on my mind as Grace discussed Detroit's agrarian turn.

"Detroit has been a symbol of American industrialization," she said.

"Now it is an international and national symbol of postindustrial society. To understand the character of a particular locality, it is important to relate it to bigger forces. We have brains that can move from the concrete to the abstract. The key is to always return to the concrete."

"Some people are just interested in gardening. But the way it came about is key to thinking about organizing. When my husband worked at Chrysler, he used to say if you threw a stone up in the air, you'd hit a Chrysler worker. There were three thousand workers under one roof. When you throw a stone up in the air now, it is not landing on a factory but an empty building."

Grace explained that when Jimmy wrote *The American Revolution: Pages from a Negro Worker's Notebook*, he was trying to think through these precise questions.[14] The book offered one of the earliest leftist analyses of the far-reaching implications of American industrial transformation and postindustrial decline.[15] This was several years before their publication of "The City Is the Black Man's Land" (1966), which, recall from chapter 2, issued a sweeping call to politically and territorially reorganize the city from the bottom up.

The *American Revolution* captured not only a local but also a world phenomenon, said Grace, remarking on its translation into six different languages—French, Italian, Japanese, Spanish, Catalan, and Portuguese. As evidence of its continued import, just a few years prior, in 2009, Monthly Review Press had issued a new edition. New commentary—by Grace and other Detroit activists associated with the Boggs Center—insisted that the questions Jimmy had been asking a half century ago had only grown more urgent, as had his analysis of what it meant to confront them.[16]

Originally from Marion Junction, Alabama, Jimmy Boggs joined the Great Migration north in search of employment in 1937. He became a lifelong autoworker, political activist, and public intellectual. Laboring under the specter of automation, Jimmy foresaw the collapse of industrial labor long before most.[17]

Detroit, once a heartland of industry and unionism, was fertile ground for thinking not only about their decline but also about the revolutionary possibilities that came with the advent of so-called postindustrial society. That term is often associated with two landmark texts—Daniel Bell's *The Coming of the Post-Industrial Society* (1973) and Alain Touraine's *The Postindustrial Society* (1971). The phenomenon was debated decades before the publication of these works, however, particularly among liberals and the New Left.[18]

In the 1950s and 1960s, the rise of cybernetics and automation gave rise to both dystopian and utopian visions of how technological changes would affect labor relations and society writ large. Would automation bring affluence or social exclusion? Would it improve or deteriorate working conditions—or end work altogether? How would the new leisure classes spend their time? How might progressive visions for social change be articulated through technological transformation?[19]

These questions motivated an ad hoc committee of thirty-two social critics, educators, economists, and scholars to issue the *Manifesto for Triple Revolution*.[20] Among the authors were James Boggs, economist and sociologist Gunnar Myrdal, and democratic socialist writer and activist Michael Harrington. The manifesto sought to address the social dilemmas associated with automation and the implications of three intertwined revolutions—"the cybernation revolution of increasing automation; the weaponry revolution of mutually assured destruction; and the human rights revolution."[21]

Among the policy changes needed, the committee argued, was for every American to have the right to a guaranteed adequate income. "The traditional link between jobs and incomes is broken," they wrote. The committee worked to widely disseminate the manifesto, which was originally published in the New Left magazine *Liberation* in 1964, including presenting it to then-president Lyndon B. Johnson and circulating it to members of Congress.[22]

The concerns of the *American Revolution* run through the manifesto. One of Boggs's insights was that automation and the decentralization of production were counterrevolutionary responses to the growing power of radical labor and Black liberation movements. Detroit was a case in point. Recognized internationally as a hub of militant organizing, by 1947 it was also the site of

Ford Motor Company's first Automation Department, an attempt to fix the crisis of labor power by replacing workers with machines.[23]

As an autoworker himself, Boggs was fundamentally concerned with how automation affected the lives of workers, especially their ability to resist and organize.[24] He was adamant that technological restructuring represented a new stage in industrial production, one that dramatically diminished worker power within the factory and in US politics generally. Boggs worried that under automation, workers, particularly Black workers, would go from exploited to redundant. He also predicted accurately that automation would increase racial and ethnic tensions among workers, creating challenges for solidarity.

Notably, Boggs did not simply criticize automation and cybernetic command. He was optimistic about their revolutionary potential to abolish capitalism. This, however, required rethinking Leftist strategies rooted in Marxist traditions that focused on uniting the working class. Specifically, he grappled with the social and political implications of obsolescence. What happens when people don't need to work anymore? How should the Left— long rooted in labor politics—develop new social movement–organizing infrastructures for an age of permanent unemployment? Could young people who were unable to find work be transformed into agents of social change? Might the decrease in socially necessary labor time lead to new anticapitalist, cooperative arrangements?

These were the kinds of immodest questions and propositions to which the Boggses dedicated their lifework. In their writings, they laid bare the interconnectivity of production, governance, and social reproduction that some advocates of urban agriculture in early twenty-first-century Detroit overlooked when localizing production was seen as progressive politics unto itself. They argued that the postindustrial conjuncture required people to confront their own consumerism, individualism, and moral depravity. Cooperative relationships were needed that would foment and sustain a new value system, new modes of being, and new visions for society.[25]

The Boggses, in an effort to cultivate and sustain such changes, as I discussed in chapter 2, helped form groups to remove drug dealers from Detroit's neighborhoods. They led study groups. They theorized and wrote prolifically. They served as mentors and teachers for generations of activists. They set up youth programs to reimagine activism and political participation.[26] They saw activism with Black youth and youth engagement in general as part of a strategy to break from racial capitalism and to restructure community values, actions, institutions, and systems of governance. It was with this orientation toward the future, grounded in the Black radical tradition and dialectical thinking, that Grace approached Detroit's contemporary agrarian questions.

When I asked Grace about Hantz's proposal, her answer was succinct: "We will learn a lot from the struggle. It's a question of how the struggle will be used for learning."

I suspected Grace was right. Neither Hantz nor the future of Detroit were forgone conclusions. Rather, they would emerge, to be sure, from the articulation of multiple local struggles, the outcomes of which could not be known in advance.[27]

One thing I took away from my time in Detroit was that struggles are important sites of learning because they reveal lines of force, antagonisms, and possibilities for organizing power relations differently. There is a "collective intelligence gathered from struggle," to borrow the words of philosopher Ernst Bloch, that can inform efforts to build community in ways that counter and heal the damage caused by oppressive systems. This is why Grace's question of *how* the country was being brought back into the city was so important. It was not just a question of land control but a foundational question of what it takes to cultivate community capacities capable of revolutionary change and sustaining new modes of life.

Making Sense of the Country in the City

Detroit's postindustrial landscape confounded sensibilities born from the city/country divide. Cultural theorist Raymond Williams argued decades ago that the boundary between them was central to how society conceptualized changes associated with capitalist development. Sixteenth-century English novels, for example, obscured class conflict in the countryside, portraying rural life as pure and unadulterated. By contrast, the city was cast as its "dark mirror," rife with exploitation and alienation. Williams was interested not in the veracity of such myths, nor am I, but rather in how they index society's consciousness of itself and shared interpretations of the animating crises of different historical moments.[28]

For many Detroiters, debates over the place of agriculture in the city turned on the future of "good quality jobs" and the lack of state services and infrastructure. Seen in this light, the acceptance of large-scale urban agriculture signified the acceptance of something bigger: that the industrial era would not be returning.

Hantz marked a shift in postindustrial agrarian capitalism. If the city's rurality had been born from postindustrial obsolescence and people striving to get by, before Hantz, no one planned it as an extractive economy or redevelopment strategy. Agriculture was not new to Detroit, but the proposed scale of it was, as were the hype and tensions surrounding it. As one interviewee said of the publicity that surrounded Detroit's so-called transition from Motown to Growtown, "It's bullshit. People in Detroit have gardened forever." It was true. Gardens had been a mainstay of urban living, if state support waxed and waned. For example, Mayor Hazen Pingree's Potato Patch program in the 1890s encouraged unemployed residents to grow food on public land. The program tapered off in the early 1900s as the economy improved. Then, during World War II, the federal government encouraged the establishment of Victory Gardens, which were planted in the city; but when the war ended, the government stopped its promotion. In the 1970s, Mayor Coleman Young started the Farm-A-Lot program, an effort to put vacant land to use and reconnect city dwellers with their rural Southern roots.[29]

But significantly, residents had also always farmed informally outside these state-supported programs. Local activist Rosa Clayton explained in a Uniting Detroiters interview in 2012 that urban gardens were a part of everyday life. "I think [gardening's] current resurgence comes out of our [Black] resiliency. . . . I think half of Detroit is from Alabama, and they had kitchen gardens. So, you come here, you have a pear tree—you grew tomatoes, you grew peppers."[30]

Some traced Detroit's recent resurgence of agriculture to the 1980s, when the Gardening Angels, a group of mainly African American elders who had grown up farming in the South, began planting flowers and gardens on vacant lots to combat crime and drugs. The Gardening Angels cared for the community by caring for land. They trained young people in agrarian practices and food preservation techniques.[31] Their name and orientation recalled the Guardian Angels, vigilantes in the late 1970s who responded to high crime and the need for safety by organizing foot patrols on the subway and city streets in New York City and then in more than fifty other cities across the United States and Canada.[32] Debates raged over the Guardian Angels—could a volunteeristic bottom-up approach guarantee public safety to millions of urban residents? Simlar questions dominated debates over the form urban agriculture would take in Detroit. Was it a retreat from politics or a political act, as many growers proclaimed?[33] There was no one-size-fits-all answer to this question.

In the early 2010s, people gardened for many reasons: lifestyle, sustenance, income, nutrition, education, resistance, beautification, and sense of community. For some residents, gardening was part of a larger underground economy. Food produced in gardens offered a form of alternative exchange, beyond the capitalist, profit-driven market. Clayton explained it this way,

> On the bartering and economic order, for the thousands of people who do not have a job, so they are here. They eat, and some of them spare change like that is a hustle, like people spare change. But also, people, they fix, they repair. I just left a guy on Gratiot [Street] in an old broke-down parking lot of a business that closed, a lawn mower repair. So, he pulls up in his minivan and puts a sign out, make-a-do, and he just repairs small engines. We got people selling stuff on the side of the road, children selling stuff; we got handy man, handy women; we got fix-it services. Kind of feels like Havana, Cuba, where you get these resiliencies.[34]

Others too explained the gardens as a central way Detroiters grappled with the effects of postindustrial society and labor precarity. As resident Faye Moore put it, gardens were one way of expanding community control over the means of production. "There's no jobs dropping out of the sky, and we've tried this business of being a casino town, an entertainment town, and clearly that's not it. Meanwhile, technology has been evolving in ways that are allowing us on small scales to start producing things we need, . . . which would address not only questions of personal health, but questions around the use of a petroleum-based food production system. . . . When I envision [the future of] Detroit I envision a Detroit of producers and consumers being the same thing."[35]

Food security was high on the list of why people farmed; gardens provided an essential nutritional supplement for poor people. Sam Johnson, who maintained three urban garden plots, explained to us in a Uniting Detroiters interview that urban farming continued a long tradition of Black resilience and self-sufficiency. "I grew up around Tuskegee [Alabama] surrounded by agriculture," he said, "Black boys and Black girls need to be taught how to farm and how to survive. It's necessary for Blacks and Latinos and other poor people in Detroit, but primarily it's good for anyone who's on food stamps."[36] In many Detroit neighborhoods, the primary food outlets have been "party stores" (liquor stores that carry some food items), gas stations, fast-food restaurants, and grocery stores notorious for price gouging. Thus, food justice advocates argued that Detroit suffered from supermarket redlining, meaning that after assessing risks and profits, supermarkets relocate or raise prices.[37] With an inadequate public transportation system and high rates of poverty, access to nutritional, culturally appropriate food was an urgent matter.

For many Black growers, urban agriculture was an important practice of political self-determination. Sociologist Monica White has shown how Black farming is a strategy of resistance and how urban farms act as community centers where participants work to constructively improve the daily existence of residents.[38] Malik Yakini, director of the Detroit Black Community Food Security Network, which runs a seven-acre farm called D-Town in Rouge Park on the city's far West Side, explained their work this way: "One of the major messages we carry is that we have the capacity to produce our own food, to distribute our own food, to process our own food, that we're not just victims or pawns on the chess board where these more powerful forces move us around, that we actually have the capacity to define our own reality."[39]

Cultivating such capacity entailed developing a robust, community-controlled urban agriculture system, challenging systemic inequities in access to capital and grant funding, and securing land tenure. Many small farmers rented land, had informal agreements with owners, leased land from the city, or, in some cases, squatted on land. Concerns among smallholders over precarious land tenure became more pronounced as the city's agricultural potential attracted young (mostly white) idealistic farmers from outside the city interested in market gardens, along with entrepreneur-investors, who saw Detroit's condemned lots as a prime location for the large-scale production of food, fuel, and fiber.

Hantz Farms represented the latter. By the time I sat down with Grace, tensions had grown over this sleek, well-financed, and wildly speculative form of postindustrial agrarianism. The best way to understand these antagonisms—and more importantly, to understand why some community gardens served as everyday sites of radical resistance—is to visit one.

Plotting the World Anew

Feedom Freedom Growers is a small place. Founded in 2009 by Wayne Curtis and Myrtle Thompson-Curtis, the community garden located in the Jefferson Chalmers neighborhood on the city's East Side, consists of about two dozen raised garden beds, a large hoop house, and an extensive composting station. A dozen or more wooden crated bins hold organic material in various states of decomposition. Brightly colored benches and signs are interspersed throughout the garden, which had become a gathering spot for local residents and passersby. The smallness of the plot belied the extensive networks that Wayne and Myrtle had developed in their neighborhood, throughout the city, and beyond.

As part of the garden, they offered various programming: art in the garden days, cooking classes, a winter coat drive, and a youth program that integrated agricultural training and political education. The impetus for projects like Feedom Freedom contrasted sharply with that of Hantz Farms. While for Hantz, the goal of urban farming was a property market correction, for Feedom Freedom and other Black radical farming projects like D-Town Farms, it was about political organizing via agriculture and creating a community infrastructure that supported Black life.[40]

During my fieldwork, I occasionally volunteered at Feedom Freedom and became friendly with Wayne and Myrtle, who are part of the Black radical intelligentsia and activist community in Detroit. They are capacious thinkers who engage in theorizing as a part of everyday life. Feedom Freedom served as a community classroom without walls. It was common for Wayne and Myrtle to invite volunteers to join in collective study. They made reading recommendations and solicited them from others. They approached newcomers like me with an openness and generosity that suggested the garden was as much about growing relationships and expanding collective consciousness as it was about food.

One morning in November 2011, I asked Wayne about the origins of Feedom Freedom. It was a warm day in the garden under a blue sky. A slight breeze rustled the trees, making rays of sunlight dance over the vegetable beds that we were preparing for winter. Wayne is an artist. He is quick to smile and has gray dreadlocks that reach down his back. He often philosophized as he worked, drawing visitors into deep analyses of the contemporary political conjuncture and what it means to effect change.[41]

Wayne described how Feedom Freedom stemmed, in part, from his involvement in the Black Panther Party, which he had joined in 1970. "I sold newspapers, which is important. I read. I talked to people, created an environment so that the survival programs could operate here in Detroit. Going door to door, downtown, creating routes for people to contribute to the program."

"What did the configuration of the party look like here when you joined?" I asked.

"It looked like, it looked like war," Wayne replied, pausing. "Because that's the frame of mind I was in. That's how I saw it. But as I became more involved . . . war took on a different concept. War of offense, war of defense, war of strategy, there was a whole infrastructure, which I . . . I didn't know those words then."

Between 1968 and 1972, the Black Panther Intercommunal News Service distributed more than 200,000 copies of its weekly newspaper. The periodical featured current events relevant to the party's struggle and highlighted their service to the community.[42] Wayne emphasized that the aim of the publication was not simply to disseminate the news but also to establish community relationships, cultivate an ethic of responsibility, and create an infrastructure that would support the party's survival programs. The survival programs, as explained in chapter 2, were designed to raise political consciousness while providing for basic needs, for example, food, shoes, health care, education, and various services (plumbing, legal, and electrical). Through political education and everyday social reproduction, the BPP sought to create liberated territory and escape the oppression of US empire.

Like the BPP, Feedom Freedom has a basic-needs orientation and a crucial, if humble, agenda for community self-determination, which began with creating spaces that fostered "face-to-face relationships in the neighborhood." It is also oriented by a radical engagement with ecology and a recognition of the entanglement of human and environmental futures. While Wayne drew connections between Feedom Freedom and the BPP's conceptualization of liberated territory, he was quick to point out that times had changed. In its heyday the BPP received donations from businesses (sometimes under extortion) for its survival programs. But, as Wayne pointed out, many of those businesses no longer existed. He wanted me to understand that the situation had changed, but the same political economic forces persisted. "The plantation is still here, the relationship between us and the corporate community is still here, the suffering . . . lack of ability to determine your own destiny."

Wayne challenged me to think more deeply about what it takes to undo regimes of racial and spatial violence and their associated systems of knowledge. The shift in land and labor regimes—from the plantations in which enslaved people were forced to labor, to automotive "plants" that drew masses of laborers, to Hantz's proposed woodlands, which required little labor but lots of land—suggested that their undoing was multilayered. It required reworking not only extractive spatial and ecological relationships but also forms of political subjectivity and personhood and ways of inhabiting the earth that had been forged through violence.

"The garden is a weapon in the war," Wayne said to me. "The struggle is nothing new. We've been struggling for a long time."

Wayne's poetic inversion of the *garden as a weapon* upturned images typically associated with war: guns, bombs, maimed bodies. It was a political commentary on the permanent war on Black life since slavery and Emancipation, and the everyday war of power relations that we are all subject to and participants in, in ways that result in drastically different life and death outcomes. It also indexed the garden as a historical infrastructure of Black resistance.

In the eighteenth and nineteenth centuries, garden plots on plantations and in work camps were where enslaved people and laborers nurtured life on their own terms. J. T. Roanne writes, following Sylvia Wynter, that it was through the plot and "fugitive practices of plotting" that "captive Black communities renegotiated the terrain of radical exploitation and totalizing social control envisioned by slave masters . . ."[43] After Emancipation, the Black community continued "plotting," in Roanne's terms, to acquire land and build their own community infrastructures to ensure some measure of self-determination.

This infrastructural work was extensive, as political economist Jessica Nembhard has documented. It included Black cooperative grocery stores, warehouses, and credit unions; mutual insurance companies; gas stations; schools; and, notably, farm co-ops. The BPP continued the tradition of cooperative economics through cooperative housing, cooperative bakeries, the free breakfast program for children, among other services, and notably by weaving political education into its programs.[44]

Wayne recalled how study groups were central to the BPP. "It was so painstaking reading out loud, and, oh God, they wouldn't tolerate anything else." They would read texts, line by line, and talk about them. Wayne told me that if he didn't understand something, he'd read the passage again and again for the next few days. His comrades told him he didn't need to do this, but he explained that at the time, he thought he needed to correct himself. "If we want to have community control, we all we got, " Wayne explained. "We're going to have to find ways of healing ourselves going forward."

For me, Wayne's comment about healing conveyed a broader concept: the ways people respond to stimuli and conflicts, human codes of conduct and behavior, are inherited. They are, as he puts it, "physiological hand-me-downs." But they are also adaptive. New feedback loops and behaviors—and ways of being human—can be established.[45]

Indeed, the days I spent at Feedom Freedom taught me that the garden was about more than growing vegetables; it was about growing new socioecological relationships beyond proprietary logics. At a time when collective gathering spaces were shrinking, Feedom Freedom was a space for community. It was a space that nurtured the reinvention of selves and worlds. Jessi

Quizar has aptly described the work of Feedom Freedom as offering a "logic of care," which she describes as a "system of analysis, politics, collective understanding, and collective common sense."[46] Such embodied and emplaced care work suggests the necessity of reciprocal socio-ecological relationships to sustaining modes of life that can flourish as antidotes to abandonment.

I finished the work day at Feedom Freedom by gathering armfuls of sweet-smelling straw to cover the upturned soil, leaving it to rest until the ground thawed in the spring. Wayne went to check the compost. Myrtle finished her work in the greenhouse, harvesting salad greens with a group of young people. A neighbor dropped by to say hello. Wayne went to greet him, and it was not long before they had leaped deep into conversation.

The Forest for the Trees, and the Politics of Improvement

Days at Feedom Freedom and my chats with Wayne often made me ponder philosophical questions about the long, slow work of building community and the importance of place. They also attuned me to the normative moral assumptions that undergirded competing imaginaries for the city's future. These thoughts were on my mind when I interviewed Mike Score, the president of Hantz Farms, in June 2012.

The company's office was in an unassuming windowless brick building on Detroit's East Side. Its front held a hardware store set up to service the hundreds of properties that Hantz owned. It was also open a few days a week to the community. Score, a white man with a long thin face and trimmed gray beard, was clad in Carhartt workwear. We chatted in his office over a wooden table with coffee brewing at one end.

Score was born in Detroit. In the 1960s, his family moved to the suburban town of Warren, on the outskirts of the city. He spent decades working on rural development projects that ranged from cattle production in the Congo to mining reclamation in West Virginia. In 1997, Score took a job with Michigan State University. He was working in agricultural extension and outreach when Hantz approached the agency about developing a business plan. Score took the job. He considered it an opportunity to apply his expertise in a very different context.[47]

John Hantz's vision had changed forms over time, Score explained. The most grandiose was a plan for a five-thousand-acre complex to integrate vegetable, fruit, timber, and biofuels production, agritourism, and a hydroponic

Figure 8.2 | Hantz demonstration area in 2012 with skinny saplings spaced twelve feet apart. *Source:* Author photo.

and aeroponic research center. Hantz ultimately settled on a comparatively humble plan to establish 180 acres of woodlands.

Score led me across the street to tour their demonstration plot. From afar, it looked like any other vacant lot in Detroit. Once I got closer, I was able to see the skinny saplings. Score noted that they mowed it once a week, explaining that it used to be overgrown with a thicket of paulownia trees, mulberries, and box elders. It was a quiet afternoon save the staccato rhythm of crickets. I noticed the Queen Anne's lace blooming, the wind swaying its white tops. The sight of the juvenile trees, held up by poles (figure 8.2), seemed at odds with the outsized controversy that surrounded them. Score told me that the plan was to buy tax-foreclosed lots from the city, demolish any buildings, and then plant native hardwoods: sugar maples, swamp oaks, bur oaks, white birch, flowering dogwoods. In sixty years, the trees would be sold for lumber. After they planted the full woodlands, they planned to intercrop hostas, ginseng, and morels. They also hoped to sell carbon credits. Score was passionate about the project, and his enthusiasm felt contagious. I tried to imagine walking through the forest understory, picking mushrooms and prying ginseng root from the dirt. In many ways, it was easy to be attracted to the design. Cities, after all, are more hospitable with green space; morels are also delicious.

That said, to be seduced by the projected landscape would be to miss the end game and bigger meaning of the story: how, that is, the fledgling forest was a means of instantiating a new property regime and form of capitalist accumulation and extraction. If the woodlands tapped the agrarian pastoral idyll that Williams critiqued and Ford yearned for, the trees' gridlike formation suggested a form of control that was inherently capitalist. That said, the primary intention of the project was not timber production, per se, but a green fix for depressed real estate markets.

As Score walked me around the plot, I thought about how postindustrial forests—like all managed forests—are not simply resources or environmental goods. Rather, they reflect how formations of capital accumulation shift in response to crisis. Hantz's new form of urban forestry, like its precursors, turned on racialized dispossession, exploitation, and extraction couched in the vernacular of improvement. Take, for instance, the early lumber boom in Michigan. After the Erie Canal opened in 1825, logging companies, unable to meet growing demand for lumber by clearing the forests of New York and Maine, moved west to the next stretch of the great pine belt. On the logging frontier, lumber extraction and property making went hand in hand. Indeed, lumber extraction was a huge motivation for the government's establishment of a regional private property system. The incipient state and federal government used complex bureaucratic maneuvers and violence to break Indigenous control over the forest, including creating allotments and codifying rules about who could and could not own property as a pretext for opening the land to lumber capitalists.[48]

The Great Lakes lumber frontier was lucrative. By the late 1860s, Michigan emerged as the number one lumber-producing state in the nation. *Pinus strobus* logs, known as "green gold," filled the 130-mile length of the Tittabawasee River from Midland to Saginaw, where it was said one could walk from log to log without touching water or land.[49] Midwestern cities were built on Michigan's lumber trade, supposedly creating more millionaires than the California gold rush. The boom quickly went bust, however, leaving behind barren and eroded landscapes, which by the 1970s were ablaze with wildfire. Meanwhile, capital moved on. Lumber barons, needing places to invest, turned to the emerging automobile industry in Detroit, including Ford Motor Company, demonstrating the power of finance capital to weather economic crisis by seeking out new frontiers. As the company grew, so too did the modern liberal state, with its infrastructural investments, including establishing a commission to oversee the city's parks and a nursery for growing tress (one of the first municipally-owned nurseries in the country). Elms, maples, oaks, and chestnuts soon shaded Detroit's wide boulevards.[50]

If in the twentieth century, urban trees stood for the extended realm of the state, by the twenty-first century, they indexed its rollback—but a green version of it. The rollback, however, was highly uneven. Austerity, after all, is not the retreat of the state writ large but a reduction of its welfare and distributional capacities in favor of private interests. The neatly demarcated rows of trees in Hantz's woodlands were a reminder of how, under austerity urbanism, capitalists make use of ecological fixes as they wait for markets to ripen. The woodlands abstracted green space to facilitate the eventual extraction of exchange value. It should come as no surprise, then, that the land was in an area deemed a distressed market according to the Market Value Analysis. Recall from chapter 7 that the local government wanted to provide few services in these areas. It was also slated for "innovative green production" as part of the broader city planning process.

The project was clearly about capital accumulation, but profit seeking didn't explain it all. Hantz could have made money off his money in other ways. As a multimillionaire, Hantz didn't need to make money with this project, said Score. He just wanted to break even and have a positive impact by making the city more "livable."

From Livability to Living Otherwise

Livability has become a catchall term for urban improvement. In the face of rapid urbanization, livable indices are often associated with greening and sustainability. But livability discourses, as Aimi Hamraie reminds us, are loaded with racial, economic, gendered, and ability exclusions. Places deemed unlivable cannot be separated from the marginalized bodies who occupy those spaces.[51]

According to Score, many of Detroit's neighborhoods were not livable because the city owned most of the land. Blight decimated the exchange value of homes. It also spread negative perceptions about the people who lived nearby.

"Imagine if you had a family reunion, and people were coming from Chicago and Columbus, Atlanta. You can't host a family reunion at your house because it's an embarrassment. People will think you've failed in life because none of the lots next to your house are mowed. There are boats and tires and cars parked in the field next to your house." Crucially, for Score, making Detroit more livable meant transferring property from the city to private ownership because the government didn't have resources, staff, or expertise to manage it, nor did they care. "The dangerous structures have to be taken out. The thickets in the alleys have to be taken out. The lots need to be cleaned up. The grass needs to be mowed. So that when a private homeowner maintains their house, it retains value."

Hantz's first proposal was not for a farm but a Homesteading Office, which would transfer foreclosed de facto public property into responsible private hands; applicants would have to prove they could maintain and upgrade the property. It was a logic that recalled John Locke's theory that property ownership makes civilized and rational subjects who strive to "improve" (i.e., productively use) their land. Private property, in short, becomes a means of inducing progress and economic prosperity; the function of government is to protect and administer property rights.

"This is the problem in Detroit—the city does not exist," Score said to me. "We keep on trying to figure out where the eyes are on this entity sitting across the table from us. We want to have eye contact. Where are the eyes? . . . When you start, you say, 'I'll go to the mayor's office,' then you've made council angry. You should have started with them. You start with them, and you make the mayor's office angry. It's like, who is running the city?"

Score explained how hard it was to get the city to sell them thirty-five lots for the demonstration plot. They acquired another fifteen from other property owners. Meanwhile, the city was considering a request to sell Hantz Farms another approximately 180 acres, or 1,900 properties, for only $520,000 ($275 per parcel), even though the city planning commission had publicly advised against it, calling it "premature" and "speculative."[52]

"Government has to improve if the marketplace is going to thrive," said Score. He was frustrated. In contrast to the government, he insisted, they cared about what life was like for people in the neighborhood. They were improving the lots they owned. They planned for the trees to be spaced twelve feet apart so they could mow in between them; the spacing would also create visibility like a park. "To give people a neighbor that actually cares about what life is like for them is a big part of making the city more livable." If they could accomplish this, said Score, Detroit could be a "new type of city," because it would incentivize other prominent Detroiters to make similar investments in green redevelopment.

In this sense, the project was about fostering livability through "positive scarcity," which, according to Hantz, would raise property values and, in turn, induce people to "take action." It was also a private sector solution to the city's infrastructural challenges. "With a farm, you can turn the sewage and the water off; it takes care of blight—it's really the cheapest option you have," said Hantz.[53] Livable for whom? Livable for what?

Once new metrics deem places "livable," they often become unlivable for longtime residents. When activists and residents talked about their visions for the city as part of the Uniting Detroiters project, they used a different vocabulary. They didn't talk about livability, at least not in terms of property values and market logics. Rather, they talked about living otherwise.

Their analyses were as precise in diagnosing the current conjuncture as they were capacious in envisioning alternatives. They rooted their reflections in their lived experiences engaging in place-based community development, from cleaning up neighborhoods to building bookstores and gardens, establishing community spaces, and developing youth programs.

They wanted to see changes in the city. They wanted access to resources: high-quality water, public education, fresh food, childcare, adequate housing, transportation, electricity, small businesses that met community needs, and a responsive public safety system. One person imagined a city where "our children would be able to play on the streets and be children," and as another put it, a city where "youth walk safely with their grandparents. Where they're able to cook together with their families and their neighbors. Where people commune together and share ideas."

They also had critiques of the local government, but they didn't argue for privatization. That was part of the problem. They argued instead for government that cared about the people. They understood the inadequacy of electoral politics and that voting alone was insufficient. Rather, they argued for the primacy of community self-determination and an active citizenry of which the history of Black struggle provided models. "The only way you can have a responsible and accountable government is to have a conscious and mobilized populace," said Dee Rollins, a member of the city's Black farming movement. "If the people are not mobilized and conscious, then the government kind of runs roughshod over them."[54]

Developing an activity citizenry involved dealing with issues of complacency and the fact that many people didn't feel heard. As Lila Cabill, a *People's Atlas of Detroit* contributor and longtime activist who focused on antiracist organizing and self-development, put it, people needed to wake up to their consumer power in terms of how they participate in their own oppression and in terms of how elected officials represent or do not represent their interests.[55] Intervention in electoral politics could not be sustained by one-off voting alone but required sustained Black organization.

At a time of when civic power was being usurped by the state and corporate capital, no one was under the illusion that the government or representative democracy was going to save them. John Darby, who directed a community center, which offered adult recreation programs and other social services, explained it this way:

> A lot of people used to think that the messiah was coming . . . in terms of a president, in terms of a governor, in terms of a mayor, in terms of a county executive. Or we were one corporate executive away, whether it be General Motors, Chrysler, Ford, Google, e-Bay. They were going to come and save us, right? And so, increasingly year after year, development idea after development idea, we've come to the realization in our community that the cavalry is not coming to save us. And, in fact, if the cavalry does come, it's only a courtesy call to say, "We've gotten your phone calls, we've gotten your letters, we ain't coming. We just came to tell you we ain't coming. Go on without us." So, we have to figure out how can we find different ways through different relationships, through innovation, through a lot of thinking. How can we create the type of community that we want to see?[56]

None of this was easy, John admitted. It required not only conviction but materials, facilities, computers, money, health care, infrastructure, and revenue streams to pay people living wages. It also required a shift in consumer-driven values and lifestyles.

Others talked about the need for cultural transformation. Activists like Mary Hawthorne, who worked on housing issues, argued for a shift from a social order rooted in the dream of individual home ownership to one in which "we have our dream neighborhood, our dream community."[57]

Nurturing such an ethos, as others argued, required attention to trauma and healing at the psychic level. "We're damaged. Our humanity has been damaged," Lila Cabill said. "It's damaged from racism, and it's damaged from our spirituality; you know people's spirits are low, but they aren't feeding their spirit. They aren't feeding their human spirit and their humanity. And I think that's going to have to be a part of that vision. What can we do to heal and repair human relations?"[58]

As Cabill argued, it is the relationships that come out of that healing process that will restore community. People's values will shift. What they think they need to sustain themselves will be different, she said.

Other people we interviewed also framed direct democracy and the restoration of participation as healing work. Many of them envisioned a city in which the needs of everyday people were of concern to the larger community in which individuals felt heard and valued, in which they could express their dreams and what they needed to thrive, in which they could work through conflicts and heal fractured relationships. Cara May put it succinctly: "On a very basic level, I believe that people need to love, be loved, to belong, and to be of use."[59] As Yusef Shakur, an author, educator, community organizer, and *Atlas* contributor, said, "We have to start thinking outside the box, reclaiming our soul, reclaiming our connection to each other, developing trust within each other."[60]

Developing such trust was the elemental but necessary work of building a community's capacity for self-determination and collective decision-making. As Detroiters suggested, such capacity and power is generated by people being accountable to place.

Doug Collins, the pastor of a local church, explained that, for him, community was a network of place-based relationships: "A community is such a living thing that it's not easily defined, but it basically has to do with relationships, with knowing one another, with a shared 'our,' and to a certain degree common shared vision. You know Martin Luther King used the phrase 'the beloved community,' and I think we're talking about love here. It's a social expression of love."[61]

Collins and others challenged me to think more deeply about how one's relationship to oneself and others is produced in common and how the power to create revolutionary change grows in place, within block clubs, neighborhoods, places of faith, and sometimes gardens. Such visions were not utopian like Howard's, Ford's, or Hantz's. Rather they were forged in the present from the accumulated knowledge of struggle and through persistent questioning and experimentation about how life could be lived otherwise amid life-threatening forces, in ways that interrupted and ran counter to relations of abandonment. They revealed a city that was rooted in radical relationality, a city built from collective daily practices of care, a city where Black life flourished—a city after property.

The City Not Given

By the time I arrived, throngs of people snaked out the front door of Timbuktu Academy of Arts and Sciences, a golden-hued concrete building with a modern facade. Named after the famed scholastic center for learning in what is now Mali, Timbuktu Academy was one of three remaining African-centered schools in the city. It was a cold Midwestern evening in December 2012, but indignation and camaraderie warmed the gymnasium, where more than three hundred people had gathered to protest the city council's upcoming vote on Hantz's proposal.

"Hantz off our land!" The woman stood with a microphone addressing the crowd as they erupted with enthusiastic cheers. I joined others sitting in hard plastic folding chairs that fanned out across the basketball court. Those without seats lined the periphery. Shoulder to shoulder they leaned against walls painted with African proverbs, iconography, and murals.

Activists had spent the week knocking on doors, passing out fliers, and talking to residents in the project's proposed footprint, notifying many for the first time about the development. The rally was the culmination of this last-minute organizing push and an effort to get people energized for a public city council hearing in advance of the vote. Judging by the size of the crowd, they had succeeded.

One after another, participants walked to the front of the room to register dissent in the form of short speeches, testimonials, and poetry. They drew attention to the smallholders, community gardeners, homeowners, and renters who faced precarious land tenure and housing situations. They emphasized that many residents had tried to buy lots for projects that would create community opportunities, but with little success. They decried the lack of transparency and the lengthy and ambiguous land acquisition process. They argued that citizens should have equal rights and access to opportunities. They called for an impact assessment. They insisted that the land Hantz sought to purchase was spectacularly undervalued, given its prime location outside of downtown and a half mile from the riverfront.

"It sets a precedent for other sales," said one woman. "He doesn't have to move anyone out. When property values go up, gentrification will remove us."

Applause and uplifting shouts followed each speaker, echoing off the concrete walls.

Many called into question the legal systems that permitted real estate developers and speculators to prey on their community. Some referred to Hantz's project as a "neocolonial land grab," drawing connections to the spate of large-scale land acquisitions by corporate, state entities, and finance capital for agricultural production, particularly in Africa and Latin America. They made it clear that while global land grabs, or "green grabs," under the guise of sustainability, may be novel, Black dispossession had a long history, but so did Black resistance.[62]

"We are opposed to this land grab," said a representative from D-Town Farms. "It has citywide, local implications, national, and also international. They are doing land grabs in Africa, Latin America, and urban areas of the United States. The international community is looking at us for how we decide to repurpose all this vacant land. We support a community land trust where land benefits the community."

"What's happening is deeper than saying no to a land grab," one resident added. "It's about having an ability to develop our own plan."

Collectively, the speakers made clear that Hantz Farms symbolized a development paradigm that threatened alternative visions, which residents had been cultivating in neighborhoods in the wake of political and economic abandonment. Many of them had been at the forefront of community-building efforts from service-based community organizing to waging campaigns for food security, affordable housing, running water, and government accountability to creating neighborhood-level institutions like bookstores, schools, community spaces, and gardens.

In response to Hantz's project, residents started calling for "land justice." My colleague Linda put it this way: "I'm not fighting for cheap land for you to grow [food], I'm fighting for land justice. I want to go from 'I want to be able get cheap land like Hantz' to thinking about land differently in Detroit: how land-use decisions are being made, who's benefiting, who is not benefiting. What does a land justice paradigm look like, as opposed to cheap land for individuals?"

On the surface, such calls were demands for equity in the distribution of land. Yet to understand the struggle over Hantz Farms simply in terms of land distribution would be to miss something important. Land justice was as much about alternative forms of sovereignty, political subjectivity, and personhood as about rights to landed property. As people's enunciations of grief and grievance suggested, their visions for the city's future could not be contained by the logics of possessive individualism and market values. They were premised on a foundational belief that all residents deserved the right to decide what development would look like for themselves and their communities. Activists demanded that the city council create a community land trust instead of selling the land to Hantz. They issued an open call to the Detroit community:

We, the Community Trust, are a coalition of organizations that have done sustained, substantial work on the east side of Detroit for many decades. We have established youth programs, worked on anti-violence efforts, organized business initiatives, encouraged economic innovation, established gardens, reclaimed homes, planted trees, developed new models of education, and supported artistic and creative activities. Like all Detroiters, we have contributed to the support of public lands, and we have all suffered from their neglect.[63]

The letter argued that public land should be used for community health, welfare, beauty, independence, and interconnection and that a community land trust was the best path for the future development of the city. The dissent against Hantz reminded me that through quotidian practices of claiming space within contested landscapes, residents were transforming their communities.

The day after the rally at the Timbuktu Academy, more than four hundred residents gathered at Bethel Baptist Church to voice their concerns about Hantz Farms, this time to Detroit city council members. A map hung on the back wall of the church illustrating the proposed development zone. It showed that in addition to the initial sale of 1,900 lots, under the proposed agreement, after four years, Hantz Farms would also be given the right of first refusal to buy any city-owned lots within a one-mile buffer zone. A hand-drawn line showed how the zone encircled most of Detroit's lower East Side (figure 8.3). By 2016, as one city planner put it, Hantz Farms could potentially own 1/14 of Detroit. Despite the widespread opposition, the next day the city council narrowly voted to approve the project. Hantz was one among a rising class of land barons rapidly acquiring vast swaths of the city with implications for years to come.

✳

As Grace asked: What is to be learned from the struggle? The stakes of Hantz's project were much bigger than the woodlands itself. If, in the 1960s, urban struggles turned on race and labor relations on the factory floor, by the 2010s, they turned on who would control social reproduction in the neighborhood. Urban land and nature had become key sites of struggle because they were the grounds from which residents were building the city anew. Indeed, the fight over the fledgling woodlands indicated the extent to which urban greening had emerged as a contested mode of governance. It also illustrated how urban greening risks co-opting grassroots activism and obscuring radically different socio-ecological vision for the future.

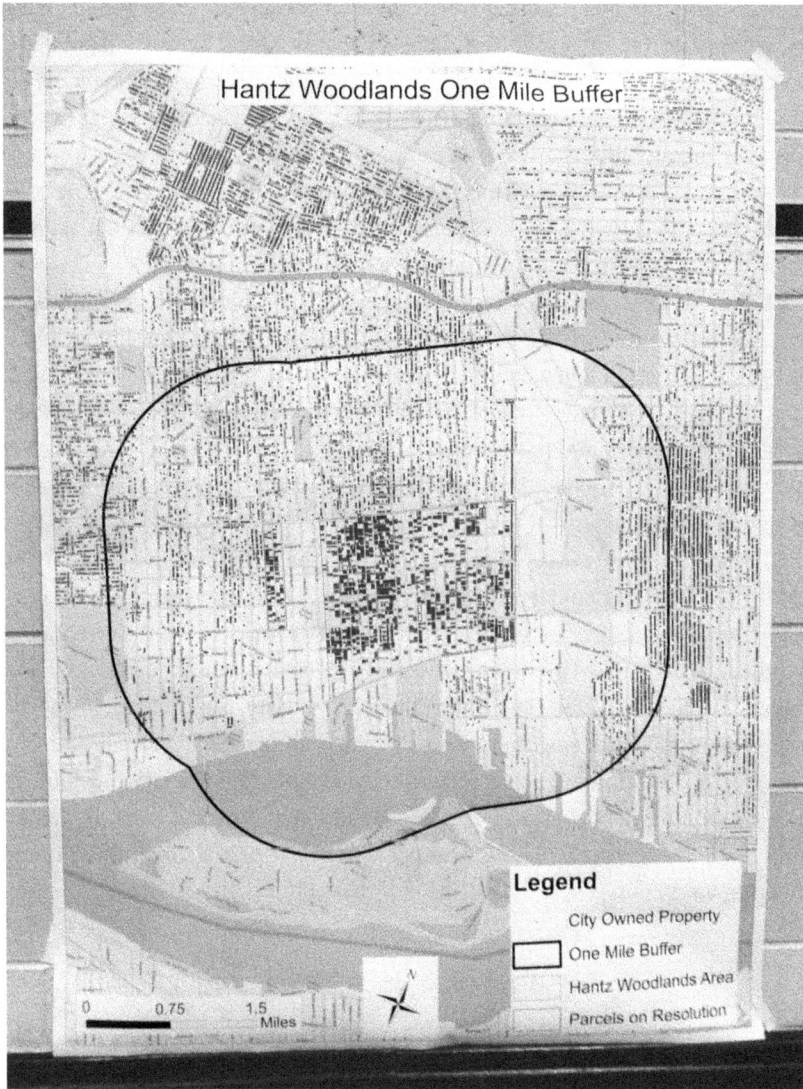

Figure 8.3 | The map depicts Hantz Woodland's proposed development site. The hand-drawn line encircles most of Detroit's lower East Side. It traces a one-mile buffer around the footprint of the woodlands. In addition to the initial sale of 1,900 lots, after four years, Hantz would be given the right of first refusal to buy any city-owned lots within the buffer zone. Darkened parcels indicated city-owned land. The map hung at the back of the Bethel Baptist Church, where a public hearing about Hantz was hosted by the city council on December 12, 2012. *Source:* Author photo.

The struggle over Hantz brought into stark relief how the construction of a "new Detroit" was manifesting as an assault on Black life and poor life. The assault came in different forms: evictions, the closures of schools, police violence, layoffs, and stripping elected officials of decision-making power. It often seemed like there weren't enough people to sustain resistance, to protest at this meeting or that meeting, not enough people to fight back and to also do the work to tend the spaces—the houses, churches, gardens, schools—that were the foundation for a different future city.

Yet people showed up. They made signs. They took their two minutes at the microphone before the gavel pounded. They marched. They linked arms. They got arrested. They chained themselves to buildings. They preached. They prayed. They sang. They studied. They did research. They wrote. They cooked. They engaged in visionary organizing. Their refusal underscored that another city was not only possible but that it already existed and that it must be defended.

The chant "Hantz off our land" made clear that residents did not cede the land. They did not consent for it to be given. Their invocation of *our* land challenged proprietary notions of personhood. It was an assertation that the land should not be an abstract commodity for speculators, developers, and financial markets. It was their home, their community, their refuge. It was the material, ecological, spiritual, and psychic grounds for beloved community.

"Hantz off our land" was a refusal to cede a vision for a city in which all people could assert their full humanity and lived dignified lives. It was an affirmation that whether Hantz's proposal passed or not, they would continue making a way out of no way, for the city that could be otherwise.

reconstructing
the world epilogue

In March 2014, red Homrich trucks started appearing in Detroit's neighborhoods. The city, under the auspices of a state-appointed emergency manager, had paid the company more than $5 million to shut off the water of up to three thousand households per week. The Detroit Water and Sewerage Department (DWSD) aimed to collect on ninety thousand accounts. It instructed Homrich to turn off water to any household with an overdue bill of at least sixty days or debts exceeding $150. Homrich was in the demolition business, not the water business. The wrecking company had another contract with the city to bulldoze thousands of buildings. The simultaneity of the contracts highlights a broader politics of abandonment that has concerned me in this book.

How do you unbuild a city? Urban infrastructures materialize visions for how social worlds should be organized. The water shutoffs brought into stark relief how a policy of disconnection stood in for urban governance. They also underscored that abandonment is an active political project.

This book has attempted to rethink narratives of postindustrial decline. Detroit is often cast as a place left behind by people and capital. My focus on contemporary land and property politics offers a more complicated story that allows us to see the water shutoffs as a situated manifestation of a global racial capitalist system that sustains itself through social abandonment.

Detroit's water infrastructure was designed at the scale of the city, but shutoffs happened at the point where the public water pipes crossed private property lines.[1] When Homrich trucks arrived, residents watched from windows, porches, and yards as workers shut off home water valves using long turnkeys. The process took under five minutes. Some residents confronted Homrich laborers during this procedure or afterward, as the company's workers painted a pale blue line on the sidewalk in front of the property, a method of record keeping that publicly marked delinquency and shamed and stigmatized the occupants.

The blue line also marked a more profound political shift. It signaled an inversion of civic commitments and promises of universal public services that had defined liberal urbanism since the late nineteenth century.[2] It was a grim reminder of what happens when the market rationalities that subtend neoliberalism are unleashed.

The water shutoffs, contrary to some rumors, were not part of the Detroit Future City (DFC) plan. Like the DFC, however, they were part of a larger redevelopment strategy aimed at making the city more attractive to transnational capital. The disconnection laid bare by both the DFC and the water shutoffs should be understood as the outgrowth of a broader realignment of power that began in the 1960s, when corporate capital and the state, seeking to retain power and profitability, launched a counterrevolutionary attack on labor, Black liberation, and other radical movements. The combination of state warfare and economic restructuring manifested in a dramatic shift in domestic urban policy toward the kinds of punitive and market-oriented governance that predominates today.

All told, Homrich turned off water to twenty-seven thousand households between March and October 2014. Though half of the households were reconnected after residents paid their bills, the shutoffs were one of the largest utility disconnection campaigns in US history.

The shutoffs meant that thousands of the city's poorest residents did not have potable water, shower water, or flushable toilets. Many were reduced to hauling water in five-gallon buckets from their neighbors' outdoor spigots. They bathed at the houses of friends and family. Even those who still had water began rationing, fearing the possibility of disconnection. Without water, some parents were anxious that Child Protective Services could remove their children from their homes. Other homeowners worried that the water department might put a lien on their houses for overdue bills, making them vulnerable to the tax-foreclosure process and auction.

Residents started to organize locally. Scores of people engaged in acts of civil disobedience, like blocking water shutoff trucks. Advocacy groups like We the People of Detroit developed a Water Hotline and water deliveries.

Residents filed lawsuits that put the morals and ethics of the state and political leaders under scrutiny.[3] They also launched a campaign to protect the commons and "wage love" against the shutoffs.[4]

The shutoffs drew national and international condemnation. Marches attracted thousands of demonstrators. The National Nurses United declared a "public health emergency," citing not only water insecurity, but the spread of disease and the corrosion and toxic buildup that can happen when water is not moving through pipes. The United Nations sent rapporteurs to Detroit who declared the shutoffs a human rights violation and called for a total prohibition on disconnections for people who couldn't afford to pay.

If water—the so-called liquid of life—often invites political convergence and religious sentiments (universality, purification, healing, revival), the shutoffs were a potent symbol of disposability and the meta-materiality of austerity.[5] Water made abandoned people visible in a way that other, arguably equally detrimental policies had not, for example, policies that caused people to lose their homes, emergency management, cutbacks in unemployment benefits and food stamps, rightsizing plans based on market-based algorithms, corporate tax incentives, and the development of managed forests where houses once stood.

At the end of summer 2014, a coalition of more than thirty community groups organizing under the name of Detroiters Resisting Emergency Management (D-REM) issued a statement entitled "Whose City? Our City!" in which they insisted that austerity measures must be resisted. "We must . . . use our collective power," they wrote, "to create our City, a city of self-government, public accountability, and protection of one another."[6]

"In places long abandoned and forgotten by corporate development we have established visionary ways to address the needs of our community," they argued. Needs were being met through gardens that fostered food security; the restoration of homes, parks, and schools that made neighborhoods more livable; the creation of African-centered and place-based educational institutions; block clubs and neighborhood associations that fostered public safety; church groups that developed grassroots plans for supporting local economies; and myriad community groups that encouraged young people to stay in school, fought to keep libraries open, and raised money for students to study beyond high school.

"Whose City? Our City!" uplifted a proposal for what urban governance, planning, and development could look like if they weren't tethered to protecting capitalist interests and the commodification of property and real estate values but were based instead on the needs of the most vulnerable. It was a proposal for reimagining the city by *unbuilding* structures of oppression through radical reconstruction rather than by disconnecting people from vital resources. It was a vision for *the city after property*—the possibility of a new city, in their words, "our city," in which "all of us live in dignity, mutual respect, and love."

The "Whose City? Our City!" statement and the campaign to wage love both tapped love as the spiritual grounds for liberation. Reverend Dr. Martin Luther King Jr. used the term *beloved community* to name a society organized around interdependence and shared humanity. His usage of *beloved* merged African American values of community connectedness with biblical notions of love and redemption.

Agape denotes a wide-open love. But it is distinguished from eros. It is not sexual or romantic love. Nor is it fraternal love, nor unconditional love. It contains a challenge to act. It is a demand to move from abstract to concrete freedom, a call to struggle against oppression by fighting for new laws, policies, and structures that enable better living for all. This looks like joining mass movements like those underway today to decommodify housing, defund the police, and reimagine public safety, movements that underscore the importance of contending with policy but whose visions and blueprints extend beyond state reform toward an anti-capitalist and anti-racist politics capable of supporting radical democratic governance. The demand to move from abstract to concrete freedom is also a demand to recognize that culture is at the foundation of structure.

Changing culture requires remembering and fostering ways of knowing, being, and world-building that connect us to place and one another beyond dominion. It requires a recognition of our relationality, a recognition that freedom rooted in the self-possessed individual is a seductive lie, that no one is free until the least among us are free. If racial capitalism—and private property as its form and function—organizes abandonment, and if abandonment is enabled through the severing of mutuality, then, as Detroiters show, radical repair and love are central to constructing the world anew.

notes

Prologue

1 Beaver, "Civil War on the North Fork," 98–100; Crawford, *Ashe County's Civil War*, 34; Our State Staff, "Invisible Appalachia: Junaluska," *Our State*, February 2015, https://www.ourstate.com/junaluska/.

2 On representations of Appalachia, see Billings, "Economic Representations in an American Region," 172–85.

3 On thinking about theory and study as liberatory practice, see hooks, "Theory as Liberatory Practice," 59–75; Harney and Moten, *Undercommons*.

4 Campbell et al., *People's Atlas of Detroit*. The companion documentary is *A People's Story of Detroit*, video, 1:02:00, Detroit People's Platform, September 12, 2015, https://www.youtube.com/watch?v=qcAvvr6yYjM. Andrew Newman and I have also written about the Uniting Detroiters project here: Newman and Safransky, "Remapping the Motor City," 17–28.

Chapter One. Unbuilding a City

1 Jonathan Oosting, "Urban Farming Entrepreneur John Hantz Suggests Homestead Act for Detroit," *MLive*, April 8, 2010, https://www.mlive.com/business/detroit/2010/04/urban_farming_entrepreneur_joh.html; "Michigan Governor Seeks Visas to Lure Skilled Immigrants to Detroit," *Aljazeera America*, January 23, 2014, http://america.aljazeera.com/articles/2014/1/23/michigan-governoreyes50000visastoattractimmigrants.html; "Zombie Apocalypse Theme Park Could Take Over Abandoned Neighborhood in Detroit," *HuffPost*, July 2, 2012, https://www.huffpost.com/entry/zombie-apocalaypse-detroit-theme-park_n_1644298; Rick Perlstein, "Hell Isle," *Nation*, January 28, 2013, accessed June 27, 2020, https://www.thenation.com/article/archive/hell-isle/; Detroit Future City, *2012 Detroit Strategic Framework Plan* (Detroit, MI: Inland Press, 2013), https://detroitfuturecity.com/wp-content/uploads/2017/07/DFC_Full_2nd.pdf.

2   I am indebted to Erin Collins for conversations early on about abandonment and an American Association of Geographers conference session that we organized on the "Social Geographies of Urban Abandonment."

3   Several scholars have analyzed how Detroit has become a spectacle, including Herron, "Detroit," 663–82; Herron, "Forgetting Machine"; Herron, "Motor City Breakdown"; John Patrick Leary, "Detroitism," *Guernica,* January 15, 2011, http://www.guernicamag.com/features/leary_1_15_11/; Kinney, "Longing for Detroit," 1–14; and Millington, "Post-Industrial Imaginaries," 279–96.

4   More than half of the city's children lived at or below the poverty rates (which, in 2010, was less than $22,050 per year for a family of four). *State of the Detroit Child: 2010* (Detroit, MI: Data Driven Detroit, 2011), https:// datadrivendetroit.org/web_ftp/Project_Docs/DETKidsDrft_FINAL.pdf.

5   On precarity being a permanent state of exception under capitalism, see Mahmud, "Precarious Existence and Capitalism," 699–726.

6   In addition to economic obsolescence, postindustrial society flagged a general set of claims about shifts in the nature of work and labor relations, including the predominance of the service sector (versus agricultural or industrial); the rise of white-collar work over blue; and the growing economic importance of research, technology, financial services, and associated institutions (universities, hospitals, banks).

7   Charlie LeDuff, "What Killed Aiyana Stanley-Jones?," *Mother Jones*, November/December 2010, https://www.motherjones.com/politics/2010/09/aiyana -stanley-jones-detroit/.

8   Andrew Clark and Jill Treanor, "Greenspan—I Was Wrong about the Economy, Sort of," *Guardian* (UK), October 23, 2008, https://www.theguardian .com/business/2008/oct/24/economics-creditcrunch-federal-reserve -greenspan.

9   For instance, we might recall Daniel Moynihan, who as President Richard Nixon's counselor took the controversial and since disgraced stance of "benign neglect" regarding issues of race. See Peter Kihss, "'Benign Neglect' on Race Is Proposed by Moynihan," *New York Times*, March 1, 1970, 1, 69, https://timesmachine.nytimes.com/timesmachine/1970/03/01/90600209 .html. Also see "Text of the Moynihan Memorandum on the Status of Negroes," *New York Times*, March 1, 1970, 69.

10 Wallace and Wallace, *Plague on Your Houses*. Also see Starr, *Urban Choices*; and Roger Starr, "Making New York Smaller," *New York Times*, November 14, 1976, https://www.nytimes.com/1976/11/14/archives/making-new -york-smaller-the-citys-economic-outlook-remains-grim.html.

11 As Alesia Montgomery has argued in the case of Detroit, sustainability became its own regime of capitalist growth. Montgomery, *Greening the Black Urban Regime*.

12 On the shrinkage debate, see Jennifer Bradley, "We Need a New Mindset to Unbuild Cities," *New York Times*, March 28, 2011, https://www.nytimes.com

/roomfordebate/2011/03/28/the-incredible-shrinking-city/we-need-a-new
-mindset-to-unbuild-cities. Also see Nate Berg, "Next Steps for Shrinking
Cities: Results from a Planetizen Brainstorm," *Planetizen*, July 9, 2009,
https://www.planetizen.com/node/39619.

13 See, for example, Dillard, *Faith in the City*; Fine, *Violence in the Model City*;
Georgakas and Surkin, *Detroit, I Do Mind Dying*; Hartigan, *Racial Situations*; Shaw, *Now Is the Time*; and Thompson, *Whose Detroit?*

14 Including Thomas Sugrue's now classic *Origins of Urban Crisis*, June Manning Thomas' seminal *Redevelopment and Race*, and Freund's monumental
Colored Property.

15 Important exceptions include recent books by Herbert, *Detroit Story*;
Kinder, *DIY Detroit*; and Montgomery, *Greening the Black Urban Regime*.

16 See, for example, Harvey, "Spatial Fix," 1–12; Mezzadra and Neilson, "Operations of Capital," 1–9; and Brenner and Schmid, "Planetary Urbanization,"
449–53; for debates over the planetary urbanization concept, see Oswin,
"Planetary Urbanization," 540–46; and the entire issue of *Society and Space*
36, no. 3 (2018).

17 Mishuana Goeman's concept of "storied land" has helped me understand
the processes of meaning making that happen vis-à-vis land. To understand
"land as a storied site of human interaction," Goeman writes, is to "(re)open
its meaning beyond territory, property, or location while retaining its political vitality." Recognizing land beyond property and territory involves understanding land as a "meaning making process rather than a claimed object."
See Goeman, "Land as Life," 72–73. This work requires, as she explains
elsewhere, "reaching back across generations, critically examining our use
of the word land in the present, and reaching forward to create a healthier
relationship for future generations." See Goeman, "From Place to Territories and Back Again," 24. Also see Tuck, Guess, and Sultan, "Not Nowhere,"
1–11; Tuck et al., "Geotheorizing Black/Land," 52–74; and La Paperson,
"Ghetto Land Pedagogy," 115–30.

18 This framing of seeing landscapes in terms of loss is indebted to sociologist
Montgomery, "Sight of Loss," 1828–50.

19 Hurricane Katrina ravaged the Gulf Coast in 2005. Flooding precipitated
intense depopulation. New Orleans's population decreased by over half.
Seventy percent of the city's occupied housing was damaged by the storm.

20 Horowitz, *Katrina*, 3.

21 To be clear, from colonial forts to postindustrial cities, urban plans and policies have always been shaped within geographies of comparison.

22 For comparison of Detroit to post-Katrina New Orleans, see, for example, Dan Kildee, interview by Craig Fahle, *The Craig Fahle Show*, WDET,
August 2, 2013, http://archives.wdet.org/shows/craig-fahle-show/episode
/callers-on-dan-kildee-comments/. In 2011, weeks before Mayor David Bing
launched the Detroit Works Project with the aim of shrinking Detroit, he

met with New Orleans Mayor Mitch Landrieu to talk about downsizing strategies. On the meeting between Bing and Landrieu, see Campbell Robertson, "A Lesson for Detroit in Efforts to Aid a New Orleans Devastated by Katrina," *New York Times*, February 22, 2014, https://www.nytimes.com/2014/02/23/us/a-lesson-for-detroit-in-efforts-to-aid-a-new-orleans-devastated-by-katrina.html. The German Marshall Fund of the United States has funded a number of comparative programs and partnerships between cities. See, for example, *GMF 2010 Annual Report* (Washington, DC: German Marshall Fund, 2010), https://www.gmfus.org/sites/default/files/2010gmf_annual_final_0.pdf.

23 Critical literature on post-Katrina reconstruction provides useful insights into Detroit. Plans to "rightsize" New Orleans were stopped by popular protests; however, the plan to rebuild everywhere did not produce a more just city. In the wake of Katrina, the widespread volunteerism that followed was taken by many as a sign of democratic popular reconstruction, yet studies of its impact tell a different story. The embrace of volunteerism coincided with an intensified assault on and privatization of the public realm, such as the demolition of public housing complexes, closures of the city's public hospital, and school privatization. See, for example, Johnson, *Neoliberal Deluge*; Arena, *Driven from New Orleans*; Adams and Sakakeeny, *Remaking New Orleans*; and Adams, *Markets of Sorrow, Labors of Faith*. Thanks to the anonymous reviewer who directed me to these sources.

24 See Nicholas Blomley on how the survey acts as a "form of organized forgetting." Blomley, *Unsettling the City*, 112.

25 This truism about systems breakdown—often observed in studies of infrastructure (e.g., power grids, water pipes, bridges, dams) and political collapse—is also useful for thinking about property regimes. Star and Ruhleder, "Steps toward an Ecology of Infrastructure," 111–34; Graham and Thrift, "Out of Order," 1–2.

26 The sanctity of landed private property obscures its peculiarity. As the political economist Karl Polanyi wrote, "What we call land is an element of nature inextricably interwoven with man's institutions. To isolate it and form a market for it was perhaps the weirdest of all the undertakings of our ancestors." Polanyi, *Great Transformation*, 187.

27 Notions of scarcity are deeply rooted when it comes to land, extending at least as far back as the physiocrats, who in the eighteenth century argued that wealth originated in the land, that land was finite, and that private property was central to societal well-being.

28 See, for example, C. M. Rose, *Property and Persuasion*; Hann, "Introduction," 1–47; Hann, "Property: Anthropological Aspects," 153–59; von Benda-Beckmann, von Benda-Beckmann, and Wiber, "Properties of Property," 1–39; Singer, *Entitlement*; and van de Walt, *Property in the Margins*.

29 Locke, *Two Treatises of Government*.

30 Redecker, "Ownership's Shadow," 43. If settler colonialism turned on (turns on) the possession of land and territory, then "property law was [and is] the primary means of realizing this desire," as Bhandar writes. "There cannot be a history of private property law. . . . in early modern England that is not at the same time a history of land appropriation in Ireland, the Caribbean, North America, and beyond." Indeed, the granting of land in Detroit by the French and then British Crown was coincident with enclosures in Europe. Bhandar, *Colonial Lives*, 3. Also see Wolfe, "Settler Complex," 1–22; Wolfe, "Land, Labor, and Difference," 866–905; and Wolfe, *Settler Colonialism*.

    In Detroit, as historian Tiya Miles shows, settler colonial expansion depended on the displacement and forced labor of both Indigenous peoples and Africans. See Miles, *Dawn of Detroit*. Also see Kyle T. Mays's *City of Dispossessions* for an examination of how Black and Indigenous dispossession shape contemporary Detroit and the development of modern US cities more generally. On scholarship that questions how to best analyze the complex relationships among whiteness, Blackness, and Indigeneity, see Kelley, "Rest of Us"; Byrd, "Weather with You"; C. I. Harris, "Of Blackness and Indigeneity"; and King, *Black Shoals*.

31 Locke, *Two Treatises of Government*.

32 Bhandar, *Colonial Lives*, 4.

33 Bhandar, *Colonial Lives*. Also see Wynter, "Unsettling the Coloniality of Being," 257–337.

34 C. I. Harris, "Whiteness as Property," 1707–9. Harris argues that whiteness, which begins as a type of status property, becomes an entitlement to social goods, continuing today, for example, in affirmative action litigation. Like property, whiteness shares the characteristics of the right to use and enjoyment, the power to exclude, and reputational value.

35 On foundational works in geography, see for example, H. M. Rose, "Geography of Despair," 453–64; Blaut, *Colonizer's Model of the World;* Woods, *Development Arrested*; B. M. Wilson, *America's Johannesburg*; Kobayashi and Peake, "Racism out of Place," 392–403; Pulido, "Reflections on a White Discipline," 42–49; Delaney, "Space That Race Makes," 6–14; and Gilmore, *Golden Gulag*.

36 Hong, "Property."

37 A proliferation of important early twenty-first century work in geography, influenced by the rise of Black, Indigenous, and Latinx geographies, has directed renewed attention to land and property relations in North American cities and between urban and rural areas. Recent examples of scholarship include but are not limited to studies that direct attention to land and property in relationship to haunting (Best and Ramírez, "Urban Specters," 1043–54); settler colonialism (Blatman-Thomas and Porter, "Placing Property," 30–45; Hugill, "What Is a Settler-Colonial City?," 1–11; Dorries, Hugill,

and Tomiak, "Racial Capitalism," 263–70); policing, gentrification, and the carceral state (Bonds, "Race and Ethnicity I," 574–83); white propertied power and the valorization of whiteness (Brand, "Sedimentation of Whiteness as Landscape," 276–91); Black, Latinx, and Indigenous geographies and urban futures (Ramírez, "City as Borderland," 147–66; Ramírez, "Take the Houses Back," 682–93); vacancy (Noterman, "Taking Back Vacant Property," 1079–98; Noterman, "Speculating on Vacancy," 123–38; McClintock, "Nullius No More?," 91–108); racial liberalism and water crisis (Ranganathan, "Thinking with Flint," 17–33); foreclosures and racial banishment (Roy, "Dis/possessive Collectivism," A1–A11); abolition ecology (Heynen, "Urban Political Ecology II," 839–45); narratives and storytelling (Brahinsky, "Story of Property," 837–55); social reproduction and informality (Goffe, "Capture and Abandon"); appraisal science and predatory property relations (Zaimi, "Rethinking 'Disinvestment,'" 245–57); technology (McElroy, "Property as Technology," 112–29); housing financialization (Fields and Raymond, "Racialized Geographies of Housing Financialization," 1625–45); Black liberation theology and Black agrarian futures (McCutcheon, "Growing Black Food on Sacred Land," 887–905); and the relationship between urban and rural property relations (Van Sant, Shelton, and Kay, "Connecting Country and City," 1–15).

38 Read, "Enclosing the Spirit," 163; Fullilove, *Root Shock*, 11.

39 See Salerno, *Landscapes of Abandonment*, 3. Notably, the French word *banlieue* (literally "banned place") is also link to the word abandon. *Banlieue* is the name given to the urban outskirts in France where much public housing is concentrated and many people whose families immigrated from West Africa, North Africa, and Southeast Asia live. In this sense, as my colleague Andrew Newman pointed out to me, the racist aspects of the word's history extend beyond English.

40 Salerno, *Landscapes of Abandonment*, 3.

41 See Wynter, "Unsettling the Coloniality of Being," 263. Wynter is engaging Aníbal Quijano and Walter Mignolo's work on coloniality, particularly papers presented at the Conference on Coloniality Working Group at SUNY-Binghamton in 1999 and 2000. As Wynter notes, Quijano used the phrase "coloniality of power" and Mignolo, "colonial difference."

42 Salerno, *Landscapes of Abandonment*, 4.

43 Salerno, *Landscapes of Abandonment*, 4.

44 Severalty means the conditions of being separate or distinct, as in severed. In property law, for example, "property in severalty" signifies individual or sole ownership, without joined interest with anyone else. See "severalty" in *The American Heritage Dictionary of the English Language*, 5th ed. (New York: HarperCollins, 2022).

45 This sense of freedom associated with the rise of liberalism represented a new way of thinking about economic affairs. While the term *laissez-faire*

capitalism (free-market capitalism) suggests nonintervention, as Perelman has noted, the early political economists systematically engaged in projects to make society more market oriented by urging measures to deprive people of any alternatives to wage labor. They advocated simultaneously for laissez-faire ideology and for policies that were at odds with laissez-faire principles. These policies were focused on undermining people's ability to provide for themselves and keeping people from finding alternative survival strategies outside the system of wage labor. People were driven to wage labor through brutal discipline. If the poor were taken to not be sufficiently industrious, their want of discipline was criminalized and medicalized. Thus, the violent dispossession of the people and the creation of free-market economics was a dual, complementary project. In other words, the invisible hand only operated in the framework of contrived law and order. See, e.g., Perelman, *Invention of Capitalism.*

46 Harvey, *Limits to Capital*, 397.

47 Povinelli, Economies of Abandonment, 29.

48 Gilmore, "Forgotten Places," 31–61. For other interpretations of abandonment, see Biehl, "Technologies of Invisibility," 248–71; Giroux, "Reading Hurricane Katrina," 171–96.

49 See Bhandar, *Colonial Lives*, on the coevolution of racial and property regimes.

50 See, for example, Jenkins and Leroy, "Introduction," 1–26; Melamed, "Racial Capitalism," 76–85; and *Boston Review*'s 2017 special issue, "Race, Capitalism, Justice," Forum 1.

51 Bledsoe and Wright, "Anti-Blackness of Global Capital," 8–26.

52 Gross-Wyrtzen, "Contained and Abandoned in the 'Humane' Border," 893. As Geraldine Pratt writes, "Abandonment is not equivalent to exclusion. It has a more complex topological relation of being neither inside nor outside the juridical order. The difference between exclusion and abandonment turns on the fact that abandonment is an active, relational process. The one who is abandoned remains in a relationship with sovereign power: included through exclusion." Pratt, "Abandoned Women and Spaces of the Exception," 1054.

53 As Gilmore writes, "The quality of having been forgotten that materially links such places is not merely about absence or lack. Abandoned places are also planned concentrations or sinks—of hazardous materials and destructive practices that are in turn sources of group-differentiated vulnerabilities to premature death (which, whether state-sanctioned or extra-legal, is how racism works, regardless of the intent of the harms' producers, who produce along the way racialization and therefore race)." See Gilmore, "Forgotten Places," 35–36.

54 My thinking here is related to Biehl's conceptualization of "technologies of invisibility." In "Technologies of Invisibility," Biehl asks how social and

scientific technologies are combined into governance to make people invisible. Biehl is concerned with how technical-political dynamics make people invisible and how they are dying—its experience, distribution, and social representation. For Biehl, "technologies of invisibility" are the bureaucratic procedures, informational difficulties, sheer medical neglect, moral contempt, and unresolved disputes over diagnostic criteria that turn people into absent things. Similarly, I am interested in how vacancy and abandonment discourses work to make people invisible.

55 I draw on ideas of "being in-difference" from Gordon, *Ghostly Matters*, v, 48–49. Gordon writes, "Being in-difference is a political consciousness and a sensuous knowledge: a standpoint and a mindset for living on better terms than what we're offered, for living as if you had the necessity and the freedom to do so. By better, I mean a collective life without misery, deathly inequalities, mutating racisms, social abandonment, endless war, police power, authoritarian governance, heteronormative impositions, patriarchal rule, cultural conformity, and ecological destruction" (v).

56 Povinelli, *Economies of Abandonment*, 30; Gilmore, "Forgotten Places," 36.

57 Gilmore, "Forgotten Places," 34. Gilmore is drawing on Ganz, "Resources and Resourcefulness," 1003–62.

Chapter Two. On Our Own Ground

1 Much has been written about the 1967 uprising in Detroit. See, in particular, these excellent sources: Hersey, *Algiers Motel*; Fine, *Violence in the Model City*; J. M. Thomas, *Redevelopment and Race*; Georgakas and Surkin, *Detroit, I Do Mind Dying*.

2 The terminology also conflated the uprisings of the 1960s with race riots of earlier decades, when white people exacted raw violence on Black people. There were those of 1918 in East St. Louis; Chester, Pennsylvania; and Lexington, Kentucky. The next year, riots erupted in scores of cities and towns across the country when white soldiers returning from World War I accused African Americans of taking their jobs. It was dubbed the Red Summer of 1919. Two years later, in 1921, there was the massacre in Tulsa, Oklahoma; and then, in Detroit, the riots of 1943, to name but a few. Thus, riots could not be used to describe 1967 because riots were, in short, the outcome of white rage.

3 In July of the same year, California passed the Mulford Bill (aka the Panther Bill), which criminalized the open display of firearms.

4 Shelia Porter is a pseudonym. I use a combination of interviewees' real names and pseudonyms throughout the book. Whenever I use pseudonyms, I indicate them as such. In some instances, I use the interviewees' real names, specifically when one's identity cannot be easily masked or is central to the analysis. As mentioned in the prologue, I draw on interviews that were

conducted as part of the Uniting Detroiters project. Some interviews are published in Campbell et al., *People's Atlas of Detroit*, and are cited accordingly under the contributor's name.

5 In response to worker dissatisfaction and the organizing efforts of the Industrial Workers of the World, Ford offered workers five dollars for an eight-hour workday (a lot at the time, given that the average wage in the industry was $2.34 for a nine-hour shift). Ford workers received the full five dollars, however, only if they met certain conditions. Workers earned a regular wage for working a full day—$2.34; they would earn an additional $2.66 if Ford determined the worker was living "right."

To determine who was living "right," Ford established a Sociological Department. A project of civic reform and surveillance, the program aimed to Americanize immigrants and mold "good Ford men." Ford assumed a sound home environment produced an efficient worker and a good citizen. If the worker were living in an "unsound" home environment, he would bring a bad attitude and habits to work. Under the auspices of the Sociological Department, hundreds of inspectors studied and kept tabs on Ford workers across the Detroit region. They took inventory, asking questions pertaining to bank accounts, debts, marriage status, and how workers spent their income. Agents discouraged drinking, smoking, and gambling and encouraged wholesome lifestyle habits, including cleanliness, sleeping in beds, and thriftiness. They also advised workers against spending money on "trunkery and trinkets" and advocated instead the consumption of vacuum cleaners, washing machines, houses, and Model Ts.

This focus on consumption best distinguished Fordism as a model of economic development. Ford's philosophy was that if workers were able to consume the goods they produced, their consumption would help stabilize and stimulate supply and demand. See Hooker, "Ford's Sociology Department"; also see Grandin, *Fordlandia*.

6 The NAACP's the *Crisis* reported sixty-nine persons lynched in 1920 alone, sixty of whom were Negroes. The report includes a listing of those lynched by date, place, name, and their alleged charges. It also includes a map of Georgia, "The 'Empire State' of Lynching," with black dots denoting the location of the lynching of 460 persons between 1885 and 1920. The paper reports that between 1885 and 1920, a total of 3,112 Negroes were lynched nationally. See M. G. Allison, "The Lynching Industry—1920," *Crisis* 21, no. 4 (February 1921): 160–62. See also W. E. B. Du Bois's account of his seven-thousand-mile journey by way of Fitchburg, Massachusetts, to Charleston, New Orleans, Oklahoma, Duluth, and New York, during which he delivered thirty-eight lectures. W. E. B Du Bois, "Opinion," *Crisis* 22, no. 1 (May 1921): 5–9.

7 On railroad companies sponsoring free passage, see Robinson, *Black Movements in America*, 115. Ads run by Detroit-based Michigan Land and

Homestead Company, for example, can be viewed in the *Richmond Planet* 38, no. 52 (November 5, 1921), and in the NAACP's *Crisis Advertiser* 21, no. 4 (February 1921): 280.

8 Between 1915 and 1925, the percentage of all US autoworkers who lived in Michigan increased from 23 to 55 percent. Before the Great Migration, Detroit's small community of Black residents were dispersed throughout the city. For example, in the late nineteenth century, it was even common for Black elites to be more integrated with white society than Black. Black physicians, dentists, and attorneys were more likely to have white clientele than Black. Black managers and clerks worked for white businesses. Black elites attended white churches. They also lived separately from most Black residents, who lived in scattered pockets in white neighborhoods, often in substandard housing. Things dramatically changed with the Great Migration. At the time, immigrants from southern and eastern Europe were not seen as white. Understood as racial threats, they were also barred from native-born white neighborhoods. Yet, they still had more mobility than African Americans. Whereas ethnic enclaves formed across the city, Black migrants' housing options were limited to two concentrated neighborhoods on the downtown East Side called Black Bottom and Paradise Valley. See Zunz, *Changing Face of Inequality*, 373; on racial classification, see Freund, *Colored Property*, 4–5.

9 Detroit's all-white real estate board threatened to expel realtors who sold homes to Blacks in all-white neighborhoods, claiming a home sale to a Negro family would deteriorate property values. When upwardly mobile African Americans purchased homes in all-white neighborhoods, it was common for angry mobs made up of hundreds of whites, sometimes thousands, to terrorize the newcomers for transgressing the color line. *Corrigan v. Buckley* (271 US 323 [1926]) upheld restrictive covenants, arguing that unlike racial zoning, covenants did not violate the Fourteenth Amendment because they were not considered part of "state action." See Alexander von Hoffman, "Like Fleas on a Tiger? A Brief History of the Open Housing Movement," Harvard Joint Center for Housing Studies, W98-3, August 1998. While the NAACP had successfully challenged racial zoning years earlier in the Supreme Court case *Buchanan v. Warley* (245 US 60 [1917]), restrictive covenants remained legal until the late 1940s.

In Detroit, neighborhoods instituted racially restrictive covenants that defined a "'Negro' as any person with '1/8 or more of Negro blood.'" See Freund, *Colored Property*, 16. The famous case of Ossian and Gladys Sweet, an African American couple who in 1925 bought a new house in a white neighborhood on the city's East Side points to how even for Blacks with economic standing—Ossian was a Howard-educated physician—home purchases in white neighborhoods still prompted threats and violence. On moving day, a small group of whites tried to scare the Sweets away. By evening, the group had grown to a mob of eight hundred. The mob dispersed the next day and returned in the evening, stoning the house and chanting, "Niggers! Niggers . . . Get the Niggers!" As the crowd advanced, two shots were fired by Ossian's brother and a police officer. Two white men were shot, one died, and the Sweet family was arrested. The public began passing judgment immediately, including the mayor of Detroit, who laid down his color-line policy in no uncertain terms: "Any colored person who endangers life and property simply to gratify his personal pride, is an enemy of his race as well as an incitant of riot and murder." See Freund, *Colored Property*, 1–4.

10 For instance, while Ford was lauded for hiring African Americans when other factories refused, management consigned them to the most grueling work, including janitorial and labor in the furnaces, foundries, print shops, and wet standing operations. Moreover, Ford strategically separated workers at plants by race and then used Black workers as strikebreakers, increasing whites' fears that Blacks were taking their jobs. From 1937 to 1941, Ford employed almost half of all African Americans in the industry, 99 percent of whom worked at the River Rouge plant, which employed more than one hundred thousand laborers. Ford colluded with pro-Republican and antiunion ministers in an attempt to recruit a "docile" Black labor force. Sugrue, *Origins of the Urban Crisis*, 25–26.

11 The *Messenger* was an African American periodical founded and edited by labor activist A. Philip Randolph and economist Chandler Owen with support from the Socialist Party. "Coming Race Riots: A Few Cities in Which We May Expect Them," *Messenger*, July 1921, 210–11. The KKK's support in Detroit was evidenced by the near victory of the KKK write-in candidate for mayor, Charles Bowles. See Zunz, *Changing Face of Inequality*, 324, 402.

12 The Klan's membership, along with the white supremacist terrorist organization the Black Legion, swelled with disaffected "native-born" white factory workers who felt economically threatened by the arrival of new immigrants. They boasted thousands of members in the city and tens of thousands more in Michigan. To assuage their anxieties, they turned against Catholics, Jews, and, especially, Blacks. By the mid-1920s, the Klan nationwide had gained more than four million members. The Black Legion was in Ohio, Michigan, Indiana, and Kentucky. In the mid-1930s, the organization claimed sixty thousand to one hundred thousand members. See Amann, "Vigilante Fascism," 490–524. See also Freund, *Colored Property*, 14–15.

13 The campaign dovetailed with an organization called Better Homes in America, which was headed by Secretary of Commerce Herbert Hoover and promoted exclusionary zoning as a solution to "racial strife." Rothstein, *Color of Law*, 60–61. Excerpts from the "Guidebook of Better Homes in America: How to Organize the 1926 Campaign: Better Homes Week: April 25 to May 1, 1926" are illustrative of the massive amounts of resources and energy the federal government devoted to hetero- and racial-norming of what it meant to have better homes. See "Better Living through Home Ownership," Hoover

Heads, National Archives, June 24, 2020, https://hoover.blogs.archives.gov/2020/06/24/better-living-through-home-ownership/.

14 The Communist Party, entrenched in local auto unions, did speak to racism, but their key platform was arguing for "self-determination for the Black Belt"—a separate Black republic in the Southern states. Sharon Smith, "The 1930s: Turning Point for U.S. Labor," *Internationalist Socialist Review* 25 (September–October 2002), https://isreview.org/issues/25/The_1930s/.

15 As historian Kenneth Jackson writes, "The element of novelty did not lie in the appraisal requirement itself—that had long been a required real estate practice. Rather, it lay in the creation of a formal and uniform system of appraisal, reduced to writing, structure in defined procedures, and implemented by individuals only after intensive training. The ultimate aim was that one appraiser's judgment of value would have meaning to an investor located somewhere else." Jackson, *Crabgrass Frontier*, 197.

16 FHLBB Division of Research and Statistics 1937, quoted in Hillier, "Residential Security Maps," 217.

17 Hillier, "Residential Security Maps," 33. See Hillier's argument on not overprivileging HOLC maps and other ways in which redlining happened. Also see Freund, *Colored Property*, 33, in which he argues that the federal government used zoning and mortgage politics to suggest that segregation and exclusion were driven by land-use science, economics, and the "market imperative," not racism or their own interventions.

18 For example, the National Urban League reported in the *Crisis* in 1921, "That Negroes are taking pride in financing philanthropic ventures is evinced by their contributions in campaigns for community budgets. In Kansas City they have given in excess of $10,000; in Louisville, $3,000; in St. Louis, $5,000; and in Detroit, $6,300." See "National Urban League" entry in "The Horizon" section of the *Crisis* 21, no. 4, 176.

19 At start of the war, for example, Chrysler's Jefferson Avenue plant in Detroit employed 7,000 workers. As it shifted to wartime production, it expanded its workforce to 9,500, hiring twice as many Black workers and three times as many women. By March 1945, Black workers in Detroit made up 15 percent of workers at the city's largest plants, reflecting roughly the city's racial demography. See Ward, *In Love and Struggle*, 37–38.

20 The growing power of Black workers was demonstrated in 1941 when President Roosevelt issued an executive order banning discrimination in the war industry, preemptively responding to the call of A. Philip Randolph of the Brotherhood of Sleeping Car Porters for a march on Washington to demand the end of segregation in the armed forces and federal wartime jobs. See Ward, *In Love and Struggle*, 38–46.

21 As Black workers organized within and beyond the factory, they continued to be met by white violence. For example, white workers held "hate strikes." Hate strikes were exactly what they sounded like: when management hired

Black workers at all-white factories, white workers held sit-down strikes or walked off the job in protest. On May 24, 1943, at the Packard Motor Car Company, twenty thousand white unionists walked out after three Black workers were upgraded. In a sign that labor relations were changing, the company's five thousand Black workers also staged a walkout. Racial tensions within the plants were felt outside. On June 22, less than three weeks after the Packard walkout, skirmishes erupted between Blacks and whites on Belle Isle, Detroit's island-park, which quickly escalated into one of the nation's worst riots to that point in time. Three days of rioting left 34 dead, 25 of whom were African American, 17 killed by white police officers. An additional 675 people were seriously injured and 1,893 arrested. When federal troops came to quell the disorder, the state attorney general blamed Black people for instigating the riots, insinuating that they had stepped out of place, and had the audacity to argue that FDR could prevent future rioting if he simply barred Black urban migration using the same emergency war powers exercised to intern the Japanese. See Sugrue, *Origins of the Urban Crisis*, 29; and Rahman, "Marching Blind," 181–82.

22 Sugrue, *Origins of Urban Crisis*, 73–75.

23 R. W. Thomas, *Life for Us Is What We Make It*, 146–48.

24 Anonymous, "Danger in Detroit," *Negro: A Review* 11, no. 3 (1944): 12.

25 Self and Sugrue, "Power of Place."

26 Darden et al., *Detroit: Race and Uneven Development*, 16.

27 Consider the famous case of Minnie and Orsel McGhee. In 1945, the Mc-Ghees, an upwardly mobile Black family, bought a house at 4626 Seabaldt Street on Detroit's West Side. Immediately following their purchase, their new next-door neighbor, Benjamin Sipes, in partnership with the all-white Northwest Civil Association, legally challenged their occupancy on the grounds that it violated a neighborhood covenant that homes could be sold only to those of the "Caucasian race." The Wayne County Circuit Court agreed with Sipes, validating the covenant. The McGhees, who were represented by the NAACP Legal Department, appealed to the Michigan Supreme Court (*Sipes v. McGhee*, 316 Mich. 614, 628, 25 N.W.2d 638, 644), arguing that racial covenants violated state antidiscrimination laws and the Fourteenth Amendment. The conservative court remained unconvinced, leaving the NAACP attorneys no other recourse than to bring the case to the Supreme Court. In 1948, the Court heard the *Sipes* case, bundled with three others, including *Shelley v. Kraemer*, 443 U.S. 1 (1948), a similar case from Saint Louis, and ruled unanimously that restrictive covenants were illegal.

Shelley v. Kraemer marked a key turning point in the growth of a Black middle and elite class, members of which moved proportionally farther from the city center as income allowed, often into neighborhoods recently vacated by well-to-do whites. For Black families, like for their white counterparts, homeownership was a sign of status and respectability. As more and more Black families rose to the ranks of middle class and breached the ghetto walls, new class-based spatial divisions emerged within the Black community. Sugrue, *Origins of the Urban Crisis*, 181–83.

28 Sugrue, *Origins of the Urban Crisis*, 212, 194–97.

29 Sugrue, *Origins of the Urban Crisis*, 63–72.

30 Freund, *Colored Property*, 10.

31 Freund, *Colored Property*, 23. As Freund argues, "Rhetorically, at least, whites focused not on the threat that Black people posed to white people but on the threat that Blacks' presence posed to white-owned property, white neighborhoods, and other supposedly white 'places'" (18). Moreover, whites claimed that Black people were incapable of becoming good, responsible home-owning citizens because they perceived them as having an inability to care for their neighborhoods and achieve ownership without "government handouts." They were in short incapable of functioning in the free market— an argument that reflected, as Freund writes, "their fundamental misunderstanding of the forces driving metropolitan change" (19), or, perhaps, this can be better understood as their willful ignorance.

32 "Dr. Tommie Johnson," *Detroit Historical Society Oral History Archive*, accessed August 29, 2021, https://detroit1967.detroithistorical.org/items/show/748.

33 Sugrue, *Origins of Urban Crisis*, 143.

34 For historical analysis of this period of American urbanism and politics beyond Detroit, see Massey and Denton, *American Apartheid*; and Self, *American Babylon*.

35 On tensions between generations, see J. M. Thomas, *Redevelopment and Race*, 128. For more on Black politics and grassroots activism in Detroit, particularly the Freedom Now Party, see Shaw, *Now Is the Time*. Uhuru was led by Luke Tip, John Williams, John Watson, Charles Johnson, General G. Baker, and Gwen Kemp. Some members of Uhuru later went on to join the Revolutionary Action Movement. In 1965, they reformed as the Afro-American Student Movement and put out a journal called *Black Vanguard*, edited by John Watson and distributed to Black workers in plants. See, for example, Dillard, *Faith in the City*, 263–68.

36 Carmichael, "Stokely Carmichael Explains Black Power," 87. See also Tyner, *Geography of Malcolm X*, 76–78.

37 Boggs and Boggs, "City Is the Black Man's Land," 162–70.

38 Maxwell, *New Negro, Old Left*.

39 Boggs and Boggs, "City Is the Black Man's Land," 163.

40 Boggs and Boggs, "City Is the Black Man's Land," 168.

41 Ward, "Introduction," 22.

42 Woodard, "It's Nation Time in NewArk," 289.

43 Shellow, *Harvest of American Racism*, 1–2.

44 Quoted in Marable, *Race, Reform, and Rebellion*, 90.

45 Quoted in Kelley, *Freedom Dreams*, 78.

46 Plummer, *In Search of Power*, 10.

47 Marable, *Race, Reform, and Rebellion*, 84.

48 Following World War II, a global period of decolonization ensued with forty former colonies gaining independence between 1945 and 1960. To be clear, internationalism preceded World War II, but it became more pronounced in its aftermath. For example, after World War I, W. E. B. Du Bois helped organize the Congress in Paris in 1919 that revived the Pan-African movement. In the 1920s, Marcus Garvey's Universal Negro Improvement Association garnered the support of millions. In the twenties and thirties, George Padmore founded the Communist International and Pan-African workers movement. The Fifth Pan-African Congress at Manchester was organized by Padmore, Kwame Nkrumah, and W. E. B. Du Bois and helped set the stage for US postwar liberation struggles, including national independence, civil rights, Black power, and Pan-Africanism.

49 US state officials kept the UN from considering the petition, which was filed in both Paris and New York at the same time.

50 In April 1967, three months before the uprising in Detroit, Martin Luther King Jr. delivered his now famous "Beyond Vietnam: A Time to Break the Silence" speech at New York City Riverside Church, in which he connected domestic struggles for racial equality to unjust war abroad.

51 In an effort to reduce urban violence and amid international pressure to confront racism and inequality at home, in 1964, Congress passed the Civil Rights Act, and the following year, the Economic Opportunity Act and the Voting Rights Act. The Economic Opportunity Act and the newly created Office of Economic Opportunity sought to reduce urban violence by eliminating poverty. Antipoverty programs focused primarily on poor urban Black people, who were seen as an essential and volatile electoral base.

Detroit had one of the first tactical assistance grants for training staff to work with local Community Action agencies as part of the Community Action Program. The city, led by white liberal Democratic mayor Jerome Cavanaugh, a charismatic and crusading integrationist, was poised for revitalization. Touted as a "model city" of race relations, it was even being considered for the 1968 Olympics. As elsewhere, the Community Action Program in Detroit sought to implement a strategy of "maximum feasibility participation" to contain insurgency and integrate radical groups that were seen as a threat to the security of liberal democracy and the project of expanding the national economy. On the politics of community action, see Plummer, *In Search of Power*; A. Goldstein, *Poverty in Common*; and Immerwahr, *Thinking Small*.

52 J. M. Thomas, *Redevelopment and Race*, 130, 132–38.

53 Immerwahr, *Thinking Small*.

54 Rickford, "We Can't Grow Food on All This Concrete," 963.

55 "Jerome Pikulinski, August 14th, 2015," interview transcript and video, Detroit Historical Society Oral History Archive, https://detroit1967 .detroithistorical.org/items/show/295.

56 The notion that community was dissenting and full of difference comes from Plummer, *In Search of Power*, 10.

57 Rahman, "Marching Blind," 184.

58 In the words of Ahmad Rahman, "Black Detroiters had always had a 'place,' and white policemen had confined and controlled them there, in their traditional role as protectors of the security and safety of whites and their property. The 1967 rebellion had been, in effect, an extremely destructive attempt by the black community to violate those boundaries of 'place,' raising the question of who would rule, and under what conditions." See Rahman, "Marching Blind," 189. Also see anthropologist John Hartigan Jr.'s argument that the uprisings were more about class than race, and his point, drawing on Sydney Fine, that it is myth that looting was directed only at white merchants. Hartigan, *Racial Situations*, 310n82.

59 Fine, *Violence in the Model City*, 384.

60 Chafets, *Devil's Night*, 21.

61 Darden and Thomas, *Detroit: Race Riots*, 7, citing Fine, *Violence in the Model City*, 384.

62 Fine, *Violence in the Model City*, 351.

63 Kerner Commission, *Report of the National Advisory Commission on Civil Disorders* (Washington, DC: GPO, 1968), 1.

64 M. McLaughlin, *Long, Hot Summer of 1967*, 45.

65 M. McLaughlin, *Long, Hot Summer of 1967*, 46. The social scientists included David Boesel, Louis Goldberg, Gary T. Marx, and David Sears.

66 See especially Fine, "Meaning of Violence," in *Violence in the Model City*, 351, for survey data. Fine is citing a Campbell and Schuman survey done by the Inter-University Consortium for Political and Social Research. Black File, No. 232, Detroit data for Angus Campbell and Howard Schuman, "Racial Attitudes in Fifteen American Cities," in *Supplemental Studies for the National Advisory Committee on Civil Disorders* (Washington, DC: GPO, 1968).

67 Fine, *Violence in the Model City*, 356.

68 Fine, *Violence in the Model City*, 359.

69 These quotations come from a sermon called "Samson" that Agyeman delivered. The full sermon is published as "No Halfway Revolution" in his first book: Cleage, *Black Messiah*, 122–28. I am quoting from the republication of parts of the sermon in the *Michigan Citizen*. See Paul Lee, "UPRISING! Rare Testimonies and Reports in the '67 Detroit Rebellion, Part 8," *Michigan Citizen*, October 14–20, 2007.

70 The conference, held in July 1967, was part of series of political conventions that took place between 1966 and 1980 modeled on the nineteenth-century National Negro Conventions. See Veroni-Paccher, "Black Power 1968," para. 10.

71 Sherman Adams wrote in the October 20, 1967, issue of the *Inner-City Voice*, "Every major black organization in the U.S. was represented: H. Rap Brown of SNCC, Floyd McKissick of CORE, Watts' nationalist leader Ron Karenga, Dr. Martin Luther King's top troubleshooter Rev. Jesse Jackson and representatives from the Urban League were all official delegates. The delegates emphasized the role of Black Americans in the international struggle for human rights, a theme which earlier was developed by the late Malcolm X." Quoted in Azikiwe, *Rebellion, Crises and Social Transformation*, 107.

72 The Newark uprisings lasted from July 12 to July 17, 1967.

73 Adams's *Inner-City Voice* article quoted in Azikiwe, *Rebellion, Crises and Social Transformation*, 108.

74 "The First Black Power Conference of Newark Is Held," July 22, 1967, African American Registry, https://aaregistry.org/story/black-power-conference-of-newark-held/.

75 In doing so, they countered the economist Gunnar Myrdal, author of the Carnegie Corporation of New York study-turned-book *The American Dilemma*. See Carmichael and Hamilton, *Black Power*, 5.

76 Cleaver, "Land Question," 186.

77 For analysis of the relationship between urban crisis and the Southern land strategy, see Hickmott, "Black Land, Black Capital," 504–34. Hickmott writes, "In emphasizing both the economic possibility of rural spaces and the national implications of agricultural transformation, southern-oriented development workers offered a self-conscious alternative to contemporary celebrations of urbanity and municipal self-government as cornerstones of the Black Power Project" (506). On post-Emancipation calls for land redistribution and calls for an African American state, see L. A. Harris, "Political Autonomy as a Form of Reparations."

78 Singh, *Black Is a Country*, 193.

79 Kelley, *Freedom Dreams*, 125.

80 As James Brown puts it in "Funky President" (1974), "We got to get together and buy some land / Raise our food just like the man / Save our money, do like the mob / Put up your fight, and own the job."

81 Fanon, *Wretched of the Earth*.

82 Early RNA members included Imari Obadele and Gaidi Obadele (cofounders, formerly known as the Henry brothers, who had been active in Detroit's organizing scene, for example, assuming leadership roles in the formation of the Group on Advanced Leadership and the Freedom Now Party), Robert Williams (president elect), members of RAM, Amiri Baraka, H. Rap Brown of the Student Nonviolent Coordinating Committee, Betty Shabazz (Malcolm

X's widow), and members of the Black Panther Party for Self-Defense. See Berger and Dunbar-Ortiz, "Struggle Is for Land!," 57–76. The Obadele brothers argued that the group's claims to Southern land were justified because Black people had lived there traditionally, worked and improved it, and fought to stay there. "This is the civilized rule of land possession," they wrote, "sanctioned by international practices, and it is quite clear that Black people in many northern cities, but especially in the Black Belt of the South, meet all these criteria." Quoted in Densu, "Patchin," 135–36.

83 Berger and Dunbar-Ortiz write, "The RNA argued that black people in the United States constituted a new political subject: The New Afrikan, an identity born within the confines of the United States as a result of the trans-Atlantic slave trade and the ensuing centuries of white supremacy. . . . [T]he New Afrikan could only achieve independence here through claiming the territory that slaves had built and that therefore had been historically home to large populations of black people. . . . [like the American Indian Movement, established in the same year, the RNA] viewed land reclamation as essential to dismantling the US empire from within its domestic colonial boundaries." See Berger and Dunbar-Ortiz, "Struggle Is for Land!," 59.

The American Indian Movement (AIM) and RNA were just two social movements struggling for territory at the time. Other groups also advocated for the redistribution of land. For example, land was the fulcrum of struggle for groups such as the Crusade for Justice (Chicano); the Movimiento de Liberación Nacional (Puerto Rican and Chicano groups); and Prairie Fire Organizing Committee (whites). As Berger and Dunbar-Ortiz write, "These groups, independently and sometimes in coalition, argued that radicalism in the United States must contend with and ultimately overturn the country's settler-colonial roots" ("Struggle Is for Land!," 75nn53–54). In 1972, the RNA unveiled an Anti-Depression Program—they demanded (1) that the US government cede land and sovereignty to the RNA in places where Black people vote for independence through a plebiscite; (2) that it pay $300 billion in reparations; and (3) that a procedure be established to determine payments. In March 1974, the RNA held elections in Mississippi in more than thirty counties. More than five thousand Black people voted for reparations. Karolczyk, *Subjugated Territory*, 163–65; Kelley, *Freedom Dreams*, 124–27.

84 Republic of New Afrika advertisement, Robert Williams Archive, University of Michigan, Ann Arbor.

85 For more on the history of RNA, see Onaci, *Free the Land*.

86 Rahman, "Marching Blind," 189.

87 On the BPP's extensive survival programs, see Dr. Huey P. Newton Foundation, *Black Panther Party*.

88 See Reyes, "Can't Go Home Again," 217–18.

89 Newton, "Intercommunalism," 181–99. Also see John Narayan's writing on intercommunalism: Narayan, "Huey P. Newton's Intercommunalism,"

57–85; Narayan, "Wages of Whiteness in the Absence of Wages," 2482–2500; and Delio Vasquez, "Intercommunalism: The Late Theorizations of Huey P. Newton, 'Chief Theoretician' of the Black Panther Party," *Viewpoint Magazine*, June 11, 2018, https://www.viewpointmag.com/2018/06/11/intercommunalism-the-late-theorizations-of-huey-p-newton-chief-theoretician-of-the-black-panther-party/.

90 Quoted in Kelley, *Freedom Dreams*, 99.

91 The Dodge Revolutionary Union Movement was founded in 1968 after Black workers were overwhelmingly punished for a general walkout strike at the Dodge plant, when neither the local union nor Chrysler met the group's demands. As the LRBW centralized leadership, they expanded their programming into community organizing and legal defense. They founded a bookstore and organized book clubs. It was common for up to two hundred people to attend their book club meetings, including many white suburbanite sympathizers. The league also organized to produce and control their own media, establishing a printing press and embarking on film production. In 1970, they released *Finally Got the News*, a documentary about the league's political program that garnered international interest, particularly in Italy, where since the 1950s, transnational labor radicals in Turin had been in engaged in conversation and critique with radicals in Detroit about the failures of trade unions and Soviet-inspired parties.

    In Detroit, much of this early critique was developed by a small group who published under the name of Correspondence; the group originally included C. L. R. James, Raya Dunayevskaya, and Grace Lee Boggs. Correspondence, in collaboration with Socialisme ou Barbarie, a group of French political militants, faulted unions for failing to address speed-ups and for being "body guards of capital." They also put forth a vision of class struggle in which workers had the capacity to resist and self-organize outside the traditional labor movement. See, for example, Romano and Stone, *American Worker*; and James and Lee, *Facing Reality*. For an in-depth analysis of this transnational exchange, see Pizzolato, *Challenging Global Capitalism*.

    By 1973, the LRBW succumbed to several challenges, including the loss of jobs from continued deindustrialization, the decline in influence of RUM groups within existing plants, particularly Chrysler's change in hiring practices of Black foremen on its assembly lines (which effectively diffused one of RAM's key demands), and, finally, organizational issues within the LRBW itself, including its rapid expansion, related questions of capacity, and internal divisions over political strategy. For a wonderful oral history media project about the LRBW, see General Baker Institute, https://www.revolutionaryblackworkers.org/.

92 On the Black Manifesto, see Forman, "Black Manifesto," 36–44; Kelley, *Freedom Dreams*, 120–21; Lechtreck, "We Are Demanding $500 Million for Reparations," 39–71. At the same conference, Robert Browne put forth

a similar vision, which did not receive as much attention. As Hickmott argues, Browne saw Forman as putting forward a program that sounded good but with little organizational capacity to bring it about. In response, Browne sought to organize the Emergency Land Fund. Hickmott writes, "In many respects, a new era of rural development was born with the issuance of a $4,500 check, sent from NBEDC organizers to the ad-hoc Southeast Regional Economic Development Association (SREDA), to fund 'research preliminary to the formulation of the proposed Southern Land Bank.'" Hickmott, "Black Land, Black Capital," 513.

93 In 1969, Forman famously presented the manifesto to the congregation at New York Riverside Church. For more on the Black Manifesto, see Dye, "Black Manifesto for Reparations in Detroit," 53–83.

94 The manifesto followed closely on the heels of what's become known as the New Bethel Baptist Church incident. A month earlier, on March 29, 1969, supporters of the RNA had gathered at the church in Detroit for an anniversary meeting, when upward of forty police officers stormed the church, fired on the crowd, and arrested almost 150 people. The assault galvanized support for the RNA and the Black Manifesto. Reverend C. L. Franklin (the father of Aretha and head of the church) declared afterward that he shared the goals of the RNA, if not their methods. Like the BPP, the group expanded its base, establishing consulates in New York City, Philadelphia, Chicago, Pittsburgh, San Francisco, Los Angeles, Baltimore, Cleveland, and Washington, DC. In an attempt to garner international support, they also met with foreign governments, including those of the Soviet Union, Tanzania, Sudan, and China. Emboldened by the Black Manifesto, the RNA demanded $400 billion in reparations for the establishment of the republic. Dye, "Black Manifesto for Reparations in Detroit," 53–83; Berger and Dunbar-Ortiz, "Struggle Is for Land!," 57–76; Dawson and Popoff, "Reparations," 53.

95 On coalitional politics, see Berger and Dunbar-Ortiz, "Struggle Is for Land!," 57–76; also see Fung, "This Isn't Your Battle or Your Land," 163–64.

96 Quoted in Flamm, *Law and Order*, 173.

97 Lassiter and the Policing and Social Justice HistoryLab, "STRESS on Trial." Also see Camp, *Incarcerating the Crisis*, 5.

98 J. M. Thomas, *Redevelopment and Race*, 150.

99 "Black Seeks Mayor's Office," *Chicago Defender (Big Weekend Edition)*, June 2, 1973, 5.

100 Heather Thompson writes: "By 1981, 1,126 out of 5,013 police officers were African American, and 10 of the 20 police commanders were black as well. Whereas women comprised only 2 percent of the department in 1967, by 1987 they made up a full 20 percent of the force and, in addition, there were three female commanders and a female deputy chief." Thompson, *Whose Detroit?*, 204.

101 Editorial, "Young Has Set the Stage for a Bitter Campaign," *Detroit Free Press*, May 12, 1973.

102 J. M. Thomas, *Redevelopment and Race*, 199.

103 Thompson, *Whose Detroit?*, 206.

104 Darden et al., *Detroit: Race and Uneven Development*, 24–27. They write: "Metropolitan industrial investment targeted to Detroit fell from 44 percent in 1958 to 22 percent in 1977—a decline of 50 percent in just two decades" (24). At the same time, Detroit's share of commercial sales generated by the region's major shopping areas decreased from 65.7 percent to 9.8 percent. They continue, "In 1968, 10 of the region's 20 major shopping areas were located in the city of Detroit. By 1977 that number had dropped to 1, and with the closing of Hudson's in 1983, the central city—with a population of 1.2 million people—was no longer home to even 1 major shopping area" (26).

105 In *Milliken v. Bradley*, 433 U.S. 267 (1977), the Supreme Court held that desegregation plans to deal with segregation in the metropolitan Detroit school system were not legal. It essentially ruled that the right of a child to attend a desegrated school meant only the right to attend a school where no vestiges of state-imposed segregation still existed. The case has had an enormous effect on ensuring segregated school districts across the nation. See Sedler, "Profound Impact of Milliken v. Bradley," 1693–1722.

106 In 1983, the gap was $11,685. For overall Metro Detroit, average household income was $33,241, whereas in Detroit, it was $21,556. Darden et al., *Detroit: Race and Uneven Development*, 206.

107 For UAW figures, see Thompson, *Whose Detroit?*, 216. For national union figures, see Kris Warner, *Protecting Fundamental Labor Rights* (Washington, DC: Center for Economic and Policy Research, 2012), http://www.cepr .net/documents/publications/canada-2012-08.pdf; and Mahmud, "Debt and Discipline," 18–19n117. In the private sector, the decline in unionization rates was even more dramatic, falling from 25 percent in 1975 to 6.9 percent in 2010. Thompson summarizes the stakes of this period: "African Americans finally had real power in Detroit, and liberalism had survived a conservative attack. But because the national conservative war against liberal, and particularly African American, power never ended, Detroit was doomed to experience severe economic distress and social isolation" (193).

108 See Austin McCoy, "A Socialist Oasis in Detroit in the 1970s?," *Metropole: The Official Blog of the Urban History Association*, November 4, 2019, https://themetropole.blog/2019/11/04/a-socialist-oasis-in-detroit-in-the -1970s/.

109 "Conference Draws a Crowd," *Dispatch: The Newsletter of the Detroit Alliance for a Rational Economy (DARE)* 1, no. 10 (October 1979).

110 McCoy, "A Socialist Oasis," 110.

111 SOSAD's archive can be found at the Bentley Historical Library, 1987–1992.

112 On the power of bond-rating agencies over municipal governance, see Hackworth, "Local Autonomy, Bond-Rating Agencies," 707–25; and Lake, "Financialization of Urban Policy," 75–78.

113 On Detroit's credit-rating debacle, see Sinclair, *New Masters of Capital*, 106. Sinclair argues that rating agencies have "epistemic authority," meaning they significantly discipline the thinking and action of municipal leaders. The creation of ratings depends on value-laden algorithms to assess and minimize investor risk, which has a disciplinary effect on sovereign governments and other borrowers. See Sinclair, "Passing Judgment," 133–59.

114 Deploying the discourse of multiculturalism and regional cooperation, Archer promised to "transcend old racial divides, work with a Republican governor, and spur new business investment." Quoted in Shaw, *Now Is the Time*, 166. His deracialized campaign infuriated many Black Detroiters, but he still won by a narrow margin. For political and corporate leaders in the suburbs, Archer's election marked the dawn of a new day in Detroit. Sinclair, *New Masters of Capital*, 106, 170.

115 If demolition did not altogether cease, it happened on a more ad hoc basis under the pretense of economic development, like the razing of the Poletown neighborhood for the GM assembly plant expansion and the destruction of public housing under the HOPE VI program. See Hackworth, "Demolition as Urban Policy," 2205. In 2002, as a mayoral candidate, Kilpatrick promised to take down five thousand homes during his first year in office. Residents initially supported demolitions as a strategy in the local war on drugs. But as the Kilpatrick administration edged on, residents were troubled by the lack of redevelopment plans. Many neighborhoods were left pockmarked with upturned dirt where houses had sat before. See Bergmann, *Getting Ghost*, 81. Nevertheless, demolitions as urban redevelopment continued throughout the Kilpatrick administration and beyond. While Kilpatrick was seen as an up-and-coming Black politician—being eyed by national Democratic leadership—his political career began to unravel at the start of a narrowly secured second term when he became caught up with his chief of staff in a sex scandal. Detroit became politically paralyzed as the mayor bungled his way through the controversy, refusing to resign for almost a year and reinforcing perceptions of the city government as corrupt and inept.

116 Stein, *Capital City*.

Chapter Three. Stealing Home

1 The opening scene comes from a description of the auction in an article by Laura Gottesdiener, "A Foreclosure Conveyor Belt: The Continuing Depopulation of Detroit," *TomDispatch*, April 19, 2015, http://www.tomdispatch.com/blog/175983/.

2 As Woods argues, capitalist societies develop through the reorganization of property relations and social-spatial enclosures. Multiple mechanisms enable wealth extraction, including asset stripping, which has functioned as a key pillar of neoliberalism via privatization. Woods writes, "The stripping of

assets from racially enclosed communities presents another dimension of the question. Although there is a complex legal regime in the United States to enforce laws against racial discrimination, racialized groups are targeted by the policies of blocs which are designed for specific racial-spatial enclosures (neighborhoods, regions, etc.), and for those economic sectors, occupations, institutions, and policy arenas where African Americans and subordinated groups are concentrated." The subprime foreclosure crisis, which disproportionately affected low-income people of color, was a prime example. Banks issued subprime loans to Latinx and Black people at rates 2.5 to 3 times higher than those issued to whites. Across the country the total loss of wealth for people of color was devastating. As cited by Woods, a report issued by United for a Fair Economy estimated the figure to be between $164 to $213 billion. See Woods, "Les Misérables of New Orleans," 775–76; and for the report, see Amaad Rivera, Brenda Cotto-Escalera, Anisha Desai, Jeannette Huezo, and Dedrick Muhammad, *Foreclosed: State of the Dream 2008* (Boston: United for a Fair Economy, January 15, 2008), vii, https://d3n8a8pro7vhmx.cloudfront.net/ufe/pages/2157/attachments/original/1442675896/StateOfDream_01_16_08_Web.pdf?1442675896.

3 Christine MacDonald and Joel Kurth, "Foreclosures Fuel Detroit Blight, Cost the City $500 Million," *Detroit News*, June 3, 2015, https://www.detroitnews.com/story/news/special-reports/2015/06/03/detroit-foreclosures-risky-mortgages-cost-taxpayers/27236605/.

4 Nationally, according to the US Census, Black homeownership peaked at about 50 percent in 2004. In 2016, Black households had a homeownership rate of 41.7 percent, which was a fifty-year low. In 1990, the percentage of African Americans who owned their own homes in Michigan was 47.7 percent. In Detroit, it was 49 percent. See Carl Hedman and Rolf Pendall, "Rebuilding and Sustaining Homeownership for African Americans," Southeast Michigan Housing Futures, Brief 3, June 2018, https://www.urban.org/sites/default/files/publication/98719/rebuilding_and_sustaining_homeownership_for_african_americans.pdf.

5 Michelle Morris is a pseudonym. Uniting Detroiters project interview, December 2012.

6 In 2007, Black people constituted 82 percent of the city's population and received 75 percent of all home loans and loan dollars, representing relative parity. The subprime crisis and recession, however, regressed this progress. By 2017, Black people received just 48 percent of home loans and only 34 percent of loan dollars, even though they still made up the majority of the city's population (79 percent). In 2007, 52 percent of home loan applications in the region (including Wayne, Oakland, Macomb, and Washtenaw Counties) were for homes in Detroit. Ten years later, this figure stood at a mere 14 percent. Home Mortgage Disclosure Act data can be found here: "Download HDMA Data," Consumer Financial Protection Bureau, accessed

October 1, 2022, https://www.consumerfinance.gov/data-research/hmda
/historic-data/?geo=mi&records=all-records&field_descriptions=labels. For
a summary of findings, see Mike Wilkinson, "Whites Get Half of Mortgages
in Detroit, Nation's Largest Majority Black City," *Bridge Michigan*, June 13,
2019, https://www.bridgemi.com/urban-affairs/whites-get-half-mortgages
-detroit-nations-largest-majority-black-city. Also see Campbell et al.,
"Black Homeownership in Detroit," 198–201.

7   Claude Faye is a pseudonym. Uniting Detroiters project interview,
    November 2012.

8   Glenda is a pseudonym.

9   Kahrl, "Unconscionable," 911.

10 Connolly, *World More Concrete*, 208.

11 *Online Etymology Dictionary*, s.v. "foreclosure (n.)," updated July 27, 2012,
    https://www.etymonline.com/word/foreclosure.

12 *Online Etymology Dictionary*, s.v. "eviction (n.)," updated April 27, 2020,
    https://www.etymonline.com/word/eviction.

13 While tenants could be expelled, as Claire Priest has shown, English tradi-
    tion protected land-owning families from loss due to nonpayment of debt.
    Priest, "Creating an American Property Law," 385–459. Also see Park,
    "Money, Mortgages, and the Conquest of America," 1006–35.

14 Christine MacDonald, "Persistent Evictions Threaten Detroit Neighbor-
    hoods," *Detroit News*, October 5, 2017, https://www.detroitnews.com
    /story/news/special-reports/2017/10/05/detroit-evictions-threaten
    -neighborhoods-rentals/106315064/. Also see "Fact Sheet on City of Detroit
    Conditions," Moratorium NOW!, July 2018, https://moratorium-mi.org/wp
    -content/uploads/2018/07/Detroit-fact-sheet.pdf.

15 Woods, "Life after Death," 63. See also Eve Tuck's important call for a focus
    on desire-centered research. Tuck, "Suspending Damage," 409–27.

16 Rode, *Poems at My Doorstep*. Poem can be read in full online here:
    "Playing with Big Numbers," Poetry International, 2008, https://www
    .poetryinternational.org/pi/poem/11871/auto/0/0/Ajmer-Rode/PLAYING
    -WITH-BIG-NUMBERS/en/tile.

17 Rode, *Poems at My Doorstep*.

18 Matthew Bloch and Haeyoun Park, "Here Are the 43,634 Properties in
    Detroit That Were on the Brink of Foreclosure in 2014," *New York Times*,
    June 26, 2014, https://www.nytimes.com/interactive/2014/06/27/us/detroit
    -foreclosure-photo-mosaic.html.

19 Calculations are based on federal minimum wage ($7.25) and monthly aver-
    age disability at the time of writing. In 2014, minimum wage in Michigan was
    $8.14.

20 Alana Davis is a pseudonym. Uniting Detroiters project interview, March 2012.

21 On the moral valences of debt and homeownership following the subprime
    crisis, see Stout, "Indebted," 82–106.

22 On unemployed councils, see Lorence, *Organizing the Unemployed.*

23 On mortgage moratorium foreclosure statutes in the 1930s, see D. P. K., "Constitutional Law," 71–80.

24 At the same time, it is important to recognize that low-rent housing remained segregated and access to it was limited by "selectivity and moral judgement," in the words of urban studies scholar and public housing historian Lawrence Vale. Public housing, as Vale shows, was intended not for the poorest of the poor but rather for working-class families who could afford modest rent and who demonstrated promise for upward economic mobility. Vale, *Purging the Poorest,* 3.

25 Blackmar, "Appropriating 'the Commons,'" 57–58.

26 Ben Austen, "The Towers Came Down, and with Them the Promise of Public Housing," *New York Times Magazine,* February 6, 2008.

27 On dismantling the projects, see Fennell, *Last Project Standing.* On dismantling public housing, see Goetz, *New Deal Ruins;* on taxes, imagined publics, and racialized notions of citizenship, see C. Walsh, "White Backlash," 237–47.

28 This section is indebted to an excellent paper by geographer Joshua Akers about the auction, which at the time of writing was the only extensive research that existed on its history. For a more nuanced political history of the auction and to better understand the stake of market-centric policy transfers through think tanks, see Akers "Making Markets," 1070–95. From property rights movement adherents, see Steven J. Eagle, "The Birth of the Property Rights Movement," *Policy Analysis,* no. 404, June 26, 2001, http://www.cato.org/sites/cato.org/files/pubs/pdf/pa404.pdf. Also cf. Jacobs and Paulsen, "Property Rights," 134–43. Other names for the property rights movement include the *land rights movement* and the *wise use movement.*

29 Akers, "Making Markets," 1070–95. In 1981, Detroit started an urban homesteading program (now defunct) following the enactment of the federal Housing and Community Development Act of 1974. See Christensen, "Securing the Momentum," 241–60. As part of the program, the federal government transferred ownership of eighty-one single-family residences to the City of Detroit to be used for homesteading, of which thirty-eight were transferred conditionally to homesteaders and only twelve became occupied. See Office of Program Analysis and Evaluation, *Consolidated Annual Report to Congress on Community Development Programs,* Department of Housing and Urban Development, March 31, 1982, http://archives.hud.gov/offices /cpd/communitydevelopment/congress/1982.pdf. On the Michigan Urban Homestead Act, see Reno, "Floor without a Ceiling," 137–54.

30 Akers "Making Markets," 1070–95.

31 Akers "Making Markets," 1078.

32 Schuette quoted in Akers, "Making Markets," 1079.

33 Akers, "Making Markets," 1079.

34 Under the Dawes Severalty Act of 1887, modeled on the first Homestead Act, tribal land was divided into allotments for which Native Americans could then apply for individual title; however, one had to first prove one's "Indianness." Prior to application for land, Native Americans were subjected to blood quantum testing. Pugliese, *Biometrics*, 44.

35 Bill Schuette, "Urban Homesteading: An Urban Policy for a New Century," *American Outlook* (Spring 1998): 1–3.

36 Akers, "Making Markets, 1080.

37 Quoted in Akers, "Making Markets, 1080.

38 Hartman, *Scenes of Subjection*, 118.

39 Mark Schmidt is a pseudonym.

40 On the entertainment-led development and rise of the casino industry, see McCarthy, "Entertainment-Led Regeneration," 105–11; and Ryan, "From Cars to Casinos," 91–106.

41 Every March, the county started doing title searches. It hired three companies that went through all the legal records to see who had an interest in a property. Did someone perform work and take out a lien? Was there a mortgage? Who owned it? At the end of November, they notified everyone who had an interest in (or lien on) the property. It could be one person or fifteen. Someone might put a lien on a property for nonpayment of a bill. If there was a lien, it meant that the property had a "cloud" on the title.

42 Sarah Cwiek, "Citizen Research Links Detroit Water Shutoffs, Tax Foreclosures," Michigan Radio, August 12, 2016, https://www.michiganradio.org /post/citizen-research-links-detroit-water-shutoffs-tax-foreclosures. Also see the excellent work of We the People of Detroit Community Research Collective and their 2016 report "Mapping the Water Crisis: The Dismantling of African American Neighborhoods in Detroit," We the People of Detroit, https://www.wethepeopleofdetroit.com/product-page/mapping-the-water -crisis-ebook.

43 On debtor-creditor relations under neoliberalism, see, for example, Mahmud, "Debt and Discipline," 469–94; and Lazzarato, *Making of the Indebted Man*.

44 See Hull, "File," 287–314; and Hull, *Government of Paper*.

45 By comparison, in 2000, the Big Three employed 435,000. To be sure, the dominance of the Big Three had been shrinking since 1965, when it commanded the vast majority (91 percent) of the US auto market. But the losses in the last decade were striking. By 2009, the figure stood at 45 percent, with devasting effects for those employed by the automobile sector. Employment rose abroad for the Big Three, from 249,622 in 2000 to 276,800 in 2010. See Ryan, "From Cars to Casinos," 93–94.

46 Ghazavi, "Ethics at a Distance."

47 "Interview with Jill Stauffer, author of Ethical Loneliness," *Columbia University Press Blog*, October 1, 2015, https://www.cupblog.org/2015/10/01/interview-with-jill-stauffer-author-of-ethical-loneliness/.

48 Bhandar et al., "Unsettling our Relationship to Things and People," 174.

49 Joel Kurth, Mike Wilkinson, and Laura Herberg, "Sorry We Foreclosed Your Home, but Thanks for Fixing Our Budget," *Bridge Michigan*, June 6, 2017, https://www.bridgemi.com/detroit-journalism-cooperative/sorry-we-foreclosed-your-home-thanks-fixing-our-budget.

50 Kurth, Wilkinson, and Herberg, "Sorry We Foreclosed Your Home." Also see Stephen Henderson interview with Wayne County executive Warren Evans on WDET's *Detroit Today*, March 2, 2016, https://wdet.org/posts/2016/03/02/82625-warren-evans-says-wayne-county-in-much-better-fiscal-health/.

51 Christopher F. Petrella, "Wealth, Slavery, and the History of American Taxation," *Black Perspectives*, April 20, 2017, https://www.aaihs.org/wealth-slavery-and-the-history-of-american-taxation/.

52 Henricks and Seamster, "Mechanisms of the Racial Tax State," 175. They attribute "killing them softly" to Bonilla-Silva, *Racism without Racists*.

53 See, for example, Sears and Citrin, *Tax Revolt*.

54 Rothstein, *Color of Law*, 170–72.

55 Lincoln Institute of Land Policy and Minnesota Center for Fiscal Excellence, *50-State Property Tax Comparison*, April 2015, accessed November 27, 2022, https://www.lincolninst.edu/sites/default/files/pubfiles/50-state-property-tax-study-2015-full_0.pdf. The city's high tax rate is driven by multiple factors but is largely attributable to the downward spiral that comes with population loss. Simply put, originally the flight of business and whites led to new taxes to cover city services. Higher taxes led to more outmigration followed by a further reduction in the quality of services and then more people leaving. Moreover, one-fifth of the city's land area is not taxable, including schools, colleges and universities, religious and charitable organizations, nonprofits, and a sizable number of properties with tax abatements. The fewer the entities paying taxes, the more the burden falls on a smaller number of payers. In 2013, Detroit had the ninth highest property taxes in the country for a large city according to the report "10 U.S. Cities with the Highest Taxes," *Market Watch*, March 11, 2013, http://www.marketwatch.com/story/10-us-cities-with-the-highest-taxes-2013-03-02.

56 Millage rates are tax rates that are applied to the assessed value of real estate. The rate is the amount of tax, in dollars, on every $1,000 of taxable value, meaning in the example above, $60,000 is multiplied by 0.06774.

57 The millage rate listed here is for the portion of Portland in Multnomah County. The other half of Portland is in Washington County and has an

even lower millage rate. Notably, Portland's low millage rate is the result of the same sort of homeowner tax revolt, which led to Prop 5 in Oregon and froze property taxes. This had the effect of subsidizing the gentrification of Black neighborhoods in Portland, providing white newcomers with extremely low property taxes, while those who were displaced faced higher overall tax rates in their new neighborhoods. See Mark Henkels, "Measure 5 (Property Taxes)," *Oregon Encyclopedia*, January 22, 2021, https://www.oregonencyclopedia.org/articles/measure_5_property_taxes/# .YNNmmBNKii4.

58 Median household income data for all three cities comes from the US Census Bureau, American Community Survey, 2008–2012. Even though property taxes are high in Detroit, they are a small percentage of the city's general fund revenues compared to other cities. In 2012, property taxes in other US cities constituted between 48 and 77 percent of general fund revenues. In Detroit, they made up a mere 13 percent. The general fund is used to account for general municipal operations and activities, for example, police, fire, parks, planning, community development, and administrative support services. Cf. Sands and Skidmore, "Making Ends Meet," 682–700.

59 Christine MacDonald and Mike Wilkinson, "Half of Detroit Property Owners Don't Pay Taxes," *Detroit News*, February 21, 2013, https://www.detroitnews .com/story/news/local/detroit-city/2018/06/13/detroit-property-owners-tax -delinquency/700005002/.

60 Atuahene and Hodge, "Stategraft," 263–302. They estimate that 90 percent of properties valued at less than $18,500 were assessed in violation of the Michigan Constitution (272n31). See also Atuahene, "Our Taxes Are Too Damn High," 1501–64.

61 The property reappraisal happened in 2017 (the first in almost sixty years) after a 2013 *Detroit News* investigation revealed the problem. See Mac-Donald and Wilkinson, "Half of Detroit Property Owners." Also see a 2020 news report on overtaxation by Christine MacDonald, "Detroit Homeowners Overtaxed $600 Million," *Detroit News*, January 9, 2020, https://www .detroitnews.com/story/news/local/detroit-city/housing/2020/01/09/detroit -homeowners-overtaxed-600-million/2698518001/. Read about ACLU case here: "Discriminatory Tax Foreclosures," ACLU Michigan, accessed October 1, 2022, https://www.aclumich.org/en/cases/discriminatory-tax -foreclosures. And for more on the announcement of the lawsuit, see Christine MacDonald, "Class Action Lawsuit: Detroiters Prevented from Appealing Inflated Tax Assessments," *Detroit News*, February 13, 2020, https://www.detroitnews.com/story/news/local/detroit-city/2020/02 /13/class-action-lawsuit-accuses-officials-overtaxing-detroit-residents /4723186002/.

62 Kevin Krolicki, "Detroit House Auction Flops for Urban Wasteland," *Reuters*, October 26, 2009, para. 6, https://www.reuters.com/article/us

-usa-housing-detroit/detroit-house-auction-flops-for-urban-wasteland
-idUKTRE59O17F20091026.

63 Quoted in Krolicki, "Detroit House Auction Flops," paras. 2–3.

64 Christine MacDonald, "Mass Foreclosure Auction Reflects Economic Fallout: Record 13,000 Properties up for Sale in Wayne Co., a 44% Jump over 2009," *Detroit News*, September 17, 2010, A8.

65 Rose Hackman, "One-Fifth of Detroit's Population Could Lose Their Homes," *The Atlantic*, October 22, 2014, https://www.theatlantic.com /business/archive/2014/10/one-fifth-of-detroits-population-could-lose -their-homes/381694/.

66 David Sands, "Kelly Parker Foreclosure: Cancer Patient Mom Renews Fight to Save Graffiti-Covered Home," *HuffPost*, September 24, 2012, https:// www.huffpost.com/entry/kelly-parker-foreclosure-graffiti-cancer-mom_n _1910412.

67 I borrow the term "fiscal disobedience" from Roitman, *Fiscal Disobedience*.

68 "Detroit—for the Ultimate Ethical Investment Opportunity," Easier.com, January 25, 2013, http://www.easier.com/111407-detroit-for-the-ultimate -ethical-investment-opportunity.html. On investors misleading international buyers, see Miles Brignall, "Beware the Detroit Buy-to-Lets Being Marketed to Unwary UK investors," *Guardian* (UK), August 2, 2014, https://www.theguardian.com/money/2014/aug/02/-sp-beware-detroit-buy -to-let-property-marketed-uk-investors; and John Gallagher, "Belgium Investors Learn It's Buyer Beware in Detroit," *Detroit Free Press*, April 6, 2017, https://www.freep.com/story/money/business/john-gallagher/2017/04/06 /detroit-investment-belgium/99823810/.

69 Christine MacDonald, "Persistent Evictions Threaten Detroit Neighborhoods," *Detroit News*, October 5, 2017, https://www.detroitnews.com /story/news/special-reports/2017/10/05/detroit-evictions-threaten -neighborhoods-rentals/106315064/; Hedman and Pendall, "Rebuilding and Sustaining Homeownership"; Akers and Seymour, "Instrumental Exploitation," 127–40; Seymour and Akers, "Portfolio Solutions," 46–56; Seymour and Akers, "Building the Eviction Economy," 35–69.

70 Christine MacDonald, "Detroit Landlords Cash in on Rent Aid, Ignore Tax Bills," *Detroit News*, March 28, 2014. For example, in 2014, 26 percent of Section 8 landlords were tax delinquent. City ordinances required rentals to be registered, livable, and inspected annually; however, lack of regulation and enforcement meant most landlords escaped scrutiny, despite complaints from tenants.

71 Alba is a pseudonym.

72 Jameelah is a pseudonym.

73 Jay Scott Smith, "Highland Park Goes Dark: City Removes Lights to Pay Bills," *The Grio*, October 11, 2011, https://thegrio.com/2011/10/11/highland -park-goes-dark-city-removes-lights-to-pay-bills/

Chapter Four. White Picket Fences

1 See, for example, Herscher, *Unreal Estate Guide to Detroit*.

2 On the transfer of rights and relationship to new forms of political authority, see Verdery, "Obligations of Ownership," 139.

3 On state formation through the production of property and citizenship, see Lund, "Rule and Rupture," 1199–1228.

4 According to an interview with a city planner, when the land holdings of other city departments were factored in—Water and Sewerage, Police, Fire, Housing Commission—the city owned more than sixty-two thousand parcels, and this figure didn't even count the hundreds of school closures.

5 Ben Price is a pseudonym.

6 As I discuss further in chapter 8, at the time, urban agriculture sat a crossroads between state and local power. Urban farming was widespread, but zoning did not support it. City officials had a policy of looking the other way. An urban agricultural ordinance was being developed but had not yet been formalized.

7 I couldn't help but note, paradoxically, that more than a few of the companies featured in the book had recently been ensconced in accusations of swindling and racism, with some conspicuously around issues of housing (e.g., Fannie Mae and Wells Fargo).

8 The program was located in demonstrations areas of the Detroit Works Project and was first piloted in Southwest Detroit. The city allowed the disposition of vacant lots only in areas considered "transitional" or of better value, according to the Market Value Analysis, which I discuss in chapter 7.

9 There was a large black market for steel and other salvaged valuables sourced from vacated homes and factories, such as pipes, sinks, toilets, tubs, hot water tanks, and furnaces.

10 On the complexities of blight and eminent domain, see Murray, "Detroit Looks toward a Massive, Unconstitutional Blight Condemnation."

11 See Kinder, *DIY Detroit*.

12 This section relies in part on Uniting Detroiters Project interview. It appears in abbreviated form in *A People's Atlas of Detroit*. Ada and Rosalind are pseudonyms. See Foster, Marble, and Williamson, "Riverfront East Congregation Initiative," 222–26.

13 Freire, *Pedagogy of Hope*, 3.

14 Cowen, Garelli, and Tazzioli, "Editors' Interview with Deborah Cowen," 402.

15 Historically, there were bars to owning property. Indeed, those outside of whiteness and masculinity were outside of property or were property themselves. As Grace Hong writes, "Propertylessness was not only an economic category (i.e., the condition of not owning particular things) but became a form of illegible and despised subjectivity (the inability to own) mapped onto race and gender." Hong, "Existentially Surplus," 89.

16 Davis and Williams, "Fences and Between Fences," 247.

17 Blomley, "Performing Property," 5.

18 *Picket* itself references the historical French *piquet*, a pointed stake atop which a soldier stood for military punishment.

19 Hutchinson, "White Picket Fences, White Innocence," 622.

20 Roy, "Urban Informality," 149.

21 C. M. Rose, *Property and Persuasion*, 3.

22 Frost, "Mending Wall," 11–13.

23 This conversation with Kathleen is excerpted from a longer interview that appears in *A People's Atlas of Detroit*. See Foster, Marble, and Williamson, "Riverfront East Congregation Initiative," 222–23.

24 Pinto, *Daughters of Parvarti*, 256–57.

25 Goffe, "Capture and Abandon," 63.

26 Katherine McKittrick shows how what gets perceived as empty space or vacant space by contemporary planners is neither. Rather, there are different coordinates, secret histories, ways of relating and surviving that produce differential space, illegible within the contours of redevelopment maps born from a colonial European lineage of ownership, private property, and exchange value. Such alternate ways of knowing is what Clyde Woods calls a "blues epistemology." Like the plot on the plantation, Detroiters have forged new social orders/infrastructures in the face of expropriation, dispossession, and dehumanization that challenge proprietary notion of personhood and ownership and suggest other ways of organizing social relationships and ways of being. McKittrick, "Plantation Futures," 1–15; Woods, *Development Arrested*.

27 McClellan, "This Is What We Call Home," 87–93.

28 Martinez, "We Need to Put a Plan Together," 111–15.

29 Robinson, *Black Marxism*, especially chapter 6, 121–66.

30 Martinez, "We Need to Put a Plan Together," 111–15.

31 Hosbey and Roanne, "A Totally Different Form of Living," 70.

32 See for example, Winston, "Maroon Geographies," 2185–99; and Wright, "Morphology of Marronage," 1134–49.

33 Uniting Detroiters project, Land Conversations, August 2012.

34 Curtis and Quizar, "Detroit-Opoly," 83.

35 Lee Gaddies quoted in Campbell et al., *People's Atlas of Detroit*, 90. Many African Americans in Detroit, like Gaddies, are only one or two generations removed from land in the South. Given this, it was common for people to talk about how their families lost land during the massive waves of northern migration. Indeed, Black farmers were often encouraged to sell land cheaply. In the early 1900s, Black farmers owned 15.6 million acres of land. By the end of the twentieth century, they owned only 2 million acres. See Center for Social Inclusion, *Regaining Ground: Cultivating Community Assets and Preserving Black Land* (New York: Center for Social Inclusion, 2011).

36 Uniting Detroiters project, Land Conversations, August 2012. Their conversation made me think about a point that Bhandar makes: "The ways in which we understand, practice, and perform modes of subjectivity that are rooted in possession and domination are intimately bound to the juridical apparatus of private property relations. One cannot be done without dismantling the other." Bhandar, *Colonial Lives of Property*, 199. As philosopher Emmanuel Levinas writes, "Self is not a substance but a relation." According to Levinas, ethics unfold within relationships of responsibility. Subjectivity is constituted by our intersubjective encounters. To abjure this relationality and our entangled responsibility to others—to act as if one were alone—is violence. Levinas quoted in Bird Rose, *Reports from a Wild Country*, 13.

37 Hunter et al., "Black Placemaking," 31–56.

Chapter Five. Accounting for Unpayable Debt

1 Pew Charitable Trusts, *The Local Squeeze: Falling Revenues and Growing Demand for Services Challenging Cities, Counties, and School Districts* (Washington, DC: Pew Charitable Trusts, 2012), http://www.pewtrusts.org /~/media/Assets/2012/06/Pew_Cities_Local-Squeeze_report.pdf.

2 On unpayable debt, see Haiven, "Art of Unpayable Debts," 195–230; Joseph, *Debt to Society*; Lazzarato, *Making of the Indebted Man*; Graeber, *Debt*; and Ross, *Creditocracy*.

3 Chakravartty and Ferreira da Silva, "Accumulation, Dispossession, and Debt," 362–71.

4 As Seamster writes, "Consider Black enslaved people working for years to purchase freedom for themselves and their families (earning the right to start at zero). Later, debt was the key mechanism in sharecropping, wherein Black families wound up trapped by having to pay off the previous year's expenses with the next year's crop (all via balance sheets controlled by White overseers)." When the Freedman's Savings Bank was created as an "alternative to reparations," Blacks deposited money and USDA loans continued the cycle when sharecropping ended. The expropriation continues, at the individual level up to towns and entire cities. See Seamster, "Black Debt, White Debt," 35.

5 According to 2010 US Census, only 14.3 percent of the state identified as Black or African American.

6 As Paula Chakravartty and Denise Ferreira da Silva argue, the contemporary global financial order is built on legacies of racism and colonialism, producing racialized financial subjects, including nonwhite and poor people who are saddled with unpayable debts and those who profit off their failure. Chakravartty and Ferreira da Silva, "Accumulation, Dispossession, and Debt," 362–71.

7 Stauffer, *Ethical Loneliness*, 45.

8 Stauffer, *Ethical Loneliness*, 45.

9 Alfred Frankowski writes, "Social forgetting is far more political than we might initially think since it includes not only what is forgotten, but also the way in which events are remembered." See Frankowski, "Violence of Post-racial Memory," para. 2.

10 Said, "Invention, Memory, and Place," 185.

11 For more on Halbwachs's biography, see Friedmann and Mueller, "Maurice Halbwachs," 509–17.

12 Halbwachs, *On Collective Memory*, 183.

13 For more on the Maine Wabanaki TRC process, see Collins, McEvoy-Levy, and Watson, "Maine Wabanaki-State Child Welfare Truth and Reconciliation Commission," 140–69.

14 Moments like these filled me with a sense of urgency and responsibility to make analytical space for them in my writing. Scholars have sought to name these impulses in a number of ways—through the telling of counter-histories or people's histories to draw attention to subjugated knowledges and to the framework of haunting. My thinking here is shaped by scholars such as Gordon, *Ghostly Matters*; Bird Rose, *Reports from a Wild Country*; Foucault, "Nietzsche, Genealogy, History"; McKittrick, "Plantation Futures"; and Lowe, "History Hesitant."

15 Derek H. Alderman writes, "The potential struggle to determine what (and whose) conception of the past will prevail constitutes the politics of memory." Alderman, "Surrogation and the Politics of Remembering," 90.

16 See Coser, "Introduction," 25.

17 Schwartz and Heinrich, "Shadings of Regret," 116.

18 Soyinka, *Burden of Memory*, 90.

19 For analysis of the Detroit and Greensboro TRC processes, see Inwood, Alderman, and Barron, "Addressing Structural Violence." For more information about the Michigan Roundtable's effort to facilitate the truth commission process in the Detroit metro region, see Jason Reece and Dwight Holley, *Detroit at a Crossroad: Emerging from Crisis and Building Prosperity for All* (Columbus, OH: Kirwan Institute for the Study of Race and Ethnicity, 2013), http://www.racialequitytools.org/resourcefiles/DetroitatCrossroads.pdf; and Tom Costello, "We Don't Want Them: Race and Housing on Trial," Michigan Roundtable for Diversity and Inclusion, October 17, 2019, https://miroundtable.wordpress.com/2009/10/17/we-dont-want-them-race-and-housing-on-trial/.

20 Metropolitan Detroit Truth and Reconciliation Commission, "Charter for the Metropolitan Detroit Truth and Reconciliation Commission on Racial Inequality," April 2011.

21 Metropolitan Detroit Truth and Reconciliation Commission, "Charter."

22 Music, "Kidnapped Children of Detroit," 22.

23 Music, "Kidnapped Children of Detroit," 21.

24 Gilmore, "Fatal Couplings of Power and Difference," 15. Gilmore's definition of racism—as "a practice of abstraction, a death-dealing displacement of difference into hierarchies that organize relations within and between the planet's sovereign political territories"—underscored the steep challenges of the commission's charge. Gilmore, "Fatal Couplings of Power and Difference," 16.

25 On child poverty, see Data Driven Detroit, *State of the Detroit Child: 2010*. The median household income in Detroit of $28,000 stands in stark contrast to that in adjacent counties, where median incomes range from $54,000 (Macomb) to $66,000 (Oakland). Data from US Census, 2010. On racial divides in Detroit, see, for example, Darden et al., *Detroit: Race and Uneven Development*; Farley, Danziger, and Holzer, *Detroit Divided*; and Sugrue, *Origins of the Urban Crisis*.

26 Gilmore, "Fatal Couplings of Power and Difference," 16.

27 House gave this address at the inaugural event. A version of it is also published in *A People's Atlas of Detroit*. House, "Corporate Power and the Reinvention of Detroit," 204–7.

28 Chakravartty and Ferreira da Silva, "Accumulation, Dispossession, and Debt," 372.

29 See chapter 4 ("Suspending Democracy Is Violence") of Campbell et al., *A People's Atlas of Detroit* for a detailed timeline of the state takeover, 160–92. On revanchism, see N. Smith, *New Urban Frontier*, 43–45.

30 Yusef Bunchy Shakur, "Black and White, What Is All the Fuss About? Truth and Reconciliation!" *Critical Moment*, February 23, 2012, https://critical -moment.org/2012/02/23/black-white-what-is-all-the-fuss-about-truth -reconciliation/.

31 On disappointment over Detroit's TRC process and differences from Greens-boro's TRC, see Inwood, Alderman, and Barron, "Addressing Structural Violence," 57.

32 Doxtader, "Potential of Reconciliation's Beginning," 380.

33 Sitze, *Impossible Machine*.

34 Mamdani, *When Victims Become Killers*.

35 *Merriam-Webster*, s.v. "reconcile (v.)," accessed November 27, 2022, https:// www.merriam-webster.com/dictionary/reconcile; and "redress (v., n.)," accessed November 27, 2022, https://www.merriam-webster.com/dictionary /redress.

36 Inwood, "Righting Unrightable Wrongs," 1465.

37 Gil Scott-Heron, "We Almost Lost Detroit," on *Bridges*, co-produced by Gil Scott-Heron and Brian Jackson, Arista, 1977.

38 On "freedom dreams," see Kelley, *Freedom Dreams*.

39 Among the leaders mentioned were Martin Luther King, Rosa Parks, Coleman Young, Erma Henderson, Paul Robeson, Malcolm X, Hon. Elijah Muhammed, Rev. Albert Cleage, Dr. Imari Obadele, Rev. Gaide Obadele,

Richard Henry, Rev. Milton Henry, Ray Jenkins, General Baker, Marian Kramer, and James and Grace Lee Boggs.

40 Pontiac was under emergency management from 2009 through 2013.

41 Another financial review team process that extended from December 2012 to January 2013 concluded that the city was in a financial crisis. The review team report can be found here: "Report of the Detroit Financial Review Team," State of Michigan, February 19, 2013, https://www.michigan.gov/-/media/Project/Websites/treasury/Reports/2013/2013_ReviewTeamReport21913.pdf. The financial review team unanimously determined that a government financial emergency existed in Detroit and that the city had no satisfactory plan in place to resolve it. As Dillon stated, "The team collectively believes the city needs assistance in making the difficult decisions necessary to achieve the significant reforms that are so crucial to the city's long-term viability." Ronald Goldsberry, a member of the review team, argued that the city's governance structure resisted "meaningful, structural change." See "Detroit Review Team Finds 'Financial Emergency' in City," *ClickOnDetroit*, February 19, 2013, https://www.clickondetroit.com/news/2013/02/19/detroit-review-team-finds-financial-emergency-in-city/.

42 A report by Demos contested the debt calculations as being inflated. The bankruptcy case dealt with a figure of $12 billion and settled $7 billion of that. Wallace C. Turbeville, "The Detroit Bankruptcy," Demos, November 20, 2013, https://www.demos.org/sites/default/files/publications/Detroit_Bankruptcy-Demos.pdf.

43 Eaves, "We Wear the Mask," 23; Coulthard quoted in Stauffer, *Ethical Loneliness*, 108.

44 Paula Ioanide writes: "I liken the legacies of ethical witnessing to what M. Jacqui Alexander calls 'pedagogies of the sacred' or 'pedagogies of crossing'— epistemologies and practices that tirelessly work to cultivate structures of feeling, faith, hope, and sociality that align with justice, with survival, and with healing. . . . [T]he legacy of ethical witnessing foregrounds the political and social collective responsibilities to redress past wrongs and develops mechanisms through which to implement such collective responsibilities. Cedric Robinson and Robin D.G. Kelley have likewise traced these legacies of ethical witnessing in the cosmologies, epistemologies, and practices of people in the African Diaspora." See Ioanide, "Alchemy of Race and Affect," 163–64.

45 On "limited emancipation," see Hartman, *Lose Your Mother*, 170. Also see Hartman, *Scenes of Subjection*, 6. She writes, "I think it is important to consider the failure of Reconstruction not simply as a matter of policy or as evidence of a flagging commitment to black rights, which is undeniably the case, but also in terms of the limits of emancipation, the ambiguous legacy of universalism, the exclusions constitutive of liberalism, and the blameworthiness of the freed individual. . . . [E]mancipation appears less the grand event of liberation than a point of transition between modes of servitude and racial subjection."

Chapter Six. Conjuring Terra Nullius

1 Claire Pfeiffer Ramsey and Marvin Shaouni, "Merry Detroit Mob Chases Nain Rough through Cass Corridor, Burns Him to a Crisp," *Model D Media*, March 23, 2010, https://www.modeldmedia.com/features/nain032310.aspx.

2 Quoted in Paul Abowd, "Marche du Nain Rouge: Keep on Truckin?'" *Critical Moment*, April 17, 2011, https://critical-moment.org/2011/04/17/marche-du -nain-rouge-keep-on-truckin/.

3 Hamlin, *Legends of Le Détroit*, 22–39.

4 Hamlin, *Legends of Le Détroit*, 22–39.

5 Watson, *Legends of Le Détroit*, 22–39.

6 Said, *Culture and Imperialism*, 6.

7 Seed, *Ceremonies of Possession in Europe's Conquest*.

8 This chapter draws on my own analysis of primary documents as well as on critiques made by residents. It extends the fantastic work of other scholars and cultural critics of Detroit, including Dora Apel, Rebecca Kinney, Emma Slager, Nate Millington, and Liev Cherry, by directing more attention to cultural production of property and urban *re*settlement at the beginning of the twenty-first century. See Apel, *Beautiful Terrible Ruins*; Kinney, *Beautiful Wasteland*; Kinney "'America's Great Comeback Story,'" 777–806; Slager, "Ruin Tours," 124–42; Millington, "Post-Industrial Imaginaries," 279–96; and Cherry, "Construction of Emptiness."

9 As Jane M. Jacobs argues in *Edge of Empire*, "Colonial constructs not only belong to a past that is being worked against in the present, but also to a past that is being nostalgically reworked and inventively adapted in the present" (14).

10 Watson, *Legends of Le Détroit*, 22–39.

11 Hamlin primarily gathered the legends from family narratives, which she then supplemented with additional research and input from individuals who had memories of the eighteenth century.

12 M. W. Walsh, "Revenge against the Idol," 56–57.

13 Galinée, "Journey of Dollier and Galinée."

14 On Indigenous names of Detroit, see Petch, "Detroit as Treatied Space," 9.

15 Galinée, "Journey of Dollier and Galinée," 204.

16 Galinée, "Journey of Dollier and Galinée," 204. Also see Larzelere, "Teaching of Michigan History," 312.

17 Watson, *Legends of Le Détroit*, 5–6. In my own reading of Dollier and Galinée's travelogue, I did not find evidence of the planting of arms directly after destroying the idol, though they did record another instance of the planting of arms on Lake Erie. Regardless, if their destruction of the manitou happened in conjunction with such ceremonial land claims or not, their recorded justification of their own violence represents how Christian imaginaries of the demonic were deeply entangled with colonial conquest and the imperial enterprise.

While Hamlin's account of the destruction of the idol does not appear in the travelogue, her account is repeated verbatim in a *Chronography of Notable Events in the History of the Northwest Territory and Wayne County*, published by the local History and Pioneer Society in 1890, seven years after the publication of Hamlin's work, suggesting that even it was not accurate, it had import for regional lore. Carlisle, *Chronography of Notable Events*, 16–17.

18 In 1493, the pope issued five papal bulls (i.e., public decrees) before the conquistadores left Spain that granted sovereignty of any land to its discoverer. The decree left the question open, however, as to what counted as discovery. The English argued that only discovery combined with possession should confer clear sovereign title. The rule became that if a territory was not claimed by a European power, then whichever power first discovered and occupied it could lay claim to it. North American colonization is often defended on the grounds that it existed in a "state of nature." The state of nature was both a material and a political claim: it was claimed that land was empty and uncultivated and that Indigenous populations did not have recognizable forms of sovereign government. In the 1600s and 1700s, following the Peace of Westphalia in 1648, European political and legal theory grappled with developing an international system for sovereign states. The new colonies, as Carole Pateman argues, were integral to the development of an international system. Given this, the actualization and justification of territorial claims by European powers varied greatly by time and place. In Australia, for example, the British government did not enter any treaties with Aboriginal people, whereas in North America, hundreds of treaties with Indigenous people were negotiated. By the early 1700s, the British Crown, seeking to gain the upper hand in territorial struggles with France, insisted on the development of policies that recognized Indigenous sovereignty. The Royal Proclamation of 1763 ruled that territory needed to be purchased rather than possessed via invasion or occupation. "Such restrictions on expansion and appropriation of land were," as Pateman writes, "anathema to colonial elites and the Proclamation became a precipitating cause of the American Revolution" (58). See Pateman, "Settler Contract."

19 There was a close relationship between terra nullius and wasted land. Waste stands in for the political other of capitalist value and suggests the necessity for an ordering rule of property. See Gidwani and Reddy, "Afterlives of 'Waste.'"

20 Pateman, "Settler Contract," 39.

21 Dollier and Galinée's travelogue highlights how missionaries mapped Old World heretics onto people in new lands, slotting them into categories of otherness and demonizing their cultures and ways of being human. See Wynter, "Unsettling the Coloniality of Being," 257–337. In Hamlin's retell-

ing of the encounter, after the priests had planted the cross, deposited the broken idol in the river, and departed, a band of Indians returned and found the fragments. Summoned by the Spirit of the Manitou, who resided under Belle Isle, they brought the broken idol to the bank, where the shards were transformed into rattlesnakes—"a sentinel to guard the sacredness of his domain from the profaning foot of the white man." Hamlin, *Legends of Le Détroit*, 6.

22 The site would allow the French to monitor canoe traffic and thwart contact between the British and Native tribes in the west. It would also position the French to gain the upper hand in fur markets by blocking exchanges between Anishinaabe and Iroquois traders. See Toups, "More Than Just a Missionary," 5.

23 Miles, *Dawn of Detroit*.

24 "According to the Northwest Ordinance," as Miles writes, "these remaining Indian lands could not be taken without 'consent,' except in the case of 'lawful wars authorized by Congress,' language that anticipated and justified further territorial expansion by the U.S. government." Miles, *Dawn of Detroit*, 139.

25 James W. Perkinson offers an analysis of the *nain rouge* in Norman and Indigenous traditions. See Perkinson, *Political Spirituality for a Century of Water Wars*, 125–72. On Nanabush in Nishnaabeg traditions see Simpson, "Land as Pedagogy."

26 Shoemaker, "How Indians Got to Be Red," 624–44.

27 Between 1501 and 1875, some 12.3 million African people were forcibly taken from their homelands and shipped to the Americas, but only 10.5 million of them arrived. The majority of enslaved Africans sent to British North America arrived between 1720 and 1780. Elite Detroiters owned more than two hundred enslaved people of Native and African descent. Many of the city's streets to this day are named after slaveholders.

   See embarkment estimates at "Trans-Atlantic Slave Trade—Estimates," Slave Voyages: The Trans-Atlantic Slave Trade Database, accessed October 1, 2022, http://www.slavevoyages.org/estimates/RoGD05Wu; for disembarkment estimates, see "Trans-Atlantic Slave Trade—Estimates," Slave Voyages: The Trans-Atlantic Slave Trade Database, accessed October 1, 2022, http://www.slavevoyages.org/estimates/Gx3vZ7H3. Also see Miles et al., "Mapping Slavery in Detroit," 20–24.

28 In exchange, they were guaranteed ten thousand dollars that could be disbursed in money, goods, husbandry tools, or animals to be divided among all the nations. The treaty stipulated that Indian nations would "enjoy the privilege of hunting and fishing on the lands ceded . . . as long as they remain the property of the United States." See "Detroit, 1807," Michigan Related Treaties 1795–1864, Clarke Historical Library, Central Michigan University, accessed October 1, 2022, https://www.cmich.edu/research/clarke-historical

-library/explore-collection/explore-online/native-american-material/native
-american-treaty-rights/text-of-michigan-related-treaties#a3. The Treaty
of Detroit was just the beginning of the land cessions in what would become
the state of Michigan. It was followed by the Maumee Treaty of 1817; the
Saginaw Treaty of 1819; the Chicago Treaty of 1821 and 1833; the Carey
Mission Treaty of 1828; the Washington Treaty of 1836; the Cedar Point
Treaty of 1836; and the La Point Treaty of 1842. The text of Michigan-
related treaties can be read here: Michigan Related Treaties 1795–1864,
Clarke Historical Library, Central Michigan University, https://www.cmich
.edu/research/clarke-historical-library/explore-collection/explore-online
/native-american-material/native-american-treaty-rights/text-of-michigan
-related-treaties.

29 Bohaker, "Reading Anishinaabe Identities," 11–33.
30 Bohaker, "Reading Anishinaabe Identities," 11–33.
31 Byrd, Goldstein, Melamed, and Reddy, "Predatory Value," 1–18.
32 See Bronner, "Challenges of American Folklore to the Humanities," 3–7;
    Skinner, *Myths and Legends of Our Own Land*, 308–10. White possession,
    as Goenpul Indigenous studies scholar Aileen Morten Robinson argues,
    turns not only on violence, coercion, and displacement but also, crucially, on
    cultural practices that work to normalize both appropriation and the logics
    of possessive individualism. See Morten-Robinson, *White Possessive*.
33 Bronner, "Challenges of American Folklore to the Humanities," 3–4.
34 As historian Nathan Petch observes, in Michigan state history, the presence
    of Indigenous people as agents of history ceases after the War of 1812, when
    political hegemony is achieved in the Northwest Territory. After Michigan
    becomes a state in 1837, Indigenous presence is elided altogether. As Petch
    writes, "Fundamentally, indigenous peoples' history and Michigan's history
    remain separate." Petch, "Detroit as Treatied Space," 6–7.
35 This is a history that scholars have recently sought to correct. See, for exam-
    ple, Tiya Miles's *Dawn of Detroit*, and Kyle Mays's new book *City of Disposses-
    sion: Indigenous Peoples, African Americans, and the Creations of Modern
    Detroit*. On settler-colonial urbanism, see Dorries, Hugill, and Tomiak,
    "Racial Capitalism," 263–70.
36 D. J. R. Bruckner, "Detroit Fights against Slow Community Decay," *Los An-
    geles Times*, February 5, 1967, D12; William Serrin, "The Detroit Disease: An
    American Infection," *New York Times*, January 30, 1975, 34.
37 Serrin, "Detroit Disease," 34.
38 "Detroit and America's Future," *Los Angeles Times*, July 26, 1967, A4.
39 Jerry M. Flint, "Humphrey Urges New Aid to Poor: In Detroit, He Says
    Nation Must Pay to Set Up an American Marshall Plan," *New York Times*,
    August 3, 1967, 1.
40 As legal scholar Amy Lavine argues, "Just as the destruction of all possi-
    ble host plants within a given geographical area was considered to be an

appropriate governmental response to the outbreaks of plant disease, planners and sociologists claimed that slum clearance was necessary to prevent the spread of urban blight" ("Urban Renewal," 434–35). Even though the widespread slum clearance of urban renewal years has been publicly reviled, property law has continued to uphold the government's use of eminent domain to curtail blight. The 1954 Supreme Court ruling in *Berman v. Parker,* 348 U.S. 26 (1954), marked a turning point in that it allowed the government to take blighted properties and turn them over to private developers for the purposes of abating public nuisance. It also permitted the taking of non-blighted properties if doing so prevented the spread of blight. The Supreme Court's 2005 ruling in *Kelo v. City of New London,* 545 U.S. 469 (2005), further extended permissible takings, setting precedent for municipal governments to take unblighted private property for private development as long as it economically benefited the city. See Lavine, "Urban Renewal," 423–75.

41 Jungle metaphors had long been used to mark the difference between those considered to be fully human and racialized others, for example, in travel and colonial writing and in analyses of slums in public health and urban sociology. See, for example, J. McLaughlin's *Writing the Urban Jungle*; and Valverde, "Dialectic of the Familiar," 493–509. The jungle has often been invoked, to draw on the words of Andrew Light, as a "wild place, not fit for human habitation except for those beings who were not really fully human, that is, for savages." "This *classical* wilderness was the jungle," writes Light. "Wilderness did not just mark the geographical boundaries between human settlements and wild nature, but also a cognitive boundary between the civilized explorers and the 'savages' that were being encountered. The wilderness was in short, the mental and physical boundary between humans and the radical/racial others." A. Light, "Metaphorical Drift of Classical Wilderness," 15.

42 Rebecca Kinney also notes this shift in her wonderful book *Beautiful Wasteland*, ix–x.

43 See Fabian, *Time and the Other*, 31.

44 On urban exploration, see Mott and Roberts, "Not Everyone Has (the) Balls."

45 Slager, "Ruin Tours," 4–5. In contrast to the naturalization of ruins discussed above, tour operators, as Slager argues, tended to not aestheticize ruins but instead offered place narratives that confronted ruination and suggested a range of responses from encouraging tour goers to relocate to Detroit to insisting on a more complex historical understanding of ruins than that offered by ruin porn.

46 On ruin art in Detroit, see John P. Leary, "Detroitism," *Guernica*, January 15, 2011, http://www.guernicamag.com/features/leary_1_15_11/. On theorizing ruins beyond Detroit, also see DeSilvey and Edensor, "Reckoning with

Ruins," 465–85; Dawney, "Decommissioned Places," 33–49; and Stoler, "Imperial Debris," 191–219.

47 Andrew Nelson, "Rise and Shine Detroit," *National Geographic Traveler*, March/April 2012, https://www.nationalgeographic.com/travel/city-guides /detroit-traveler/.

48 Bradford Frost, "Envisioning the Millennial Frontier," *Detroit Opportunity Project*, January 31, 2011, https://detroitopportunityproject.com/post /3032599063/envisioning-the-millennial-frontier.

49 Aaron Renn, "Detroit: A New American Frontier," *Yes! Magazine*, July 20, 2011.

50 N. Smith, *New Urban Frontier*, xvi. On frontier mythology, see Richard Slotkin's classic *Fatal Environment*. Slotkin argued that myths made history cliché. Drawing on Slotkin, geographer Neil Smith, in his seminal *New Urban Frontier*, added that "myth is constituted by the loss of the *geographical* quality of things as well. . . . [T]he more events are wrenched from their constitutive geographies, the more powerful the mythology" (11). Smith argued that "the social meaning of gentrification is increasingly constructed through the vocabulary of the frontier myth" (11). According to Smith, "Gentrification portends a class conquest of the city. The new urban pioneers seek to scrub the city clean of its working-class geography and history. By remaking the geography of the city they simultaneously rewrite its social history as a preemptive justification for a new urban future" (25).

51 Kinney, *Beautiful Wasteland*, xx.

52 Tsing, *Friction*, 68.

53 "Detroit: The Ghost City Gradually Being Reclaimed by Nature," *Scribol*, May 20, 2011, https://scribol.com/anthropology-and-history/urban -exploration/detroit-the-ghost-city-gradually-being-reclaimed-by-nature/.

54 La Paperson makes a similar argument that such discourses "collapse Native land and black space together, leading once again to re-settlement." La Paperson, "Ghetto Land Pedagogy," 117.

55 As Millington writes, "While the nature found in Detroit is decidedly murky, one nevertheless glimpses in these comments a lurking desire for nature to reclaim the city from the impure human touch. Given Detroit's long and ugly history of racial antagonism and the fact that it is at present nearly 90% African-American, it is possible to see these comments as part of an attempted erasure of African-American Detroiters from the landscape. In the case of Detroit, residents of the city are written out of the scene, replaced by a concern for decaying architecture rather than the lives of those who inhabit these buildings." See Millington, "Post-industrial Imaginaries," 290.

56 *Sweet Juniper* blog, 2010, cited in Millington, "Post-industrial Imaginaries," 290.

57 Kisa Lala, "Detroit—the Ruins of an Empire: A Conversation with Photographers Marchand and Meffre," *HuffPost*, January 31, 2011, http://www.huffingtonpost.com/kisa-lala/detroit-the-ruins-of-an-e_b_810688.html.

58 On the sublime and the frontier, see Cronon, "Trouble with Wilderness."

59 In the words of La Paperson, "The duality of land as desecrated, in pain, in need of rescue; and land as sacred, wild, and preserve-able; are contemporary discourses that justify re-invasion." La Paperson, "Ghetto Land Pedagogy," 117.

60 Bledsoe and Wright, "Anti-Blackness of Global Capital," 13.

61 Wood, *Rethinking the Power of Maps*, 15

62 Sarah Hulett, "Inchvesting in Detroit: A Virtual Realty," March 4, 2010, https://www.npr.org/templates/story/story.php?storyId=124252909.

63 Their combined square-mile area was just over 118. By contrast, Detroit's population of under a million was spread out over 138 square miles.

64 The "Time to End Blight" report, Detroit Blight Removal Task Force Plan, accessed November 11, 2014, http://jack-seanson.github.io/taskforce/funding/.

65 According to the "Time to End Blight" report, of the blighted areas, 73,035 are residential structures, 6,135 are vacant lots that require clearing, and 5,471 are nonresidential structures (commercial, civic, church). It estimated that it would cost approximately one billion dollars to remove all the blighted property. The approximate cost of a single house demolition was ten thousand dollars. The planned demolition timeline was a formidable task given that if demolition teams worked every day for three years, they'd need to disassemble eighty-four structures per day.

66 Quoted in Tom Walsh, "Thrills and Danger Ahead in Detroit's Wild Bankruptcy Ride," *Detroit Free Press*, December 28, 2013; italics added.

67 The Uniting Detroiters project was a community-based participatory research project, which, as I discuss in the prologue, I helped codevelop early in my fieldwork. The project aimed to use the research process as a means of movement building.

68 Joann Muller, "Why One Rich Man Shouldn't Own an International Bridge," *Forbes*, January 12, 2012, https://www.forbes.com/sites/joannmuller/2012/01/12/why-one-rich-man-shouldnt-own-an-international-bridge/?sh=394f37706c18.

69 Rector, "Toxic Debt," 265–68.

70 Kinney, *Beautiful Wasteland*, xv, 131.

71 See *7.2 SQ MI: A Report of Greater Downtown Detroit* (Detroit, MI: Hudson-Webber Foundation, 2015), https://static1.squarespace.com/static/5ab01e379d5abb3869926931/t/5babece5e79c704c5f3f7565/1537993966446/7.2SQ_MI_Book_FINAL_LoRes.pdf.

72 Clyde Woods writes about how the history of capitalist societies has evolved through a series of racialized "socio-spatial enclosures," including "colonization, slavery, ghettos, company towns, redlining, benign neglect, suburbs,

gated communities, and prison complexes," from which wealth is extracted and assets are stripped. Woods, "Les Misérables of New Orleans," 774.

73 For more on the walkout, see this video-recorded panel: the 1966 Northern Senior High School Walkout and The Freedom School Movement Forum, featuring Judy Walker and Chuck Colding (leaders of the 1966 Northern High School boycott) and Karl Gregory and Frank Joyce (administrators of Freedom Schools in 1966), held on May 25, 2017, at Charles H. Wright Museum of African American History: "Panel: The 1966 Northern Senior High School Walkout / Boycott and Freedom School Movement Snippets," video, 1:08:18, MacSpeaking, May 27, 2017, https://www.youtube.com/watch?v =X63Y9NhFBzE.

74 See S. E. Smith, *Dancing in the Streets*, for more about Motown.

75 Chakrabarty, *Provincializing Europe*, 109.

76 Massey, *For Space*, 92.

77 McKittrick, *Demonic Grounds*, xix.

78 McKittrick, *Demonic Grounds*, xix; Gilmore, "Fatal Couplings," 16.

79 Moulton, "Black Monument Matters," 5. A fantastic resource is the Black Geographies Reading List curated by LaToya Eaves since 2016, online at https://drive.google.com/file/d/0B1CIBgdeHdAPUHBZcmNIX19wSXc /view?resourcekey=0-0R0nkFcmwr5O4nLzM84egQ.

80 North End Gardens were eventually renamed Oakland Avenue Farm.

81 Other sites included Central United Methodist, Fishing Community, Feedom Freedom, Messiah Church, Genesis Hope, Earthworks, Eastern Market, Wright African Museum, the DIA, the public library, and the mosque at Division E M8.

82 Gordon argues for attending to the power that is held in communities—"to a power that is constantly denied and said we do not possess: the power to create life on our own terms." Drawing on Massimo De Angelis, she argues that "'revolution' is not struggling for the commons but through the commons, not for dignity, but through. . . . Life despite capitalism, as a constituent process, not after capitalism, as a constituted future state of things." Gordon, *Hawthorne Archive*, 137.

83 Gordon, *Ghostly Matters*, xvi.

84 Gordon, *Ghostly Matters*, xvi.

85 Gordon, *Ghostly Matters*, 8.

86 As Asha Best and Margaret Ramírez argue, engagement with the spectral can be generative for rethinking entanglements among race, property, and the urban, "Urban Specters," 1043–54.

87 Ghezzi, "Nanabush Stories from the Ojibwe," 445. Also see Hardin, "Trickster of History," 25–45.

88 Simpson, "Land as Pedagogy," 18.

Chapter Seven. Political Ecologies of Austerity

1 For more on the consent agreement and Detroit's fiscal crisis, see chapter 5 herein, "Accounting for Unpayable Debt."

2 In 1993, Detroit ombudsman Marie Farrell-Donaldson proposed in a 1993 report, *Management by Commonsense*, that residents be moved from abandoned neighborhoods into city-owned homes and that their old neighborhoods be razed and fenced off. See Stephen Advokat and Constance C. Prater, "City Divided on Closing of Areas," *Detroit Free Press*, April 29, 1993. She later submitted a dossier to city council; see David Usborne, "Motor City Fights against Fulfilling a Death Wish," *Independent* (London), May 31, 1993. Mothballing had been a popular strategy in post–World War II cities in Europe and was controversially deployed under the name of "urban triage" in some American cities in the mid-1970s, like St Louis and Cleveland. See Cooper-McCann, "Trap of Triage," 149–69.

3 Sociologist Michel Callon argues that to ensure the functioning of a market, agents mobilize "boundary-objects," a term he takes from Susan Leigh Star and James R. Griesemer. As Callon writes, "These objects allow the framing and stabilization of actions, while simultaneously providing an opening on to other worlds" ("Introduction," 18). Objects—be it people, houses, or land—are always entangled. They become commodities through an active process of alienation and dissociation. For things to be brought into market transactions, they must be tied to other objects, and people's relationships to them must be disentangled and severed. Marketization is, thus, a process of disentangling and framing anew social relationships to allow for calculation and calculative agencies (19). The MVA can be understood, in Callon's language, as a "calculating tool" that is not simply measuring reality but shaping a reality it purports to measure (23). Also see Star and Griesemer, "Institutional Ecology," 387–420.

4 *New Oxford American Dictionary* on Apple, s.v. "value (n.)," accessed June 14, 2022. On "regimes of value," see Appadurai, *Social Life of Things*, 3–30; and Bigger and Robertson, "Value Is Simple." Appadurai argues that "valuation regimes" create rules and modes of comparison by which things are differentiated and made commensurable. They give meaning to life and tell you how to live, shaping the priorities around which social orders are organized. When valuation regimes become dominant, they can be taken for granted as simply the way of things. For this reason, David Graeber argues, "It is value that brings universes into being." Graeber, "It Is Value That Brings Universes into Being," 231.

5 J. Cranshaw, "Whose 'City of tomorrow' Is It? On Urban Computing, Utopianism, and Ethics." In "13 Proceedings of the 2nd ACM SIGKDD International Workshop on Urban Computing," 2013, Article 17, http://dl.acm.org/citation.cfm?doid=2505821.2505838.

As early as the 1960s and 1970s, urban administration relied upon cybernetics, GIS, modeling, and urban control rooms. See Batty, *New Science*. Indeed, usage of geo-demographics, GIS, and other planning software tools to make decisions about investment and disinvestment in cities has existed for decades—a famous example being RAND Corporation's joint endeavor with New York City in 1968 to use advanced computer models to make public policy decisions and streamline management along rational-scientific lines. See Flood, *Fires*.

6   Thrift and French, "Automatic Production of Space"; Kitchin et al., "Knowing and Governing Cities"; and Shelton et al., "'Actually Existing Smart City.'"

7   Quoted in Jonathan Oosting, "Detroit Works: Bing Asks for Ideas, Residents Demand Answers at First Community Meeting," *MLive*, September 15, 2010.

8   Jane M. Jacobs writes that changes in city space often "result in protracted struggle." "This politics is rarely only about how space is to look and function, about competing architectural aesthetics or urban planning ideologies, although such concerns may well provide the dominant discursive form of these struggles. These place-based struggles are also arenas in which various coalitions express their sense of self and their desires for the spaces which constitute their 'home'—be it the local neighborhood or the nation home, an indigenous home or one recently adopted. This politics produced by places in the process of becoming or being made anew is, then, also a politics of identity in which ideas of race, class, community and gender are formed. This politics of identity and place is not simply built around structures of power internal to the city itself or even to globally linked processes of urbanization. It is undeniably a politics that occurs in and is concerned with the city, but for many groups it is also a politics constituted by a broader history and geography of colonial inheritances, imperialist presents and postcolonial possibilities." See Jacobs, *Edge of Empire*, 2.

9   Bing is quoted in M. W. Anderson, "New Minimal Cities," 1166. Also see Chris McGreal, "Detroit Mayor Plans to Shrink by Cutting Services to Some Areas," *Guardian* (UK), December 17, 2010, https://www.theguardian.com /world/2010/dec/17/detroit-shrinking.

10   Jay Hammond is a pseudonym.

11   Jorge Rees is a pseudonym.

12   The organization has changed names over time. Originally, it was the Delaware Valley Community Reinvestment Fund. In 1999, it became The Reinvestment Fund, and in the 2010s, it became simply, Reinvestment Fund. See here for history: "The Reinvestment Fund at 30: Insights and New Directions," Federal Reserve Bank Philadelphia, Fall 2015, https:// www.philadelphiafed.org/community-development/credit-and-capital/the -reinvestment-fund-at-30-insights-and-new-directions.

13 *Disintermediation* is an economic term that refers to reducing intermediaries between producers and consumers, or simply, cutting out the middlemen.

14 Hackworth, "Local Autonomy, Bond Rating Agencies."

15 Lake, "Financialization of Urban Policy."

16 Benjamin, Rubin, and Zielenbach, "Community Development Financial Institutions," 177–95.

17 Jeremy Nowak, "Civic Lessons: How CDFIs Can Apply Market Realities to Poverty Alleviation," Brookings, March 1, 2001, https://www.brookings.edu/articles/civic-lesson-how-cdfis-can-apply-market/.

18 By the early 2000s, some 550 CDFIs managed US$6.5 billion in investments. On the history of community development and its trajectory toward market-based development, see DeFilippis, "Paradoxes of Community-Building," 223–34.

19 See "New Year, New Look," Reinvestment Fund, January 4, 2016, https://www.reinvestment.com/news/2016/01/04/new-year-new-look/.

20 Ira Goldstein and C. Sean Closkey, "Market Value Analysis: Understanding Where and How to Invest Limited Resources," Federal Reserve Bank of St. Louis, June 30, 2006, https://www.stlouisfed.org/publications/bridges/summer-2006/market-value-analysis-understanding-where-and-how-to-invest-limited-resources. Reinvestment Fund makes five normative assumptions when analyzing markets: (1) "Public subsidy is scarce and it alone cannot create a market"; (2) "Public subsidy must be used to leverage, or clear the path for, private investment"; (3) "In distressed markets, invest into strength (e.g., major institutions of place, transportation hubs, environmental amenities)"; (4) "All communities and residents are customers of the programs and services of the local government"; and (5) "Decisions to invest and/or deploy governmental programs must be based on objectively gathered data and sound quantitative and qualitative analysis" (Goldstein and Closkey, "Market Value Analysis," 5).

21 Block groups are statistical divisions of census tracts. They consist of clusters of blocks within the same census tract. They generally contain between six hundred to three thousand people; "Block Group," Glossary, US Census Bureau, accessed October 1, 2022, https://www.census.gov/programs-surveys/geography/about/glossary.html#par_textimage_4.

22 Rob Kitchin has argued for more critical analyses of algorithms and algorithmic governance across the humanities and social sciences. Kitchin, "Thinking Critically about and Researching Algorithms," 26. Meanwhile, Brian Jordan Jefferson has urged urban geographers to attend to the "interfaces between data-driven governance and sociospatial differentiation, particularly differentiations along axes of ethnicity, gender, race, and class." Jefferson, "Policing, Data, and Power-Geometry," 1259. A substantial body of literature addresses the technical perspective of the study of algorithms. More recently scholars have started to attend to concerns about algorithmic

bias (for example, Garcia's article "Racist in the Machine"), algorithmic in-equity (like O'Neil's *Weapons of Math Destruction* and Wachter-Boettcher's *Technically Wrong*), automating inequality (see Eubanks, *Automating Inequality*), and algorithmic oppression and technological redlining (Noble's *Algorithms of Oppression*). Simone Browne's *Dark Matters* offers critical analyses of how histories of racial formation shape surveillance technolo-gies and practices. Jefferson extends this focus by calling for attention to how "power-geometries" (Massey, "Power Geometry") or what he calls "racialized geometries of power" (Jefferson, "Policing, Data, and Power-Geometry," 1248) inscribed in urban space prefigure the use of data-driven analytics in urban administration.

23 I. Goldstein, "Maximizing the Impact of Federal NSP Investments."

24 Graeber, "It Is Value That Brings Universes into Being."

25 To be clear, RF produces the analysis, which city officials then use to develop strategies for investment and service delivery. The designation "distressed" does not necessarily mean disinvestment. City officials could, in theory, de-cide to develop a plan of strategic investment for these areas. Reinvestment Fund describes the MVA as follows: "It is a unique approach using spatial and statistical analysis that is field validated and reviewed by local subject matter experts to identify and characterize local conditions throughout a locality, creating an internally-referenced index of residential real-estate markets. The MVA provides stakeholders with a common understanding of market types that allows public, nonprofit, and community organizations to engage in productive dialogue around the creation of a coordinated investment and service-delivery strategy. The MVA also provides a baseline against which community change over time can be measured." For more information, see "Market Value Analysis," Reinvestment Fund, accessed October 2, 2022, https://www.reinvestment.com/policy-solutions/market -value-analysis/.

26 Jaqueeta White, "Blight in New Orleans Is Back to Pre-Katrina Levels, but Challenges Remain," *New Orleans Advocate*, August 25, 2015, https:// www.theadvocate.com/baton_rouge/news/article_91d27e96-ec2f-50bb -a205-48a394d128ab.html.

27 T. Logan, "St. Louis Turns to Data to Guide Development," *St. Louis Post Dispatch*, January 29, 2014, https://www.stltoday.com/business/local/st -louis-turns-to-data-to-guide-development/article_88e96f4f-7f8f-5f31-b4a3 -50f73dfob28d.html.

28 Reinvestment Fund, "Market Value Analysis: Using Data and Market Map-ping to Identify Public and Private Investment Opportunities in Cities," pre-sentation to the Federal Reserve Bank of Philadelphia's "Reinventing Older Communities: How Does Place Matter?," Philadelphia, PA, January 4, 2008.

29 In 2012, the Manhattan Institute—a conservative think tank that advocates for the privatization of public infrastructure, school vouchers, and cuts in

social welfare programs—had a partnership with the Detroit Police Department to pilot a "broken windows" program. The "broken windows" program and "zero tolerance" policing—pioneered in New York City in the 1990s—are based on the argument that if officers patrol by foot and crack down on smaller nuisances like broken windows, crime will be reduced. According to the policy's theorists, crime is more likely to happen in blighted neighborhoods. The policy has come under much damning critique for enforcing vagrancy laws, criminalizing the homeless, and increasing incarceration rates among Black, Latinx, and poor populations.

30 "Do Black Lives Matter? Robin D. G. Kelley and Fred Moten in Conversation," video, 1:25:36, Critical Resistance, January 6, 2015, https://vimeo.com/116111740.

31 Quoted in Logan, "St. Louis Turns to Data."

32 Gillespie, "Relevance of Algorithms," 179.

33 Beer, "Social Power of Algorithms," 7.

34 Matthew Stinton is a pseudonym.

35 Armstrong, "Race and Property Values," 1051–65; C. I. Harris, "Whiteness as Property," 1707–91; Barrett, *Blackness and Value*, 19.

36 J. Light, "Discriminating Appraisals," 485–522.

37 J. Light, "Discriminating Appraisals," 485–522. Also see Brown, "Appraisal Narratives," 211–34. The racially discriminatory appraisals became policy when the Federal Housing Administration and the Federal Home Loan Bank Board began using them to make decisions about where to insure long-term mortgages. As discussed in chapter 2, HOLC hired appraisers in every major American city to produce color-coded risk assessment maps. Their decision to withhold financing from red zones led to long-term disinvestment and instability in neighborhoods deemed risky, as well as undercutting intergenerational wealth accumulation for residents of these neighborhoods.

38 Rutan and Glass, "Lingering Effects of Neighborhood Appraisal," 339–49. As David Freund has argued, federal programs helped codify and promote the real estate industry's new science of urban development, "subsum[ing] myths about racial difference within a supposedly objective analysis of housing markets and property values." Freund, *Colored Property*, 116.

39 I. Goldstein, "Making Sense of Markets," 84.

40 Wolfink, "What's the Matter with Value?"

41 Bowker and Star, *Sorting Things Out*, 13, 14.

42 See "Strategic Renewal Is Right-Sizing" flier in Campbell et al., *People's Atlas of Detroit*, 218. As part of the Uniting Detroiters project, we analyzed the Detroit Works Project dataset and found that over 19 percent of the city's residents lived in areas slated for decommission, whereas only 6.68 percent of the city's population lived in areas slated for upgrade. Decommission areas were on average 91.93 percent Black, 5.72 percent white, and 45.68 percent

in poverty. Upgrade areas, by contrast, were on average 66.68 percent Black, 19 percent white, and 37.34 percent in poverty.

43 K. Mitchell, "Pre-Black Futures," 239–61.

44 Best and Ramírez, "Urban Specters," 1045; Roy, "Dis/possessive Collectivism."

45 Angie Mead is a pseudonym. At the time I met Angie, Belle Isle's future as a city asset was in peril as part of the state takeover. It came under state control in 2014.

46 As Calvário, Velegrakis, and Kaika argue in "Political Ecology of Austerity," the tensions and contradictions arising from austerity generated new environmental conflicts, as well as new forms of social mobilization and resistance.

47 The emotionally charged debates over Detroit's strategic abandonment recall James Ferguson's writing about prolonged economic decline and abjection in Zambia. Abjection seeks to capture the act of not just being "thrown out" but "thrown *down*"—back into a past world in which the color bar kept Africans in their place, experiencing a sense of "humiliating expulsion," as the promises of modernization betrayed them, and they scrambled to merely get by. Ferguson, *Expectations of Modernity*, 236. I have written about "infrastructural displacement" in Safransky, "Rethinking Land Struggle," 1089. On "infrastructural violence," see Rodgers and O'Neill, "Infrastructural Violence," 401–12.

48 In the words of the plan's authors, land was Detroit's "greatest asset" and "greatest liability." Detroit Future City, *2012 Detroit Strategic Framework Plan*, 95.

Rightsizing's green turn could be explained in part by a recent holy union between landscape urbanism and urban shrinkage. Landscape urbanism dates to Frederick Law Olmsted's vision of integrating landscape and urban life (take, for example, his design of Central Park in New York, or Detroit's own Belle Isle, also his creation). Likewise, twenty-first-century landscape urbanism sought to rehabilitate relics of the early and mid-twentieth-century industrial economy (e.g., derelict railways and expressways) by integrating natural landscape features and transforming them into recreational spaces and parks. Think the Atlanta BeltLine and the High Line in Chelsea in Manhattan. The journalist Nikil Saval has described the turn to landscape urbanism as "post-post-industrial" planning—"trying to make whole the freeway-carved cities that date from an era when car-centric planning was in vogue." But for whom and for what? That sustainability was fast becoming the new guiding principle for urban regeneration in postindustrial cities raised important questions about the shifting value of urban nature. Nikil Saval, "Uncommon Ground: Our New Urban Oases," *New York Times Magazine*, November 10, 2016, https://www.nytimes.com

/interactive/2016/11/13/magazine/design-issue-redesigned-public-spaces
.html.

49 The DFC proposed a new land-use typology, which included four neighborhood types—mixed medium, green mixed use, live + make, and innovative
production. Detroit Future City, *2012 Detroit Strategic Framework Plan*, 199.

50 As discussed in the previous chapter, more than 100,000 people lived in
neighborhoods slated for disconnection. Yet no money was set aside for the
relocation of residents. Urban studies scholars have most often theorized
displacement in terms of people being pushed out of places (e.g., from
gentrification, urban renewal, disasters). The DFC represented a new type
of displacement in which residents were not displaced but left behind as the
services and infrastructures that served them were retracted. The DFC was
the result of an extensive regime of participation orchestrated by the Detroit
Works Project and bankrolled by foundations. The design and rollout of the
DWP signaled the ascent of foundations and large nongovernmental organizations (NGOs)—as opposed to the municipal government—as the key
institutions managing the "comeback" of Detroit.

   Foundations serve as proxies for government in Detroit, creating a development landscape dominated by the NGO and foundation sector reminiscent
of that found in many countries in the global South. As anthropologist James
Ferguson writes in *Anti-Politics Machine*, the development apparatus—and
here I'd add the nonprofit and philanthropic industrial complex—works as
an "anti-politics machine," transforming highly political planning projects to
"technical problems" and "technical solutions." Like the MVA and resulting
remapping of service provision and investment in Detroit, the antipolitics
machine depoliticizes the operation of power through projects and deflects
attention from their crucial side effects.

   In 2007, private foundations began pouring massive amounts of money
into the city, including the long-term planning process. The Ford, Charles
Stewart Mott, and John S. and James L. Knight Foundations, all national
organizations, played a key role. Between 2007 and 2014, the Ford Foundation alone invested $60 million in the region, an almost twofold increase in
foundation giving to Detroit over the previous ten years. Meanwhile, regional
foundations like Hudson-Webber, Skillman, Kresge, and W. K. Kellogg poured
more than $628 million into Detroit. Among these, several large foundations
(Kresge, Ford, and Kellogg) and a number of smaller foundations supported
the long-term engagement (i.e., participation) process and then pledged
over $150 million dollars so the DWP plan could be rolled out. In short, private
foundations, along with Detroit's numerous real estate–driven community
development corporations, have played a significant role in shaping the
city's planning process, including a participation regime that raises serious
questions about democratic accountability. See Whyte, "Philanthropy Keeps
the Lights on in Detroit." Also see Suzanne Perry, "Detroit Tests What

Foundations Can Do to Rescue Troubled Cities," *Chronicle of Philanthropy*, October 20, 2013, https://www.philanthropy.com/article/detroit-tests-what -foundations-can-do-to-rescue-troubled-cities/.

51 Bélanger, "Landscape as Infrastructure," 8–15.

52 Urban nature is often considered to be an unequivocal good, for recreation, aesthetics, and public health (e.g., parks, tree-lined boulevards). But it has also had a sordid history within urban planning, long serving as a proxy for managing racialized groups. Planners, city officials, and other land management bureaucrats have called on urban nature time and again not only to purify, contain, civilize, improve, and uplift racialized others but also to regenerate the built environment amid fears of social degeneration.

Chapter Eight. The Garden Is a Weapon in the War

1 Boggs and Kurashige, *Next American Revolution*; G. L. Boggs, *Living for Change*.

2 Boggs and Boggs, *Revolution and Evolution*, 138.

3 Colasanti, Hamm, and Litjens, "City as an 'Agricultural Powerhouse'?," 348–69. Meanwhile, planners and policy makers proposed new land-use policies, such as agricultural enterprise zones with tax abatements. On the potential of agricultural enterprise zones, see Mogk, Kwiatkowski, and Weindorf, "Promoting Urban Agriculture as an Alternative Land Use."

4 The American Institute of Architects is quoted in David Whitford, "Can Farming Save Detroit?," *Fortune*, December 29, 2009, https://money.cnn .com/2009/12/29/news/economy/farming_detroit.fortune/.

5 See, for example, Choo, "Plowing Over."

6 For a sympathetic critique of urban agriculture, see Stehlin and Tarr, "Think Regionally, Act Locally?," 1329–51. Also see Tornaghi, "Critical Geography of Urban Agriculture," 551–67.

7 For Howard, as David Pinder writes, "Re-ordering the city was a means of re-ordering society, as he cast his vision of cities as both the symbol and materialisation of a more balanced, co-operative and 'healthy' society. . . . Howard argued that land should be brought into ownership of the whole community and that rents should flow back into communities to be used to finance public services. He therefore argued that garden cities should be established on these principles, placing the interests of the community above those of private landlords who would in due course cease to exist. His aim was that the cities would embody the values of a more just and equitable social order, and that they would set in train a process of social reform that would ultimately be a means of superseding the class conflicts of capitalism" (*Visions of the City*, 40). Pinder continues with the question of land control: "Most importantly the experiment was meant to break up

interests of property and capital, and to unite and inspire workers, bringing them together as a group with the owners of capital and of agricultural land and thus creating a broad-based force for change" (41). Pinder makes the important point that over time, the socialist sensibilities and radical edge of Howard's vision were lost, and the garden city was invoked as environmental reformism and the new town movement rather than a challenge to capitalism (46). Howard's ideas—particularly his organic and bodily metaphors and classification and exclusion of social groups—also appealed to eugenicists, who in the early 1900s promoted garden cities as means of "purifying men's blood" by bringing them closer to the soil (51). Pinder, *Visions of the City*, 29–56. Also see Amanda Kolson Hurley, "The Machine Is a Garden," *Foreign Policy*, September/October 2014, 71–77. She describes how since the early 2000s, garden cities have been making a comeback from "England to India to Cambodia" and, in particular, in China.

8 On Village Industries, see Mullin, "Henry Ford and Field and Factory," 419–31. Also see Segal, *Recasting the Machine Age*.

9 The phrase "spatial palliative" comes from Clevenger and Andrews, "'Peaceful Path to' Healthy Bodies," 141–45. Also see Brunetta and Moroni, "Proposal of Ebenezer Howard," 65–74.

10 In *Progress and Poverty* (1879), Henry George argued that if the Constitution was to live up to the political rights it supposedly guaranteed, working people needed to be able to have economic security and independence, which he understood, like many of his time, as embodied in the rights to land. His saw the single tax as a replacement for all other taxes as a mechanism for turning land into "common property." As he writes, "The result of this investigation . . . shows that nothing short of making land common property can permanently relieve poverty and check the tendency of wages to the starvation point." See George, *Progress and Poverty*, xv.

11 Jonathan Oosting, "Jesse Jackson on Urban Farming: Detroit Needs Investment and Industry—'Not Bean Patches,'" *MLive Michigan*, September 8, 2010, https://www.mlive.com/news/detroit/2010/09/jesse_jackson_on _urban_farming.html.

12 On ecomodernism, see "An Ecomodernist Manifesto," accessed October 2, 2022, http://www.ecomodernism.org/.

13 See *Machine in the Garden*, in which Leo Marx analyzes how American writers from the 1830s to the 1850s dealt with issues of alienation and environmental destruction that accompanied industrialization (e.g., a steam locomotive in interrupting Nathaniel Hawthorne's daydreams in Sleepy Hollow; an enormous ash dump marring the main Manhattan through Queens portrayed by F. Scott Fitzgerald; a steamboat threatening the tranquil raft of Huck Finn drifting down the Mississippi). Marx was primarily concerned with the dissonance Americans experienced with rampant industrialization, immigration, and urbanization and how they responded by inventing new

cultural symbols to make sense of altered landscapes. When *The Machine in the Garden* was published in 1964, he hoped his exploration of the anxieties that accompanied an earlier era might provoke debate over late twentieth-century technological changes and global capitalism.

14 It was first published in *Monthly Review* in a combined July–August 1963 issue and later as a slim standalone book. As Leo Huberman and Paul M. Sweezy wrote in the editor's foreword to the *Monthly Review* issue,

> The fact that we are devoting an entire double issue of *Monthly Review* to one man's assessment of our present national condition does not mean that we agree with everything James Boggs has to say, any more than publication of this work in *MR* means that Mr. Boggs shares all the views of the editors. Our reason for publishing these pages is that we think Mr. Boggs has things to say that all Americans, and especially Americans of the Left, ought to listen to. He knows the American labor movement from the inside, and he knows the mood of working-class Negroes because he is one. When he speaks of the American Revolution, he is not using a figure of speech. He means it quite literally. In fact, he thinks that the American Revolution has already begun. He also thinks that it will be a protracted, painful, violent process in which not only will Negroes clash with whites but Negroes will clash with Negroes and whites with whites. And there is no end in sight and will not be until Americans finally come to realize that their responsibility is nothing less than the building of a classless society capable of making use of the prodigious powers of modern technology for genuinely human ends. They will not come to this realization and assume this responsibility except to the extent that they purge themselves of the accumulated corruption not of years or decades but of centuries, and this can be achieved only through struggle, suffering, and sacrifice. To this, we can only say amen. (9)

15 J. Boggs's *American Revolution* anticipated later works, such as *Who Needs the Negro* (1970), *Labor and Monopoly* (1976), *Adieux au Proletariate* (1980), *The Jobless Future* (1994), and *The End of Work* (1995). Johnson, "James Boggs, the 'Outsiders,'" 303–26.

16 The new edition included commentary from Shea Howell, Carl Edwards, Larry Sparks, Julia Pointer-Putnam, Jenny Lee, and Richard Feldman.

17 Boggs worked at the plant for twenty-eight years, from 1940 to 1968. Ward, *In Love and Struggle*, 2.

18 Bell and Touraine saw postindustrial society as a new societal model that differed significantly from agrarian and industrial societies. Its key characteristics included the predominance of the service sector (over manufacturing), white collar work (over blue), and the proliferation of knowledge-based firms such as research and development, insurance, financial, and telecommunications (over factories). Bell's 1973 book was not his first foray into

analyzing postindustrial society. It was preceded by *The End of Ideology* (1960), which also analyzed the implications of automation. In contrast to Boggs, Bell decries socialist revolution and the failures of Marxism and argues that automation will end class struggle. See Bell, *End of Ideology*; Touraine, *Postindustrial Society*; Bell, *Coming of the Post-Industrial Society*.

19 On the imaginaries and anxieties that pervaded this period, see Brick, "Optimism of the Mind," 348–80; and Bix, *Inventing Ourselves Out of Jobs*.

20 The Triple Alliance's Manifesto can be found here: "The Triple Revolution," Mississippi Freedom School Curriculum, accessed June 4, 2021, http://www .educationanddemocracy.org/FSCfiles/C_CC2a_TripleRevolution.htm. The ad hoc committee included the following members: Donald G. Agger, Dr. Donald B. Armstrong, James Boggs, W. H. Ferry, Todd Gitlin, Roger Hagan, Michael Harrington, Tom Hayden, Ralph L. Helstein, Dr. Frances W. Herring, Brig. General Hugh B. Hester, Gerald W. Johnson, Irving F. Laucks, Gunnar Myrdal, Gerard Piel, Michael D. Reagan, Ben B. Seligman, Robert Theobald, William Worthy, Alice Mary Hilton, David T. Bazelon, Maxwell Geismar, Philip Green, H. Stuart Hughes, Linus Pauling, and John William Ward.

21 Quotation from James Boggs, "The Negro and Cybernation," Proceedings of the April 21–23, 1964, Spring Joint Computer Conference, AFIPS, ACM, New York, cited in Bassett and Roberts, "Automation Now and Then," 17.

22 John D. Pomfret, "Guaranteed Income Asked for All, Employed or Not," *New York Times*, March 23, 1964, https://nyti.ms/3iXFYX9.

23 Johnson, "James Boggs, the 'Outsiders,'" 306. The struggles were also playing out at ports with containerization, an antilabor technology recognized as such by longshore unions. See Levinson, *Box*.

24 Boggs argued that the power of unions, particularly the UAW, had largely been compromised before automation by integrating their demands into the capitalist model rather than attacking its base.

25 Boggs and Boggs, "City Is the Black Man's Land," 162–70.

26 Lee, "Humanizing Schooling in Detroit," 281–84.

27 There was nothing absolute, no guarantees, as Stuart Hall used to say. See Grossberg, "Learning from Stuart Hall," 3–11.

28 Williams, *Country and the City*, 289.

29 Detroit Food Policy Council, *Detroit Food System Report 2011–2012* (Detroit: Detroit Food Policy Council, 2012). See also Pothukuchi, "Five Decades of Community Food Planning," 419–34.

30 Rosa Clayton is a pseudonym.

31 Boggs and Kurashige, *Next American Revolution*, 115.

32 Thanks to anonymous reviewers for raising questions about the Gardening Angels' namesake, the Guardian Angels. On the Guardian Angels' approach to crime prevention, see Pennell et al., "Guardian Angels," 378–400.

33 See Baker, "Racial Capitalism and a Tentative Commons," 25–36.

34 Rosa Clayton is a pseudonym.

35 Faye Moore is a pseudonym.

36 Sam Johnson is a pseudonym.

37 Morales, "Growing Food and Justice," 151.

38 White, "D-Town Farm," 406–17.

39 Interview is published in excerpted form in Campbell et al., *A People's Atlas of Detroit*. Yakini, "We Actually Have the Capacity to Define Our Own Reality," 124–28.

40 See Jessi Quizar's scholarship for fuller treatment and insightful analysis of urban agriculture and Feedom Freedom Growers. Quizar, who has engaged in long-standing study with Feedom Freedom, describes their work "as a means of survival and security; as a route toward reframing what it means to live a fulfilling life; and as a tool for promoting self-determination for Black and poor people. These views are rooted in a long Black radical tradition of challenging racial capitalism." Quizar, "Working to Live," 77.

41 The interview is published in excerpted form in Campbell et al., *A People's Atlas of Detroit*. See Curtis, "Liberated Territory Is a Means of Survival," 130–35.

42 On the Intercommunal News Service, see Hilliard, *Black Panther*.

43 Roanne, "Plotting the Black Commons," 4.

44 Nembhard, *Collective Courage*.

45 Philosopher Sylvia Wynter has argued that regimes of truth define modes of being human. The struggle of our time, according to Wynter, is a struggle over the overrepresentation of a secular, rational Man rooted in anti-Blackness and ways of being that threaten the human-species habitat. But it's possible, she argues, for culture and biological feedback loops to foster the reinvention of a more human humanism. I understand her provocation to be similar to the Boggses' call for a new human and Wayne's insight about healing as part of community control. See Wynter, "Unsettling the Coloniality of Being," 257–337.

46 See Quizar's fantastic *Antipode* article "A Logic of Care and Black Grassroots Claims to Home in Detroit" for more on how she theorizes a "logic of care." She applies the concept to thinking about property politics and claiming land in ways that resonate with and go beyond what I have been attempting to communicate here about how activists in Detroit seek to counter abandonment. Also see Curtis and Quizar, "Detroit-Opoly," 79–86.

47 As a Mennonite, he also took it as a message from God. Anna Groff, "Detroit Mennonite Runs Largest Urban Farm," *Mennonite*, June 2013.

48 To be sure, Indigenous tribes resisted and attempted to manipulate the strategies of a US government intent on their removal to gain more power amid the shifting political economy of the antebellum era. See Karamanski, "Settler Colonial Strategies," 27–51.

49 Dustin Dwyer, "From Wilderness to Wasteland: How the Destruction of Michigan's Forests Shaped Our State," Michigan Radio, Stateside podcast, 9:08, October 17, 2018, https://www.michiganradio.org/post/wilderness

-wasteland-how-destruction-michigan-s-forests-shaped-our-state. Also see Cronon's chapter "The Wealth of Nature: Lumber," in *Nature's Metropolis*, 148–206.

50 On Detroit's history of forestry, see Amy Elliot Bragg, "How Detroit Became a City of Trees," *Model D Media*, March 29, 2016.

51 On livability discourses, see Hamraie, "Enlivened City," 77–104.

52 The city planning commission argued in a November 13, 2012 letter to city council for its rejection based on the unprecedented nature of the proposal, the city's lack of an urban agriculture ordinance, that only five jobs were anticipated to be created, and that the project would affect the equitable access to city-owned land for other purchasers, community-based interests, and developers. Letter can be read here in appendix D: https://www .detroitfoodpc.org/sites/default/files/pdfs/DFPC%20Report-Public%20 Land%20Sale%20Process%20in%20Detroit.pdf.

53 Quoted in Editors, "A New Harvest for Detroit," *Atlantic*, May 27, 2010, http://www.theatlantic.com/special-report/the-future-of-the-city/archive /2010/05/a-new-harvest-fordetroit/57308/.

54 Dee Rollins is a pseudonym.

55 Excerpted interview is published in Campbell et al., *A People's Atlas of Detroit*. See Cabill, "We're Just Beginning the Journey," 136–38.

56 John Darby is pseudonym.

57 Mary Hawthorne is a pseudonym.

58 Excerpted interview is published in Campbell et al., *A People's Atlas of Detroit*. See Cabill, "We're Just Beginning the Journey," 136–38.

59 Cara May is a pseudonym.

60 See Shakur, "Reclaiming Our Souls," 293–95.

61 Doug Collins is a pseudonym.

62 Fairhead, Leach, and Scoones, "Green Grabbing," 237–61.

63 A textual version and oral delivery of this call can be viewed at "Community! Land! Trust! Video Rally—Charity Hicks," YouTube, accessed January 11, 2023, https://www.youtube.com/watch?v=7_eImVNFAks.

Epilogue. Reconstructing the World

1 Since 1836, Detroit had managed its own water system. Indeed, the expansion of the suburbs could not have happened without DWSD's willingness to build and manage a regional infrastructure, enabling new municipalities to avoid great capital expenditures. As the system aged and needed upgrades, DWSD struggled to cover its costs, and Detroiters' water rates were raised, reflecting a disproportionate responsibility for regional upkeep.

Between 1955 and 1973, DWSD added fifty-one municipalities to its system, leading to the claim made by many that Detroit subsidized the suburbs. By 2014, the regional water system served 3.8 million people through 2,700 miles of transmission and distribution mains and 3,000 miles of sewage collection pipes. Eighty percent of DWSD users lived outside Detroit. By 2012, 40 percent of DWSD revenue went to debt service. Their revenue was strained further when the city of Flint, seventy miles north, changed its water source from Lake Huron and the Detroit River (serviced by DWSD) to the Flint River. The reasons for water insecurity are complex, but the water shutoffs can be attributed in large part to the predatory nature of finance capital, emergency management and bankruptcy, and a management approach that sought to balance debt on the backs of the poor. Joseph Recchie, Anna Recchie, john a. powell, Lauren Lyons, Ponsella Hardaway, and Wendy Ake, *Water Equity and Security in Detroit's Water and Sewer District*, Othering and Belonging Institute (Berkeley: University of California, Haas Institute for a Fair and Inclusive Society, 2019), https://haasinstitute.berkeley.edu/detroitwaterequity.

2   Melosi, *Sanitary City*.

3   We the People of Detroit is an organization that was cofounded in 2008 by Chris Griffith, Aurora Harris, Monica Lewis-Patrick, Cecily McClellan, and Debra Taylor in response to the imposition of emergency management of Detroit Public Schools. Amid the water shutoffs, the organization put together a research collective called We the People of Detroit Research Collective, made up of scholars and residents. They have produced research related to emergency management across Michigan and the water shutoffs in Detroit. We the People of Detroit Community Research Collective, "Mapping the Water Crisis."

4   Charity Hicks, a lifelong Detroiter and leader of the People's Water Board, is credited with the initial call to wage love. Hicks had been organizing Detroiters around the right to water long before the shutoffs received global attention during Detroit's bankruptcy. In March 2014, Hicks was arrested and detained overnight for speaking out against the Detroit Water and Sewerage Department shutting off her neighbors' water access because they couldn't afford their bills. The phrase "wage love" recalls Ruth Wilson Gilmore's argument that "feelings" serve as the basis of struggle. It is urgent, therefore, to understand "how ordinary people," as she writes, "who lack resources but who do not necessarily lack 'resourcefulness' . . . develop the capacity to combine themselves into extraordinary forces and form the kinds of organizations that are the foundation of liberatory social movements." Gilmore, "Forgotten Places," 33–34.

5   Weston, "Lifeblood, Liquidity, and Cash Transfusions."

6   Detroiters Resisting Emergency Management, "Whose City? Our City!," D-REM, October 15, 2014, http://www.d-rem.org/whose-city-our-city-by-detroiters-resisting-emergency-management/.

bibliography

Adams, Thomas, and Matt Sakakeeny, eds. *Remaking New Orleans: Beyond Exceptionalism and Authenticity*. Durham, NC: Duke University Press, 2019.

Adams, Vincanne. *Markets of Sorrow, Labors of Faith: New Orleans in the Wake of Katrina*. Durham, NC: Duke University Press, 2013.

Akers, Joshua M. "Emerging Market City." *Environment and Planning A: Economy and Space* 47, no. 9 (2015): 1842–58. https://doi.org/10.1177/0308518x15604969.

Akers, Joshua M. "Making Markets: Think Tank Legislation and Private Property in Detroit." *Urban Geography* 34, no. 8 (2013): 1070–95. https://doi.org/10.1080/02723638.2013.814272.

Akers, Joshua, and Eric Seymour. "Instrumental Exploitation: Predatory Property Relations at City's End." *Geoforum* 91 (May 2018): 127–40.

Alderman, Derek H. "Surrogation and the Politics of Remembering Slavery in Savannah, Georgia (USA)." *Journal of Historical Geography* 36, no. 1 (2010): 90–101.

Alkon, Alison Hope, and Julian Agyeman, eds. *Cultivating Food Justice: Race, Class, and Sustainability*. Cambridge, MA: MIT Press, 2011.

Amann, Peter. "Vigilante Fascism: The Black Legion as an American Hybrid." *Comparative Studies in Society and History* 25, no. 3 (1983): 490–524.

Anderson, Carol. *White Rage: The Unspoken Truth of Our Racial Divide*. New York: Bloomsbury, 2016.

Anderson, Michelle Wilde. "The New Minimal Cities." *Yale Law Journal* 123, no. 5 (2014): 1118–27.

Apel, Dora. *Beautiful Terrible Ruins: Detroit and the Anxiety of Decline*. New Brunswick, NJ: Rutgers University Press, 2015.

Appadurai, Arjun, ed. *The Social Life of Things*. Cambridge: Cambridge University Press, 1986.

Arena, John. *Driven from New Orleans: How Nonprofits Betray Public Housing and Promote Privatization*. Minneapolis: University of Minnesota Press, 2012.

Armstrong, Margalynne. "Race and Property Values in Entrenched Segregation." *University of Miami Law Review* 52, no. 4 (1997): 1051–65.

Atuahene, Bernadette. "Our Taxes Are Too Damn High: Institutional Racism, Property Tax Assessments, and the Fair Housing Act." *Northwestern University Law Review* 112, no. 6 (2018): 1501–64.

Atuahene, Bernadette, and Timothy R. Hodge. "Stategraft." *Southern California Law Review* 91, no. 2 (2018): 263–302.

Azikiwe, Abayomi. *Rebellion, Crises and Social Transformation: Lessons from the Detroit July 1967 Rebellion and Beyond*. Detroit, MI: Panafnewswire Press, 2017.

Baker, Rachael. "Racial Capitalism and a Tentative Commons: Urban Farming and Claims to Space in Post-Bankruptcy Detroit." In *Commoning the City: Empirical Perspectives on Urban Ecology, Economics and Ethics*, edited by Derya Özkan and Güldem Baykal Büyüksaraç, 25–26. New York: Routledge, 2020.

Baldwin, James. *Tell Me How Long the Train's Been Gone*. New York: Vintage Books, 1968.

Barrett, Lindon. *Blackness and Value: Seeing Double*. Cambridge: Cambridge University Press, 2009.

Bassett, Caroline, and Ben Roberts. "Automation Now and Then: Automation Fevers, Anxieties and Utopias." *New Formations: A Journal of Culture, Theory, Politics* 98 (Winter 2019): 9–28.

Batty, Michael. *The New Science of Cities*. Cambridge, MA: MIT Press, 2013.

Beauregard, Robert A. "Representing Urban Decline: Postwar Cities as Narrative Objects." *Urban Affairs Quarterly* 29, no. 2 (1993): 187–202. https://doi.org/10.1177/004208169302900201.

Beauregard, Robert A. *Voices of Decline: The Postwar Fate of US Cities*. New York: Routledge, 2012.

Beaver, Patricia D. "The Civil War on the North Fork of the New River: The Cultural Politics of Elevation and Sustaining Community." *Appalachian Journal* 34, no. 1 (2006): 98–116.

Beer, David. "The Social Power of Algorithms." *Information, Communication and Society* 20, no. 1 (2017): 1–13. https://doi.org/10.1080/1369118X.2016.1216147.

Bélanger, Pierre. "Landscape as Infrastructure." *Landscape Journal* 28, no. 1 (2009): 79–95.

Bell, Daniel. *The Coming of the Post-Industrial Society*. New York: Basic Books, 1973.

Bell, Daniel. *The End of Ideology: On the Exhaustion of Political Ideas in the Fifties*. Cambridge, MA: Harvard University Press, 1960.

Benjamin, Lehn, Julia Sass Rubin, and Sean Zielenbach. "Community Development Financial Institutions: Current Issues and Future Prospects." *Journal of Urban Affairs* 26, no. 2 (2004): 177–95.

Berger, Dan, and Roxanne Dunbar-Ortiz. "'The Struggle Is for Land!': Race, Territory, and National Liberation." In *The Hidden 1970s: Histories of Radical-*

ism, edited by Dan Berger, 57–76. New Brunswick, NJ: Rutgers University Press, 2010.

Bergmann, Luke. *Getting Ghost: Two Young Lives and the Struggle for the Soul of an American City*. Ann Arbor: University of Michigan Press, 2010.

Best, Asha, and Margaret M. Ramírez. "Urban Specters." *Environment and Planning D: Society and Space* 39, no. 6 (2021): 1043–54.

Best, Stephen, and Saidiya Hartman. "Fugitive Justice." *Representations* 92, no. 1 (2005): 1–15. https://doi.org/10.1525/rep.2005.92.1.1.

Bhandar, Brenna. *Colonial Lives of Property: Law, Land, and Racial Regimes of Ownership*. Durham, NC: Duke University Press, 2018.

Bhandar, Brenna, Eva von Redecker, Harrison Lechley, and Hannah Voegele. "Unsettling Our Relationship to Things and People: A Conversation with Brenna Bhandar and Eva von Redecker." *Interfere: Journal for Critical Thought and Radical Politics* 2 (2021): 166–79.

Biehl, Joao. "Technologies of Invisibility." In *Anthropologies of Modernity: Foucault, Governmentality, and Life Politics*, edited by Jonathan Xavier Inda, 248–71. Malden, MA: Blackwell.

Bigger, Patrick, and Morgan Robertson. "Value Is Simple; Valuation Is Complex." *Capitalism Nature Socialism* 28, no. 1 (2017): 68–77. https://doi.org /10.1080/10455752.2016.1273962.

Billings, Dwight B. "Economic Representations in an American Region: What's at Stake in Appalachia?" In *Economic Representations*, edited by David F. Ruccio, 172–85. New York: Routledge, 2008.

Bird Rose, Deborah. *Reports from a Wild Country: Ethics of Decolonisation*. Sydney: University of New South Wales Press, 2004.

Biss, Eula. *Notes from No Man's Land: American Essays*. Minneapolis: Graywolf Press, 2018.

Bix, Amy Sue. *Inventing Ourselves Out of Jobs? America's Debate over Technological Unemployment, 1929–1981*. Baltimore, MD: Johns Hopkins University Press, 2002.

Blackmar, Elizabeth. "Appropriating 'the Commons': The Tragedy of Property Rights Discourse." In *The Politics of Public Space*, edited by Setha Low and Neil Smith, 57–58. New York: Routledge, 2006.

Blatman-Thomas, Naama, and Libby Porter. "Placing Property: Theorizing the Urban from Settler Colonial Cities." *International Journal of Urban and Regional Research* 43, no. 1 (2019): 30–45. https://doi.org/10.1111/1468 -2427.12666.

Blauner, Robert. "Internal Colonialism and Ghetto Revolt." *Society for the Study of Social Problems* 16, no. 4 (1969): 393–408. https://doi.org/10.2307 /799949.

Blaut, James Morris. *The Colonizer's Model of the World: Geographical Diffusionism and Eurocentric History*. New York: Guilford, 1993.

Bledsoe, Adam, and Willie J. Wright. "The Anti-Blackness of Global Capital." *Environment and Planning D: Society and Space* 37, no. 1 (2019): 8–26. https://doi.org/10.1177/0263775818805102.

Blomley, Nicholas. "Cuts, Flows, and the Geographies of Property." *Law, Culture and the Humanities* 7, no. 2 (2010): 203–16. https://doi.org/10.1177/1743872109355583.

Blomley, Nicholas. "Enclosure, Common Right, and the Property of the Poor." *Social and Legal Studies* 17, no. 3 (2008): 311–31. https://doi.org/10.1177/0964663908093966.

Blomley, Nicholas. "Land Use, Planning, and the 'Difficult Character of Property.'" *Planning Theory and Practice* 18, no. 3 (2017): 351–64. https://doi.org/10.1080/14649357.2016.1179336.

Blomley, Nicholas. "Law, Property, and the Geography of Violence: The Frontier, the Survey, and the Grid." *Annals of the Association of American Geographers* 93, no. 1 (2003): 121–41.

Blomley, Nicholas. "Performing Property: Making the World." *Canadian Journal of Law and Jurisprudence* 26, no. 1 (2013): 23–48.

Blomley, Nicholas. *Unsettling the City: Urban Land and the Politics of Property*. New York: Routledge, 2003.

Boggs, Grace Lee. "Introduction to the New Edition." In *The American Revolution: Pages from a Negro Worker's Notebook*, by James Boggs, vii–xvii. New York: Monthly Review Press, 2009.

Boggs, Grace Lee. *Living for Change: An Autobiography*. 1998. Minneapolis: University of Minnesota Press, 2016.

Boggs, Grace Lee, and Scott Kurashige. *The Next American Revolution: Sustainable Activism for the Twenty-First Century*. Berkeley: University of California Press, 2012.

Boggs, James. *The American Revolution: Pages from a Negro Worker's Notebook*. New York: Monthly Review Press, 1963.

Boggs, James, and Grace Lee Boggs. "The City Is the Black Man's Land (1966)." In *Pages from a Black Radical's Notebook: A James Boggs Reader*, edited by Stephen M. Ward, 162–70. Detroit, MI: Wayne State University Press, 2011.

Boggs, James, and Grace Lee Boggs. *Revolution and Evolution in the Twentieth Century*. 1975. New York: Monthly Review Press, 2008.

Bohaker, Heidi. "Reading Anishinaabe Identities: Meaning and Metaphor in Nindoodem Pictographs." *Ethnohistory* 57, no. 1 (2010): 11–33.

Bonds, Anne. "Race and Ethnicity I: Property, Race, and the Carceral State." *Progress in Human Geography* 43, no. 3 (2019): 574–83.

Bonilla-Silva, Eduardo. *Racism without Racists: Color-Blind Racism and the Persistence of Racial Inequality in America*. 2003. Lanham, MD: Rowman and Littlefield, 2014.

Bowker, Geoff, and Susan L Star. *Sorting Things Out: Classification and Its Consequences*. Cambridge, MA: MIT Press, 1999.

Boyd, Herb. *Black Detroit: A People's History of Self-Determination*. New York: Amistad, 2017.

Brahinsky, Rachel. "The Story of Property: Meditations on Gentrification, Renaming, and Possibility." *Environment and Planning A: Economy and Space* 52, no. 5 (2020): 837–55.

Brand, Anna Livia. "The Sedimentation of Whiteness as Landscape." *Environment and Planning D: Society and Space* 40, no. 2 (2022): 276–91. https://doi.org/10.1177/02637758211031565.

Brenner, Neil, and Christian Schmid. "Planetary Urbanization." In *The Globalizing Cities Reader*, edited by Xuefei Ren and Roger Keil, 449–53. New York: Routledge, 2017.

Brick, Howard. "Optimism of the Mind: Imagining Postindustrial Society in the 1960s and 1970s." *American Quarterly* 44, no. 3 (1992): 348–80.

Bronner, Simon J. "The Challenges of American Folklore to the Humanities." *Humanities* 7, no. 17 (2018): 1–31. https://doi.org/10.3390/h7010017.

Brown, Adrienne. "Appraisal Narratives: Reading Race on the Midcentury Block." *American Quarterly* 70, no. 2 (2018): 211–34. https://doi.org/10.1353/aq.2018.0015.

Browne, Simone. *Dark Matters: On the Surveillance of Blackness*. Durham, NC: Duke University Press, 2015.

Brunetta, Grazia, and Stefano Moroni. "The Proposal of Ebenezer Howard." In *Contractual Communities in the Self-Organising City: Freedom, Creativity, Subsidiary*, edited by Grazia Brunetta and Stefano Moroni, 65–74. New York: Springer, 2012.

Byrd, Jodi A. "Weather with You: Settler Colonialism, Antiblackness, and the Grounded Relationalities of Resistance." *Critical Ethnic Studies* 5, no. 1–2 (2019): 207–14.

Byrd, Jodi A., Alyosha Goldstein, Jodi Melamed, and Chandan Reddy. "Predatory Value: Economies of Dispossession and Disturbed Relationalities." *Social Text* 36, no. 2 (2018): 1–18.

Cabill, Lila, "We're Just Beginning the Journey." In *A People's Atlas of Detroit*, edited by Linda Campbell, Andrew Newman, Sara Safransky, and Tim Stallmann, 136–38. Detroit, MI: Wayne State University Press, 2020.

Callon, Michel. "Introduction: The Embeddedness of Economic Markets in Economics." In *Laws of the Markets*, edited by Michel Callon, 1–57. Malden, MA: Blackwell, 1998.

Calvário, Rita, Giorgos Velegrakis, and Maria Kaika. "The Political Ecology of Austerity: An Analysis of Socio-Environmental Conflict under Crisis in Greece." *Capitalism, Nature, Socialism* 28, no. 3 (2017): 69–87. https://doi.org/10.1080/10455752.2016.1260147.

Campbell, Linda, Andrew Newman, Sara Safransky, and Tim Stallmann. "Black Homeownership in Detroit." In *A People's Atlas of Detroit*, edited by Linda Campbell, Andrew Newman, Sara Safransky, and Tim Stallmann, 198–203. Detroit, MI: Wayne State University Press, 2020.

Campbell, Linda, Andrew Newman, Sara Safransky, and Tim Stallmann, eds. *A People's Atlas of Detroit*. Detroit, MI: Wayne State University Press, 2020.

Carlisle, Fred, comp. *Chronography of Notable Events in the History of the Northwest Territory and Wayne County, 1531–1890*. Detroit, MI: Gulley, Bornman, 1890.

Carmichael, Stokely. "Stokely Carmichael Explains Black Power to a Black Audience in Detroit." In *The Rhetoric of Black Power*, edited by Robert L. Scott and Wayne Brickriede, 84–95. New York: Harper and Row, 1969.

Carmichael, Stokely, and Charles V. Hamilton. *Black Power: The Politics of Liberation in America*. 1968. New York: Vintage, 1992.

Chafets, Ze'ev. *Devil's Night: And Other True Tales of Detroit*. New York: Random House, 1990.

Chakrabarty, Dipesh. *Provincializing Europe*. Princeton, NJ: Princeton University Press, 2000.

Chakravartty, Paula, and Denise Ferreira da Silva. "Accumulation, Dispossession, and Debt: The Racial Logic of Global Capitalism—An Introduction." *American Quarterly* 64, no. 3 (2012): 361–85.

Cherry, Liev. "The Construction of Emptiness and the Re-Colonisation of Detroit." PhD diss., Queen Mary University of London, 2018.

Choo, Kristin. "Plowing Over: Can Urban Farming Save Detroit and Other Declining Cities? Will the Law Allow It?" *ABA Journal of Labor and Law* 97 (2011): 42–70. https://www.abajournal.com/magazine/article/plowing_over_can _urban_farming_save_detroit_and_other_declining_cities_will.

Christensen, Dana M. "Securing the Momentum: Could a Homestead Act Help Sustain Detroit Urban Agriculture?" *Drake Journal of Agricultural Law* 16, no. 2 (2011): 241–60.

Cleage, Albert B., Jr. *The Black Messiah*. New York: Sheed and Ward, 1968.

Cleaver, Eldridge. "The Land Question." In *What Country Have I? Political Writings by Black Americans*, edited by Herbert J. Storing, 183–92. New York: St. Martin's Press, 1970.

Clevenger, Samuel Martin, and David Lawrence Andrews. "'A Peaceful Path to' Healthy Bodies: The Biopolitics of Ebenezer Howard's Garden City." *Urban Planning* 2, no. 4 (2017): 141–45. https://doi.org/10.17645/up.v2i4.1251.

Colasanti, Kathryn J. A., Michael W. Hamm, and Charlotte M. Litjens. "The City as an 'Agricultural Powerhouse'? Perspectives on Expanding Urban Agriculture from Detroit, Michigan." *Urban Geography* 33, no. 3 (2012): 348–69. https://doi.org/10.2747/0272-3638.33.3.348.

Cole, Teju. *Blind Spot*. New York: Random House, 2016.

Coletta, Claudio, and Rob Kitchin. "Algorhythmic Governance: Regulating the 'Heartbeat' of a City Using the Internet of Things." *Big Data and Society* 4, no. 2 (2017): 1–16. https://doi.org/2053951717742418.

Collins, Bennett, Siobhan McEvoy-Levy, and Alison Watson. "The Maine Wabanaki–State Child Welfare Truth and Reconciliation Commission: Perceptions and Understandings." In *Indigenous Peoples' Access to Justice, Including Truth and Reconciliation Processes*, edited by Wilton Littlechild and Elsa Stamatopoulou, 140–69. New York: Institute for the Study of Human Rights, Columbia University, 2015.

Connolly, N. D. B. *A World More Concrete: Real Estate and the Remaking of Jim Crow South Florida*. Chicago: University of Chicago Press, 2014.

Cooper-McCann, Patrick. "The Trap of Triage: Lessons from the 'Team Four Plan.'" *Journal of Planning History* 15, no. 2 (2016): 149–69.

Coser, Lewis A. "Introduction: Maurice Halbwachs 1877–1945." In *On Collective Memory*, by Maurice Halbwachs, edited and translated by Lewis A. Coser, 1–36. Chicago: University of Chicago Press, 1992.

Coulthard, Glen S. "Subjects of Empire: Indigenous Peoples and the 'Politics of Recognition' in Canada." *Contemporary Political Theory* 6 (2007): 437–60.

Cowen, Deborah, Glenda Garelli, and Martina Tazzioli. "Editors' Interview with Deborah Cowen." *South Atlantic Quarterly* 117, no. 2 (2018): 397–403.

Crawford, Martin. *Ashe County's Civil War: Community and Society in the Appalachian South*. Charlottesville: University Press of Virginia, 2001.

Cronon, William. "The Trouble with Wilderness; Or, Getting Back to the Wrong Nature." *Environmental History* 1, no. 1 (1996): 7–28.

Cronon, William. *Nature's Metropolis: Chicago and the Great West*. W. W. Norton and Company, 2009.

Cruse, Harold. *Rebellion or Revolution?* New York: Morrow, 1968.

Curtis, Kezia, and Jessi Quizar. "Detroit-Opoly." In *A People's Atlas of Detroit*, edited by Linda Campbell, Andrew Newman, Sara Safransky, and Tim Stallmann, 79–86. Detroit, MI: Wayne State University Press, 2020.

Curtis, Wayne. "Liberated Territory Is a Means of Survival." In *A People's Atlas of Detroit*, edited by Linda Campbell, Andrew Newman, Sara Safransky, and Tim Stallmann, 130–35. Detroit, MI: Wayne State University Press, 2020.

Daigle, Michelle. "The Spectacle of Reconciliation: On (the) Unsettling Responsibilities to Indigenous Peoples in the Academy." *Environment and Planning D: Society and Space* 37, no. 4 (2019): 703–21.

Daniel, Pete. *Dispossession: Discrimination against African American Farmers in the Age of Civil Rights*. Chapel Hill: University of North Carolina Press, 2013.

Darden, Joe T., Richard C. Hill, June Thomas, and Richard Thomas. *Detroit: Race and Uneven Development*. Philadelphia: Temple University Press, 1987.

Darden, Joe T., and Richard W. Thomas. *Detroit: Race Riots, Racial Conflicts, and Efforts to Bridge the Racial Divide*. East Lansing: Michigan State University Press, 2013.

Darden, Joe, and Elvin Wyly. "Cartographic Editorial—Mapping the Racial/
Ethnic Topography of Subprime Inequality in Urban America." *Urban Geography* 31, no. 4 (2010): 425–33. https://doi.org/10.2747/0272–3638.31.4.425.

Davis, Robbie, and Ed Williams. "Fences and Between Fences: Cultural, Historical, and Smithsonian Perspectives." *Journal of the Southwest* 50, no. 3 (2008): 243–61.

Dawney, Leila. "Decommissioned Places: Ruins, Endurance and Care at the End of the First Nuclear Age." *Transactions of the Institute of British Geographers* 45, no. 1 (2020): 33–49.

Dawson, Michael C., and Rovana Popoff. "Reparations: Justice and Greed in Black and White." *Du Bois Review: Social Science Research on Race* 1, no. 1 (2004): 47–91.

Dear, Michael, and Steven Flusty. "Postmodern Urbanism." *Annals of the Association of American Geographers* 88, no. 1 (1998): 50–72.

DeFilippis, James. "Paradoxes of Community-Building: Community Control in the Global Economy." *International Social Science Journal* 59, no. 192 (2008): 223–34.

Delaney, David. "The Space That Race Makes." *Professional Geographer* 54, no. 1 (2002): 6–14.

Deloria, Vine, Jr. *Custer Died for Your Sins: An Indian Manifesto*. New York: Macmillan, 1969.

Densu, Kwasi. "Patchin: Towards a Theory and Political History of Africana Agrarianism." PhD diss., Clark Atlanta University, 2011.

Derickson, Kate D. "Urban Geography II: Urban Geography in the Age of Ferguson." *Progress in Human Geography* 41, no. 2 (2017): 230–44. https://doi.org/10.1177/0309132515624315.

DeSilvey, Caitlin, and Tim Edensor. "Reckoning with Ruins." *Progress in Human Geography* 37, no. 4 (2013): 465–85.

Dillard, Angela D. *Faith in the City: Preaching Radical Social Change in Detroit*. Ann Arbor: University of Michigan Press, 2007.

Dorries, Heather, David Hugill, and Julie Tomiak. "Racial Capitalism and the Production of Settler Colonial Cities." *Geoforum* 132 (June 2022): 263–70. https://doi.org/10.1016/j.geoforum.2019.07.016.

Doxtader, Erik. "The Potential of Reconciliation's Beginning: A Reply." *Rhetoric and Public Affairs* 7, no. 3 (2004): 378–90.

Dozier, Deshonay. "Contested Development: Homeless Property, Police Reform, and Resistance in Skid Row, LA." *International Journal of Urban and Regional Research* 43, no. 1 (2019): 179–94.

D. P. K. "Constitutional Law: Mortgage Foreclosure Moratorium Statutes." *Michigan Law Review Association* 32, no. 1 (1933): 71–80.

Dr. Huey P. Newton Foundation. *The Black Panther Party: Service to the People Programs*. Edited by David Hilliard. Albuquerque: University of New Mexico Press, 2008.

Du Bois, W. E. B. *Darkwater: Voices from Within the Veil*. 1920. New York: Verso, 2016.

Dunbar-Ortiz, Roxanne. *An Indigenous People's History of the United States*. Boston: Beacon Press, 2014.

Dye, Keith. "The Black Manifesto for Reparations in Detroit: Challenge and Response, 1969." *Michigan Historical Review* 35, no. 2 (2009): 53–83.

Eaves, LaToya. "We Wear the Mask." *Southeastern Geographer* 56, no. 1 (2016): 22–28.

Eubanks, Virginia. *Automating Inequality: How High-Tech Tools Profile, Police, and Punish the Poor*. New York: St. Martin's, 2017.

Fabian, Johannes. *Time and the Other: How Anthropology Makes Its Market*. New York: Columbia University Press, 2014.

Fairhead, James, Melissa Leach, and Ian Scoones. "Green Grabbing: A New Appropriation of Nature?" *Journal of Peasant Studies* 39, no. 2 (2012): 237–61.

Fanon, Frantz. *The Wretched of the Earth*. Translated by Richard Philcox. 1961. New York: Grove, 2004.

Farley, Reynolds, Sheldon Danziger, and Harry Holzer. *Detroit Divided*. New York: Russell Sage Foundation, 2002.

Fennell, Catherine. *The Last Project Standing: Civics and Sympathy in Post-Welfare Chicago*. Minneapolis: University of Minnesota Press, 2015.

Ferguson, James. *The Anti-Politics Machine: "Development," Depoliticization, and Bureaucratic Power in Lesotho*. Minneapolis: University of Minnesota Press, 1994.

Ferguson, James. *Expectations of Modernity: Myths and Meanings of Urban Life on the Zambian Copperbelt*. Berkeley: University of California Press, 1999.

Fields, Desiree, and Elora Lee Raymond. "Racialized Geographies of Housing Financialization." *Progress in Human Geography* 45, no. 6 (2021): 1625–45.

Fine, Sidney. *Violence in the Model City: The Cavanagh Administration, Race Relations, and the Detroit Riot of 1967*. Ann Arbor: University of Michigan Press, 1989.

Flamm, Michael W. *Law and Order: Street Crime, Civil Unrest, and the Crisis of Liberalism in the 1960s*. New York: Columbia University Press, 2005.

Florida, Richard. *The Rise of the Creative Class: And How It's Transforming Work, Leisure, Community, and Everyday Life*. Basic Books: New York, 2002.

Flood, Joe. *The Fires*. Riverhead Books: New York, 2010.

Forman, James. "The Black Manifesto." *Review of Black Political Economy* 1, no. 1 (Spring–Summer 1970): 36–44.

Foster, Kathleen, Jeanette Marble, and Deborah Williamson. "Riverfront East Congregation Initiative: 'Do They Have Our Community's Best Interests at Heart?'" In *A People's Atlas of Detroit*, edited by Linda Campbell, Andrew Newman, Sara Safransky, and Tim Stallmann, 222–26. Detroit, MI: Wayne State University Press, 2020.

Foucault, Michel. "Nietzsche, Genealogy, History." In *The Foucault Reader*, edited by Paul Rabinow, 76–100. New York: Pantheon, 1984.

Frankowski, Alfred. "The Violence of Post-Racial Memory and the Political Sense of Mourning." *Contemporary Aesthetics* 11 (2013). http://hdl.handle.net /2027/spo.7523862.0011.012.

Freire, Paulo. *Pedagogy of Hope: Reliving Pedagogy of the Oppressed*. 1994. New York: Bloomsbury Academic, 2021.

Freund, David M. P. *Colored Property: State Policy and White Racial Politics in Suburban America*. Chicago: University of Chicago Press, 2007.

Friedmann, Georges, and John H. Mueller, "Maurice Halbwachs, 1877–1945." *American Journal of Sociology* 51, no. 6 (1946): 509–17.

Frost, Robert. "Mending Wall." In *North of Boston*, 11–13. New York: Henry Holt, 1914.

Fullilove, Mindy Thompson. *Root Shock: How Tearing Up City Neighborhoods Hurts America, and What We Can Do about It*. New York: New York University Press, 2016.

Fung, Catherine. "'This Isn't Your Battle or Your Land': The Native American Occupation of Alcatraz in the Asian-American Political Imagination." *College Literature* 41, no. 1 (2014): 149–73. https://doi.org/10.1353/lit.2014 .0006.

Galinée, René de Bréhan de. "Journey of Dollier and Galinée, 1669–1670." In *Early Narratives of the Northwest, 1634–1699*, edited by Louise Kellogg, 163–209. New York: Scribner, 1917. https://www.americanjourneys.org/aj -049/.

Gallagher, Victoria J., and Margaret R. LaWare. "Sparring with Public Memory: The Rhetorical Embodiment of Race, Power, and Conflict in the Monument to Joe Louis." In *Places of Public Memory: The Rhetoric of Museums and Memorials*, edited by Greg Dickinson, Carole Blair, and Brian L. Ott, 87–112. Tuscaloosa: University of Alabama Press, 2010.

Ganz, Marshall. "Resources and Resourcefulness: Strategic Capacity in the Unionization of California Agriculture, 1959–1966." *American Journal of Sociology* 105, no. 4 (2000): 1003–62.

Garcia, Megan. "Racist in the Machine: The Disturbing Implications of Algorithmic Bias." *World Policy Journal* 33, no. 4 (2016): 111–17.

Georgakas, Dan, and Marvin Surkin. *Detroit, I Do Mind Dying*. Cambridge, MA: South End Press, 1998.

George, Henry. *Progress and Poverty.* New York: Doubleday, 1879. New York: Robert Shalkenbach Foundation, 1966.

Ghazavi, Vafa. "Ethics at a Distance." *Boston Review*, April 21, 2020. https:// bostonreview.net/philosophy-religion/vafa-ghazavi-ethics-distance.

Ghezzi, Ridie Wilson. "Nanabush Stories from the Ojibwe." In *Coming to Light: Contemporary Translations of the Native Literatures of North America*, edited by Brian Swann, 443–63. New York: Random House, 1994.

Gidwani, Vinay, and Rajyashree N. Reddy. "The Afterlives of 'Waste': Notes from India for a Minor History of Capitalist Surplus." *Antipode: A Radical Journal of Cartography* 43, no. 5 (2011): 1625–58.

Gillespie, Tarleton. "The Relevance of Algorithms." In *Media Technologies: Essays on Communication, Materiality, and Society*, edited by Tarleton Gillespie, Pablo J Boczkowski, and Kirsten Foot, 167–94. Cambridge, MA: MIT Press, 2014.

Gilmore, Ruth Wilson. "Fatal Couplings of Power and Difference: Notes on Racism and Geography." *Professional Geographer* 54, no. 1 (2002): 15–24. https://doi.org/10.1111/0033-0124.00310.

Gilmore, Ruth Wilson. "Forgotten Places and the Seeds of Grassroots Planning." In *Engaging Contradictions*, edited by Charlie Hale, 31–61. Berkeley: University of California Press, 2008.

Gilmore, Ruth Wilson. *Golden Gulag: Prisons, Surplus, Crisis, and Opposition in Globalizing California*. Berkeley: University of California Press, 2007.

Gilmore, Ruth Wilson. "What Is to Be Done?" *American Quarterly* 63, no. 2 (2011): 245–65.

Giroux, Henry A. "Reading Hurricane Katrina: Race, Class, and the Biopolitics of Disposability." *College Literature* 33, no. 3 (2006): 171–96.

Goeman, Mishuana. "From Place to Territories and Back Again: Centering Storied Land in the Discussion of Indigenous Nation-Building." *International Journal of Critical Indigenous Studies* 1, no. 1 (2008): 23–34.

Goeman, Mishuana. "Land as Life: Unsettling the Logics of Containment." In *Native Studies Keywords*, edited by Stephanie Nohelani Teves, Andrea Smith, and Michelle Raheja, 71–89. Tucson: University of Arizona Press, 2015.

Goetz, Edward G. *New Deal Ruins: Race, Economic Justice, and Public Policy*. Ithaca, NY: Cornell University Press, 2013.

Goffe, Rachel. "Capture and Abandon: Social Reproduction and Informal Land Tenure in Jamaica." PhD diss., City University of New York, 2017.

Goffe, Rachel. "Reproducing the Plot: Making Life in the Shadow of Premature Death." *Antipode: A Radical Journal of Cartography* (2022). https://onlinelibrary.wiley.com/doi/epdf/10.1111/anti.12812.

Goldstein, Alyosha. "Finance and Foreclosure in the Colonial Present." *Radical History Review* 2014, no. 118 (2014): 42–63. https://doi.org/10.1215/01636545-2349095.

Goldstein, Alyosha. "The Ground Not Given Colonial Dispositions of Land, Race, and Hunger." *Social Text* 36, no. 2 (135) (2018): 83–106. https://doi.org/10.1215/01642472-4362373.

Goldstein, Alyosha. *Poverty in Common: The Politics of Community Action during the American Century*. Durham, NC: Duke University Press, 2012.

Goldstein, Ira. "Making Sense of Markets: Using Data to Guide Reinvestment Strategies." In *What Counts: Harnessing Data for America's Communities*, 74–87. San Francisco: Federal Reserve Bank of San Francisco and the Urban Institute, 2014. https://www.researchgate.net/profile/Ira_Goldstein3

/publication/282860303_Making_Sense_of_Markets_Using_data_to_guide
_reinvestment_strategies/links/5e303781a6fdccd9657099bd/Making-Sense
-of-Markets-Using-data-to-guide-reinvestment-strategies.pdf.

Goldstein, Ira. "Maximizing the Impact of Federal NSP Investments through the Strategic Use of Local Market Data." In *REO Vacant Properties: Strategies for Neighborhood Stabilization*, edited by Prabl Chakrabarti, Matthew Lambert, and Mary Helen Petrus, 65–75. Philadelphia: Federal Reserve Board and Federal Reserve Banks of Boston and Cleveland, 2010.

Gordon, Avery F. *Ghostly Matters: Haunting and the Sociological Imagination*. Minneapolis: University of Minnesota Press, 2008.

Gordon, Avery F. *The Hawthorn Archive: Letters from the Utopian Margins*. New York: Fordham University Press, 2017.

Gotham, Kevin Fox. "Creating Liquidity out of Spatial Fixity: The Secondary Circuit of Capital and the Restructuring of the US Housing Finance System." In *Subprime Cities: The Political Economy of Mortgage Markets*, edited by Manuel B. Aalbers, 25–52. Malden, MA: Blackwell, 2012.

Graeber, David G. *Debt: The First 5,000 Years*. Brooklyn, NY: Melville House, 2012.

Graeber, David G. "It Is Value That Brings Universes into Being." *HAU: Journal of Ethnographic Theory* 3, no. 2 (2013): 219–43. https://doi.org/10.14318 /hau3.2.012.

Graham, Stephen, and Nigel Thrift. "Out of Order: Understanding Repair and Maintenance." *Theory: Culture and Society* 24, no. 3 (2007): 1–25.

Grandin, Gregg. *Fordlandia: The Rise and Fall of Henry Ford's Forgotten Jungle City*. New York: Picador, 2009.

Greenstone, David, and Paul Peterson. *Race and Authority in Urban Politics*. New York: Russell Sage Foundation, 1973.

Grossberg, Lawrence. "Learning from Stuart Hall, Following the Path with Heart." *Cultural Studies* 29, no. 1 (2015): 3–11. https://doi.org/10.1080 /09502386.2014.917228.

Gross-Wyrtzen, Leslie. "Contained and Abandoned in the 'Humane' Border: Black Migrants' Immobility and Survival in Moroccan Urban Space." *Environment and Planning D: Society and Space* 38, no. 5 (2020): 887–904.

Haase, Dagmar. "Urban Ecology of Shrinking Cities: An Unrecognized Opportunity?" *Nature and Culture* 3, no. 1 (2008): 1–8. https://doi.org/10.3167/nc .2008.030101.

Hackman, Rose. "One-Fifth of Detroit's Population Could Lose Their Homes." *The Atlantic*, October 22, 2014. https://www.theatlantic.com/business/archive /2014/10/one-fifth-of-detroits-population-could-lose-their-homes/381694/.

Hackworth, Jason. "Demolition as Urban Policy in the American Rust Belt." *Environment and Planning A: Economy and Space* 48, no. 11 (2016): 2201–22. https://doi.org/10.1177/0308518×16654914.

Hackworth, Jason. "Local Autonomy, Bond-Rating Agencies and Neoliberal Urbanism in the United States." *International Journal of Urban and Regional*

Research 26, no. 4 (2002): 707–25. https://doi.org/10.1111/1468-2427 .00412.

Haiven, Max. "The Art of Unpayable Debts." In *The Sociology of Debt*, edited by Mark Featherstone, 195–230. Bristol: Policy Press, 2021.

Halbwachs, Maurice. *On Collective Memory*. Translated by Lewis A. Coser. Chicago: University of Chicago Press, 1992.

Hamlin, Marie Caroline Watson. *Legends of Le Détroit*. Detroit, MI: Thorndike Nourse, 1884.

Hamraie, Aimi. "Enlivened City: Inclusive Design, Biopolitics, and the Philosophy of Liveability." *Built Environment* 44, no. 1 (2018): 77–104. https://doi.org /10.2148/benv.44.1.77.

Hann, Chris. "Introduction: The Embeddedness of Property." In *Property Relations: Renewing the Anthropological Tradition*, 1–47. New York: Cambridge University Press, 1998.

Hann, Chris. "Property: Anthropological Aspects." In *International Encyclopedia of the Social and Behavioral Sciences*, edited by James D. Wright, vol. 19, 153–59. 2nd ed. Oxford: Elsevier, 2015.

Hardin, Michael. "The Trickster of History: *The Heirs of Columbus* and the Dehistorization of Narrative." Special issue, *MELUS* 23, no. 4 (1998): 25–45. https://doi.org/10.2307/467826.

Harney, Stefano, and Fred Moten. *The Undercommons: Fugitive Planning and Black Study*. New York: Minor Compositions, 2013.

Harris, Cheryl I. "Of Blackness and Indigeneity: Comments on Jodi A. Byrd's 'Weather with You: Settler Colonialism, Antiblackness, and the Grounded Relationalities of Resistance.'" *Critical Ethnic Studies* 5, no. 1–2 (2019): 215–28. https://doi.org/10.5749/jcritethnstud.5.1-2.0215.

Harris, Cheryl I. "Whiteness as Property." *Harvard Law Review* 106, no. 8 (1993): 1707–91.

Harris, Lee A. "Political Autonomy as a Form of Reparations to African-Americans." *Southern University Law Review* 29, no. 1 (2001): 25–56.

Hartigan, John, Jr. *Racial Situations: Class Predicaments of Whiteness in Detroit*. Princeton, NJ: Princeton University Press, 1999.

Hartman, Saidiya. *Lose Your Mother: A Journey along the Atlantic Slave Route*. New York: Farrar, Straus and Giroux, 2007.

Hartman, Saidiya. *Scenes of Subjection: Terror, Slavery, and Self-Making in Nineteenth-Century America*. New York: Oxford University Press, 1997.

Hartman, Saidiya. "Venus in Two Acts." *Small Axe: A Caribbean Journal of Criticism* 12, no. 2 (2008): 1–14.

Harvey, David. *The Limits to Capital*. New York: Verso, 2018.

Harvey, David. *New Imperialism*. New York: Oxford University Press, 2003.

Harvey, David. "The Spatial Fix—Hegel, von Thunen, and Marx." *Antipode: A Radical Journal of Cartography* 13, no. 3 (1981): 1–12. https://doi.org/10 .1111/j.1467-8330.1981.tb00312.x.

Henricks, Kasey, and Louise Seamster. "Mechanisms of the Racial Tax State." *Critical Sociology* 43, no. 2 (2017): 169–79.

Herbert, Claire W. *A Detroit Story: Urban Decline and the Rise of Property Informality*. Oakland: University of California Press, 2021.

Herron, Jerry. "Detroit: Disaster Deferred, Disaster in Progress." *South Atlantic Quarterly* 106, no. 4 (2007): 663–82. https://doi.org/10.1215/00382876 -2007-040.

Herron, Jerry. "The Forgetting Machine: Notes toward a History of Detroit." *Places Journal*, January 2012. https://doi.org/10.22269/120109.

Herron, Jerry. "Motor City Breakdown." *Places Journal*, April 2013. https://doi .org/10.22269/130423.

Herscher, Andrew. *The Unreal Estate Guide to Detroit*. Ann Arbor: University of Michigan Press, 2012.

Hersey, John. *Algiers Motel*. 1968. Baltimore, MD: Johns Hopkins University Press, 1998.

Heynen, Nik. "Urban Political Ecology II: The Abolitionist Century." *Progress in Human Geography* 40, no. 6 (2016): 839–45. https://doi.org/10.1177 /0309132515617394.

Hickmott, Alec F. "Black Land, Black Capital: Rural Development in the Shadows of the Sunbelt South, 1969–1976." *Journal of African American History* 101, no. 4 (2016): 504–34. https://doi.org/10.5323/jafriamerhist.101.4.0504.

Hilliard, David. *The Black Panther: Intercommunal News Service, 1967–1980*. New York: Atria, 2007.

Hilliard, David. "Introduction." In *The Huey P. Newton Reader*, edited by David Hilliard and Donald Weise, 9–24. New York: Seven Stories Press, 2002.

Hillier, Amy E. "Residential Security Maps and Neighborhood Appraisals: The Home Owners' Loan Corporation and the Case of Philadelphia." *Social Science History* 29, no. 2 (2005): 207–33. https://doi.org/10.1017 /S014555320001292X.

Hinton, Elizabeth. *From the War on Poverty to the War on Crime*. Cambridge, MA: Harvard University Press, 2016.

Hong, Grace Kyungwon. "Existentially Surplus: Women of Color Feminism and the New Crises of Capitalism." *GLQ: A Journal of Lesbian and Gay Studies* 18, no. 1 (2012): 87–106.

Hong, Grace Kyungwon. "Property." In *Keywords for American Cultural Studies*, edited by B. Burgett and G. Hendler. 2nd ed. New York: New York University Press, 2014. Accessed November 10, 2017. http://key words.nyupress .org/american-cultural-studies/essay/property/.

Hooker, Clarence. "Ford's Sociology Department and the Americanization Campaign and the Manufacture of Popular Culture among Assembly Line Workers c. 1910–1917." *Journal of American Culture* 20, no. 1 (March 1997): 47–53.

hooks, bell. "Introduction: Theory as Liberatory Practice." In *Teaching to Transgress*, 1–12. New York: Routledge, 1994.

Horowitz, Andy. *Katrina: A History, 1915–2015*. Cambridge, MA: Harvard University Press, 2020.

Hosbey, Justin, and J. T. Roane. "A Totally Different Form of Living: On the Legacies of Displacement and Marronage as Black Ecologies." *Southern Cultures* 27, no. 1 (2021): 68–73.

House, Gloria. "Corporate Power and the Reinvention of Detroit." In *A People's Atlas of Detroit*, edited by Linda Campbell, Andrew Newman, Sara Safransky, and Tim Stallmann, 205–9. Detroit, MI: Wayne State University Press, 2020.

Hugill, David. "What Is a Settler-Colonial City?" *Geography Compass* 11, no. 5 (2017). https://doi.org/10.1111/gec3.12315.

Hull, Matthew S. "The File: Agency, Authority, and Autography in an Islamabad Bureaucracy." *Language and Communication* 23, nos. 3–4 (2003): 287–314.

Hull, Matthew S. *Government of Paper: The Materiality of Bureaucracy in Urban Pakistan*. Berkeley: University of California Press, 2012.

Hunter, Marcus A., Mary Pattillo, Zandria F. Robinson, and Keeanga-Yamahtta Taylor. "Black Placemaking: Celebration, Play, and Poetry." *Theory, Culture and Society* 33, nos. 7–8 (2016): 31–56. https://doi.org/10.1177/0263276416635259.

Hutchinson, Sikivu. "White Picket Fences, White Innocence." *Journal of Religious Ethics* 42, no. 4 (2014): 612–39.

Immerwahr, Daniel. *Thinking Small: The United States and the Lure of Community Development*. Cambridge, MA: Harvard University Press, 2015.

Inwood, Joshua. "Righting Unrightable Wrongs: Legacies of Racial Violence and the Greensboro Truth and Reconciliation Commission." *Annals of the Association of American Geographers* 102, no. 6 (2012): 1450–67. https://doi.org/10.1080/00045608.2011.603647.

Inwood, Joshua, Derek Alderman, and Melanie Barron. "Addressing Structural Violence through US Reconciliation Commissions: The Case Study of Greensboro, NC and Detroit, MI." *Political Geography* 52 (May 2016): 57–64. https://doi.org/10.1016/j.polgeo.2015.11.005.

Ioanide, Paula. "The Alchemy of Race and Affect: 'White Innocence' and Public Secrets in the Post–Civil Rights Era." *Kalfou* 1, no. 1 (2014): 151–68. https://doi.org/10.15367/kf.v1i1.14.

Jackson, Kenneth T. *Crabgrass Frontier: The Suburbanization of the United States*. New York: Oxford University Press, 1985.

Jacobs, Harvey, and Kurt Paulsen. "Property Rights: The Neglected Theme of 20th-Century American Planning." *Journal of the American Planning Association* 75, no. 2 (2009): 134–43.

Jacobs, Jane M. *Edge of Empire: Postcolonialism and the City*. New York: Routledge, 1996.

James, Cyril L. R., and Grace C. Lee. *Facing Reality*. 1958. Chicago: Charles H. Kerr, 2006.

James, Sheryl. *Michigan Legends: Folktales and Lore from the Great Lakes State*. Ann Arbor: University of Michigan Press, 2013.

Jefferson, Brian Jordan. "Policing, Data, and Power-Geometry: Intersections of Crime Analytics and Race during Urban Restructuring." *Urban Geography* 39, no. 8 (2018): 1247–64. https://doi.org/10.1080/02723638.2018.1446587.

Jenkins, Destin, and Justin Leroy. "Introduction: The Old History of Capitalism." In *Histories of Racial Capitalism*, edited by Destin Jenkins and Justin Leroy, 1–26. New York: Columbia University Press, 2021.

Jessop, Bob. "Rethinking the Diversity and Varieties of Capitalism: On Variegated Capitalism in the World Market." In *Capitalist Diversity and Diversity within Capitalism*, edited by Christel Lane and Geoffrey T. Wood, 209–37. Abingdon: Routledge, 2011.

Johnson, Cedric. "James Boggs, the 'Outsiders,' and the Challenge of Postindustrial Society." *Souls* 13, no. 3 (2011): 303–26. https://doi.org/10.1080/10999949.2011.601705.

Johnson, Cedric, ed. *The Neoliberal Deluge: Hurricane Katrina, Late Capitalism, and the Remaking of New Orleans*. Minneapolis: University of Minnesota Press, 2011.

Joseph, Miranda. *Debt to Society: Accounting for Life under Capitalism*. Minneapolis: University of Minnesota Press, 2014.

Kahrl, Andrew W. "Unconscionable: Tax Delinquency Sales as a Form of Dignity Taking." *Chicago-Kent Law Review* 92, no. 3 (2017): 905–35.

Karamanski, Theodore J. "Settler Colonial Strategies and Indigenous Resistance on the Great Lakes Lumber Frontier." *Middle West Review* 2, no. 2 (2016): 27–51. https://doi.org/10.1353/mwr.2016.0007.

Kelley, Robin D. G. *Freedom Dreams: The Black Radical Imagination*. Boston: Beacon, 2002.

Kelley, Robin D. G. "The Rest of Us: Rethinking Settler and Native." *American Quarterly* 69, no. 2 (2017): 267–76. https://doi.org/10.1353/aq.2017.0020.

Kincaid, Jamaica. "In History." *Callaloo* 20, no. 1 (1997): 1–7.

Kincaid, Jamaica. *My Garden (Book)*. New York: Farrar, Straus and Giroux, 1999.

Kinder, Kimberley. *DIY Detroit: Making Do in a City without Services*. Minneapolis: University of Minnesota Press, 2016.

King, Tiffany Lethabo. *The Black Shoals: Offshore Formations of Black and Native Studies*. Durham, NC: Duke University Press, 2019.

Kinney, Rebecca J. "'America's Great Comeback Story': The White Possessive in Detroit Tourism." *American Quarterly* 70, no. 4 (2018): 777–806. https://doi.org/10.1353/aq.2018.0063.

Kinney, Rebecca J. *Beautiful Wasteland: The Rise of Detroit as America's Postindustrial Frontier*. Minneapolis: University of Minnesota Press, 2016.

Kinney, Rebecca J. "Longing for Detroit: The Naturalization of Racism through Ruin Porn." *Media Fields Journal*, no. 5 (2012): 1–14.

Kipfer, Stefan, and Kanishka Goonewardena. "Colonization and the New Imperialism: On the Meaning of Urbicide Today." *Theory and Event* 10, no. 2 (2007): 1–39. https://doi.org/10.1353/tae.2007.0064.

Kitchin, Rob. "Thinking Critically about and Researching Algorithms." *Information, Communication and Society* 20, no. 1 (2017): 14–29. https://doi.org/10.1080/1369118X.2016.1154087.

Kitchin, Rob, Tracey P. Lauriault, and Gavin McArdle. "Knowing and governing cities through urban indicators, city benchmarking and real-time dashboards," *Regional Studies, Regional Science* 2 (2015): 1–28.

Kobayashi, Audrey, and Linda Peake. "Racism out of Place: Thoughts on Whiteness and an Antiracist Geography in the New Millennium." *Annals of the Association of American Geographers* 90, no. 2 (2000): 392–403.

Kosek, Jake. *Understories: The Political Life of Forests in Northern New Mexico*. Durham, NC: Duke University Press, 2006.

Kurashige, Scott. *The Fifty-Year Rebellion: How the US Political Crisis Began in Detroit*. Oakland: University of California Press, 2017.

Lake, Robert. "The Financialization of Urban Policy in the Age of Obama." *Journal of Urban Affairs* 37, no. 1 (2015): 75–78. https://doi.org/10.1111/juaf.12167.

Lampland, Martha, and Susan L. Star. "Reckoning with Standards." In *Standards and Their Stories*, edited by Martha Lampland and Susan L. Star, 3–34. Ithaca, NY: Cornell University Press, 2009.

La Paperson. "A Ghetto Land Pedagogy: An Antidote for Settler Environmentalism." *Environmental Education Research* 20 no. 1 (2014): 115–30.

Larzelere, Claude. "The Teaching of Michigan History." In *Michigan Historical Collections*, vol. 39. Lansing, MI: Wynkoop Ballenbeck Crawford, 1915.

Lassiter, Matthew D., and the Policing and Social Justice HistoryLab. "STRESS on Trial." *Detroit under Fire: Police Violence, Crime Politics, and the Struggle for Racial Justice in the Civil Rights Era*. Ann Arbor: University of Michigan Carceral State Project, 2021. https://policing.umhistorylabs.lsa.umich.edu/s/detroitunderfire/page/the-stress-trial.

Lavine, Amy. "Urban Renewal and the Story of *Berman v. Parker*." *Urban Lawyer* 42, no. 2 (2010): 423–75.

Lazzarato, Maurizio. *The Making of the Indebted Man*. Los Angeles: Semiotext(e), 2012.

Lechtreck, Elaine Allen. "'We Are Demanding $500 Million for Reparations': The Black Manifesto, Mainline Religious Denominations, and Black Economic Development." *Journal of African American History* 97 (Winter–Spring 2012): 39–71.

Lee, Jenny. "Humanizing Schooling in Detroit." In *A People's Atlas of Detroit*, edited by Linda Campbell, Andrew Newman, Sara Safransky, and Tim Stallmann, 281–84. Detroit, MI: Wayne State University Press, 2020.

Lefebvre, Henri. *The Production of Space*. Translated by Donald Nicholson-Smith. Malden, MA: Blackwell, 1991.

Levinson, Marc. *The Box: How the Shipping Container Made the World Smaller and the World Economy Bigger*. Princeton, NJ: Princeton University Press, 2016.

Li, Tania M. "What Is Land? Assembling a Resource for Global Investment." *Transactions of the Institute of British Geographers* 39, no. 4 (2014): 589–602. https://doi.org/10.1111/tran.12065.

Light, Andrew. "The Metaphorical Drift of Classical Wilderness." *Geography Research Forum* 15 (1995): 14–32.

Light, Jennifer. "Discriminating Appraisals: Cartography, Computation, and Access to Federal Mortgage Insurance in the 1930s." *Technology and Culture* 52, no. 3 (2011): 485–522. https://doi.org/10.1353/tech.2011.0111.

Linebaugh, Peter, and Marcus Rediker. *The Many-Headed Hydra: Sailors, Slaves, Commoners, and the Hidden History of the Revolutionary Atlantic*. Boston: Beacon Press, 2000.

Lipsitz, George. *The Possessive Investment in Whiteness: How White People Profit from Identity Politics*. Philadelphia: Temple University Press, 2006.

Lipsitz, George. *How Racism Takes Place*. Philadelphia: Temple University Press, 2011.

Lipsitz, George. "The Racialization of Space and the Spatialization of Race." *Landscape Journal* 26, no. 1 (2007): 10–23.

Locke, John. *Two Treatises of Government*. 1689. Edited by Peter Laslett. Cambridge: Cambridge University Press, 1988.

Lorence, James J. *Organizing the Unemployed: Community and Union Activists in the Industrial Heartland*. Albany: State University of New York Press, 1996.

Lowe, Lisa. "History Hesitant." *Social Text* 33, no. 4 (125) (2015): 85–107. https://doi.org/10.1215/01642472-3315790.

Lund, Christian. "Rule and Rupture: State Formation through the Production of Property and Citizenship." *Development and Change* 47, no. 6 (2016): 1199–1228. https://doi.org/10.1111/dech.12274.

Mahmud, Tayyab. "Debt and Discipline: Neoliberal Political Economy and the Working Classes." *Kentucky Law Journal* 101, no. 1 (2013). https://digitalcommons.law.seattleu.edu/faculty/125.

Mahmud, Tayyab. "Precarious Existence and Capitalism: A Permanent State of Exception." *Southwestern Law Review* 44, no. 4 (2015): 699–726.

Mamdani, Mahmood. *When Victims Become Killers: Colonialism, Nativism, and the Genocide in Rwanda*. Princeton, NJ: Princeton University Press, 2014.

Marable, Manning. *Race, Reform, and Rebellion: The Second Reconstruction and Beyond in Black America, 1945–2006*. 3rd ed. Jackson: University of Mississippi Press, 2007.

Marchand, Yves, and Romain Meffree. *The Ruins of Detroit*. Göttingen, Germany: Steidl, 2010.

Martinez, Michelle. "'We Need to Put a Plan Together That Honors People in This Place, on This Land.'" In *A People's Atlas of Detroit*, edited by Linda Campbell, Andrew Newman, Sara Safransky, and Tim Stallmann, 111–15 Detroit, MI: Wayne State University Press, 2020.

Marx, Leo. *The Machine in the Garden: Technology and the Pastoral Ideal in America*. New York: Oxford University Press, 1964.

Massey, Doreen. *For Space*. Thousand Oaks, CA: Sage, 2005.

Massey, Doreen. "Power Geometry and a Progressive Sense of Place." In *Mapping the Futures: Local Cultures, Global Change*, edited by Jon Bird, Barry Curtis, Tim Putnam, George Robertson, and Lisa Tickner, 59–69. London: Routledge, 1993.

Massey, Douglas, and Nancy Denton. *American Apartheid: Segregation and the Making of the Underclass*. Cambridge, MA: Harvard University Press, 1993.

Maxwell, William J. *New Negro, Old Left: African-American Writing and Communism between the Wars*. New York: Columbia University Press, 1999.

Mays, Kyle T. *City of Dispossessions: Indigenous Peoples, African Americans, and the Creations of Modern Detroit*. Philadelphia: University of Pennsylvania Press, 2022.

McCarthy, John. "Entertainment-Led Regeneration: The Case of Detroit." *Cities* 19, no. 2 (2002): 105–11. https://doi.org/10.1016/S0264-2751(02)00005-7.

McClintock, Nathan. "Nullius No More? Valorising Vacancy through Urban Agriculture in the Settler-Colonial 'Green City.'" In *The New Urban Ruins: Vacancy, Urban Politics and International Experiments in the Post-Crisis City*, edited by Cian O'Callaghan and Cesare Di Feliciantonio, 91–108. Bristol: Policy Press, 2021.

McCutcheon, Priscilla. "Growing Black Food on Sacred Land: Using Black Liberation Theology to Imagine an Alternative Black Agrarian Future." *Environment and Planning D: Society and Space* 39, no. 5 (2021): 887–905.

McElroy, Erin. "Property as Technology: Temporal Entanglements of Race, Space, and Displacement." *City* 24, nos. 1–2 (2020): 112–29.

McKittrick, Katherine. *Demonic Grounds: Black Women and the Cartographies of Struggle*. Minneapolis: University of Minnesota Press, 2006.

McKittrick, Katherine. "Plantation Futures." *Small Axe: A Caribbean Journal of Criticism* 17, no. 3 (42) (2013): 1–15. https://doi.org/10.1215/07990537-2378892.

McKittrick, Katherine, and Clyde Woods, eds. "No One Knows the Mysteries at the Bottom of the Ocean." In *Black Geographies and the Politics of Place*, 1–13. Cambridge, MA: South End Press, 2007.

McLaughlin, Joseph. *Writing the Urban Jungle: Reading Empire in London from Doyle to Eliot*. Charlottesville: University Press of Virginia, 2000.

McLaughlin, Malcolm. *The Long, Hot Summer of 1967: Urban Rebellion in America*. New York: Palgrave Macmillan, 2014.

Melamed, Jodi. "Racial Capitalism." *Critical Ethnic Studies* 1, no. 1 (2015): 76–85. https://doi.org/10.5749/jcritethnstud.1.1.0076.

Melamed, Jodi. "The Spirit of Neoliberalism from Racial Liberalism to Neoliberal Multiculturalism." *Social Text* 24, no. 4 (89) (2006): 1–24. https://doi.org /10.1215/01642472-2006-009.

Melosi, Martin V. *The Sanitary City: Environmental Services in Urban America from Colonial Times to the Present*. Pittsburgh, PA: University of Pittsburgh Press, 2008.

Mezzadra, Sandro, and Brett Neilson. "Operations of Capital." *South Atlantic Quarterly* 114, no. 1 (2015): 1–9. https://doi.org/10.1215/00382876-2831246.

Mezzadra, Sandro, and Brett Neilson. *The Politics of Operations: Excavating Contemporary Capitalism*. Durham, NC: Duke University Press, 2019.

Miles, Tiya. *The Dawn of Detroit: A Chronicle of Slavery and Freedom in the City of the Straits*. New York: New Press, 2017.

Miles, Tiya, Michelle Cassidy, Emily MacGillivray, Paul Rodriguez, Sarah Khan, Alexandra Passarelli, and Kaisha Brezina. "Mapping Slavery in Detroit." In *A People's Atlas of Detroit*, edited by Linda Campbell, Andrew Newman, Sara Safransky, and Tim Stallmann, 20–24. Detroit, MI: Wayne State University Press, 2020.

Millington, Nate. "Post-Industrial Imaginaries: Nature, Representation and Ruin in Detroit, Michigan." *International Journal of Urban and Regional Research* 37, no. 1 (2013): 279–96. https://doi.org/10.1111/j.1468-2427.2012.01206.x.

Mills, Charles W. "Racial Liberalism." *PMLA* 123, no. 5 (2008): 1380–97.

Mills, Charles W. "White Ignorance." In *Race and Epistemologies of Ignorance*, edited by Shannon Sullivan and Nancy Tuana, 11–38. Albany: State University of New York Press, 2007.

Mitchell, Katharyne. "Pre-Black Futures." *Antipode: A Radical Journal of Cartography* 41, no. S1 (2010): 239–61. https://doi.org/10.1111/j.1467-8330 .2009.00724.x.

Mitchell, Timothy. "The Properties of Markets." In *Do Economist Make Markets?*, edited by Donald MacKenzie, Fabian Muniesa, and Lucia Siu, 244–76. Princeton, NJ: Princeton University Press, 2007.

Mogk, John E., Sarah Kwiatkowski, and Mary J. Weindorf. "Promoting Urban Agriculture as an Alternative Land Use for Vacant Properties in the City of Detroit: Benefits, Problems, and Proposals for a Regulatory Framework for Successful Land Use Integration." *Wayne Law Review* 56, no. 4 (2010): 1521–80. http://digitalcommons.wayne.edu/lawfrp/109.

Montgomery, Alesia F. *Greening the Black Urban Regime: The Culture and Commerce of Sustainability in Detroit*. Detroit, MI: Wayne State University Press, 2020.

Montgomery, Alesia F. "The Sight of Loss." *Antipode: A Radical Journal of Cartography* 43, no. 5 (2011): 1828–50. https://doi.org/10.1111/j.1467-8330 .2011.00856.x.

Morales, Alfonso. "Growing Food and Justice: Dismantling Racism through Sustainable Good System." In *Cultivating Food Justice: Race, Class, and*

Sustainability, edited by Alison Hope Alkon and Julian Agyeman, 149–76. Cambridge, MA: MIT Press, 2011.

Moreton-Robinson, Aileen. *The White Possessive: Property, Power, and Indigenous Sovereignty*. Minneapolis: University of Minnesota Press, 2015.

Mott, Carrie, and Susan M. Roberts. "Not Everyone Has (the) Balls: Urban Exploration and the Persistence of Masculinist Geography." *Antipode: A Radical Journal of Cartography* 46, no. 1 (2014): 229–45. https://doi.org/10.1111/anti.12033.

Mullin, John Robert. "Henry Ford and Field and Factory: An Analysis of the Ford Sponsored Village Industries Experiment in Michigan, 1918–1941." *Journal of the American Planning Association* 48, no. 4 (1982): 419–31.

Murray, Yxta Maya. "Detroit Looks toward a Massive, Unconstitutional Blight Condemnation: The Optics of Eminent Domain in Motor City." *Georgetown Journal on Poverty Law and Policy* 23 (2015): 395–461.

Music, Marsha. "The Kidnapped Children of Detroit." In *Voices from the Rustbelt*, edited by Anne Trubek, 18–31. New York: Picador, 2018.

Narayan, John. "Huey P. Newton's Intercommunalism: An Unacknowledged Theory of Empire." *Theory, Culture and Society* 36, no. 3 (2019): 57–85. https://doi.org/10.1177/0263276417741348.

Narayan, John. "The Wages of Whiteness in the Absence of Wages: Racial Capitalism, Reactionary Intercommunalism and the Rise of Trumpism." *Third World Quarterly* 38, no. 11 (2017): 2482–2500. https://doi.org/10.1080/01436597.2017.1368012.

Nembhard, Jessica G. *Collective Courage: A History of African American Cooperative Economic Thought and Practice*. University Park: Pennsylvania State University Press, 2014.

Newman, Andrew, and Sara Safransky. "Remapping the Motor City and the Politics of Austerity." *Anthropology Now* 6, no. 3 (2014): 17–28. https://doi.org/10.1080/19492901.2014.11728447.

Newton, Huey P. "Intercommunalism." In *The Huey P. Newton Reader*, edited by David Hilliard and Donald Weise, 181–99. New York: Seven Stories Press, 2011.

Newton, Huey P. "Speech Delivered at Boston College: November 18, 1970." In *The Huey P. Newton Reader*, edited by David Hilliard and Donald Weise, 160–75. New York: Seven Stories Press, 2002.

Nixon, Rob. *Slow Violence and the Environmentalism of the Poor*. Cambridge, MA: Harvard University Press, 2011.

Noble, Safiya U. *Algorithms of Oppression: How Search Engines Reinforce Racism*. New York: New York University Press, 2018.

Noterman, Elsa. "Speculating on Vacancy." *Transactions of the Institute of British Geographers* 47, no. 1 (2022): 123–38. https://doi.org/10.1111/tran.12477.

Noterman, Elsa. "Taking Back Vacant Property." *Urban Geography* 42, no. 8 (2021): 1079–98. https://doi.org/10.1080/02723638.2020.1743519.

Omi, Michael, and Howard Winant. *Racial Formation in the United States: From the 1960s to the 1990s*. New York: Routledge, 1994.

Onaci, Edward. *Free the Land: The Republic of New Afrika and the Pursuit of a Black Nation-State*. Chapel Hill: University of North Carolina Press, 2020.

O'Neil, Cathy. *Weapons of Math Destruction*. New York: Broadway Books, 2016.

Onuoha, Mimi. "Notes on Algorithmic Violence." Accessed July 10, 2018. https://github.com/MimiOnuoha/On-Algorithmic-Violence.

Oswin, Natalie. "Planetary Urbanization: A View from Outside." *Environment and Planning D: Society and Space* 36, no. 3 (2018): 540–46. https://doi.org/10.1177/0263775816675963.

Outka, Paul. *Race and Nature from Transcendentalism to the Harlem Renaissance*. New York: Palgrave MacMillan, 2008.

Park, K-Sue. "Money, Mortgages, and the Conquest of America." *Law and Social Inquiry* 41, no. 4 (Fall 2016): 1006–35.

Pateman, Carole. "The Settler Contract." In *Contract and Domination*, edited by Carole Pateman and Charles Wade Mills, 35–78. Malden, MA: Polity, 2007.

Peck, Jamie. "Austerity Urbanism." *City* 16, no. 6 (2012): 626–55. https://doi.org/10.1080/13604813.2012.734071.

Peck, Jamie. "Struggling with the Creative Class." *International Journal of Urban and Regional Research* 29, no. 4 (2005): 740–70. https://doi.org/10.1111/j.1468-2427.2005.00620.x.

Peck, Jamie, and Nik Theodore. "Variegated Capitalism." *Progress in Human Geography* 31, no. 6 (2007): 731–772. https://doi.org/10.1177/0309132507083505.

Pennell, Susan, Christine Curtis, Joel Henderson, and Jeff Tayman. "Guardian Angels: A Unique Approach to Crime Prevention." *Crime and Delinquency* 35, no. 3 (1989): 378–400.

Perelman, Michael. *The Invention of Capitalism*. Durham, NC: Duke University Press, 2000.

Perkinson, James W. *Political Spirituality for a Century of Water Wars: The Angel of the Jordan Meets the Trickster of Detroit*. New York: Palgrave Macmillan, 2019.

Petch, Nathan J. "Detroit as Treatied Space." Master's thesis, University of Hull, 2018.

Pinder, David. *Visions of the City: Utopianism, Power, and Politics in Twentieth-Century Urbanism*. New York: Routledge, 2005.

Pinto, Sarah. *Daughters of Parvati: Women and Madness in Contemporary India*. Philadelphia: University of Pennsylvania Press, 2014.

Pizzolato, Nicola. *Challenging Global Capitalism: Labor Migration, Radical Struggle, and Urban Change in Detroit and Turin*. New York: Palgrave Macmillan, 2013.

Plummer, Brenda G. *In Search of Power: African Americans in the Era of Decolonization, 1956–1974*. Cambridge: Cambridge University Press, 2013.

Polanyi, Karl. *The Great Transformation: The Political and Economic Origins of Our Time*. Boston: Beacon Press, 1944.

Porter, Libby. *Unlearning the Colonial Cultures of Planning*. Burlington, VT: Ashgate Publishing Company, 2010.

Pothukuchi, Kameshwari. "Five Decades of Community Food Planning in Detroit: City and Grassroots, Growth and Equity." *Journal of Planning Education and Research* 35, no. 4 (2015): 419–34.

Pottage, Alain, and Martha Mundy. *Law, Anthropology, and the Constitution of the Social: Making Persons and Things*. New York: Cambridge University Press, 2004.

Povinelli, Elizabeth A. *Economies of Abandonment: Social Belonging and Endurance in Late Liberalism*. Durham, NC: Duke University Press, 2011.

Pratt, Geraldine. "Abandoned Women and Spaces of the Exception." *Antipode: A Radical Journal of Cartography* 37, no. 5 (2005): 1052–78.

Priest, Claire. "Creating an American Property Law: Alienability and Its Limits in American History." *Harvard Law Review* 120, no. 2 (December 2006): 385–459.

Pugliese, Joseph. *Biometrics: Bodies, Technologies, Biopolitics*. New York: Routledge, 2010.

Pulido, Laura. "Flint, Environmental Racism, and Racial Capitalism." *Capitalism Nature Socialism* 27, no. 3 (2016): 1–16. https://doi.org/10.1080/10455752.2016.1213013.

Pulido, Laura. "Reflections on a White Discipline." *Professional Geographer* 54, no. 1 (2002): 42–49.

Quizar, Jessi. "A Logic of Care and Black Grassroots Claims to Home in Detroit." *Antipode: A Radical Journal of Cartography* (2022). https://doi.org/10.1111/anti.12842.

Quizar, Jessi. "Who Cares for Detroit? Urban Agriculture, Black Self-determination, and Struggles over Urban Space." PhD diss., University of Southern California, 2014.

Quizar, Jessi. "Working to Live: Black-Led Farming in Detroit's Racialized Economy." In *Racial Ecologies*, edited by Leilani Nishime and Kim D. Hester Williams, 76–89. Seattle: University of Washington Press, 2018.

Rahman, Ahmad. "Marching Blind: The Rise and Fall of the Black Panther Party in Detroit." In *Liberated Territory*, edited by Yohuru Williams and Jama Lazerow, 181–231. Durham, NC: Duke University Press, 2008.

Ramírez, Margaret M. "City as Borderland: Gentrification and the Policing of Black and Latinx Geographies in Oakland." *Environment and Planning D: Society and Space* 38, no. 1 (2019): 147–66. https://doi.org/10.1177/0263775819843924.

Ramírez, Margaret M. "Take the Houses Back/Take the Land Back: Black and Indigenous Urban Futures in Oakland." *Urban Geography* 41, no. 5 (2020): 682–93. https://doi.org/10.1080/02723638.2020.1736440.

Ranganathan, Malini. "Thinking with Flint: Racial Liberalism and the Roots of an American Water Tragedy." *Capitalism Nature Socialism* 27, no. 3 (2016): 17–33. https://doi.org/10.1080/10455752.2016.1206583.

Read, Peter. "Enclosing the Spirit." In *Landscapes of Clearance: Archaeological and Anthropological Perspectives*, edited by Angele Smith and Amy Gazin-Schwartz, 154–63. New York: Routledge, 2016.

Rector, Josiah. "Toxic Debt: The Detroit Incinerator, Municipal Bonds, and Environmental Racism." In *A People's Atlas of Detroit*, edited by Linda Campbell, Andrew Newman, Sara Safransky, and Tim Stallmann, 265–68. Detroit, MI: Wayne State University Press, 2020.

Redecker, Eva von. "Ownership's Shadow: Neoauthoritarianism as Defense of Phantom Possession." *Critical Times* 3, no. 1 (2020): 33–67.

Reno, B. Jeffrey. "A Floor without a Ceiling: Balancing Normative and Strategic Goals in Policy Design." *Polity* 39, no. 2 (2007): 137–54. https://doi.org/10.1057/palgrave.polity.2300078.

Revel, Judith. "Identity, Nature, Life: Three Biopolitical Deconstructions." *Theory, Culture and Society* 26, no. 6 (2009): 45–54.

Reyes, Alvaro. "Can't Go Home Again: Sovereign Entanglements and the Black Radical Tradition in the Twentieth Century." PhD diss., Duke University, 2009.

Rickford, Russell. "'We Can't Grow Food on All This Concrete': The Land Question, Agrarianism, and Black Nationalist Thought in the Late 1960s and 1970s." *Journal of American History* 103, no. 4 (2017): 956–80. https://doi.org/10.1093/jahist/jaw506.

Robinson, Cedric J. *Black Marxism: The Making of the Black Radical Tradition*. Chapel Hill: University of North Carolina Press, 2000.

Robinson, Cedric J. *Black Movements in America*. New York: Routledge, 1997.

Robinson, Cedric J. "Blaxploitation and the Misrepresentation of Liberation." *Race and Class* 40, no. 1 (1998): 1–12. https://doi.org/10.1177/030639689804000101.

Rode, Ajmer. *Poems at My Doorstep*. Vancouver, BC: Caitlin Press, 1990.

Rodgers, Dennis, and Bruce O'Neill. "Infrastructural Violence: Introduction to the Special Issue." In "Infrastructural Violence," edited by Bruce O'Neill and Dennis Rodgers, special issue, *Ethnography* 13, no. 4 (2012): 401–12. https://doi.org/10.1177/1466138111435738.

Roitman, Janet. *Fiscal Disobedience: An Anthropology of Economic Regulation in Central African*. Princeton, NJ: Princeton University Press, 2005.

Romano, Paul, and Ria Stone. *The American Worker*. 1947. Detroit, MI: Bewick, 1972.

Rose, Carol M. 1994. *Property and Persuasion: Essays on the History, Theory, and Rhetoric of Ownership*. Boulder, CO: Westview.

Rose, Harold M. "The Geography of Despair." *Annals of the Association of American Geographers* 68, no. 4 (1978): 453–64.

Ross, Andrew. *Creditocracy and the Case for Debt Refusal*. New York: OR Books, 2013.

Rothstein, Richard. *The Color of Law: A Forgotten History of How Our Government Segregated America*. New York: Norton, 2017.

Roy, Ananya. "Dis/possessive Collectivism: Property and Personhood at City's End." *Geoforum* 80 (March 2017): A1–A11. https://doi.org/10.1016/j.geoforum.2016.12.012.

Roy, Ananya. "Urban Informality: Toward an Epistemology of Planning." *Journal of the American Planning Association* 71, no. 2 (2005): 147–58.

Rutan, Devin Q., and Michael R. Glass. "The Lingering Effects of Neighborhood Appraisal: Evaluating Redlining's Legacy in Pittsburgh." *Professional Geographer* 70, no. 3 (2017): 339–49. https://doi.org/10.1080/00330124.2017.1371610.

Ryan, Brent. "From Cars to Casinos: Global Pasts and Local Futures in the Detroit-Windsor Transnational Metropolitan Area." In *Rethinking Global Urbanism: Comparative Insights from Secondary Cities*, edited by Xiangming Chen and Ahmed Kanna, 91–106. New York: Routledge, 2012.

Ryan, Brent D., and Daniel Campo. "Autopia's End: The Decline and Fall of Detroit's Automotive Manufacturing Landscape." *Journal of Planning History* 12, no. 2 (2013): 95–132.

Safransky, Sara. "Geographies of Algorithmic Violence: Redlining the Smart City." *International Journal of Urban and Regional Research* 44 no. 2: (2019) 200–218. https://doi.org/0.1111/1468-2427.12833.

Safransky, Sara. "Grammars of Reckoning: Redressing Racial Regimes of Property." *Environment and Planning D: Society and Space* 40, no. 2 (2022): 292–305.

Safransky, Sara. "Greening the Urban Frontier: Race, Property, and Resettlement in Detroit." *Geoforum* 56 (2014): 237–48. https://doi.org/10.1016/j.geoforum.2014.06.003.

Safransky, Sara. "Land Justice as a Historical Diagnostic: Thinking with Detroit." *Annals of the American Association of Geographers* 108, no. 2 (2018): 499–512. https://doi.org/10.1080/24694452.2017.1385380.

Safransky, Sara. "Rethinking Land Struggle in the Postindustrial City." *Antipode: A Radical Journal of Cartography* 49, no. 4 (2017): 1079–1100. https://doi.org/10.1111/anti.12225.

Said, Edward W. *Culture and Imperialism*. New York: Vintage Books, 1993.

Said, Edward W. "Invention, Memory, and Place." *Critical Inquiry* 26, no. 2 (2000): 175–92.

Salerno, Roger A. *Landscapes of Abandonment*. Albany: State University of New York Press, 2003.

Sands, Gary, and Mark Skidmore. "Making Ends Meet: Options for Property Tax Reform in Detroit." *Journal of Urban Affairs* 36, no. 4 (2014): 682–700.

Sassen, Saskia. *Expulsions: Brutality and Complexity in the Global Economy*. Cambridge, MA: Harvard University Press, 2014.

Schwartz, Barry, and Horst-Alfred Heinrich. "Shadings of Regret: America and Germany." In *Framing Public Memory*, edited by Kendall R. Phillips, 115–47. Tuscaloosa: University of Alabama Press, 2004.

Scott, James C. *Seeing Like a State: How Certain Schemes to Improve the Human Condition Have Failed*. New Haven, CT: Yale University Press, 1998.

Seamster, Louise. "Black Debt, White Debt." *Contexts* 18, no. 1 (2019): 30–35. https://doi.org/10.1177/1536504219830674.

Sears, David O., and Jack Citrin. *Tax Revolt: Something for Nothing in California*. Cambridge, MA: Harvard University Press, 1982.

Sedler, Robert A. "The Profound Impact of *Milliken v. Bradley*." *Wayne Law Review* 33, no. 5 (1987): 1693–1722.

Seed, Patricia. *Ceremonies of Possession in Europe's Conquest of the New World, 1492–1640*. Cambridge: Cambridge University Press, 1995.

Segal, Howard P. *Recasting the Machine Age: Henry Ford's Village Industries*. Amherst: University of Massachusetts Press, 2005.

Self, Robert O. *American Babylon: Race and the Struggle for Postwar Oakland*. Princeton, NJ: Princeton University Press, 2003.

Self, Robert O., and Thomas J. Sugrue. "The Power of Place: Race, Political Economy, and Identity in the Postwar Metropolis." In *A Companion to Post-1945 America*, edited by Jean Christophe Agnew and Roy Rosezweig, 20–43. Malden, MA: Blackwell, 2002.

Seymour, Eric, and Joshua Akers. "Building the Eviction Economy: Speculation, Precarity, and Eviction in Detroit." *Urban Affairs Review* 57, no. 1 (2021): 35–69.

Seymour, Eric, and Joshua Akers. "Portfolio Solutions, Bulk Sales of Bank-Owned Properties, and the Reemergence of Racially Exploitative Land Contracts." *Cities* 89 (June 2019): 46–56.

Shakur, Yusef. "Reclaiming Our Souls," In *A People's Atlas of Detroit*, edited by Linda Campbell, Andrew Newman, Sara Safransky, and Tim Stallmann, 293–95. Detroit, MI: Wayne State University Press, 2020.

Shaw, Todd. *Now Is the Time: Detroit Black Politics and Grassroots Activism*. Durham, NC: Duke University Press, 2009.

Shellow, Robert, ed. *The Harvest of American Racism: The Political Meaning of Violence in the Summer of 1967*. Ann Arbor: University of Michigan Press, 2018.

Shelton, T., M. Zook and A. Wiig. "The 'Actually Existing Smart City.'" *Cambridge Journal of Regions, Economy and Society* 8, no. 1 (2015): 13–25.

Shoemaker, Nancy. "How Indians Got to Be Red." *American Historical Review* 102, no. 3 (1997): 624–44.

Simpson, Leanne. "Land as Pedagogy: Nishnaabeg Intelligence and Rebellious Transformation." *Decolonization: Indigeneity, Education and Society* 3, no. 3 (2014): 1–25.

Sinclair, Timothy J. *The New Masters of Capital: American Bond Rating Agencies and the Politics of Creditworthiness*. Ithaca, NY: Cornell University Press, 2008.

Sinclair, Timothy J. "Passing Judgment: Credit Rating Processes as Regulatory Mechanisms of Governance in the Emerging World Order." *Review of International Political Economy* 1, no. 1 (1994): 133–59.

Singer, Joseph William. *Entitlement: The Paradoxes of Property*. New Haven, CT: Yale University Press, 2000.

Singh, Nikhil P. *Black Is a Country: Race and the Unfinished Struggle for Democracy*. Cambridge, MA: Harvard University Press, 2004.

Sitze, Adam. *The Impossible Machine: A Genealogy of South Africa's Truth and Reconciliation Commission*. Ann Arbor: University of Michigan Press, 2013.

Skinner, Charles M. *Myths and Legends of Our Own Land*. Philadelphia: J. B. Lippincott Company, 1896.

Slager, Emma J. "Ruin Tours: Performing and Consuming Decay in Detroit." *Urban Geography* 41, no. 1 (2019): 124–42. https://doi.org/10.1080/02723638.2019.1637194.

Slotkin, Richard. *The Fatal Environment: The Myth of the Frontier in the Age of Industrialization, 1800–1890*. Norman: University of Oklahoma Press, 1998.

Smith, Neil. *The New Urban Frontier: Gentrification and the Revanchist City*. New York: Routledge, 1996.

Smith, Suzanne E. *Dancing in the Streets: Motown and the Cultural Politics of Detroit*. Cambridge, MA: Harvard University Press, 1999.

Soja, Edward W. "Six Discourses on the Postmetropolis." In *Imagining Cities*, edited by Sallie Westwood and John Williams, 19–31. New York: Routledge, 2003.

Soyinka, Wole. *The Burden of Memory*. New York: Oxford University Press, 1999.

Spivak, Gayatri. "Can the Subaltern Speak?" In *Marxism and the Interpretation of Culture*, edited by C. Nelson and L. Grossberg, 271–316. Urbana: University of Illinois Press, 1998.

Star, Susan Leigh, and James R. Griesemer. "Institutional Ecology, 'Translations' and Boundary Objects: Amateurs and Professionals in Berkeley's Museum of Vertebrate Zoology, 1907–39." *Social Studies of Science* 19, no. 3 (1989): 387–420.

Star, Susan Leigh, and Karen Ruhleder. "Steps toward an Ecology of Infrastructure: Design and Access for Large Information Spaces." *Information Systems Research* 7, no. 1 (1996): 111–34.

Starr, Roger. *Urban Choices: The City and Its Critics*. Baltimore, MD: Pelican, 1966.

Stauffer, Jill. *Ethical Loneliness: The Injustice of Not Being Heard*. New York: Columbia University Press, 2015.

Stehlin, John G., and Alexander R. Tarr. "Think Regionally, Act Locally? Gardening, Cycling, and the Horizon of Urban Spatial Politics." *Urban Geography* 38, no. 9 (2017): 1329–51. https://doi.org/10.1080/02723638.2016.1232464.

Stein, Samuel. *Capital City: Gentrification and the Real Estate State*. New York: Verso Books, 2019.

Steinmetz, George. "The Colonial State as a Social Field: Ethnographic Capital and Native Policy in the German Overseas Empire before 1914." *American Sociological Review* 73, no. 4 (2008): 589–612. https://doi.org/10.1177/000312240807300404.

Stoler, Ann Laura. "Imperial Debris: Reflections on Ruins and Ruination." *Cultural Anthropology* 23, no. 2 (2008): 191–219.

Stout, Noelle. "Indebted: Disciplining the Moral Valence of Mortgage Debt Online." *Cultural Anthropology* 31, no. 1 (2016): 82–106. https://doi.org/10.14506/ca31.1.05.

Strang, Gary. "Infrastructure as Landscape." *Places* 10, no. 3 (1995): 8–15.

Strathern, Marilyn. "Potential Property: Intellectual Rights and Property in Persons." In *Property, Substance, and Effects*, edited by Marilyn Strathern, 161–78. London: Althone Press, 1999.

Sugrue, Thomas J. *The Origins of the Urban Crisis: Race and Inequality in Postwar Detroit*. Princeton, NJ: Princeton University Press, 2005.

Sum, Ngai-Ling, and Bob Jessop. *Towards a Cultural Political Economy: Putting Culture in Its Place in Political Economy*. Northampton, MA: Edward Elgar Publishing, 2013.

Taylor, Keeanga-Yamahtta. *Race for Profit: How Banks and the Real Estate Industry Undermined Black Homeownership*. Chapel Hill: University of North Carolina Press, 2019.

Thomas, June Manning. *Redevelopment and Race: Planning a Finer City in Postwar Detroit*. Detroit, MI: Wayne State University Press, 2013.

Thomas, Richard W. *Life for Us Is What We Make It: Building Black Community in Detroit, 1915–1945*. Bloomington: Indiana University Press, 1992.

Thompson, Heather Ann. *Whose Detroit? Politics, Labor, and Race in a Modern American City*. Ithaca, NY: Cornell University Press, 2001.

Thrift, Nigel and Shaun French. "The Automatic Production of Space." *Transactions of the Institute of British Geographers* 27, no. 3 (2002): 309–35.

Tornaghi, Chiara. "Critical Geography of Urban Agriculture." *Progress in Human Geography* 38, no. 4 (2014): 551–67.

Toups, Eric. "More Than Just a Missionary: The Jesuits, the Wyandot, and Colonial Crises in French Detroit, 1728–1751." *Michigan Historical Review* 46, no. 1 (2020): 1–28.

Touraine, Alain. *The Postindustrial Society: Tomorrow's Social History*. New York: Random House, 1971.

Tsing, Anna L. *Friction: An Ethnography of Global Connection*. Princeton, NJ: Princeton University Press, 2005.

Tuck, Eve. "Suspending Damage: A Letter to Communities." *Harvard Educational Review* 79, no. 3 (2009): 409–28.

Tuck, Eve, Mistinguette Smith, Allison M. Guess, Tavia Benjamin, and Brian K. Jones. "Geotheorizing Black/Land: Contestations and Contingent Collaborations." *Departures in Critical Qualitative Research* 3, no. 1 (2014): 52–74.

Tyner, James. *The Geography of Malcolm X: Black Radicalism and the Remaking of American Space*. New York: Routledge, 2013.

Tyner, James, and Joshua Inwood. "Violence as Fetish: Geography, Marxism, and Dialectics." *Progress in Human Geography* 38, no. 6 (2014): 771–84. https://doi.org/10.1177/0309132513516177.

Vaccaro, Ismael, Eric Hirsch, and Irene Sabaté. "The Emergence of the Global Debt Society." *Focaal—Journal of Global and Historical Anthropology*, no. 87 (2020): 46–60. https://doi.org/10.3167/fcl.2019.061701.

Vale, Lawrence J. *Purging the Poorest: Public Housing and the Design Politics of Twice-Cleared Communities*. Chicago: University of Chicago Press, 2013.

Valverde, Mariana. "The Dialectic of the Familiar and the Unfamiliar: The Jungle in Early Slum Travel Writing." *Sociology* 30, no. 3 (1996): 493–509. https://doi.org/10.1177/0038038596030003005.

Valverde, Mariana. "Seeing Like a City: The Dialectic of Modern and Premodern Ways of Seeing in Urban Governance." *Law and Society Review* 45, no. 2 (2011): 277–312. https://doi.org/10.1111/j.1540-5893.2011.00441.

Valverde, Mariana. "Taking Land Use Seriously: Toward an Ontology of Municipal Law." *Law Text Culture* 9 (2005): 34–59.

Van Sant, Levi, Taylor Shelton, and Kelly Kay. "Connecting Country and City: The Multiple Geographies of Real Property Ownership in the US." *Geography Compass* (2023): 1–15.

van de Walt, A. J. *Property in the Margins*. Portland, OR: Hart, 2009.

Veracini, Lorenzo. *Settler Colonialism: A Theoretical Overview*. New York: Palgrave Macmillan, 2010.

Verdery, Katherine. "The Obligations of Ownership: Restoring Rights to Land in Postsocialist Transylvania." In *Property in Question: Value Transformations in the Global Economy*, edited by Katherine Verdery and Caroline Humphrey, 115–38. New York: Bloomsbury Academic, 2004.

Verdery, Katherine. *The Vanishing Hectare: Property and Value in Postsocialist Transylvania*. Ithaca, NY: Cornell University Press, 2003.

Veroni-Paccher, Lisa. "Black Power 1968: 'To Stumble Is Not to Fall, but to Go Forward Faster'—The 1968 Philadelphia Black Power Conference and the Process from Protest to Electoral Politics." *L'Ordinaire des Amériques* 217 (2014). https://doi.org/10.4000/orda.1624.

von Benda-Beckmann, Franz, Keebet von Benda-Beckmann, and Melanie G. Wiber. "The Properties of Property." In *Changing Properties of Property*, edited by Franz von Benda-Beckmann, Keebet von Benda-Beckmann, and Melanie G. Wiber, 1–39. New York: Berghahn, 2006.

Wachter-Boettcher, Sara. *Technically Wrong: Sexist Apps, Biased Algorithms, and Other Threats of Toxic Tech*. New York: Norton, 2017.

Wallace, Deborah, and Roderick Wallace. *A Plague on Your Houses: How New York Was Burned Down and National Public Health Crumbled*. New York: Verso, 1998.

Walsh, Camille. "White Backlash, the 'Taxpaying' Public, and Educational Citizenship." *Critical Sociology* 43, no. 2 (2017): 237–47. https://doi.org/10.1177/0896920516645657.

Walsh, Martin W. "Revenge against the Idol: Competing Magical Systems on the Detroit River, 1670." *Michigan Historical Review* 43, no. 2 (2017): 55–63.

Ward, Stephen. *In Love and Struggle: The Revolutionary Lives of James and Grace Lee Boggs*. Chapel Hill: University of North Carolina Press, 2016.

Ward, Stephen M. "Introduction." In *Pages from a Black Radical's Notebook: A James Boggs Reader*, edited by Stephen M. Ward, 1–34. Detroit, MI: Wayne State University Press, 2011.

Watson, Marie Caroline. *Legends of Le Détroit*. Detroit, MI: Thorndike Nourse, 1883.

Wekker, Gloria. *White Innocence: Paradoxes of Colonialism and Race*. Durham, NC: Duke University Press, 2016.

Weston, Kath. "Lifeblood, Liquidity, and Cash Transfusions: Beyond Metaphor in the Cultural Study of Finance." *Journal of the Royal Anthropological Institute* 19, no. S1 (2013): S24–S41.

White, Monica. "D-Town Farm: African American Resistance to Food Insecurity and the Transformation of Detroit." *Environmental Practice* 13, no. 4 (2011): 406–17.

Whyte, Liz Essley. "Philanthropy Keeps the Lights on in Detroit." *Philanthropy*, Winter 2014. https://www.philanthropyroundtable.org/magazine/philanthropy-keeps-the-lights-on-in-detroit/.

Wideman, Trevor J., and Nick Lombardo. "Geographies of Land Use: Planning, Property, and Law." *Geography Compass* 13, no. 12 (2019): 1–14. https://doi.org/10.1111/gec3.12473.

Williams, Raymond. *The Country and the City*. New York: Oxford University Press, 1975.

Wilson, Bobby M. *America's Johannesburg: Industrialization and Racial Transformation in Birmingham*. New York: Rowan and Littlefield, 2000.

Wilson, Hilary. "A Way Out of No Way: Struggles for Economic Survival in Black Milwaukee." *Society and Space*, December 9, 2019. http://societyandspace.org/2019/12/09/a-way-out-of-no-way-struggles-for-economic-survival-in-black-milwaukee/.

Winston, Celeste. "Maroon Geographies." *Annals of the American Association of Geographers* 111, no. 7 (2021): 2185–99.

Wolfe, Patrick. "Settler Colonialism and the Elimination of the Native." *Journal of Genocide Research* 8, no. 4 (2006): 387–409. https://doi.org/10.1080/14623520601056240.

Wolfe, Patrick. *Settler Colonialism and the Transformation of Anthropology: The Politics and Poetics of an Ethnographic Event*. New York: Cassell, 1999.

Wolflink, Alena. "What's the Matter with Value? Anna Julia Cooper's Political-Economic Thought." *Critical Philosophy of Race* 9, no. 1 (2021): 102–25.

Wood, Denis. *Rethinking the Power of Maps*. New York: Guilford, 2010.

Woodard, Komozi. "It's Nation Time in NewArk: Amiri Baraka and the Black Power Experiment in Newark, New Jersey." In *Freedom North: Black Freedom Struggles Outside the South, 1940–1980*, edited by Jeanne Theoharis and Komozi Woodard, 287–311. New York: Palgrave Macmillan, 2003.

Woods, Clyde. *Development Arrested: The Blues and Plantation Power in the Mississippi Delta*. New York: Verso, 1998.

Woods, Clyde. "Life after Death." *Professional Geographer* 54, no. 1 (2002): 62–66.

Woods, Clyde. "Les Misérables of New Orleans: Trap Economics and the Asset Stripping Blues, Part 1." *American Quarterly* 61, no. 3 (2009): 769–96.

Wright, Willie Jamaal. "The Morphology of Marronage." *Annals of the American Association of Geographers* 110, no. 4 (2020): 1134–49.

Wynter, Sylvia. "Unsettling the Coloniality of Being/Power/Truth/Freedom: Towards the Human, after Man, Its Overrepresentation—An Argument." *CR: The New Centennial Review* 3, no. 3 (2003): 257–337. https://doi.org/10.1353/ncr.2004.0015.

Yakini, Malik. "We Actually Have the Capacity to Define Our Own Reality." In *A People's Atlas of Detroit*, edited by Linda Campbell, Andrew Newman, Sara Safransky, and Tim Stallmann, 124–128. Detroit, MI: Wayne State University Press, 2020.

Zaimi, Rea. "Rethinking 'Disinvestment': Historical Geographies of Predatory Property Relations on Chicago's South Side." *Environment and Planning D: Society and Space* 40, no. 2 (2022): 245–257. https://doi.org/10.1177/02637758211013041.

Zunz, Olivier. *The Changing Face of Inequality: Urbanization, Industrial Development, and Immigrants in Detroit, 1880–1920*. Chicago: University of Chicago Press, 1982.

Index

Note: page numbers followed by *f* refer to figures.

Village Industries, 172, 252n8

violence, 45, 62, 70, 82, 108, 110, 118–19, 126–27, 182, 186, 236n17; abstract, 8; of capitalism, 101; gun, 51, 53; of Indigenous genocide, 139; infrastructural, 249n47; Levinas on, 232n38; organized, 17; police, 53, 196; political, 19; racialized, 115; state-sanctioned, 11; symbolic, 125; uprisings of 1967 and, 38, 44; urban, 215n51; of urban renewal, 98; white, 31, 208n2, 210n9, 212n21; white possession and, 239n32

Voting Rights Act, 40, 107, 215n51

water, 4, 119, 141, 154, 189, 256n1; bills, 73; crisis, 206n37; heaters, 80, 230n9; Homrich, 197–98; lines, 153; pipes, 12, 198, 204n25; right to, 257n4; running, 193; shutoffs, 21, 97, 102, 118, 197–99, 256n1, 257n3; storm, 167

Watson, John, 48, 214n35. *See also* League of Revolutionary Black Workers (LRBW); National Black Economic Development Conference (NBEDC)

Wayne County, 62, 72, 113; tax-foreclosure auction, 57–65, 67–68, 71–72, 75–81, 83, 87, 95, 222n1, 225n28; Treasurer's Office, 57, 60, 71

white flight, 3, 5, 17, 25, 41–42, 46, 71, 112, 132, 227n55

whiteness, 9, 163, 205n30, 205n34, 206n37; as identity, 130; property and, 14, 230n15; territorialization of, 20, 133

White Picket Fence Program, 89, 90*f*, 93–95, 97

white supremacy, 44, 76, 129, 218n83

workers, 48, 51, 219n91, 251n7; automation and, 176; Big Three, 51, 74; Black, 30–31, 35, 47, 176, 211n10, 212–13nn19–21, 214n35 (*see also* League of Revolutionary Black Workers [LRBW]); Chrysler, 174, 212n19; city, 87, 158, 164; collective study among, 30; development, 217n77; effect of decline in union membership on, 51; factory, 27, 211n12; Ford, 54, 209n5, 211n10; government, 152; public, 116; unemployed councils and, 67; white, 32–33, 211n12, 212–13n21

Wyandot, 128–29; lands, 14

Young, Coleman, 50, 52–54, 178, 234n39

Main Portion

DETROIT

SCALE

Rand-McNally's 11 x 14 Map of the Main Portion of Detroit.
Copyright by Rand-McNally & Co.

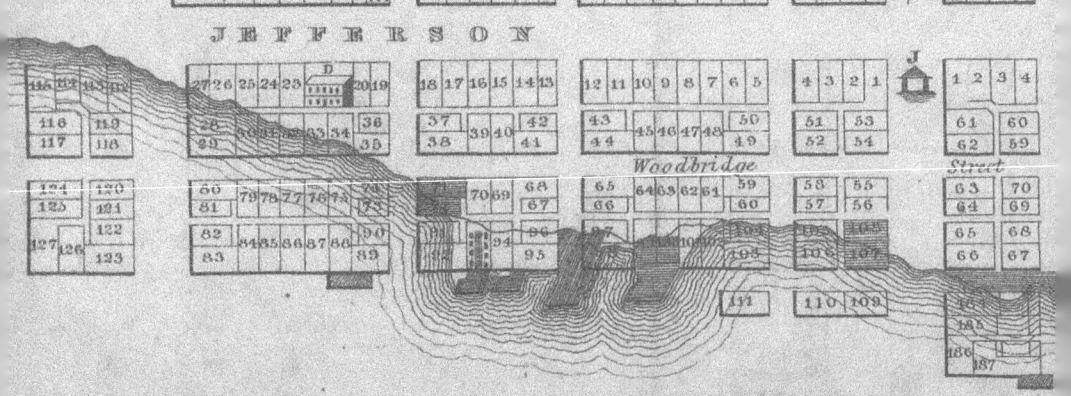